AMERICAN
NATIONAL
INTEREST

AMERICAN NATIONAL INTEREST

VIRTUE AND POWER IN FOREIGN POLICY

KARL VON VORYS

PRAEGER

New York
Westport, Connecticut
London

Library of Congress Cataloging-in-Publication Data

Von Vorys, Karl.
    American national interest : virtue and power in foreign policy /
Karl von Vorys.
          p.   cm.
    Includes bibliographical references.
    ISBN 0-275-93492-6 (alk. paper)
    1. United States—Foreign relations—1945– 2. United States
—Foreign relations—Philosophy.   I. Title.
E840.V65   1990
327.73—dc20   89-26545

Library of Congress Catalog Card Number: 89-26545
ISBN: 0-275-93492-6

First published in 1990

Praeger Publishers, One Madison Avenue, New York, NY 10010
An imprint of Greenwood Publishing Group, Inc.

Printed in the United States of America

The paper used in this book complies with the
Permanent Paper Standard issued by the National
Information Standards Organization (Z39.48-1984).

10 9 8 7 6 5 4 3 2 1

To
Dr. F. OTTO HAAS

a very gentle man
a friend in all seasons

What a boon to civilization
that a global corporation
should be guided by
a man of conscience

Contents

Figures

Preface

What this country needs, I think, is a great debate on foreign policy. Not like the one we had on Vietnam, in which we argued about specific decisions regarding a particular country, in which we pointed a finger in righteous indignation about past mistakes upsetting and dividing the nation. What would serve us well is a broad-based and thorough discussion about our visions of a congenial international environment and the practical steps that in the real world would help us get there. We would almost certainly find that most of us agree on our common national goals. We would become more sensitive about the harsh realities beyond our borders, and by exploring our options during relatively tranquil times, we could probably come together on the most suitable strategies. In the process we could build a consensus that would enormously improve both the consistency and the effectiveness of our foreign policy.

Acknowledgments

I have been very fortunate in my opportunities to become acquainted with a wide range of senior decision-makers at home and abroad. I have learned much from almost every one of them. Here I would like to express my thanks to some of my foremost teachers: Field Marshal Mohammad Ayub Khan, President of Pakistan (1958–69); The Honorable M. M. Ahmed, Deputy Chairman, Planning Commission of Pakistan (1965–70), and Economic Adviser to the President (1970–72); The Honorable Rafael Caldera, President of Venezuela (1969–74); General George Crist, USMC, Commander in Chief, Central Command (1985–88); The Honorable Dr. Lim Chong Eu, Chief Minister of Penang; Mr. Donald Gregg, Assistant to the Vice President for National Security Affairs, (1982–89); General P. X. Kelley, USMC, Commandant, U.S. Marine Corps, (1983–87); Admiral Wesley McDonald, USN, Supreme Allied Commander, Atlantic (1982–85); The Honorable George McGovern, U.S. Senator (1962–81); The Honorable Mahathir b. Mohamad, Prime Minister of Malaysia; Dr. A. Philip Odeen, Director of Program Analysis, National Security Council (1971–73); The Honorable Raymond P. Shafer, Governor of Pennsylvania (1967–71); Mr. Howard Simons, Managing Editor, *The Washington Post* (1971–84); Mr. William Small, Senior Vice President, CBS News (1974–78), and President, NBC News (1979–82); Mr. Sanford Socolow, Executive Producer, "CBS Evening News" (1979–82); The Honorable Dr. Julio Sosa Rodriguez, Venezuela's Ambassador to the United States (1969–72); and Brigade General Hasso Freiherr von Uslar-Gleichen, German Defense Attaché in Washington, D.C.

I also have learned much from my colleagues, especially Tom Davis and Milton J. Esman of Cornell University, Abdul Razzaque of the University of Dhaka, and Ivar Berg, Ed Peters, and Henry Teune of the University of Pennsylvania.

The few I have asked to read all or portions of the manuscript have been of enormous help: Professor Mauricio Baez, Simon Bolivar University of Caracas; Mr. David Harrop, author; Dr. William C. Nenno, U.S. Department of State; and members of my family, especially Eric, Beverly, and above all, its sine qua non, Barbara.

I am further indebted to Eric for the graphics and to Kathleen Kennedy Townsend for the title.

I would like to record my special thanks to David Eisenhower, with whom I held long and stimulating discussions about every aspect of foreign policy.

My manuscript could not have been prepared without Miss Jennifer Gibbons and Mrs. Judy Hoover, who typed and at times edited it so diligently and competently. My colleague Peter Swenson reminded me of the saying that no manuscript can ever be finished; it only becomes abandoned. I was most reluctant to abandon this one. Over and over I asked to make changes, insertions, or deletions, to shift footnotes, or to adjust pagination. Miss Gibbons and Mrs. Hoover responded to my interminable requests generously and with great poise and good humor. I deeply appreciate their patience and understanding, and salute their devotion to high quality.

Finally, I am grateful to my students at the University of Pennsylvania, who provided the inspiration for my work.

AMERICAN
NATIONAL
INTEREST

INTRODUCTION

These are fascinating times. Anyone can see that the world around us is changing fast. What we do not know is in what direction it is changing. Most of us are hopeful. The Cold War is over, and international cooperation may become the dominant theme. Democracy, our way of life, is on the ascendancy all over the globe. Still, there are good reasons for caution. We should not forget the troubled past. All during recent centuries Russia under czar and commissar has consistently been an unsatisfied, expansionist power. We should not ignore the ambiguities of the present. In spite of all the friendly signs and speeches, the military power of the Soviet Union has not diminished. Its government continues to develop and deploy newer and better weapons: tanks, planes, submarines, and strategic missiles. The KGB is as active as ever. And we should not discount the uncertainties of the future. The movement toward openness and democratization has already suffered some setbacks—in Tiananmen Square, for example. Whether it will resume soon or be reversed by a government anxious about losing control remains to be seen. The senior partner of the Communist enterprise is struggling with ethnic violence and labor unrest. Programs to restructure the economy so far have produced only sharpened consumer appetites and keenly felt shortages. Its Eastern European satellites are experimenting with new ventures in independence and even public expressions of hostility toward their Russian "liberators."

It is fairly certain, however, that the United States will be able to lead again. Indeed, we may be on the threshold of a new American century. We have an unusual opportunity to make a difference, to improve the prospects of peace, and to contribute to human development. Our problem is that we may blow it.

Most of us barely remember the 1970s, when our country, a modern state with enormous power, could not influence international developments to its own advantage; indeed, it could hardly influence them at all. While crises built up in different parts of the world, the American government stood by passively. When these crises blew up into revolutions, gross provocations, or outright aggressions, it had no effective options. Foreign policy became almost synonymous with explanations of why the United States could not or should not take any action. When we did act, American initiatives were limited mostly to warning of grave consequences and to sanctions that chiefly hurt American farmers, athletes, and tourists.

Vietnam, for most Americans an unusual experience of military helplessness and moral confusion, obviously contributed to this paralysis. I suggest, however, that our involvement in the war and the manner in which we managed it was less the cause than a symptom. The underlying problem was that foreign policy decision making had become visibly disconnected from its international and domestic environments. It had become grossly obsolete, producing too many policies that were inappropriate abroad and unpopular at home. A change was in order—but how and to what?

The United States meandered onto the stage of world politics in the twilight of imperialism. It was the system of major powers. They were responsible for international order; for all practical purposes they wrote international law. In case of conflict, each power, within its more or less discrete imperial sphere, was expected to be competent to resolve all disputes by persuasion if possible, by force if necessary. Crosscutting issues were settled by the major powers collectively, through negotiations at conferences (congresses) or by war. It was rather a simple system: there were few players; it was normatively cohesive; power was the universal currency. For more than a century and a half, U.S. foreign policy had learned to relate to this external environment, but given the advantage of two wide oceans, Americans could choose to ignore it.

The domestic environment of foreign policy making was not much more complicated. Americans believed in limited government; their principal concerns were economic and social. They worked very hard to make a living; a good living; they worshiped God and took pride in their honor. Politics was an occasional business with little impact on their daily lives. "If it ain't broke, don't fix it" was their attitude, and most of the time Americans thought their system was quite all right. To be sure, elections were held and issues were debated. Usually, though, they focused on local, domestic concerns. Very rarely did foreign policy attract public interest.

Foreign policy decision making was relatively simple. Most of the time the President was clearly in charge. Congress, of course, had a role. The House controlled appropriations, and the Senate had to ratify (by a two-thirds majority) all treaties. But Congress exercised its power in waves. If a matter involved special expenditures (the Louisiana and Alaska purchases), if it involved war, if it involved Great Britain, and in the special case of the League of Nations treaty, Congress was very active indeed. Otherwise it was inclined to leave the design of strategy and the conduct of diplomacy to the executive branch.

World War II marked a high point of presidential foreign policy. The attack on Pearl Harbor united the country. With the help of Senator Arthur H. Vandenberg, Jr., the senior Republican on the Senate Foreign Relations Committee, President Franklin Roosevelt forged a bipartisan foreign policy. He set the pattern of consulting with the leaders of Congress. They in turn (through party discipline) delivered to him the support of both houses. It could be said that politics stopped at the water's edge, for there was a *concurrent majority* in government and a broad public *consensus* on *national interest*.

As we moved into the second half of the twentieth century, the external environment was no longer simple. Vast empires had disintegrated into many newly independent states of all sizes and capacities, each regularly and vociferously demanding the "dignity of equality." For American foreign policy to cope with this radical expansion of essentially unintegrated diversity had become an exceptionally complex, multifaceted task. Worse still, the world had become a very dangerous place. Weapons systems capable of destroying our country and our people were now in the possession of an unfriendly power. We could ignore our international environment only at our extreme peril.

As we moved into the second half of the twentieth century moreover, the domestic environment was no longer simple either. To be sure, as all the polls repeatedly testified, the American people were still only slightly interested in events abroad. Programs featuring foreign leaders, such as "Meet the Press," invariably had small audiences. NBC's exclusive headline-making pre-summit (December 1987) interview with the Soviet party leader attracted just half the Monday night audience accustomed to watching the fictional escapades of Alf, an extraterrestrial character. But somewhere along the way *the popular consensus on national interest was lost*. People would listen to official statements on foreign policy, but they were ready to hear other authorities as well. As before, in case of war, America could be mobilized by the government, but more than before—especially in times of peace—they were ready to ask questions and to be critical, and occasionally were ready to join together in opposing official actions and policies.

More and new voices were heard throughout the land. That they increased the range of alternatives helped build dissonance. That each started from its own separate base of values and principles, and applied its own particular perspectives toward its own special goal, invited cacophony. Foreign policy *special interest* groups have always been vocal; now they pressed their parochial causes single-mindedly, with no inclination for compromise and scant courtesy to the national interest. Then a new set of lobbyists appeared, composed mostly of retired senior government officials and congressmen. They were paid handsomely by foreign governments or corporations to protect and advance their alien interests.

Television, a new and fascinating medium with unprecedented access to the electorate, developed a capability to bring events from anywhere in the world into American living rooms practically at a moment's notice. Its approach to information also was very much its own. Reporters knew that news meant stories that got on the air, and that only stories supported by pictures which grabbed immediate attention did get on the air. They had a vested interest in excitement; controversies were their meat. Criteria of national interest were rarely considered; but when they were, they were generally subordinated to the "people's right to know"—a right of which they claimed to be guardians.

Meanwhile the *academics* were also on the ascendancy. With the phenomenal expansion of the educational system, and especially with the dramatic rise in the number of college students, professors vastly increased their impact. But they, too, had their own perspectives. Their values imbued them with an idealistic view of mankind. They saw the practical hazard of the real world and man's inhumanity to man as unreasonable irritants, explained them away, or thought past them. Their training focused their attention on long-term regularities and gave them little patience with the exigencies of the moment. And their sensitivity regularly entangled them with their favorite causes. For instance, many an anthropologist who would be most reluctant to take a stand on cross-cousin marriages would not hesitate to assert and cloak in authority his or her feelings on Vietnam or disarmament.

Most important, *Congress* was no longer content with periodic forays into foreign policy. The Senate had become more active and had begun to insist on a partnership, and the House of Representatives began to demand part of the action. When foreign policy became expensive, the House had a case; when its peacetime costs ran up to a third and more of the federal budget, the House had a right. And that was not all. With the decline of political parties and discipline in both houses, individual congressmen found their career prospects (popularity) increasingly dependent on the support of special interest groups and on their own personal, dramatic initiatives. They were sorely tempted by the limelight shining on events abroad and often succumbed to it. They sought out occasions on which they could advance their private, often parochial views or chose to ride the waves of popular emotions without any concern for long-term strategy or much understanding of the intricacies of complex multilateral relations.

It all added up to a new reality. American foreign policy could no longer neglect its dangerous international environment and its fragmented domestic environment. Foreign policy needed to be both successful abroad and accepted at home.

President Lyndon Johnson did not recognize the new reality. He persisted in the traditional approach, confident that he could handle international issues by himself. "I always believed," he confided, "that as long as I could take someone into a room with me, I could make him my friend, and that included anybody, even Nikita Khrushchev." As far as Congress was concerned, he recalled that when he was majority leader in the Senate, he loyally, almost automatically, supported President Dwight Eisenhower on foreign policy and saw to it that the Senate did likewise. Sitting in the Oval Office, he expected no less from his former colleagues on the Hill. It was a big mistake. During the last years of his Presidency, when things seemed to go awry, he almost instinctively narrowed the decision structure. He retired a bitter man, certain that he had been badly treated because he was a Southerner. He blamed the media, the Eastern Establishment and the Ivy Leaguers.

President Richard Nixon was quite aware of the radical changes in the decision environments. He was shocked by the violence in the streets, the assassinations of national leaders, and the general loss of confidence in government. He was utterly appalled by the changes in the international environment. Conditions there since he first ran for the presidency in 1960 had deteriorated far beyond his worst expectations. In a few short years the United States had become mired down on the other side of the globe, suffering heavy casualties in a country about which most Americans knew little and for which they cared less, and in a war they did not know how to win or how to quit. International order had broken down; our alliances were in disarray; indeed, for the first time since independence our national existence was genuinely in peril. Something had to be done right away to reverse this trend; the future of our country demanded it. He thought he knew just what to do.

As the basis of Nixon's approach, the foreign policy decision structure would have to be reorganized into an effective modern instrument capable of dealing with the new global realities. It had become too broad, too public, too cluttered with fuzzy thinkers. The base would have to be radically narrowed. Elements outside the executive branch would be excluded altogether. Congress was petty and partisan; it might be placated by rhetoric and patronage. It would, of course, receive more or less useful and more or less truthful briefings but would not be consulted. The media was hostile; possibly they could be intimidated. Academics were irrelevant; they could safely be ignored. The electorate was ignorant and confused; it could be manipulated through public relations campaigns and encouraging news reports. There would be time, just enough time, for historic breakthroughs. Once they were accomplished, the American people would acclaim the results and forget (or care little about) the method used to bring them about.

Inside the executive branch the State Department had proven itself to be empty of new ideas but full of policy leaks. Presidents Franklin Roosevelt and John Kennedy had arrived at the same conclusion. It could still be entrusted with routine diplomatic matters but otherwise would be systematically kept in the dark and, if necessary, intentionally misled. Foreign policy would be conducted by the President from the White House, supported by a National Security Council built into a lean and tough command center, managed by a brilliant and articulate director and manned by the best talent available. Dr. Henry Kissinger promptly set out to build secret "back channels" that bypassed the entire foreign service. Indeed, there were times when foreign government officials—for example, the Soviet Ambassador in Washington or the President of Pakistan in Islamabad—were privy to secrets kept from the American Secretary of State.

Resistance in the State Department was fierce. Presidential (not to mention National Security Council) decisions often were not implemented. Presidential policies announced through the National Security Council were restated, reinterpreted, even contradicted by State Department spokesmen, at times by the Secretary himself. Meanwhile, leaking of classified information to the press reached epidemic proportions. The President, to the chagrin of his National Security Adviser, was reluctant to discipline the State Department, and then the National Security Council itself became infected. Secret deliberations by the President's closest advisers were published by columnist Jack Anderson in December 1971. Since rigorous security measures proved ineffective, extreme measures were instituted. Lie detector tests were required; the office and home telephones of senior assistants were bugged. A special White House security force ("the plumbers") was organized. More than that, it seemed necessary to engage in active deception for the good of Americans.

In January 1975 Ray Price, discussing the approach the former president should adopt in writing his memoirs, urged him that instead of being embarrassed by the "darker side" of his personality, he should acknowledge it.

If the country were ever to be restored to its senses, the public would have to recognize that a measure of scheming and duplicity is necessary in the real world of power politics. . . .

I could see some of the tension drain away, and at one point, he looked out of the window, then turned back and grinned, and commented: "Of course, it's true. We never could have brought off the opening to China if we hadn't lied a little, could we?"[1]

In the past the government had little trouble protecting its secrets and concealing its deceptions. To be sure, they were discovered, but much later—after the administration had left office or the President had died. It was too late then to charge "impeachable offenses," and the revelations were of interest mostly to historians. By the time of the Nixon presidency, however, government secrets could not be kept for long. That the office and home phones of the senior national security staff were tapped was soon discovered. So were White House efforts (under the guise of a "security check") to intimidate an unfriendly CBS reporter. So was the burglary of a psychiatrist's office in search of derogatory information on the man accused of improperly releasing the secret Pentagon Papers. And so were efforts to involve the CIA in a cover-up of Watergate. Most disappointingly, President Nixon's major and dramatic foreign policy accomplishments did not yield ex post facto validation of the procedure dominated by enhanced secrecy and the "back channel" innovation. People applauded President Nixon's foreign policy coups, but they did not forget or forgive the manner in which he went about achieving them. The congressional, media, and academic reactions were formidable.

President Nixon's foreign policy accomplishments were historic. The prohibitively high cost in public confidence in Nixon's approach, however, was dramatically demonstrated in October 1973, less than a year after his reelection by a landslide. When, during the Arab-Israeli war, in a near confrontation with the

Soviet Union, the President ordered a global nuclear alert and very much needed broad public support, he received mostly scorn and skepticism. At the State Department press conference reporters questioned whether the confrontation in general and the alert in particular were actually ploys designed to distract from the President's domestic difficulties. Henry Kissinger was close to tears:

We are attempting to conduct the foreign policy of the United States with regard for what we owe not just to the electorate but to future generations. And it is a symptom of what is happening to our country that it could even be suggested that the United States would alert its forces for domestic reasons.[2]

His response went directly to the heart of the matter. All too soon after the splendid achievements of the China trip, the Moscow summit, and the Vietnam settlement, the paralysis of U.S. foreign policy was there for all to see.

President Gerald Ford felt compelled to try a different approach. The international environment, he thought, had become manageable. What was needed was to bring the foreign policy decision-making process into harmony with the domestic environment. Henry Kissinger had in the meantime become Secretary of State. His relations with Congress were good; the President would build on them and try to restore confidence. The preoccupation with secrecy was abandoned. Congressional demands to become privy to any and all government secrets were honored to the point of severely impairing CIA overseas operations. President Ford had no intention whatsoever of deceiving the American people for their own good.

President Jimmy Carter moved even further along this path. Just before the election in 1976, Cyrus Vance, the future Secretary of State, put it plainly in a memorandum to the Democratic Presidential candidate:

The new Administration will accept the necessity *to make Congress and the American people joint partners* in foreign policy matters. To do so, the President will assume major public leadership on foreign policy matters, and make a major investment in educating the public to perceive the difference between its long-term interest and short-term interests and the difference between the interest of the nation as a whole and the interests of particular subconstituencies and interest groups within the United States.[3]

It was a move in the right direction, but in its implementation it was a failure. As far as the "joint partnerships" with Congress, the media and academe were concerned, President Carter was cautious and his staff, inept. In his partnership with the people he went to the populist extreme. He would, at least ostensibly, dissolve the boundary between decision-making structure and domestic decision environment. All American citizens would be able to participate in foreign policy making. They could do so vicariously. They were invited by gestures and style to recognize and appreciate that their President was just like them. He was Jimmy. He was opposed to luxury and ostentation; he wanted to live just like an average Joe. He complained about too many television sets in the White

House and too many large cars available in the motor pool. He demanded that their numbers be reduced and that his own black limousine be changed (it was, to a tan limousine). He sold the Presidential yacht as a luxury. Sitting before the fireplace, wearing a sweater, he discussed foreign policy (the energy crisis) with the folks. The American people did indeed recognize that their President was just another nice guy, but they did not appreciate it. Their common sense made them want to have an extraordinary person as their leader.

President Jimmy Carter, at least during the first two years of his administration, invited the American people to participate directly in foreign policy making. They were encouraged to offer their comments and suggestions directly to the President by mail and, at one point, by telephone. The President himself would travel across the country, stay in private homes and hold "town meetings" to seek the advice of the country. During his famous retreat to Camp David to ponder the causes of the "national malaise," he consulted a wide range of experts, then went into the streets of nearby Thurmont, Maryland, to tap the wisdom of the good people. No one was to be excluded. In 1980, during his debate with the Republican presidential candidate, he revealed, in all sincerity, that he had sought advice on foreign policy from his 12-year-old daughter, Amy.

Possibly President Carter never had a chance. The challenges in the domestic environment, which he had inherited from the truncated Nixon and Ford administrations, were quite probably no less intractable than those in the international environment left to President Nixon by a disoriented Johnson presidency. It takes little time to lose the confidence of the people, much more time to regain it. Determined and hard-working, meticulous in detail, President Carter did not have the skills to teach the complexities of foreign policy or the time for "a major investment in educating the public." Even so, the Carter presidency did significantly alleviate domestic tension. By the time it was over, gone was the paranoid suspicion of government and its elected leaders. Americans once again were willing to trust their government. That was no mean achievement for them and for President Carter.

In the international environment, however, the United States suffered serious setbacks. The Camp David agreement, which many hailed as an accomplishment, was gained at a cost of direct U.S. involvement in Middle East affairs on a wholly unprecedented and probably quite undesirable scale.* Soviet indirect intervention through surrogates (such as Cuba) in Angola, Ethiopia, and Yemen was exacerbated by direct intervention in Afghanistan. Meanwhile, international lawlessness was reaching new heights. American ambassadors were assassinated;

---

*Successful negotiations require a basket of issues of various degrees of difficulty. Starting with the easier ones, negotiations may build a momentum, making the difficult ones more manageable. Camp David removed all the easier, compromisable issues without building a momentum for a much-needed general settlement and left only the intractable ones. Incidentally, it was conducted in strict secrecy. And it is doubtful that Americans have yet learned its dollar cost.

some 50 diplomats were held hostage for over a year. Not an attractive state of affairs. If these were the consequences of mass participation, then few Americans really believed it was the right method for their country's foreign policy.

The Reagan Administration developed the assets accumulated by its predecessors: Nixon's détente abroad and Carter's confidence building at home. The President's values and style touched the emotional strings of the American people and built the rich resonance into a massive popular support that lasted through his second term. It so happened, moreover, that by the second Reagan Administration a very different Soviet leader emerged with a new style and, apparently, radically new approaches. He seemed to be satisfied with a militarily (and ideologically) defensive position and to rely primarily on diplomatic initiatives. He publicly espoused the principle that "nuclear war cannot be won and must not be fought," and enthusiastically endorsed former President Nixon's suggestion that an "arms race cannot be won and should not be run."[4]

International relations have become less tense but more complex. We face new challenges; we need new policies. Throughout the twentieth century the United States has grown in power and experience. The 1990s may offer us historic opportunities to exercise wisdom. That is all the more reason to harbor no illusions. The post-Vietnam syndrome may be gone, but the underlying causes have not been alleviated. We have not yet found a satisfactory answer to the central problem: *how to conduct American foreign policy that is successful in the multidimensional and still hazardous international environment and is also broadly supported by the democratic participatory domestic environment.*

As we enter the last decade of the twentieth century, we should keep in mind that, President Mikhail Gorbachev's soothing words notwithstanding, some of the traditional realities of the international environment still persist. Thus a foreign policy that to the best of our ability protects and advances our interests abroad still needs to be supported by impressive military capabilities. For the unhappy fact remains that in the world, truth and virtue rarely prevail and justice is seldom triumphant. Power is still the basic term of reference: the power of others and the limits on our own.

A foreign policy that best serves our international interests, moreover, still needs the *narrowest possible decision base.* It has to be carefully crafted to balance its various (political, economic, strategic, and so on) consequences. Its costs and benefits have to be accurately calculated, in terms not just of our bilateral relations with any specific country but also of its impact upon relations with many others. It requires special skills and experience. It is not likely to be the product of extended discussions and elaborate compromises in every segment of our democratic system.

Not least important, effective foreign policy requires *the protection of secrets.* We need to have secrets for national security reasons. Like it or not, we have enemies who want to know about us, all about us, in order to be able to take better advantage of us and do us harm. It makes no sense to help them. But that is not the only reason. Secrecy is also very useful in negotiations. History-making diplomatic breakthroughs require clandestine preparations. New ideas, new initiatives have no organized domestic constituencies; in fact, they are quite often perceived as threatening by established special interest groups. Had secret arrangements between China and the United States become prematurely known, President Nixon and Chairman Mao probably would have been prevented from proceeding by their respective domestic opponents (and supporters).

Less dramatic, incremental progress also is facilitated by secrecy. Statesmen all over the world, in democratic as well as authoritarian countries, are more comfortable when they talk in confidence, and are worried by any prospect that their remarks will become public. Negotiations necessarily involve give and take. To identify concessions (strategic or tactical) publicly is difficult in a democracy, as it exposes the government to partisan attacks by the opposition. In an authoritarian system, where they may be seen as ideological compromises, nothing short of heresies, they are more difficult still. Communist negotiators do at times compromise, not easily but they do, but only in secret. Traditionally their public position usually is a propaganda ploy frozen into the orthodox mold. It remains to be seen whether this has changed in what may become the Gorbachev era.

Meanwhile, the demands of the domestic environment keep pushing in the opposite direction. A foreign policy that is sensitive to public opinion needs to recognize *that military virtues are no longer fashionable* in America. The number of senators and congressmen who have served in the armed forces is steadily declining. Few people can now remember an experience with a good and victorious war. Fewer still consider combat an integral part of life. Americans share a profound wish that reason should prevail, and that all human conflict can, and must, be settled by negotiation and compromise. Upon reflection, they are willing to concede reluctantly that even in peacetime we must maintain military capabilities. All the same, a suspicion prevails that our armed forces ought to be kept at the minimum necessary for defense and that they bear watching. Otherwise we would spend most of our treasure on unnecessary armaments and be all too prone to project force overseas to irrelevant parts of the globe, into undeserving conflicts.

Most important, for foreign policy to gain and retain public support, *it must not be conducted in the old-fashioned exclusionary manner*. The American people do not like to be systematically kept in the dark; opinion leaders thoroughly resent secrets, and they can no longer be ignored. Pressure groups with vested interests in special foreign policy decisions are too well connected and too deeply embedded. If anything, they can be expected to multiply and become more vocal. News reporters with all their biases, brashness, errors, and excesses are too highly valued to be brought under government control. Academics with all their abstruse theories, floods of verbiage, and peculiar personal styles have developed sophisticated analytical methods and improved their societal influence. And Congress is not likely to resume its former docility. Any member of the

National Security Council staff who thinks he or she can keep secrets from the Senate or the House will soon find himself or herself on television.

So the question arises: Are the demands of the external environment and those of the domestic environment altogether irreconcilable? If they are, they will, as they did in the past, chew up presidents and produce a wildly fluctuating foreign policy that leaves most people abroad and at home uncertain about our intentions. There ought to be alternatives. We ought to try to develop an approach that will meet both sets of demands, perhaps not completely but certainly optimally.

In our search for a successful reconciliation between our international challenges and our cherished values, we shall have to give much thought to new policymaking arrangements. Within the executive branch a reassessment of the traditional hegemony of the State Department is in order. Experimentation with interdepartmental committees could prove helpful. Limits on the National Security Council's role in directing covert operations is an obvious necessity, but it seems wise to increase the Council's capacity to generate fresh approaches and innovative ideas about our overall strategy. Regarding relations between the branches, we have seen some progress recently. Still more work is needed to accomplish a satisfactory arrangement that would assure (1) that Congress is consulted early in the process and (2) that Congress refrains from using its constitutional power over the purse to manage, even micromanage, the president's constitutional power to conduct foreign policy. New ideas and more work also are needed to overcome the recent predisposition of opinion leaders to take an adversary position to presidential decisions. It might involve informal but persistent cultivation of interpersonal relations or, as President Nixon suggested, a more formal council composed of a broad selection of private sector authorities. A group that would meet regularly (for instance, twice a month) to consider foreign policy issues of the President's choosing could build valuable bridges to American society in addition to providing him with an additional dimension of advice. All these are very important questions and need to be treated by separate, further studies.

The point, however, is this: None of these revisions and innovations in the decision-making process will help much unless we can find a *common normative denominator* for the deliberations among the branches of government and the public dialogue. If any member of Congress, any newspaper pundit or television commentator, any professor of physics, English literature, or political science, any special interest lobbyist, any citizen who decides to make a pronouncement may properly choose his or her assumptions based on his or her particular values, the discussion is apt to produce more heat than light. We need to restore and *build a consensus*, at a minimum a concurrent majority among the executive branch, the Congress, and private opinion-leading groups on the *basic principles of our national interest*.

It will not be easy. One problem is that Americans have only a vague notion that it is a good thing and a proper standard for foreign policy, but not much more. A much bigger problem is that while our foreign policy makers no doubt have used it in their internal deliberations, whenever they have referred to it publicly, they rarely have done so in order to offer a standard by which policy could be evaluated. The national interest was too valuable to government as an instrument of *post-policy mobilization*. By leaving it vague, it could be fitted to suit any course decided upon. From the very beginning of the Republic, policy came first and then was (or was not) sold to the people by proclaiming it to be our national interest. By leaving it vague, moreover, it could be fitted to reflect lofty, inspiring absolutes: our manifest destiny, the tenets of Christian faith, or the will of God. Whenever publicly proclaimed, by a remarkable and felicitous coincidence our national interest was always identical with the dictates of moral law. The American people expected it and would have accepted nothing less.

Recalling briefly some of the historical highlights may illustrate this deeply embedded habit. The very first major foreign policy issue after the Constitution involved our treaty of alliance with France of 1778. The French had met their obligations handsomely and provided untold support in our struggle to gain independence from Britain. When, some 15 years later, they in turn needed help against the British and the possibility arose that they might call upon us to meet our obligations, President Washington made it clear that our national interest would not permit the extravagance of reciprocity. We could not come to the aid of France. We must be neutral between the country that helped us gain independence and the country that fought to prevent it. Lest the public mistake our motives for crass pragmatism, Alexander Hamilton hastened to explain the moral position:

Indeed, the rule of morality is in this respect not precisely the same between Nations, as between individuals. The duty of making [its] own welfare the guide of its action[s] is much stronger upon the former than upon the latter; in proportion to the greater magnitude and importance of national compared with individual happiness, to the greater permanency of the effects of national than of individual conduct. Existing Millions, and for the most part future generations, ar[e] concerned in the present measures of a government: While the consequences of private actions of [an] individual, for the most part, terminate with himself, or are circumscribed within a narrow compass.[5]

This, of course, was a case of popular mobilization behind a policy to stay out of military conflict. The position was even more clear (and more self-righteous) when it enlisted support for having engaged in conflict. By the 1830s the momentum for the United States to expand across the continent had become irresistible. Indigenous Indians had to give way, the Spanish in the Southeast (Florida) and the British to the Northwest (Oregon) had to give way, and Mexico, which nominally controlled enormous areas in the Southwest, had to give way. Mexico first faced Texan insurrection, then U.S. invasion. President James Polk was priming revolt in California, then ordered the occupation of the territory between the Nueces and Rio Grande rivers, a territory that was generally considered to be part of Mexico, but was somewhat ambiguously signed away to Texas by a captured, terrified General Santa Ana (deprived not only of his personal freedom but of his clothes as well until he signed). General Zachary Taylor, leading the U.S. forces, took up a position on the left bank of the Rio Grande with his guns aimed at the Mexican town of Matamoros, then blockaded the river to cut off food supplies for the town. When a Mexican force crossed in response, a cavalry skirmish ensued in which 16 Americans were killed or wounded. Learning of the incident, the President, who had been preparing a war message to Congress for some time, felt justified to inform the country that

now after reiterated menaces, Mexico has passed the boundary of the United States, has invaded our territory and [has] shed American blood upon American soil. . . . We are called upon by every consideration of duty and patriotism to vindicate with decision the honor, the rights and the interests of our country.[6]

About a half century later, after the Spanish-American War, the question of the ''liberated'' Philippines came up. This is how President William McKinley, who at the outbreak of the war had never even heard of the islands, explained his decision:

I walked the floor of the White House night after night until midnight; and I am not ashamed to tell you, gentlemen, that I went down on my knees and prayed [to] Almighty God for light and guidance more than one night. . . . And one night late it came to me this way—I don't know how it was but it came: (1) that we could not give them back to Spain—that would be cowardly and dishonorable; (2) that we could not turn them over to France and Germany—our commercial rivals in the Orient—that would be bad business and discreditable; (3) that we could not leave them to themselves—they were unfit for self-government—and they would soon have anarchy and misrule over there worse than Spain was; and (4) that there was nothing left for us to do but to take them all, and educate the Filipinos, and uplift and civilize and Christianize them, and by God's grace do the very best we can do by them, as our fellow-men for whom Christ also died. And then I went to bed, and went to sleep and slept soundly.[7]

The Filipinos did not receive the same message. They fought vigorously. It took 70,000 troops, four times as many as landed in Cuba, two years and more before resistance was crushed.

The twentieth century has a more secular tone, but the practice of decision followed by justification in terms of national interest has been carried on. The United States, having become a world power, wished to develop a capability to transfer its naval forces quickly between the Atlantic and Pacific oceans. It could not afford to circumnavigate South America; it needed a much shorter route: a canal across Central America. A Nicaraguan canal was the first idea, but concern about volcanic activity and aggressive lobbying by a French company shifted attention to Panama. The problem was that Panama was part of Colombia, and Colombia was uncooperative.[8] Therefore a revolution broke out in Panama City—

a revolution directed from Room 1162 of the Waldorf-Astoria Hotel in New York City and supported by a "patriot army" of 500 "bought" Colombian troops (cost about $100,000) in addition to 441 members of the local fire department. American warships prevented Colombian forces from landing. Within a day the "independent" Republic of Panama was proclaimed, and little more than an hour after receiving the news, President Theodore Roosevelt authorized formal recognition of the new "country" and its "government." Two weeks later a treaty was signed that conveyed to the United States in perpetuity a ten-mile-wide strip across the country for the price Colombia had turned down. Explained the President of the United States:

I confidently maintain that the recognition of the Republic of Panama was an act justified by the interests of collective civilization. If ever a government could be said to have received a mandate from civilization . . . the United States holds that position with regard to the interoceanic canal.[9]

Franklin Delano Roosevelt was a more complicated case. Early in his administration he apparently concluded that the rise of Hitler made U.S. intervention in Europe inevitable. By the 1930s the international stakes had grown enormously, but the traditional position of isolation was held especially fervently at home. He could not present so fundamental a reorientation as a fait accompli. Thus, when he mounted his campaign, it appeared to be an effort of pre-policy education, but in fact it was part of popular mobilization in support of his decision already made. In any case, all through his campaign he continued the tradition of presenting national interest as an expression of transcendental norms. As early as October 1937 he demanded a quarantine of states contributing to "international anarchy." As far as he (and the United States of America) was concerned:

The peace, the freedom, and the security of 90 percent of the population of the world is being jeopardized by the remaining 10 percent, who are threatening a breakdown of all international order and law. Surely the 90 percent who want to live in peace under law and in accordance *with moral standards that have received almost universal acceptance* through the centuries, can and must find some way to make their will prevail.[10]

Popular (not to mention congressional) response was generally unfavorable, and the President had to drop this theme for a while. By January 1939 he was ready to resume it. In his State of the Union address he spoke of foreign challenges to three institutions

indispensable to Americans, now as always. The first is religion. It is the source of the other two—democracy and international good faith. . . . We have learned that God-fearing democracies of the world which observe the sanctity of treaties and good faith in their dealings with other nations cannot safely be indifferent to international lawlessness anywhere. They cannot let pass, without effective protest, acts of aggression against sister nations.[11]

When war came to Europe, and especially after the fall of France, he further intensified his campaign.

The traditional approach may have served its purpose in the past. It did mobilize popular support behind policy. In our time, however, there are (at least) two things wrong with it. First, it is prone to mistreat the domestic environment. Once a decision is made, there is not much time for mobilizing popular support and no time at all for a public discussion of the pros and cons. It is disturbing enough to be presented with an accomplished fact, a decision made by an exclusive government group. But when it is cloaked in national interest to make it unassailable, when the polity is confronted with a choice between acquiescing or feeling unpatriotic, such decisions provoke vague feelings of discomfort in many citizens of the Republic.

Second, national interest as an instrument of post-policy mobilization is not without pitfalls for the government. To be sure, in case of national peril no debate is necessary. Mass support will naturally follow. Few Americans would doubt that the existence of the United States is worth defending; fewer would deny that it is the right thing to do. There are, however, very few international problems that genuinely threaten our national existence. Most of them present less drastic dangers where public opinion has no built-in response. Public debate is necessary and useful, but it runs the risk that it may not reach the same conclusion as government. Concerned with this contingency, decision makers are apt to resort to a shortcut: sound a patriotic note and redefine the issue as a threat to our national survival (for instance, the domino theory). The nation will respond by uniting behind policy.

Once public support is given, however, even if enthusiastically given, a timer will start ticking. Their attention attracted, Americans will look more closely at the issues and official justifications. The media will cover them, the academics will examine them—each from its own perspective, each with its own standards and interest. The process will take time, and periodically could be distracted by good news, but sooner or later this democratic scrutiny will expose the excesses of the official position. The claim—it was a good cause, the danger was real but it had to be exaggerated to get public attention and support—cannot prove convincing. The timer keeps ticking and winding down; popular support declines. Public confidence not only in the policy but, far worse, in the integrity of the government itself is steadily impaired.

To illustrate the point: The Nazi menace was an affront to our civilization and a mortal challenge to our friends in Europe, but there was no chance that the German forces, which could not cross the Channel, could invade the United States. The government insisted that the danger was acute. Millions of men were sent into combat in North Africa and Europe. At home volunteers watched our coasts. We blacked out our cities at night, and bought war bonds. World War II was clearly a ''good war''; the enemy was evil, no question about that—just think of the concentration camps. We fought for the right, we won glorious victories, and we had few casualties. Still, the reaction had set in. Hardly was the war won when a congressional committee began investigating its causes, soon found considerable fault with our President, even raised the specter of official deception. It was no coincidence that Congress passed, and the states hastily ratified, the 22nd Amendment (1951), limiting the President to two elected terms.

Similarly, Communist aggression in Vietnam was a serious challenge to international order, but there was no chance that it could yield strategic bases that could improve direct Soviet access to our country. Public officials spoke of dominoes that, once falling there, would soon knock us down here. As the military buildup intensified in Southeast Asia, Americans at home lined up behind the President. The Gallup Poll reported the ratio of favorable to unfavorable public reaction to be 50:28 in January 1965, 52:26 in April 1965, and 64:21 in October 1965. Vietnam was never a good war. For a while it was perceived as a necessary military action. Within two years, however, public support was rapidly eroding. By July 1967, according to the Gallup Poll, 41 percent of Americans considered our military involvement there a mistake, with 48 percent still supporting it. By October 1967 those who thought it was a mistake were in the majority (46:44). President Johnson had lost his credibility. By January 1969, when his successor took office, the opponents were in a heavy majority (52:39). In April 1971 people were asked whether they thought President Nixon was telling all they should know about Vietnam; 24 percent answered yes, and 67 percent said no. Evidently confidence in the Presidency as an institution was badly shaken.

In short, given the past record, it is not surprising that there is skepticism about the contributions of the concept of national interest to public policy. All the same, its uses in simpler times are not to the point. I propose something new. I propose to *develop national interest as a pre-policy standard*, a standard that by consensus sets the parameters for official policy, one that serves as a common base for general discussion, and one by which foreign policy can be evaluated.

To serve such a purpose, however, the concept of national interest cannot remain a vague, abstract idea; it must gain content. At the very least it must acquire an identifiable structure. All foreign policy challenges are not of the same kind. National interest needs to spell out its hierarchy quite unambiguously: (1) challenges to our vital interests, our national existence; (2) challenges to our special interests, our friends and allies; and (3) challenges to our general interests, international order. In turn, it should identify and classify the range of appropriate policy options. We have some interests for which we should be ready to fight, some for which we should be willing to pay, some for which we should be prepared to work, and some interests that should warn us to leave certain international problems alone.

NOTES

1. Raymond Price, *With Nixon* (New York: Viking Press, 1977), p. 34.
2. Henry Kissinger, *Years of Upheaval* (Boston: Little, Brown, 1982), p. 596.

3. Cyrus Vance, *Hard Choices: Critical Years in America's Foreign Policy* (New York: Simon and Schuster, 1983), pp. 441–42.

4. Conversation at the Kremlin, July 18, 1986.

5. Alexander Hamilton, *Papers*, vol. 15, edited by Harold C. Syrett (New York: Columbia University Press, 1969), p. 85.

6. Quoted in Thomas A. Bailey, *The Diplomatic History of the American People* (New York: Appleton-Century-Crofts, 1946), p. 269.

7. Quoted in ibid, p. 520.

8. The Colombian chargé in Washington was pressured into signing a treaty granting the United States a zone of six miles wide for a cash payment of $10,000,000 and an annuity of $250,000, but so strong was Colombian public opposition that their senate refused to ratify.

9. Quoted in Bailey, *The Diplomatic History of the American People*, p. 544.

10. Quoted in ibid, p. 744. Emphasis added.

11. Quoted in Charles Callan Tansill, *Back Door to War, the Roosevelt Foreign Policy, 1933–1941* (Chicago: Regnery, 1952), p. 600.

1

OUR VITAL INTEREST: NATIONAL EXISTENCE

National interest as a standard rests on one fundamental assumption: that the nation-state is for its citizens the focus of orientation or, in our specific case, that for Americans the secure existence of the United States is an altogether nonnegotiable value. It is never in the U.S. national interest to be conquered or subjugated by a foreign power. It is never in our national interest to delegate or transfer voluntarily to any foreign country or international organization our right to control our internal affairs and our right to conduct our foreign policy according to our own purposes. This, of course, is an obvious point in the age of nationalism and self-determination.

Even so, to avoid misunderstandings, some elaboration may be useful. A national focus of orientation does not shut out the universalist perspective. A foreign policy conducted according to our own purpose definitely does not mean one that callously disregards the interests of mankind. Sensitivity and concern for the needs of people throughout the world is in the best tradition of Americans. In order to help, they are prepared to bear many burdens and make many sacrifices. They are driven by altruism or motivated by enlightened self-interest. But in our national interest these sacrifices must stop short of sacrificing the United States for any purpose, however exalted. We had better be clear on this to others and to ourselves.

Nor does the preeminence of our national existence delegitimize the personal and group perspectives. The individual is a very cherished value in democracy. That a person should pursue his or her own personal happiness is an inalienable right. That it can be through free associations is constitutionally guaranteed. The standard of national interest does not contradict or threaten these values—unless they are projected into the extreme. For this right, like all rights, is not absolute. Special interest groups may lobby vigorously, but the line must be drawn when they seek to dominate and try to impose their special concerns on all others. Individual rights are limited by the rights of other individuals, and it cannot be constitutionally pushed to deny the national community its right, when its very existence is in peril, to properly demand the sacrifice of individual happiness, even individual life. The contention "better red than dead" may have merit in some private logic but is repugnant to the standard of national interest. On this, too, we had better be clear to others and to ourselves.

In the past the imperative of national existence has generally been of little concern to most Americans. We have been busy with many other things, and we have simply taken it for granted that we were safe. It was not an unreasonable assumption. Two vast oceans protect much of our borders, two more or less friendly, but in any case far weaker, countries are our neighbors. God was in His Heaven; the major powers were far away and otherwise preoccupied.

To be sure, the years just before the Monroe Doctrine or shortly after the Civil War (with Maximilian in Mexico) were potentially perilous times—but these were temporary aberrations. Soon we could put things right and return our attention to our principal preoccupation: our business at home. Admittedly we fought some wars. But at worst we fought them on the peripheries of the country (even Washington, D.C., was on the periphery in 1814; Philadelphia, Boston, and New York remained quite safe) or on someone else's land: Mexico, Cuba, the Philippines, France, Germany, or Japan.

As a matter of fact we still remain little concerned—too little concerned to examine seriously the complexities of protecting ourselves from aggression. We remain preoccupied with other matters: mostly the enjoyment of the advantages and benefits of our nation. It is a luxury we can no longer afford.

The threat of aggression has changed fundamentally. Our vulnerability to attack from a major power is no longer a rare, occasional problem. It is not one that will just go away, not one we can solve by a stroke of genius or remove by bold action, not even by a grand crusade. It presents a problem that will be with us for a long time to come. The best we can do is learn to live with it—by successfully coping with it.

Worse still, the potential consequences of being attacked also have changed fundamentally. They have become far broader in scope and far more devastating in effect than was the cost of the British burning Washington, D.C. (1814), Pancho Villa raiding into Texas (1914), or the Japanese bombing Pearl Harbor (1941). The airburst of a 1-megaton bomb "burns out" 60 square miles and destroys or radically deforms human life over a much larger area. For example, such a bomb detonated 8,500 feet above the Empire State Building "would glut or flatten almost every building between Battery Park and 125th Street, . . . and would heavily damage buildings between the northern tip of Staten Island and the George Washington Bridge." The heat from the rising fireball would be great enough to melt metal and glass from Greenwich Village to Central Park and to ignite all readily flammable materials in all five boroughs and west to the Passaic River, in New Jersey. A lethal radioactive fallout would begin almost immediately, covering an area 15 miles wide and 150 miles long (depending on the wind, from New York City to Wilmington, Delaware). Sublethal fallout that could cause serious illness and birth defects would extend another 150 miles downwind, perhaps to Washington, D.C. A single megaton bomb.[1]

The Soviet Union has an estimated 32,000 nuclear warheads, some smaller but others larger than 1 megaton. In addition to its strategic bomber force it has about 1,400 intercontinental ballistic missiles and another 1,000 submarine-launched ballistic missiles with a total of about 9,000 reentry vehicles capable of delivering nuclear warheads to the United States. Simple arithmetic quickly reveals the stark reality. For the first time in our history we are now vulnerable to attack that could effectively destroy our national existence: most of our people, much of our country, and our entire way of life. As a result the traditional policy of maintaining just sufficient capacity to *defeat* aggression, while not irrelevant, is inadequate. To *deter* aggression has become the prime requirement of national interest.

How can we avoid becoming targets of aggression? This is a vital question that raises complicated issues with considerable areas of controversy. Some of the technical details, of course, are best left to the experts to debate, but if we take a closer look at the problem, we find three identifiable preconditions to aggression.

First, aggression requires *hostility*. It stands to reason that people (or states led by people) do not attack unless they want to do so, and that takes a powerful urge.

Second, aggression requires *capability*. An enemy must be able to do serious harm to its victim. This depends fundamentally on direct access to the victim's national territory. That may explain why, in international relations, neighbors rarely have developed lasting friendships. It also may be the reason why most countries historically have sought to protect themselves with natural barriers such as swift rivers or high mountain ranges, or with weak, preferably neutral or neutralized, neighbors. Capability also depends on an exportable surplus of coercive capacity, the military forces an aggressor can bring to bear upon its target. Napoleon's armies were a formidable might, but their capability to attack England was nil. He no doubt wanted to attack, but could not. England was safe; after Trafalgar, Napoleon knew it too. Thus capability for aggression begins when the level and composition of the aggressor's forces are sufficient to overcome any physical barriers to access, it becomes significant when they can challenge the defensive forces, and it is decisive when they can overwhelm them.

Finally, aggression requires *utility*. Wanting to attack and being able to do so together may produce a powerful temptation, but as a practical matter it will rarely if ever prove irresistible unless the aggressor expects to gain by aggression. The gain may be sheer aggrandizement in the form of material benefits (better access to raw materials, markets, or cheap labor force, perhaps rich plunder) or of power and prestige. No less significantly, the gain may be defensive, the successful elimination of the constant anxiety of a perceived threat. But gain there must be. Few people and fewer governments will embark on aggression that they know will end in defeat or produce costs that will prove to be ruinous. Each of these preconditions may provide a policy focus. If any one of them could be prevented, aggression would be deterred. They are worth considering.

HOSTILITY

As a country and as a people America and Americans have a relatively favorable image abroad. In most places people are curious and pleased to meet visitors from the United States. They may find them puzzling, difficult, and even offensive at times, but usually are impressed by their open friendliness. U.S. acquaintances are often discussed and regularly quoted. Even in countries where government actively discourages it, people are attracted to the cultural and consumption patterns of the United States. American forms of entertainment, even social styles, are emulated, and American consumer products are at a premium. Many people from all walks of life want to visit, and would love to immigrate to, the United States. Thus there is a receptiveness to positive actions by the U.S. government and its representatives that are designed to generate goodwill. It seems simple enough: If we could just keep people from becoming hostile to us, we could live in peace.

Actually, it is not quite as simple as that. Part of the problem apparently lies with human personality—or, more specifically, with human greed. When their essential needs are met, other animals seem content. Monkeys play in the trees; the king of the jungle sleeps or "promenades himself." With the possible exception of most rudimentary sex, they have no ambition. Man is different. He has moments of satisfaction, even happiness, but these moments apparently are fleeting. Man is insatiable; mostly he is discontented. He wants more, much more; generally that which belongs to others. The Bible commands that a man "shalt not covet his neighbor's wife, nor his house, nor his field, nor his man servant, nor his maid servant, nor his ox, nor his ass, nor anything that is his." But it also records that he usually does. Even David, the favorite of the Lord, the gentle and innocent shepherd boy anointed by prophet Samuel, the great King of Israel with much power and glory and "exceedingly many sheep and oxen," coveted. He coveted many things, even the wife of Urias, his loyal and valiant soldier.

Human beings covet. More than that, they are prone to use violence to pursue and satisfy their wants. In the words of Freud:

Men are not gentle, friendly creatures wishing for love, who simply defend themselves if they are attacked. . . . [a] powerful measure of desires for aggression has to be reckoned with as part of their instinctual endowment. The result is that their neighbor is to them not only a possible helper or sexual object, but also a temptation to them to gratify their aggressiveness on him, to exploit his capacity for work without recompense, to use him sexually without his consent, to seize his possessions, to humiliate him, to cause him pain, to torture and to kill him.[2]

Thus Cain slew Abel and King David issued the order: "Set ye Urias in the front of the battle, where the fight is strongest: and leave ye him, that he may be wounded and die."

There are many who dispute Freud's conviction that predatory impulses are innate and fixed in human nature, but hardly anyone would seriously argue that at this point in history such impulses are not part of the personality of most human beings throughout the world. Even if they are in fact acquired, as many, including some of Freud's colleagues (such as Alfred Adler, Karen Horney, and Eric Fromm), contend and hope, predatory impulses are nevertheless very deeply rooted. The task of removing or even ameliorating them presents an enormous and prolonged challenge, indeed, nothing short of a fundamental reorientation of the historical experience. To hate is quick and easy; to love takes more time and is far more difficult.

Man, of course, is a social animal. Human beings want to love and be loved, want to be friends and have friends, want to belong, to be part of a community of fellow human beings. Even so, this sociability has not impeded, but only redirected, hostility toward one's fellows. We have not yet attained universal brotherly love. Human affection is carefully limited to a special few, and the cohesion of a community rests not only on the ties that bind the members together but also on the differences that separate them from other human beings: the nonmembers, the outsiders. The evidence abounds and is easy to find. Consider the quadrennial experience of the Olympic Games. It is a spectacle watched on television by hundreds of millions of people throughout the world. The audience knows little or nothing about the contestants, their individual integrity and character. What people look for is the national symbol worn by the athlete. But that is quite enough. The athlete, for all they know, lacks character and has an altogether unattractive personality. Possibly they would not think of inviting him into their homes and would not want to meet him at night on a lonely road. But if he wears their national symbol, they identify with him, they cheer him, they want him to win. If he does, it makes them happy, but if he loses, they feel disappointment and anger. The attitude of the same audience toward other contestants wearing other national symbols, however, is very different. The "other" may be a paragon of virtue, a thoroughly nice and altogether charming person. All the same, they want him to lose, will be happy if he does and disappointed, even angry, if he does not. (In World Cup soccer games, it seems, the audience identification with their national teams is rather more vehement.) Similarly, in social relations, in sharing a common meal, inviting a person to one's home, in selecting a marriage partner, people are sorted out more often according to group affiliation than individual characteristics. And, of course, these are mild examples. There are far worse instances of cleavages among racial, religious, ethnic, tribal, caste, and class lines. Prejudice, segregation, bigotry, and invidious discrimination are not rare aberrations on God's green earth. They are very much the rule.

Worse still, human sociability has not moderated predatory impulses. Indeed, human communities, after redirecting it, have popularized and legitimatized the use of violence. "It is one of the commonplaces of popular sociological observation," wrote Arnold J. Toynbee, "that the military peoples, castes and classes are apt to win more admiration from us than their neighbors who earn their living by occupations which do not entail the risking of one's own life in the attempt to take someone else's."[3]

Last, but not least, human hostility is not visibly diminished—quite possibly it is exacerbated—by our contemporary international environment. We live in a world dominated by ideological cleavages. Far less than a majority of mankind is committed to democracy; few countries have or want to have secular political systems. Most people believe in other values. They deride the United States as a rotten, decadent, and exploitative system or castigate it as the "Great Devil." Their righteousness moves many to a fanatical defense of their own causes, and not just a few to a passionate hatred of America.

We live in a world marked by enormous disparities in national power. We are powerful enough to bring incredible devastation to any part of the globe. Many are too weak to protect themselves from their closest neighbors. Americans really have no intention to attack anyone, and our government regularly proclaims our purest motives and our friendliest intentions. Even so, there are countries and people who fear and resent our might.

We live in a world that is aware of vast differences in the quality of human life. About 1.5 billion people in Asia, Africa, and Latin America live under conditions of relative poverty and another billion exist in abject (absolute) poverty, in which the human animal can subsist but a rational person has no chance to function. As the result of phenomenal advances in communication and transportation technology, they are becoming well acquainted with the remarkable standard of living the American people (and, of course, some others) have achieved. They are very much attracted by it and want to share in it. They resent that they have not shared in it, and that there is little chance that they in their lifetimes, probably their children in *their* lifetimes, will share in it. They have little patience with explanations, all the more so as they observe that Americans, while they zestfully enjoy their marvelous material benefits and comforts, loudly proclaim to all the world their devotion to human equality. Billions believe that they have a grievance, that they have a right to a new economic order. Their own political leaders often are pleased to promote this view. The last thing they want is popular grievances directed at themselves. Much better to point the finger at an external culprit: foreign exploitation, "American imperialism."

Clearly, strategic deterrence is well served by a policy that seeks to minimize the grievances of foreign leaders and peoples. All the same, it would be most unwise to harbor, let alone act on, the illusion that it all depends on us, that an American attitude of friendship and a fair and honorable policy will prevent (or remove) any predisposition to aggression and assure our national security. We need not explore the dynamics of "displacement" and "projection" or get into the deep and not altogether clear waters of psychology to observe that grievances may have highly subjective causes. Individuals (including those holding high office) may experience personal tragedies and failures. They may be frustrated by the conditions and consequences of economic hardship, social disruption, or political instability, and seek relief through a scapegoat. Civilization is still a precarious achievement in need of careful nurturing and is always vulnerable to radical reversal. After thousands of years of advance, on astonishingly short notice human beings turn into predators, groups become mobs, and nations are gripped by a war fever.

CAPABILITY

If we cannot be sure to prevent people from wanting to do us harm, we may try to prevent them from being able to do so.

The United States has been extraordinarily fortunate in its geopolitical location. Our northern and southern neighbors were weaker states that did not have a significant capability for aggression. To the east and west we were protected by vast oceans. In the past only the greatest powers had any capability to do us harm, and they presented only a peripheral threat. Great Britain could reach our shores, but she was a friend—indeed, throughout the nineteenth century she was our protector. Japan could bomb Pearl Harbor but could not land even on Midway. The Germans could do even less; they could only sink our ships at sea.

Most states still do not possess the capability to do us harm, but with the development of nuclear technology they could conceivably do so in the future. Graduate students engaged in research can now find out how to build nuclear bombs from publicly available sources. There is still the problem of actually building them (Israel is known to object violently), and building them in large numbers. Moreover, vehicles that would deliver nuclear bombs against American targets in large numbers are still beyond the resources of most countries. But for how long? Possibly for quite some time to come. Possibly.

Clearly it is in our national interest to prevent the proliferation of countries having strategic nuclear weapons. The task is not without problems. For one thing, it requires an intrusion into scientific progress, and that, if the past is an indicator, is not easy. Books have been burned, scientists have been persecuted, without much avail. In any case, it is not usually the American way. On the contrary.

What makes it awkward, of course, is that it is not *our* science and technology we want to restrict but *theirs*, and especially so in case of the nonnuclear powers, because we offer them nothing in return. Many countries in Asia, Africa, and Latin America are woefully short of the energy resources so essential for industrialization and the elimination of mass poverty. They desperately need nuclear science and technology. Some people and their leaders perhaps feel intensely frustrated by economic, political, and military comparisons with the United States. They may wish fervently for an equalizer: nuclear weapons. We can accept, indeed should help with, the first but resist the second. Encouraging the development of nuclear science and technology for peaceful purposes while preventing the spread of nuclear weapons is a very difficult task demanding constant attention. In 1968 we signed a treaty on the nonproliferation of nuclear weapons with the United Kingdom and the Soviet Union. In it the powers pledged not to transfer nuclear weapons or materials and technology needed for the development of nuclear weapons to other states. By the time the treaty came into force in 1970, some 100 nonnuclear weapon states had joined, promising to forgo the development of such weapons and to permit international inspection of their nuclear facilities.

Most of the signatories, probably all, kept their word. China and France, however, did not sign; they were busy building nuclear arsenals. Some other strategically important countries also did not sign, and several of them have already acquired nuclear capability. Precisely which of them also have constructed nuclear bombs is subject to lively speculation. Brazil? Pakistan? Israel? South Africa? The situation bears watching and in the meantime it might be desirable to formulate a policy and to form a consensus on what we might do in case of the emergence of a new nuclear power.

One country, the Soviet Union, already has the capability to harm us enormously, and that is of most immediate and vital concern to us. One solution suggested occasionally is a preemptive first strike. Let us take the initiative and with one fell swoop wipe out their capacity to destroy us. No fuss, no muss. Afterward, when we are safe again, we can hold seminars about the moral implications of the matter. There are two problems with this approach. First, we would not do it. It is not our way of doing things. Not in the movies: John Wayne or Gary Cooper would never draw first. Nor in reality: When during the Korean War, the subject of "preventive war" was raised by his secretary of the navy, President Harry Truman quickly and sternly disciplined him: "I have always been opposed even to the thought of such a war," he explained in his memoirs. "There is nothing more foolish than to think that war can be stopped by war. You don't 'prevent' anything by war except peace."[4] A decade later, during the Cuban missile crisis, a crisis far more perilous to our national existence, some members of the (highest level) Executive Committee urged a surprise air strike. They were firmly admonished. During the discussion Attorney General Robert Kennedy made it abundantly clear that "with all the memory of Pearl Harbor and all the responsibility we would have to bear in the world the United States could [not] possibly order such an operation. For 175 years we had not been such a country. . . . We were fighting for something more than survival, and a sneak attack would constitute a betrayal of our heritage and our ideals."[5]

The second problem is that we could not do it. It is possible, though far from certain, that in President Truman's time, or President Eisenhower's time, or even as late as President Kennedy's administration the United States could have used its enormous advantages in nuclear weapons and delivery systems to devastate the Soviet Union and cripple its capacity to do us any direct harm. This is no longer the case. No American first strike now has the remotest chance of wiping out Soviet retaliatory capacity, or even reducing it to a level at which the destruction it could wreak in the United States could be called "acceptable" by any sane person. This condition, moreover, is likely to persist into the future. In short, the option of a preemptive strike exists at best as an academic one, and is worth considering only for the brief time it takes to conclude it is altogether unrealistic.

On the opposite extreme is the disarmament approach. Its rationale is along these lines: Since we cannot compel the Soviet Union through military force to give up its capability of doing us serious, even mortal, harm, it is imperative that we make every diplomatic effort to persuade her to do so voluntarily. This means hard bargaining and predictably substantial sacrifices in our own military capabilities. If we could succeed, even if we had to give up most of our own strategic capabilities in exchange, even if we disarmed altogether, we still would have made a marvelous bargain and we could once again enjoy the conditions of a United States fully secure in its national existence. Unfortunately our reality is not quite as simple as that. Were we to disregard entirely other salient components of our national interest, such as the security of our allies, and concentrate single-mindedly on our national existence, the rationale of disarmament would still prove to be very much less than sound.

If we were to take it quite literally—that is, give up all our arms—and the Soviet Union were to do the same, we would both become militarily inferior to all other countries: large countries like China, smaller countries like Germany, Iran, or Mexico, and small countries like Cuba, North Korea, or Libya. Indeed, we would be at the mercy of any fanatic terrorist group. To have any security, we would have to compel all other countries to disarm as well, but we would have nothing left with which to compel, not even logical arguments. Alternatively, we could give up only our nuclear weapons. The zero:zero option was discussed about the time of the Reykjavik summit. It would mean that the world's only nuclear powers would be Great Britain, France, China, and possibly Israel, Pakistan, and South Africa. It also would mean that we would either have to concede enormous advantages to the much larger Soviet conventional forces or continuously spend sums on our own conventional forces that would dwarf the expenditures of the Reagan military buildup. These, of course, are absurd extremes. On the more moderate scale above the zero level, the argument for arms control and arms reduction gains plausibility. The question is: How much above the zero level?

The heart of the problem is the condition of uncertainty and its relationship to insecurity. It is not so much that most Americans do not trust the Russians—and they do not[6]—but that we and our government do not know much about them. We really do not know how their leaders make decisions—just how, for example, Gorbachev gained his ascendancy. We do not know whether the course he announced is more than a tactical maneuver (as was Lenin's New Economic Policy) and whether it will prevail over the long run, we do not know what their motives are when they undertake international commitments, and we do not know to what extent they can be relied upon to fulfill their treaty obligations. Within two years after the signing of the much heralded INF treaty, Foreign Minister Eduard Shevardnadze publicly warned that the Soviet Union may not abide by some of its provisions.

Worse still, what we do know does not help ameliorate, and actually exacerbates, uncertainty. We know that the Soviet Union possesses an advanced system of science and technology. Although in the past it apparently never originated a new weapons system, we cannot assume that it never will. The Soviets may accomplish a breakthrough in arms technology, and if they so choose, they may then break out of any arms control treaty.

We also know that normative and structural asymmetries between us give the Soviets enormous advantages for a clandestine breakout and rapid buildup. Admittedly, Gorbachev's reforms have opened up Soviet society, but there is still quite a distance to go before it can claim a free flow of information. Its values remain communist, very different from ours in their ends and means. Its government is authoritarian; indeed, in 1990 the Soviet consitution was especially amended to give Gorbachev more power than any of his predecessors had been granted. Its economy is centrally planned, capable of shifting priorities and resources from civilian consumption to military purposes without public notice and within a short time.

We may negotiate all kinds of safeguards, such as aerial (or radar) surveillance and verification by on-site inspections. The fact remains that there is no way we can eliminate altogether the uncertainty that the Soviets may break out and violate an arms control or arms reduction agreement. That we cannot be sure is a source of insecurity. We must be prepared to take risks, but the question is just how big a risk we can prudently take.

Examining this problem closely, we discover a curious effect of the level of arms on the relationship of uncertainty and insecurity. Conventional wisdom holds, and popular opinion firmly believes, that the higher the level of arms, the higher the insecurity produced by uncertainty. That is true enough—up to a point. It is true that at a low level of armaments the risks are small. Before any country could achieve a significant capability for aggression (overcoming the physical obstacles to its access and challenging existing defense forces), it would have to engage in a massive military buildup, a buildup that would be visible and would take time. It would be visible enough to be recognized and time enough for others to take countermeasures. It is also true that during the first half of this century, when the level of armaments was high, the risk was great. With large standing armies, with industry heavily engaged in arms production, and with innovations in military technology immensely profitable, the major powers were precariously balanced. The advantage needed for decisive breakthrough was relatively small and, in the midst of all the other armaments, could be gained in secret. The temptation for each of the hostile powers to do so was very great indeed, and their fear that the others would actually do so was quite

Figure 1
Level of Armaments, Risks, and Overkill

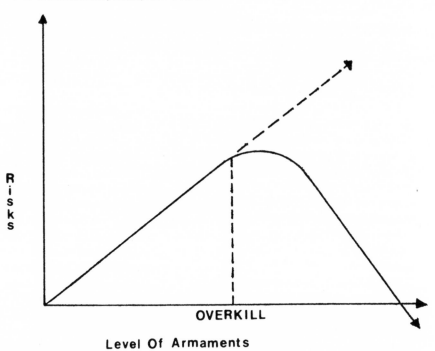

intense. The risk of trading capabilities through negotiations was too high, and all the efforts to arrive at arms reduction (disarmament) treaties proved futile.

As is so often the case, however, conventional wisdom becomes passé. During the early 1970s the strategic capabilities of the two superpowers moved beyond the level where each could destroy the other, and thus crossed the threshold into the very different realm of overkill (see Figure 1). Our current very large stockpiles of long-range missiles and nuclear warheads do not exacerbate uncertainty; paradoxically, they have actually mitigated the risks. For in the realm of mutual and multiple overkill decisive breakthroughs that would fundamentally change the balance of capabilities have become very much less likely. There is not much point in building more and more missiles, and more and more nuclear warheads, if all we gain is a capability to destroy the Soviet Union not three times but four or five times over. In turn there is not much risk in trading capabilities if the worst that could happen in case the Soviets break out of the treaty is that instead of killing us twice over they could do so four, five, even ten times over. After the first time we would not feel a thing. Here, then, is the paradox: Given our uncertainties about the Soviet Union and their systemic advantages for a clandestine breakout, treaties providing for massive arms reductions that would take us back below the overkill boundary to the pre-World War II level, where each side could not quite destroy the other, would entail extravagant risks for us. At the same time treaties that contain the race in multiples of overkill would jeopardize neither side and would save public expenditures for both.

UTILITY

Since some powerful causes for hostility against the United States are beyond our reach, and in any case their amelioration would require a determined effort over a very long time, and while the Soviet Union has developed the capability to destroy the United States, and under the prevailing condition of uncertainty, any prospect of removing this threat through diplomatic negotiations promises to be difficult, hazardous, and slow, we have no choice. For our immediate security we must focus on the third requirement of aggression. We must prevent any doubt about the disutility of an attack upon us.

It is not an altogether satisfactory solution. The problem is that cost:benefit calculations in case of national policy (ours, as well as those of a potential aggressor) are not based on some rational, universal standard but on more particularistic values. In our democratic system, for example, we place a great value on the individual, his or her life, and his or her well-being. But this is a very unusual position. Throughout much of history most people have believed— indeed, even today most people believe—that the individual is an instrument of the state and that personal interest must always be subordinated to the collective good. "You cannot make an omelet without breaking some eggs," we hear regularly from apologists of revolutionary bloodbaths. According to Soviet sources (not necessarily the most reliable on the subject), Chairman Mao was quite prepared to sacrifice millions of human lives, including millions of Chinese lives, in a nuclear war. The next war, he explained, will kill 300 million Chinese, 200 million Russians, and 200 million Americans. It will leave a few Russians, a few Americans, and 300 million Chinese!

Even in democratic countries human life is not cherished to the same extent. At the time (1983) when 241 U.S. Marines were killed in their billets in Beirut, a similar attack on French paratroop barracks cost 59 casualties. The losses of both countries were roughly proportional. Americans were shocked; Congress and the media were inflamed. The French accepted it more philosophically. *C'est la guerre*. The point is that in our efforts to identify what is an unacceptable price in human lives for a potential aggressor, we cannot simply project what we consider an unacceptable price. The aggressor's tolerance of human casualties may well be very much higher. What is unacceptable for us may seem a bargain to some.

This problem is exacerbated by the fact that decision making is never a wholly rational process, and in times of crisis the forces favoring irrationality are especially rampant. The stakes—war, the survival of the country, that of the human race—are usually incomprehensible. The pressures, often formulated in "no choice" terms, are unbelievable. The time within which a decision must be taken—if it is not, that itself becomes a decision—is extremely short. Deliberation is quickly reduced to a few tense men, and then to still fewer, still more tense and tired men. An environment ripe for miscalculation. Only wholly unambiguous evidence, recognizable even by an unstable, fanatical mind, that no attack upon the United States, under any circumstances, can possibly yield any profit—and, if attempted, there surely will be hell to pay—can assure us successful deterrence.

This may be the place to consider the piquant possibility of self-deterrence, the possibility that the United States and the Soviet Union may be restrained not just by the other's, but by their own, nuclear capabilities. According to recent calculations by a group of prominent scientists widely publicized by Dr. Carl Sagan, the detonation of 500 to 2,000 nuclear warheads would predictably induce a climatic catastrophe: a long, stark, dark, freezing nuclear winter. To quote the conclusion of the distinguished scientists who met to assess these calculations:

Species extinction could be expected for most tropical plants and animals, and for most terrestrial vertebrates of more temperate regions, a large number of plants, and numerous freshwater and some marine organisms. . . . Whether any people would be able to persist for long in the face of highly modified biological communities; novel climates; high levels of radiation; shattered agricultural, social and economic systems; extraordinary psychological stresses; and a host of other difficulties is open to question. . . . Coupled with the direct casualties of perhaps two billion people, the combined intermediate and long-term effects of nuclear war suggest that eventually there might be no human survivors in the Northern Hemisphere.[7]

Dr. Sagan's purpose, of course, was to emphasize the need to reduce strategic nuclear arms well below the "threshold" of 500 warheads. But there is another implication of these calculations as well. At present the United States and the Soviet Union each have well over 2,000 strategic targets, such as missile launchers, bomber bases, and command and communications centers. Assuming that for a successful surprise attack (first strike) an aggressor must assign at least one warhead (but for many strategic targets it probably must use two warheads), we quickly reach a total of 3,000 warheads, far above the number predicted to induce a "climatic catastrophe." This does not include warheads to be detonated over cities and economic targets, or warheads fired by the victim in retaliation. In other words, a Soviet surprise attack on us, even one so fantastically successful that the United States could not or would not retaliate with a single nuclear warhead, would nevertheless create such changes in the ecosystem of the Northern Hemisphere that the people of the Soviet Union would surely be destroyed as well—not in a quick, blinding flash but after a slower, painful agony.

Theoretical calculations by respected scientists, it goes without saying, deserve deference. Speculations about their practical implications are quite appropriate and can be fascinating. But scientists' calculations at times are conjectural and have their own uncertainties. It is even conceivable that at times—perish the thought—they are affected by partisan convictions. Thus they can be made the basis of policy only with caution—in case of national security policy, only with extreme caution. It would be marvelous if we could rely on the assumption that aggression has become synonymous with suicide and that the Soviet Union would be deterred from attacking the United States by an anxiety that its bombs dropped on U.S. targets would soon kill and maim the vast majority, if not all, of the Soviet people. Perhaps in the twenty-first century we may have reason to do so. Not now. Now, for deterrence, we must rely principally upon our own strategic forces.

NOTES

1. Jonathan Schell, *The Fate of the Earth* (New York: Alfred A. Knopf, 1982), pp. 47–51.

2. Sigmund Freud, *Civilization and Its Discontents* (London: Hogarth, 1949), p. 85.

3. Arnold J. Toynbee, *War and Civilization* (New York: Oxford University Press, 1950), pp. 12–13.

4. Harry S. Truman, *Memoirs*, vol. 2 (Garden City, N.Y.: Doubleday, 1956), p. 383.

5. Arthur M. Schlesinger, Jr., *A Thousand Days: John F. Kennedy in the White House* (Boston: Houghton Mifflin, 1965), pp. 806–7.

6. Since the 1950s the Gallup Poll has consistently found that a large majority of Americans have an unfavorable, often very unfavorable, attitude to the Soviet Union. For example, to the question "Do you think the USSR is doing all it can to keep the peace of the world?" 84 percent in November 1981 and 81 percent in November 1984 answered "no." George H. Gallup, *The Gallup Poll: Public Opinion, 1983* (Wilmington, Del.: Scholarly Resources, 1984), pp. 78–79, 227.

7. P. R. Erlich, M. A. Harnwell, Peter H. Raven, Carl Sagan, G. W. Woodwell, et al., "The Long-term Biological Consequences of Nuclear War," *Science*, 222 (December 23, 1983), p. 1299.

2

DETERRENCE BY
STRATEGIC OFFENSE

American military leaders have always had a distinct preference for the offensive. The tradition may have started shortly after the Declaration of Independence when George Washington was forced out of New York, his army a ragged remnant of 3,000 men retreating through New Jersey. It could have been the end, but Washington suddenly abandoned the defensive posture and took the initiative. On Christmas night he crossed the Delaware and captured the barracks at Trenton, taking almost 1,000 Hessian prisoners. He then withdrew to Pennsylvania, only to recross the Delaware in a few days and pounce on Cornwallis's forces at Princeton. The one lesson we can learn from our setbacks is to attack, Washington declared. It was ignored by the Union commanders in the beginning but was clearly followed by the great generals of the Civil War: Lee, Sherman, and Grant. By World War II the tradition was well established. General MacArthur defended Australia by moving into New Guinea; General Eisenhower defended "the Bulge" by ordering the historic Third Army sweep. "L'audace, toujours l'audace" exulted its commander, General George S. Patton.

Audacity, moreover, is particularly in tune with the American way of life. Americans, observed Alexis de Tocqueville, James Bryce, and Dennis William Brogan, at half-century intervals, are an extraordinarily self-confident people. When most others were content with their small, stable communities, they left their homes in the mother country, crossed the ocean against great hazards, survived, built new homes in a strange and primitive land, then picked up stakes again. They pushed the frontiers over the Alleghenies, then across the Great Plains, still further across rugged mountains and deserts, fighting off hostile attacks to the western coast of our continent. Pioneers, always on the move, always ready to take the initiative. With more temerity than courage they were always ready to challenge and conquer nature. More than that, at a time when

governments were imposed by rulers, managed by privileged classes, and sanctioned by mandates from heaven, Americans refused to acquiesce in these customs. They jumped at the chance to design their own political system, to base
its legitimacy on the consent of the common man, and to place its management
in the hands of elected officials. They knew that they would succeed. Soon
Jefferson would proclaim the United States the world's best hope, and Lincoln
would call it the last, best hope on earth.

Americans, moreover, like most people, want peace. They consider having
to think of the threat of war a rank imposition; to be willing to fight a war, they
must become "psyched-up." Being "psyched-up," they resent complex intellectual arguments of relative merit; their righteous rage sees only a simple dichotomy between themselves and the evil incarnate. They have little patience
with steady, prolonged defense producing limited or ambiguous gains, and none
with a defense marked by periodic reverses gradually leading to a stalemate.
They want to be done with war. They want to hear of grandiose initiatives filled
with glory. They want to see their cause advancing rapidly and decisively.

There can be no better example of the dominance of the strategy of offense
than the development of air power in World War II. In Europe, designated as
the principal theater of war, we would have to be on the defensive for two and
a half years, a very long time for a democracy. To sustain public persistence in
purpose, to keep the American people "psyched-up," the government mounted
a massive propaganda effort augmented by such techniques as blackout regu-
lations in Chicago and national campaigns for "pots and pans for victory."[1]
After a year there were some victories to report on the periphery, and that helped.
Still, the only way for us to strike at the heartland of the enemy was by air. We
chose to do so in the most dramatic manner, by strategic daylight bombing. The
costs in highly trained manpower and high-technology weapons were heavy, and
after the war we learned the damage to German morale and war production was
modest.[2] But those raids with hundreds and hundreds of giant four-engine bombers were grandiose; the maintenance of close formation in the face of fierce
fighter attacks was heroic; the target, German urban and industrial centers, was
unambiguous; and the result, physical devastation of the enemy's homeland,
was spectacular. The visible wrath of an aroused democracy was so satisfying.
All things considered, the strategic offensive in the air was the very best defense
in Europe. Add to this that in the Pacific the atom bomb, an offensive strategic
weapon, brought the war to a dramatic and quick end. The momentum was
entirely with the offense.

It is hardly surprising that the military strategy which won the war should be
favored when the military strategy to preserve the peace was designed. All the
more so since the United States had a clear superiority, if not monopoly, of
offensive weapons (strategic bombers and nuclear warheads). In the mid-1950s,
during Senate subcommittee hearings on the Air Force, all testimony agreed that
the next war would be won by maximum offensive power, and it could be

deterred only through an offensive capability that could inflict upon any potential aggressor a level of physical destruction that it would consider unacceptable.[3]

Conditions, however, were about to change quite fundamentally. On August 26, 1957, Moscow Radio announced the successful testing of a "super-long-distance intercontinental multistage ballistic missile." Six weeks later, when the Soviets launched Sputnik, the first man-made earth satellite, mankind entered the space age, and the strategic relationship between the United States and the Soviet Union became perilous in the extreme.

Just what, exactly, were our special problems with Soviet missiles? First, it was their range. They could bring the war to us. In the past the possibility that the United States could become vulnerable to a devastating direct nuclear attack, while worth considering, seemed a contingency with only a modest probability for some time to come. Now it became a predictable certainty in the near future. In the past strategic planning was, and could be, about "winning the war." Now a well-thought-out and highly (if not absolutely) reliable deterrence strategy became a vital imperative.

The second problem was their speed. They could surprise us. Soviet missiles could be expected to cover the entire range more than 20 times faster than a bomber. As long as the Soviets' strategic threat was based on their bombers, even if they could greatly improve them, we could have time—not much, but some. During the hours it would take for their planes to reach their targets, we could have time to remove any doubt that an attack was actually coming; we could have time to decide how to respond; we could have time to move our decision makers and our retaliatory capacity to safety; we could have time to warn the people, many of whom would have time to evacuate to safety; and we could have time to unleash a devastating counterattack. During the less than 30 minutes' flight of the missile, we would have time for few, quite possibly none, of these. Now with a surprise attack becoming a realistic possibility, the whole calculation of deterrence had to be revised. Retaliatory forces-in-being became at best only of academic significance. What counts now for deterrence is strategic offensive capability that can be expected to *survive* and can rapidly be made operational *after the absorption of a nuclear attack*.

DETERRENCE CONDITION I: SOVIET SOFT-TARGET CAPABILITY

Chairman Khrushchev's boasts and President Kennedy's campaign rhetoric notwithstanding, it was not until well into the 1960s that the Soviet Union developed the capacity for a severe, direct strategic nuclear attack on the United States. At the time of the Cuban missile crisis, the Soviet Air Force had 60–70 turboprop Bears (Tu–20) and 100–120 jet-propelled Bisons (M–4), slow and vulnerable planes that theoretically could reach the United States but could not return without refueling. The Soviet Navy had about 8 diesel-powered submarines with a total of 48 short-range (SS-N-4) ballistic missiles, none of which could be fired from a submerged position. Finally, the Soviet Strategic Rocket Forces were still in their infancy. They had probably fewer than 100 first-generation ICBMs (SS-7 and SS-8).[4] Though they were capable of carrying 3-5 megaton bombs, they were plagued by technical difficulties and were inaccurate. Moreover, they were very vulnerable. They were unprotected and freestanding, and could not store their own liquid fuel. Before firing, each had to be refueled, a prolonged, laborious, and highly visible process.

Soviet determination and its direction, however, were unmistakable. In just a few years the Soviet Union would achieve strategic soft-target capability. Its missiles could reach practically any place throughout our country. They would not be accurate enough for direct hits, but they could come close enough for their nuclear warheads to destroy our cities, our factories, our transportation networks, even some of our military establishments. We could have peace as long as our deterrence was credible, but our deterrence remained credible only as long as our retaliatory forces remained survivable.

It was an enormous challenge. First, we had to assure credible deterrence for the present (short term). Admittedly, some protection for our strategic retaliatory forces could be gained by concealing their location, since an enemy cannot hit unknown targets; by their mobility, since an enemy may find it difficult to hit moving targets; and by a defensive shield—heavy armor, sophisticated electronic countermeasures (ECM), or reinforced shelters—since an enemy may find it difficult to penetrate them. All the same, it seemed most unlikely that we could make any weapons system invulnerable. Prudence demanded that we expect losses, probably heavy losses. In order to assure that they would not become crippling, so the argument ran, we needed *redundancy*. Only if we would maintain strategic forces several times the size needed to devastate the Soviet Union, could we be sure (and what is more important for deterrence, would *they* be sure) that even after absorbing an attack the United States could still deliver a devastating blow.

Second, we had to assure a credible deterrence for the future (long run). We could not count on the Soviet Union accepting the status quo. It was wise to assume that our enemies were constantly engaged in research designed to overcome our protective measures in order to gain the critical advantage. And it was wise to assume that they would indeed, from time to time, achieve technological breakthroughs. In order to assure that these breakthroughs would not become decisive, this argument ran, we needed *diversity*. Only if we relied on several different autonomous weapons systems, could we (and they) be sure that any technological breakthrough would at most neutralize a part of our strategic forces. Neither the enormity nor the certainty of our retaliation would be decisively affected.

Specifically, the United States adopted a system of deterrence marked by redundance and diversity. It was generally referred to as the Triad, a system supported by three legs. Its air leg was provided by manned strategic bombers.

Some 538 long-range B–52s, each capable of carrying up to four multimegaton bombs, were operational shortly after President Kennedy took office. The ground leg was to be made up of fixed-site intercontinental ballistic missiles (ICBMs) placed in heavily reinforced shelters (silos). In addition to 54 heavy Titan IIs we planned to deploy 1,200 lighter Minuteman solid-fuel missiles. The former carried warheads of 9 megatons, the latter, of 1–2 megatons. Finally, the sea leg was to be composed of 45 nuclear-powered (Polaris/Poseidon) submarines with a total of 720 submarine-launched ballistic missiles (SLBMs). A formidable and credible system of deterrence. "In planning our second strike force," explained Secretary of Defense Robert McNamara to Congress in 1963, "we have provided . . . a capability to destroy virtually all of the 'soft' and 'semi-hard' military targets in the Soviet Union and a large number of their fully hardened missile sites, with an additional capability in the form of a protected force to be employed or held in reserve for use against urban and industrial areas."[5]

It was clearly a second-strike design. The United States was not trying to destroy "any very large portion of the fully hard ICBM sites," even if the Soviets were to build them in large quantities. "Fully hard ICBM sites," the secretary explained further, "can be destroyed but only at a great cost in terms of the numbers of offensive weapons required to dig them out. Furthermore, in a second strike situation we would be attacking, for the most part, empty sites from which the missiles had already been fired."[6]

For its part the Soviet Union made every effort to build up its strategic forces. It followed its own strategy, however. Unlike the United States it chose not to rely heavily on diversity. Soviet heavy bombers (the turboprop Bears and jet-powered Bisons) were inferior in performance to the B–52s and remained much fewer in number.[7] Antiquated submarines, each armed with three short-range SLBMs, accounted for much of Moscow's sea-launched missile strength as late as 1970. Half were diesel powered. In missiles, however, the Soviet effort was spectacular. From about 100 ICBMs, that is, less than a quarter of the U.S. number in 1963, the arsenal was increased to 1,300, 25 percent above the U.S. level. The improvement, moreover, was not only quantitative. Three new missiles (the SS–9, SS–11, and SS–13)—some heavier, all more accurate—were deployed. There could no longer be any question of U.S. strategic superiority, only of equivalence. We had reached the stage of mutual assured destruction. Each superpower could count upon sufficient survival second-strike capability to impose altogether unacceptable damage on the people and territory of the other.

It was something of a psychedelic experience. Quite a few people actually found the condition comforting. We could feel safe because our retaliatory forces could survive an attack and still assure the destruction of one-fifth to one-fourth of the Soviet population and one-half of Soviet industry.[8] The Soviet Union could feel safe because it, too, had a survivable retaliatory force and could be confident that we would not resort to strategic nuclear attack against her for any reason at such exorbitant costs. So everyone could feel safe and we could have peace. Mutual assured destruction would mean mutual assured deterrence. What could be better for international stability? "The doctrine," recalled Henry Kissinger, "led to the extraordinary conclusion that the vulnerability of our civilian population was an *asset* reassuring the Soviet Union and guaranteeing its restraint in a crisis. 'Assured destruction' was one of those theories that sound impressive in an academic seminar but are horribly unworkable for a decision-maker in the real world and lead to catastrophe if they are ever implemented."[9]

Indeed, there was a corollary to the theory. Mutual assured destruction *could* mean mutual assured strategic deterrence *provided* both sides were content with their own survivable second-strike capability. But only then. If either side were to move beyond that and seek to develop new weapons systems that would threaten to impair the other's retaliatory forces, it would destabilize the balance. If, to be more specific, as the result of improved Soviet weapons, our capability to deliver a devastating retaliation would be imperiled, our deterrence would be seriously degraded. We could no longer safely assume that the Soviet Union would not be tempted to attack. Still, in the late 1960s U.S. decision makers could not simply take it for granted that the Soviet Union would necessarily reject the balance of mutual assured destruction and clandestinely seek to subvert it. It was worth a try, a cautious experiment.

The United States responded to the massive Soviet missile buildup of the 1960s with remarkable restraint. It did not develop any new types of missiles. It did not seek to increase the number of its launchers. On the contrary, the Minuteman program was compressed from 1,200 to 1,000. Plans for 45 Polaris submarines with 720 missiles were cut to 41 boats with 656 missiles. All along the B–52 losses were not replaced. By 1970 their total dropped to 465.[10] Above all, we did not try to improve the accuracy of the warheads. We could have done so; we knew how—but we did not. All the United States did was develop the technology for a multiple independently targetable re-entry vehicle (MIRV). We would arm our missiles with more than one warhead: Our Minuteman III ICBMs with three, our Poseidon SLBMs with ten. In short, throughout the 1970s our strategic offensive forces significantly increased the redundancy in our second strike soft-target capability, but we (intentionally) did not improve our limited capability to destroy Soviet missiles in their heavily reinforced shelters. Thus we made a point of not threatening the survivability of their second-strike capability.

DETERRENCE CONDITION II: SOVIET HARD-TARGET CAPABILITY

It was devoutly hoped that the Soviet Union would reciprocate, though the past record was not exactly encouraging. In 1961—and this requires not only thinking of the unthinkable but also imagining the unimaginable—the Soviet Union detonated a 58 megaton weapon, almost 3,000 times the yield of the Hiroshima bomb! Then in 1967, on the fiftieth anniversary of the Bolshevik

Revolution, it unveiled the SS–9 (Scarp). It was an awesome sight. The missile was more than 100 feet long and about 10 feet in diameter, and had a throw weight (payload) of at least 12,000 pounds—twice the size and more than six times the payload of the Minuteman. It could carry a single warhead of 25 megatons, more than 12 times what the Minuteman could do.

In terms of the doctrine of mutual assured deterrence, the weapon was incomprehensible; it added neither to the survivability nor to the meaningful destructive force of Soviet second-strike capability. It was perplexing to see SS–9s being deployed at a rate of about four a month (their total reaching 308 by 1972). It was worrisome to see them being tested as satellite weapons, and it became especially worrisome to observe them being tested with three warheads, for these (dummy) giant warheads were independently targeted in a peculiar close cluster. It made no sense to target them so closely if they were intended to destroy three different cities, and it surely made no sense to use three warheads against one city. One five-megaton bomb would be quite sufficient. Could it possibly be that the Soviet Union had no intention to be constrained by the doctrine of mutually assured deterrence? Could it be possible that it was hoping to develop a first-strike capability that would cripple U.S. second strike forces?

Perhaps a point of clarification may be useful here. First strike capability is the ability to carry out a successful surprise attack. It is not enough that the victim of aggression be surprised; it is necessary that the attack be successful, and a strategic attack can be considered successful only if it paralyzes the victim's retaliatory (second-strike) capability. Both the United States and the Soviet Union, if they so chose, could plan a surprise attack on the other. After the 1960s the United States could not make it successful. Until the late 1970s it was clear that neither could the Soviet Union. But what about the 1980s?

Many Americans, including some prominent public officials, just could not believe it. They eagerly embraced arguments that the SS–9's "mammoth size could be seen as a function of Soviet technological inferiority, rather than a harbinger of Soviet strategic superiority. . . . the USSR was impelled toward a reliance on heavy missiles by the backwardness of its propulsion and guidance systems. The less accurate the warheads or clusters of warheads the bigger it has to be to destroy its target."[11] When, in January 1971, there were signs that the rapid rate of SS–9 deployment was slowing down, it was advanced by some as convincing proof that those who suspected the Soviet Union of first-strike ambitions were wrong. Indeed, the U.S. disarmament negotiator was moved to recommend to the President that *we reciprocate* in order to prove *our* good faith.[12]

As a matter of fact, Soviet missile development did not slow down. Quite the contrary. While the United States did not deploy a single new missile system, the Soviet Union deployed three: the SS–17, the SS–18, and the SS–19, each at least three times heavier than our Minuteman III, and one (SS–18) about nine times heavier. By 1977 the United States had 550 "modernized" Minuteman IIIs and the Soviet Union had 208 heavy SS–9s, plus 100 new SS–18s, 50 new

SS–17s, and 120 new SS–19s, a total of 478. A rough numerical equivalence in launchers.

The problem was that by this time the terms of relevant comparison had changed. The United States had proceeded to arm its strategic missiles with MIRVs, placing three warheads on Minuteman III. The Soviet Union soon followed suit with four warheads on the SS–17 (Mod 1), six warheads on the SS–19 (Mod 2), eight warheads on the SS–18 (Mod 2), and ten warheads on the SS 18 (Mod 4)! Since targets are destroyed by warheads, not missiles, the equivalence in missiles became irrelevant, and the disparity in warheads (by 1979 this meant a ratio of 4,306:2,154 in favor of the Soviet Union) became alarming. Unfortunately, that was not the worst of it.

It was soon noted that the new, "modernized" Soviet missiles were powered by liquid fuel. Why? some found comfort in seeing it as further evidence of the backwardness of Soviet technology; we had long since shifted to solid fuel. Others wondered. Liquid fuel cannot be stored in missiles, and it takes many hours before launch to fill the tanks. Liquid fuel missiles could not be launched in the short time available after warning of an impending attack. Were the Soviet leaders confident that their ICBMs were quite secure, that the United States not only lacked strategic hard-target capability but also could not develop one in the foreseeable future? Or could the explanation be found in a more sinister motive? Did they use liquid fuel because they expected to launch their missiles at the time of their choice? A defender does not have such a choice; only an aggressor planning a first strike does!

Most ominous, however, was the remarkable improvement of the Soviet guidance system. Its consequences were no less than the fundamental change in the conditions of deterrence. Since the mid 1960s Soviet missiles had had soft-target capabilities. They could reach our country, destroy our cities, destroy our industries, even destroy some military installations. They could not, however, hope to impair our devastating retaliatory capability. More specifically, our ICBMs (the ground leg of our Triad) were secure in their concrete-reinforced silos. The accuracy:yield ratio of Soviet missiles was not sufficient to threaten them. Their smaller warheads could come close, but their explosive yield was too small to hurt our silos. Their larger warheads could destroy them but could not come close enough. By the late 1970s, however, it had become clear that the Soviet missiles were steadily approaching the accuracy:yield ratio necessary to qualify as silo-busters.[13] And it had become clear to all but the most determined wishful thinkers that neither a 2:1 ratio in warheads in favor of the Soviet Union, nor a U.S. soft-target strategic capability matched by a Soviet soft-target capability *plus* a Soviet hard-target capability did parity make.

The combined effect of these disparities was especially serious because they added a first-strike temptation to the approaching Soviet first-strike capability. The time was rapidly approaching when the Soviet Union in a surprise attack could make the very favorable trade of warheads for missiles. For example, a single SS–18 could destroy ten Minuteman IIIs (together with their three warheads each), or, to put it in its crassest, most disturbing form: the 240 SS–18s that made up less than 20 percent of the Soviet ICBM force in 1979 could conceivably, in a sudden strike, destroy the entire U.S. ICBM force.

Threatening an important component of our retaliatory capability, the very thing that protected the American people from nuclear attack, made Soviet intentions unmistakable. They would not be content with their own security (through assured deterrence); they also wanted to be free of the high cost of aggression.

As it happened, moreover, about this time another component of the Triad, the air leg, also was beginning to cause concern. The B–52s were getting very old. The first of these planes had been delivered to the air force in 1957, the "newest" ones in 1962—the year the assembly line shut down. Arthur Hadley, a writer and journalist, described his visit to Barksdale Air Force Base, Shreveport, Louisiana, in June 1979:

We have trouble starting the engines. Bruce's [the pilot] magic finally works on number four of the left side; but number-five engine on the right is intransigent. . . . Twenty minutes later the master mechanics arrive in their truck and take the cover off the number-five engine. They stick the leads from the starting generator into the innards to jump-start it, just as you do with your car when the battery is dead. . . . Would you take off on your next civilian flight in a plane one of whose engines had to be jump-started?

Now, at 200 feet. . . . Suddenly the vital gyro instruments that show how a plane is flying, whether it is upright or turning, all begin to spin and tumble on both the pilot's and co-pilot's side. . . . Bruce opens a can of apple juice and drinks it down calmly. "This happens all the time," he says.

Obviously it does, for Bruce has no hesitation about the cure. He squeezes the can together with his hands and then jumps on it a bit, making the juice can a truncated V with a bubble at one end. He takes out his pocketknife and opens up part of the instrument panel, revealing the pumps for the worthless gyros. He wedges his sculpted juice can beneath the forward edge of the vacuum pumps. Then he ties the juice can securely in place with a bandage from the first aid kit. The gyros spin back to life. Bruce fits the instrument panel back together with his pocketknife. We go back to flying the mission.[14]

A tribute, no doubt, to the ingenuity of U.S. airmen, but a sad commentary on the strategic bombers they had to fly.

Bad as that was, unfortunately, it was not all. Even if the B–52s could fly, questions arose whether in the face of very much improved Soviet SLBM capabilities,[15] they could take off in time and whether, in the face of very much improved Soviet air defense forces,[16] they could actually reach their targets. Only the sea leg of the Triad, the SLBMs, remained safe enough; their 656 MIRVed missiles with nearly 5,000 warheads could bring awful devastation in a second strike. But the range of these missiles (2,880 miles) could not cover much strategically important Soviet territory, and their accuracy:yield ratio[17] was far from sufficient to be used against hard targets.

These potential realities of the mid 1970s produced the projected scenario of the "window of vulnerability" of the mid 1980s. Without warning, Soviet nuclear submarines just off the U.S. coastline could fire their SLBMs in a shallow, depressed trajectory at our (soft) strategic air bases. At the same time they could launch a portion of their ICBMs with sufficient warheads to destroy all our Minuteman missiles in their hardened silos. As a result practically all our ICBMs and about 70 percent of our B–52s (all those not on strip alert) would be eliminated. The decimated B–52 force would then have little chance to penetrate the fully prepared and wholly intact Soviet air defenses. We would still have available our SLBMs, which could kill a lot of Soviet citizens and devastate much of Soviet territory but could not damage Soviet strategic missile forces. Would we use them—would it be rational for us to use them? For the Soviet Union could combine its nuclear first strike with a massive propaganda campaign. Look, they would say to the American government and the American people, we have gained the decisive military advantage. We admit that you could kill many of our citizens, but we have not yet used most of our missiles; indeed, some of our missile silos can be repeatedly reloaded and you have no defense against them. Admittedly you have suffered some human casualties, but we have not yet begun to aim at your population centers. If you use your second-strike capability, we will turn our full, irresistible force against them. You Americans may start a senseless carnage, but you simply cannot gain the military advantage. Be sensible, save the lives of tens of millions of Americans and surrender. Surely you must see that being red is better than being dead.

To be sure, the scenario was not without its flaws. To begin with, it was most unlikely in the mid 1970s, and remained so in the late 1980s, that Soviet submarines could take positions off our coasts undetected. One or two might, but not many. Even the best were (and are) quite noisy, and U.S. surveillance and anti-submarine warfare capabilities were (and still are) formidable. If Soviet submarines would maneuver toward anything resembling attack position, the Navy would know about it. It quite probably would sink them, and at the very minimum our strategic bomber forces would be in the air well before any Soviet SLBMs could be launched. Then again, the destruction of our ICBM forces was (and is) far from a probable outcome. Admittedly Soviet missiles had an advantage with their high-yield warheads, and their accuracy had improved in the 1970s. All the same, it is quite unrealistic to expect the kind of performance accomplished by individual missiles, fired in peacetime over established test tracks, from all or even most missiles launched by the hundreds in wartime toward a variety of distant targets over previously untried trajectories.

The most basic flaw in the scenario of attack, however, involves the problem of timing. Just how would the attack by ICBMs and SLBMs be coordinated? Would the ICBMs with 30–minute flight times and SLBMs with 10–minute flight times be coordinated to hit their U.S. targets simultaneously? If so, the ICBMs would have to be launched 20 minutes earlier. With hundreds of ICBMs bearing down on the United States, our air defenses would know within a few minutes that something was seriously amiss. There would be time for the President to order our ICBMs to be launched and our B–52s to take off. Even if he would not be willing to make the irreversible decision to launch the missiles on warning, he would surely order the strategic bomber force, which in case of error could be recalled, into the air and out of harm's way. If, on the other hand, all Soviet missiles were launched simultaneously, Soviet ICBMs would still have 20–minute flight times when their SLBMs struck our air bases. There would be no ambiguity that we were under attack, but still enough time to launch our ICBMs before theirs could reach our silos. There are, of course, other variations in timing, but none that would not leave a high probability that not just one leg of the Triad but two of them—one with devastating soft-target and the other with significant hard-target capability—would in fact survive.

Its flaws notwithstanding, the scenario was not without lessons. It had always been recognized that designing and building a secure retaliatory capability would require a *great effort*. Once it had been built, however, it was widely assumed and fervently hoped that with reasonable maintenance it would hold up for decades. The "big push and be done with it" approach was well suited to the American temperament. It took our astronauts to the moon, and it built the Triad. Now we would have to learn that a secure retaliatory capability requires a *continuous effort* into the indefinite future. For when the Soviet Union reached assured second-strike capability, it did not stop. It pressed on toward first-strike capability. How could we trust the Soviet Union to be satisfied with strategic equivalence on any level? It could be seeking strategic superiority, and may achieve it if we let it. Thus, whether we like it or not, however much it runs against the grain, for decades to come our national existence will depend on our constant vigilance to assure that we are fully informed of all the strategic capabilities the Soviet Union is trying to develop. Our national existence will depend on our persistence of purpose in successfully countering any and all of its projected advances.

More specifically, the scenario should teach us that U.S. capability to deliver a devastating second strike on Soviet soft targets is not enough. Even if we have no first-strike intention, and we do not, credible deterrence requires that we build and maintain survivable hard-target capability. We must assure that after having absorbed a surprise first strike, we shall still have effective ways to reduce decisively (if we cannot altogether eliminate) Soviet capacity to continue the attack upon us.

Not the least important contribution of the scenario and its critics, however, was that they revealed just how fundamentally the condition of deterrence had changed in little over a decade. Until the mid 1970s Americans were confident that through strategic offensive weapons we could create an *objective certainty* that would preclude Soviet aggression. Our retaliation would be assured and horrible, no ifs, ands, or buts about it. No one, political pragmatist or ideological fanatic, calmly rational or in the grips of emotion, would take the risk. By the time of the Carter administration, however, this was no longer the case. We were still confident that the Soviets would not attack, but our confidence now rested on a *subjective probability*: our estimate that they would consider the risks too high.[18] The debate whether they would attack and whether we would actually retaliate was no longer purely academic.

Just how to proceed under such drastically altered circumstances raised many disputes. We would patch up the Triad. We would build a new, faster bomber, the B–1 (President Carter canceled the program but President Reagan reinstated it), and then the entirely new B–2 (Stealth bomber). We would build a new, more accurate intercontinental missile that could carry more warheads, the MX; and we would build a new submarine with a new, more accurate missile, the Trident, armed with much more accurate warheads (D–5s). We would even build a new category of missiles, the cruise missile, cheap, difficult to see and track by radar, and launchable from the ground, a plane, or a ship. But there were problems. Would a new SLBM, the D–5, be accurate enough to destroy Soviet ICBM silos? Though the B–1 would have twice the speed of the B–52, would it be able to penetrate Soviet airspace very much better? The B–2 could probably do so, but when it was finally rolled out in 1989 and the cost of (at a minimum) $500 million per plane was revealed, Congress had some difficulty recovering from "sticker shock."

The biggest problems, however, were with the MX. It is a better missile than the Minuteman, no question about that. But the quality of our ICBMs was not really the issue; it was their vulnerability within their silos. Originally we had hoped to turn to a mobile missile as a remedy, but as the development of the MX proceeded, and we placed more and more warheads in its nose cone, it became a fixed-base missile. So the question arose: Where could they be placed profitably? In the vulnerable silos of the Minuteman? That would not improve their survivability. In "superhardened" silos? that would not improve their survivability for long. Soon the accuracy:yield ratio of Soviet missiles could improve to the point where no concrete and steel shield could assure protection. What about "multiple protective shelters"? Build many, many silos throughout the country. Very much as in a shell game, most would be empty; only a few would actually hold MXs. The Soviets would never quite know where our missiles are, and they could never have enough missiles to target all, even most, of our silos. But it would be a very expensive undertaking. It would not be all that easy to move giant missiles from silo to silo, to truck them along I–80 or whatever, and to do so without detection. Worse still, most Americans do not want to have missile silos in their neighborhoods, whether they are filled or empty.

Then again, what about President Carter's preference for a "racetrack"? Dig a big, big hole, about 20 miles square. Place in it a circular railroad track on which flatbed cars carrying missiles could be moved around. Reinforce the whole thing with lots of steel and concrete, and top it off with a massive protective shield with a large number of doors that could be opened on command and through which missiles would be launched. The missiles underneath could be shifted regularly. No need to truck them along highways, and they could not be seen from spy satellites. But the costs would be fantastic. In any case, could we actually build such an enormous protective shelter? Where would we build it? There were no volunteers. In Nevada or Utah? When in 1981 the Republicans took control of the Senate, and those from Nevada and Utah held key chairmanships, some (not entirely in jest) suggested Georgia or Minnesota.

Another alternative would have mounted the MX on a manned aircraft. It never got off the ground. To lug a giant missile into the skies would have taken quite a plane. And it would have required some remarkable (kamikaze) volunteers to fly it. A more serious proposal urged a "dense pack." Do not disperse our missile silos; concentrate them. The first incoming Soviet missile would, predictably, destroy one of our silos. The gigantic explosion, however, would also produce colossal turbulence, intense heat, and all kinds of fallout that would decisively interfere with all other incoming Soviet missiles. On approach, if not detonated, they would be diverted and made useless. In a "fratricide" a Soviet missile would actually protect all other U.S. missiles in the vicinity. There were other suggestions as well, most recently, to make the MX mobile by placing it on railroad cars (rail garrison). A number of studies were undertaken, and reports were issued. Some were classified, others available to the public; some were technical, others readable for a layman; some were thorough and objective,[19] others, selective and partisan. It was agreed to build 100 MXs and place them in old-fashioned but further reinforced silos and in the meantime to develop a mobile, single-warhead Midgetman. Still, the controversy continues.

But while the public's attention was absorbed with this difficulty, a potentially more complicated and more formidable problem of credible deterrence was gradually becoming acute: the problem of strategic command, control, communication, and intelligence (C^3I). It started innocuously enough in July 1962. As part of its last atmospheric nuclear test, the United States detonated a 1.4–megaton hydrogen bomb 248 miles above Johnson Island in the Pacific. In Hawaii, some 800 miles away, streetlights failed, burglar alarms rang, and circuit breakers popped open in power lines. Scientists were at first puzzled; with the Nuclear Test Ban Treaty taking effect, they could not explore the phenomenon with further experiments. Soon the physicists at the Rand Corporation came up with a theory.

Earthbound gamma rays from a nuclear explosion in space eventually hit air in the upper atmosphere and knocked out compton electrons, which were deflected by the earth's magnetic field and forced to undergo a turning motion about the field lines. By a complex mechanism, these electrons emit EMP [electromagnetic pulse], which at ground level can radiate over thousands of miles with a peak strength of 50,000 volts per meter. Any metal object picks up the pulse. If the object, such as an antenna or a cable, leads to sensitive electronic components, the pulse can cause extensive damage.[20]

All of which meant that a single nuclear blast 350 miles above Missouri or Kansas could shut down the power grid and knock out communications from coast to coast. Civilian communications and possibly military communications as well.

A reliable and enduring strategic C^3I system is crucial to deterrence. (Needless to say, it is also crucial for avoiding a false alarm, which may trigger an accidental war with all its horrible consequences.) It is necessary that the National Command Authorities have early warning of an impending attack and have prompt information about the character, the progress, and the consequences of the attack. In turn, it is necessary that the President be able to send emergency action messages (EAMs) that promptly reach our strategic forces, that he be able to communicate the full range of specific responses, and that he be able to continue to do this throughout and even after a nuclear exchange.

If messages to the National Command Authorities of an impending attack can be disturbed or interrupted, our strategic forces could be caught unprepared and suffer enormous and unnecessary losses seriously reducing their second-strike capability. If the President's EAMs or their authentication could be disturbed and interrupted, his flexibility in determining the appropriate response could be lost; worse still, our second-strike capacity could become paralyzed. If the system is not enduring, the President's first EAM may well be his last. All the efforts to assure survivability and redundancy of our weapons system could be for naught. Since the electromagnetic pulse threatened all of the 43 ways that the President is supposed to have for reaching our strategic forces, it jeopardized all three legs of the Triad. It raised serious doubt about our carefully constructed system of deterrence.

One possible corrective was the use of satellites. They, too, are vulnerable to EMP but, unlike huge ground based networks, they and their ground stations can be protected from the far-flung particles of a nuclear blast. Indeed, more than 70 percent of military long-haul communications now depend on satellites. Every airborne command post and almost all B–52s and Minuteman missiles are equipped with satellite terminals. On the ground, fiber optics seem to offer some defense against EMP. The Navy uses fiber optics to connect satellite ground stations with data-processing centers for the Defense Satellite Communication System. All the same, much of our C^3I system remains vulnerable to EMP. Just how vulnerable is difficult to know and impossible to tell, because such vulnerabilities, for the sake of deterrence, must remain top secret.

As if this were not bad enough, the vulnerability of our strategic C^3I system was exacerbated by the hard-target capability of the SS–18s and SS–19s. Ground terminals for satellite communications, soft, immobile targets, were defenseless even against earlier Soviet missiles, but command centers, nodes where the channels converge and that cannot be freely multiplied, seemed safe enough. The North American Air Defense Command (NORAD) is located in a complex of steel buildings set some 1,400 feet inside the granite of Cheyenne Mountain in Colorado. The headquarters of the Strategic Air Command (SAC) is deep underground near Omaha, Nebraska, and the Alternate National Military Command Center is dug into the hills near Fort Ritchie, Maryland. They were designed to survive a direct missile attack. Whether they could actually survive 24–megaton SS 18 warheads hitting within 400 yards and 10–megaton SS–19 warheads hitting within 250 yards has become rather less certain. And whether their main sensors, upon which they depend for receiving and sending messages, would survive has become highly doubtful.

The only remedy for the vulnerability of command centers on the ground so far is provided by airborne command posts. An aircraft code-named Looking Glass is always in the air, carrying a general with a complete battle staff ready to take charge of the B–52 bombers and Minuteman missiles in case SAC headquarters is obliterated. For eight hours the aircraft follows an unpredictable course over the United States and does not land until a similar aircraft with another general and another battle staff has taken off from Omaha. There are other planes always ready on the runways to provide senior military commanders with other airborne command posts (for instance, the Airborne Launch Control System and the Post-Attack Command and Control System). They provide, however, only a partial remedy. In peacetime the system works quite well, and in war the command posts may be secure while in the air. But in war they might find it difficult to land, and there might not be any planes left on the ground that could take off and continue the relay.

By far the most perilous problem of the vulnerability of command centers, however, is the vulnerability of the ultimate command authority, the one node where all portions of the C^3I system intersect: *the President of the United States*. If the Soviet Union in a surprise move attacked Washington, D.C., there would be very little time—no more than the 30 minutes of an ICBM's flight time, and less than 10 minutes in case of an SLBM attack—from the beginning of an attack to the destruction of the President (and of his successors who were in the city). The White House shelter would be useless, and the National Military Command Center in the Pentagon not much more help. His best chance would be to fly by Marine Corps helicopter to Andrews Air Force Base, and board one of the four E–4s (converted B–747s) that are always ready to take off and are equipped as national emergency airborne command posts. "The chances of successfully evacuating the President to a survivable command center during that interval," concluded the Carnegie Endowment Report, "are not zero, but they are not high either."[21]

NOTES

1. We kept the lights from showing through the windows though no German or Japanese plane could get within thousands of miles. We collected mountains of pots, but with the installation of indoor latrines at all Army bases, there remained nothing imaginable for which they could be used.

2. Bernard Brodie, *Strategy in the Missile Age* (Princeton: Princeton University Press, 1959), pp. 107–44.

3. United States Senate, *Study of Airpower*, Hearings before the Subcommittee on

the Air Force of the Committee on Armed Services, 84th Congress, 2nd Session (Washington, D.C.: U.S. Government Printing Office, 1956).

4. John M. Collins, *U.S.–Soviet Military Balance: Concepts and Capabilities, 1960–1980* (New York: McGraw-Hill, 1980), p. 32; Stewart Menaul, *The Illustrated Encyclopedia of the Strategy, Tactics, and Weapons of Russian Military Power* (New York: St. Martin's Press, 1980), pp. 87, 91, 206. In January 1989, at a meeting in Moscow of U.S., Soviet, and Cuban officials reviewing the missile crisis, the Soviet delegation reported that in October 1962 the Soviets had installed or were about to install 42 medium-range missiles in Cuba. They had only 20 ICBMs in the Soviet Union that could reach the United States (*New York Times*, January 29, 1989, pp. 1, 10). Whether this was actually the case or just a ploy designed to persuade Americans, on the eve of arms-reduction negotiations, that we always overestimated the Soviet forces in being, is difficult to know.

5. Quoted in Harland B. Moulton, *From Superiority to Parity: The United States and the Strategic Arms Race, 1961–1971* (Westport, Conn.: Greenwood Press, 1973), p. 114.

6. Ibid.

7. A total of 210 in 1966, which then steadily declined throughout the decade.

8. This was the Pentagon definition of "assured destruction" in 1968.

9. Henry Kissinger, *White House Years* (Boston: Little, Brown, 1979), p. 216.

10. Collins, *U.S.–Soviet Military Balance*, p. 128, 454.

11. Strobe Talbott, *End Game, the Inside Story of SALT II* (New York: Harper and Row, 1979), p. 28. See also Moulton *From Superiority to Parity*, pp. 295–96. Actually, the SS–9 (circular error probable [CEP], 0.4 nautical mile) was not significantly less accurate than the Minuteman II (CEP, 0.34 nautical mile) and was actually more accurate than the Titan II (CEP, 0.8 nautical mile) or the Minuteman I (CEP, 0.5 nautical mile), which until 1970 represented about half of our ICBMs. Collins, *U.S.–Soviet Military Balance*, pp. 443, 446.

12. Kissinger, *White House Years*, p. 811.

13. The SS–19 (Mod 2) could carry a 10–megaton warhead with a CEP of only 0.14 nautical mile.

14. Arthur T. Hadley, *The Straw Giant, Triumph and Failure: America's Armed Forces* (New York: Random House, 1986), pp. 211–15.

15. From 1972 to 1980, while the number of U.S. nuclear submarines (41) and SLBM tubes (656) remained constant, Soviet nuclear submarines doubled in number (33 to 69), and so did SLBM tubes (497 to 987). Collins, *U.S.–Soviet Military Balance*, p. 748.

16. Their air defense force, PVO-Strany, was built up to 7,000 radar stations, 2,600 interceptor aircraft, and about 10,000 surface-to-air launchers. Menaul, *Illustrated Encyclopedia*, p. 51.

17. Polaris A–2, 0.5 nautical mile CEP/800 kilotons (kt); Polaris A–3, 0.5 nautical mile CEP/200 kt; Poseidon, 0.25 nautical mile CEP/40 kt.

18. See Cyrus Vance, *Hard Choices: Critical Years in America's Foreign Policy* (New York: Simon and Schuster, 1983), pp. 49–50.

19. For example, Carnegie Endowment for International Peace, *Challenges for U.S. National Security* (Washington, D.C.: Carnegie Endowment for International Peace, 1982); and United States, President's Commission on Strategic Forces, "Report," Washington, D.C., April 1983.

20. William J. Broad, ''Nuclear Pulse (I): Awakening to the Chaos Factor,'' *Science*, 212 (May 29, 1981), p. 1010.

21. Carnegie Endowment for International Peace, *Challenges for U.S. National Security*, p. 107.

3

BALANCED STRATEGIC DETERRENCE

There are still excellent reasons for maintaining massive retaliatory forces, but let us face it, they can no longer assure deterrence. Our people remain at peril, our second strike capacity is no longer invulnerable, even our President is not quite safe.

Actually the psychology was never wholly satisfactory. For the logic of deterrence by strategic offense was always entangled in the pleasures of vengeance. Marshal of the Royal Air Force Sir John Slessor wrote:

When things are really bad the people's morale is greatly sustained by the knowledge that we are giving back as good as we are getting, and this engenders a sort of combatant pride, like that of the charlady in a government office who was asked during the London blitz where her husband was—''he's in the Middle East, the bloody coward!''[1]

Air Marshal Slessor may not have been a qualified psychologist, and, of course, Americans did not have to endure heavy aerial bombardment. Still, had they been subjected to it during World War II, they might have felt much like the Londoners. Then, just after the war, while the United States had a monopoly of nuclear weapons, they might have been prepared to contemplate deterring aggression through massive retaliation or, if worse came to worst, fighting a war by devastating an enemy's homeland. But conditions have changed radically.

Until the 1960s the failure of an offense-dominated strategy might have meant heavy casualties and a battle lost, not won. But when the United States became vulnerable to nuclear attack, the perils of such a strategy escalated enormously. If it should fail to deter, a Soviet surprise attack would surely bring unimaginable horrors to our country and might conceivably impair our retaliatory capability. Even if we should have much left with which to strike back, it is doubtful that

Americans cowering in cellars or wandering about in smoldering, radioactive ruins would get much solace (let alone combatant pride) from knowing that "we are giving back as good as we are getting," that we were successfully killing tens, even hundreds, of millions of people in the Soviet Union. Even more to the point, it is doubtful that in peacetime Americans thinking of Soviet nuclear attack would feel reassured by the notion that their survival rests on the probability with which we could inflict as great or greater horrors upon an aggressor. Indeed, most Americans prefer to black out of their minds the whole nuclear problem, and those few who do think about it often become so overwhelmed as to seek refuge in such slogans as "No nukes are good nukes!"

THE FIRST STRATEGIC DEFENSE INITIATIVE

The best defense may still have been a good offense, but at the time the United States became vulnerable to nuclear attack, the need for a searching reexamination of this particular conventional wisdom became acute. If, in the logic of pragmatic calculations, maximizing the cost of aggression helps deter it, why should minimizing the benefits to the aggressor not contribute to the same purpose? Why should deterrence be determined by the masses of Soviet people we could kill? Why can't it also depend on the masses of Americans whose lives we could save? As we moved into the 1960s, scholars—Henry Kissinger, Bernard Brodie, and others—were attracted to a deterrence strategy that balanced both offensive and defensive components. And so were political decision makers— the Governor of New York, Nelson Rockefeller, and the newly elected President of the United States.

John F. Kennedy was prepared to embark on a major defense effort. President Dwight Eisenhower had already started developing the passive defense of our strategic forces. It was under his administration that the long-range ballistic missile early warning system (BMEWS) was established, that significant progress toward "hardened" protective shelters for our missiles was begun, and that, in order to ensure the survivability of our retaliatory forces through redundancy and diversity, the Triad was developed. The Kennedy administration followed through, even expanded and accelerated these programs. It did more than that. It launched what was for all practical purposes our first strategic defense initiative.

President Kennedy's program included passive measures designed to protect the American people. In order to give the urban residents a chance, it was decided to locate strategic bases as far from cities as possible. John T. McNaughton, a high Defense Department official, explained:

It is almost inevitable that military forces will be objects of attack during war; it is not inevitable that *civilian* populations will be targets—at least, not if some efforts are made to provide for the possibility of separating anti-military and anti-civilian attacks.[2]

The argument was reinforced by the suggestion that the United States should avoid targeting Soviet cities.

In order to improve the chances of survival of Americans everywhere through-out the country, a civil defense effort was launched. In May 1961, only a few months after taking office, the President urged a massive, federally sponsored shelter program. Two months later his television address to the nation on the Berlin crisis included the appeal:

In the event of an attack, the lives of those families which are not hit in a nuclear blast and fire can still be saved—if they can be warned to take shelter and if that shelter is available. We owe that kind of insurance to our families—and to our country. . . . But the time to start is now.[3]

The president's defensive initiative went further still. It also included plans for the development of active instruments: missiles that could intercept enemy ICBMs approaching the United States. The ABM (antiballistic missile), as it became known later, was to reduce further the possible damage done to the United States (primarily to its people, but also to its retaliatory capacity), and thus to reinforce the deterrent effect of our strategic offense. We seemed to be entering the era of balanced deterrence.

It was not to be. Soon the no-cities approach was challenged. American cities would be destroyed, so the argument ran, but not because they happened to be located near military installations. They would be targeted by the Soviet Union in order to increase American costs in a war and as a measure of deterring a U.S. first strike. In turn, we could not afford to forgo targeting Soviet population centers for the simple reason that for a retaliatory strike, there would not be many other meaningful strategic alternatives available. We could hardly expect to deter aggression by a capability to destroy empty Soviet silos from which missiles had already been fired at us. The Kennedy administration offered no vigorous rebuttal and quietly let its no-cities initiative drop.

Sooner still, the civil defense initiative got into trouble. The President's call for the construction of nuclear fallout shelters had an instant, dramatic effect. Some vehemently attacked it. Presidential adviser Arthur M. Schlesinger, Jr., observed:

Many on the utopian left feared that the program, if it were not actual preparation for a surprise nuclear attack on the Soviet Union, would at the very least give the American people a false sense of security and therefore encourage them in reckless foreign adven-tures. Within the United States itself they perceived it as an incitement to vigilantism, if not a means by which the radical right could seize control of local communities. The program, in short, became in their minds a portent of preventative war and fascism.[4]

Others enthusiastically embraced the President's call. Altogether too enthu-siastically. Suddenly a fallout shelter fever gripped the nation. Thinking of the unthinkable, people began acting wildly. They overwhelmed the civil defense authorities with questions; they bought thousands of home shelters, many at exorbitant prices; they dug up their suburban backyards; and they filled their basements with canned food.

People began talking wildly. A Jesuit priest offered the advice that shelter owners had the moral right to repel intrusive neighbors by "whatever means will effectively deter their assault." The civil defense coordinator of Riverside County, California, urged his constituents to arm themselves; his colleague in Las Vegas, Nevada, demanded the help of the National Guard to protect private shelters from an invasion by frantic fellow Americans from a neighboring county and a neighboring state.[5]

The lesson seemed to be that in order to sustain popular interest and popular support for a massive fallout shelter program, popular anxiety would have to be raised to so high a level and maintained for so long a time that it would tear our social and political fabric asunder. Thus, even if the technical problems of building effective fallout shelters could be solved, even if the required financial costs (through the public and/or private sectors) could be mobilized, the psychological costs to individual citizens and the political costs to our democratic system would prove to be prohibitive. In any case, the Kennedy administration apparently drew this conclusion and toned down its campaign. Public and congressional interest promptly disappeared. Three years in succession, the executive branch proposed a fallout shelter program but it did not push it, and Congress chose to ignore it. A process of identifying and licensing already existing "shelter" spaces continued, but with little interest and small appropriations.[6]

That left the ABM. The debate lasted longer, but the outcome was very much the same. The Soviets apparently thought it was a good idea. During his visit in London (February 10, 1967) Premier Aleksei Kosygin explained: "I believe that the defensive systems, which prevent attack, are not the cause of the arms race, but constitute a factor preventing the death of people." A group of distinguished American scientists vigorously disagreed. They argued that an ABM system was (1) technically impossible, (2) easily counteracted by new offensive techniques, and (3) very costly. Furthermore, it would worry the Soviet Union, and hence would exacerbate the arms race.[7]

Simply put, at the core of the problem was the very short flight time of the ICBM. Looking at it from the perspective of the defender, the flight path of an enemy missile could be divided into several segments. First, the distance it would travel before we would become aware of it. In the early 1960s, when we had to rely on radar for warning, this segment could take at least ten minutes, especially if time was taken (as it should have been) to make certain that there was no mistake. Second, the distance it would travel while we were calculating its trajectory and speed. This could take another ten minutes. Third, the distance the missile would travel while the decision was made to intercept, while the decision was communicated to the local commander, while the latter authenticated his orders, while the interceptor was launched, and while the interceptor traveled to the point of interception. Quite possibly time would have run out;

but if not, interception would take place very close to the target, less than a few hundred miles—probably over Canada, possibly over the United States.[8]

The prospect of a U.S. weapons system that could intercept a Soviet ICBM armed with a nuclear warhead in Canadian airspace did not noticeably elate our neighbors to the north (whose permission, incidentally, we needed for the installation and maintenance of our long-range radar network). Worse still, at the speeds at which ICBMs travel, interception by direct hit could not be expected. The best we could do would be a close pass. It seemed possible that an intercepting missile could approach near enough so that its thermonuclear warhead, if detonated at the right time, could through X rays, particles, and blast incapacitate the incoming warhead. In other words, if all the technological and operational difficulties could be overcome, successful interception could occur through a nuclear explosion (the larger, the surer) above our own or friendly territory. The American people understandably did not feel elated at the prospect.

Without an accompanying massive civil defense effort, an ABM system would not be a very meaningful instrument for defending the people of North America, and it soon became clear that the needed fallout shelters were not going to be built. But reinforced shelters were being built for our ICBMs. The question remained: Could the ABM at least enhance their survivability?

Not for long. It was promptly explained that a thermonuclear interception in space would "bedazzle" our radar on the ground, the radar upon which we were depending for warning and tracking. In fact, it would produce an invisible channel through which any number of Soviet missiles could be delivered against us. After the first "successful" interception we could see Soviet ICBMs when we felt them—or, rather, when we did not feel anything anymore.

It was, of course, nowhere written that such a "successful" interception would destroy even one enemy missile. The Soviet Union could launch a decoy, in which case we would succeed in incapacitating a dud—not much of a gain— while the costs to us would remain the same. This focused attention on yet another problem with the ABM. It was not so much that it would cost vast sums of money, but that for a fraction of our cost the Soviet Union could develop "penetration aids" that would make our expenditures useless.

By February 1965 the Secretary of Defense developed the most profound doubts about the ABM and other defense-oriented measures. In his testimony before the House Armed Services Committee, Robert McNamara made it clear (1) that no foreseeable defense program within the assured cost restraints could reduce American fatalities to a level much below 80 million unless an enemy delayed its attack on our cities long enough for our strategic (offensive) missile forces to reduce enemy ICBM forces substantially, and (2) that beyond a certain level of defense, the cost advantage lies increasingly with the offense, a fact that should be taken into account in any decision to commit the nation to large expenditures for additional defensive measures.[9]

With that, for all intents and purposes, the first strategic defense initiative had come to an end. The hegemony of the offense was reestablished. Typically,

Figure 2
ICBM Flight Segments, 1962

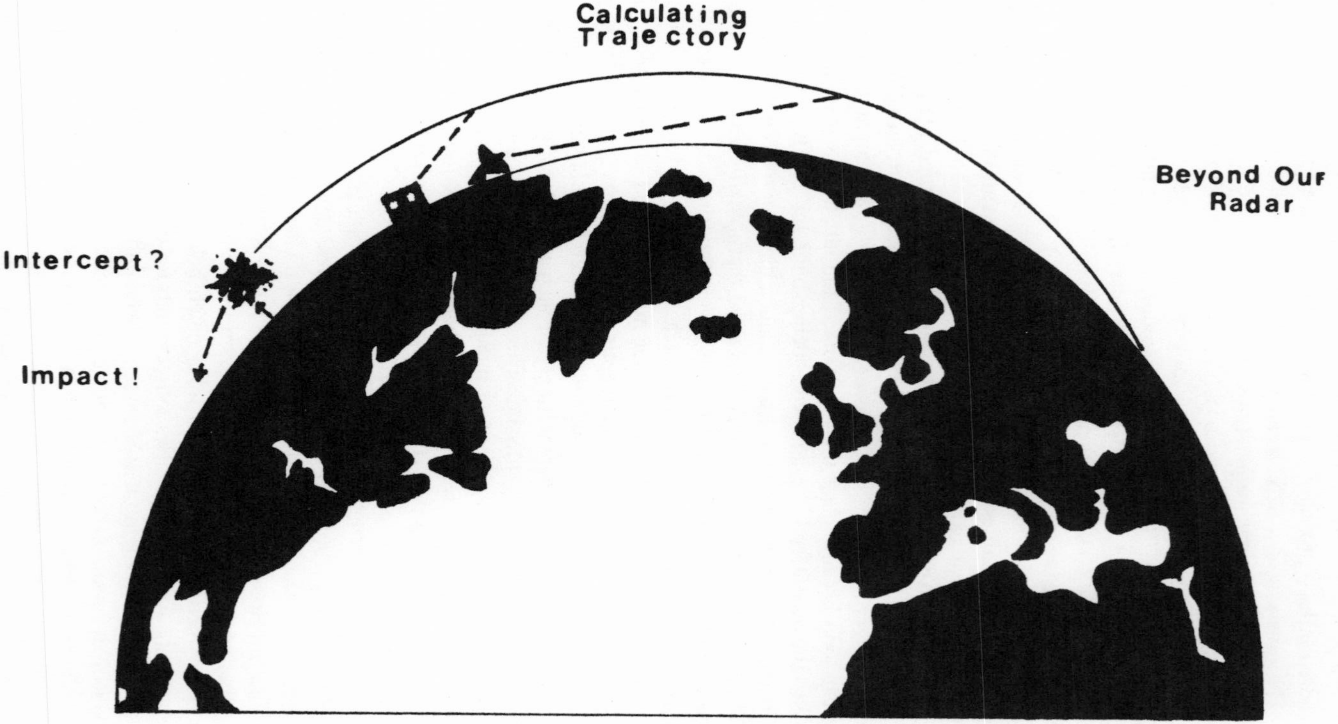

Calculating
Trajectory

Beyond Our
Radar

Intercept?

Impact!

when the evidence became unmistakable that the Soviet Union was spending much money on civil defense and was developing its own ABM, the official answer was to build additional offensive capacity. Our bombers were equipped with new penetration aids (electronic countermeasures designed to confuse enemy radar), and our ICBMs were equipped with multiple warheads, each independently targeted.

This is not to say that defense as a component of strategic deterrence was altogether ignored. Research and development of the ABM continued. In September 1967 President Johnson decided to deploy an ABM system. In March 1969, after less than two months in office, President Nixon decided to proceed with the program. Both decisions triggered intense debates among physicists, defense analysts, newspaper editors, columnists, and members of Congress. The Senate authorized funds by a one-vote majority in August 1969; resistance remained virulent, and the program was whittled down steadily by Congress.

In any case, by the time it had reached Congress, we were talking about a very different kind of ABM system. It was to be "limited" and "thin." Supposedly it would be sufficient to defend against a future nuclear attack by China (projected date the 1980s!) or an accidental attack from any source. Clearly it was not designed to reduce (significantly) the cost in American lives in case of Soviet attack. In fact, its value as a credible component of strategic deterrence was practically nil.

STRATEGIC ARMS LIMITATION TREATY I

The attitudes of Presidents Johnson and Nixon toward the ABM may have been motivated by partisan considerations. Alternatively, they may have had in mind the possibility that as a result of further development, at some future time the ABM might contribute an active defense of our ICBMs whose survivability rested entirely on passive defense. But both, and this was made perfectly clear in the case of President Nixon, saw in the ABM a "bargaining chip" in arms control negotiations.

For the failure of President Kennedy's strategic defense initiative did not restore public confidence in strategic deterrence based exclusively on offensive weapons. The psychology was still wrong. If Americans thought about it, they were still uncomfortable with the knowledge that our security rested entirely on our capability to devastate Soviet territory and destroy Soviet people. And the political coalition that fought civil defense, and especially the ABM, was prepared to lead them in another direction. Instead of our investing vast sums and much effort in building weapons that could intercept and destroy approaching Soviet missiles in the air, they insisted, we should concentrate on negotiating treaties that could obligate the Soviet Union to destroy its strategic missiles before they could take off or, better still, that could obligate them not to build strategic missiles in the first place. Surely it would be a far cheaper method of damage limitation. Thus, by the late 1960s popular pressure was building for a

strategic deterrence that balanced strong military capabilities with vigorous diplomatic initiatives. Naturally such negotiations would require goodwill and good
faith by the United States; that would be assured through popular participation
in our democratic system. It would also require goodwill and good faith by the
Soviet Union, and that would have to be assumed.

Not everyone, of course, was ready to assume the goodwill and the good faith
of the Soviet Union. Certainly President Nixon was not, but he recognized the
growing popularity of the idea of arms control. He needed to keep the intensity
of public debate and congressional opposition on foreign policy issues manageable in order to gain time to extricate the United States from Vietnam with honor.
He was confident in his own bargaining skills as a statesman and in his right as
President to determine the timing and the tempo of negotiations with a foreign
power. But he needed bargaining chips.

As a matter of fact, President Nixon could not, until practically the final
stages, control the timing or the tempo of negotiations. Pressures from the press
and politicized university communities at home, not to mention from our allies
in Western Europe, were too insistent and persistent.[10] And the President had
precious few bargaining chips. Our strategic offensive forces were holding at a
plateau; their ICBM and SLBM forces were steadily expanding. We were testing
multi-warhead missiles (MIRVs), and some in the government thought that they
could be used as bargaining chips. In fact, not once throughout the negotiations
did the Soviet delegation raise the subject, and when we did, they showed
absolutely no interest.[11] Soviet negotiators did show interest in the ABM, but
the domestic campaign against it remained virulent. Just how it could serve as
a bargaining chip when few at home believed that the system would ever be
deployed is not easy to see. Indeed, President Nixon was left with only two
major assets: (1) Soviet anxieties about improving Chinese–U.S. relations and
(2) Soviet yearning to be formally legitimized by the United States as an equal
in global affairs. He used them effectively.

At the Moscow summit in 1972 the SALT I treaty[12] was signed. It was done
in a televised atmosphere of bonhomie among equals. It limited the deployment
of ABM systems to two sites each (one around the national capital, another
around a single cluster of ICBMs). It froze for five years the total number of
strategic missiles but permitted "modernization" of ICBMs and the deployment
of a limited number of additional SLBMs, provided an equivalent number of
older ICBMs or SLBMs was taken out of service. It froze the number of heavy
missiles and prohibited the conversion of light missiles into heavies, but it did
not clearly define the weight boundary between the two. It said nothing about
warheads. Accompanying the treaty was a statement of "Basic Principles of
U.S.–Soviet Relations," which, while general in content and bland in tone, was
a joint declaration of the two superpowers on global affairs.

SALT I was a significant accomplishment. It contributed to détente, an effort
of peaceful coexistence between the ideologically divided superpowers. The
amelioration of tensions could reduce the predisposition to aggression, and that

would be a major gain. In the shorter view the treaty could serve as a means of testing Soviet intentions, and it could become a first step toward arms reduction. These would be welcome opportunities.

All the same, SALT I did not significantly affect the arms race. By the time it was signed, the leading edge of arms research and development had moved from launchers to warheads: to increase the number of reentry vehicles carried by each missile, to enhance their capacity to penetrate, and to improve their accuracy. In fact, advance along these lines accelerated. Nor did the treaty reduce our vulnerability to Soviet strategic offensive forces. The number of Soviet missiles may have remained the same, but the number of warheads they could rain upon the United States to destroy Americans nearly doubled during the five-year term of the treaty. Worse still, with their sharply improved accuracy "modernized" Soviet missiles could predictably, for the first time, seriously impair and possibly destroy vital components of our (second-strike) retaliatory capability. In this fundamental sense SALT I did not, to say the least, improve our strategic deterrence.

It did, however, fundamentally alter the scope of strategic deterrence. With the treaty, arms control negotiations became a part of our deterrence strategy. The concept was not officially stated, perhaps not even formulated, but through the multidimensional manner in which the President and his national security adviser conducted the negotiations, it became apparent that we were moving toward a broader and more complex Grand Strategic Triad: an optimal mix of strategic offense, strategic defense, and arms control.

Indeed, during the next four years all the domestic political upheaval notwithstanding, the Nixon administration, then the Ford administration, moved carefully along this road. Although it had the technology, the United States did not try to improve the accuracy:yield ratio of its strategic missiles. Nor did we increase the size of our missile forces. In November 1972, just six months after the signing of the "interim treaty" of SALT I, negotiations for a longer-term and more comprehensive arms control agreement began. During the Moscow summit in 1974, President Nixon agreed to reduce the ABM deployment from two sites to one, and even that one ABM cluster was never fully deployed. Late that year at Vladivostok, President Ford agreed to an equal total of 2,400 offensive strategic nuclear launch vehicles, including an equal subtotal of 1,320 launchers with multiple warheads.

But overall progress was slow. The United States was willing to appease the Soviet Union on legitimacy. In July 1975 President Ford traveled to Helsinki to sign the European Security Conference Charter, which spoke of human rights and the free flow of information but dramatically demonstrated American acceptance of Soviet hegemony over Eastern Europe. The United States was also prepared to offer concessions on weapons, concessions that would increase Soviet deterrence of a U.S. nuclear strike. What it was not prepared to offer were concessions that would weaken U.S. deterrence of a Soviet nuclear strike. We would agree to a straight swap: our first-strike capability for their first-strike capability, but not any deal that would trade our second-strike capability for their first-strike capability.

Secretary of State Kissinger expected the negotiations to be a slow, laborious, and gradual process. He did not disdain incremental gains toward an overall, long-term goal of a mutually acceptable and beneficial arms control agreement. Even so, all the increments did not add up to a treaty by January 20, 1977, when he had to leave office.

STRATEGIC ARMS LIMITATION TREATY II

By that time the five-year term of the Interim Treaty was about to run out. The urgency of the situation, moreover, was exacerbated by the rate and direction of Soviet military buildup. During the treaty period, in practically every category of arms the Soviet arsenal grew in numbers and/or improved in quality. In strategic weapons specifically, the number of Soviet SLBMs doubled, a new Soviet long-range bomber (TU–26 Backfire B) was introduced, and three new Soviet missiles (SS–17, SS–18, SS–19) with much improved accuracy, each with double or more than double the warheads of our ICBMs, were deployed. Since the 1960s Soviet strategic forces had posed a threat to our people; now they posed a threat to our retaliatory forces as well. Clearly our strategic deterrence was not improving.

By the time Jimmy Carter became President, it was evident that the United States had not prevented Soviet advance toward a first strike capability—not through the SALT I negotiations and not through a decade of unilateral self-restraint in its own development of a first-strike capability. Assuring that the Soviet Union could not, under any set of circumstances, see a profit in a surprise attack on our retaliatory (second-strike) forces had become an imperative of national security. The question was: Could the Soviet Union be persuaded to limit the number of its "time urgent hard target capable" missiles.

Ever since SALT I, Secretary of State Kissinger had been trying to accomplish this by persuading the Soviet leaders to reduce the number of their "heavy" missiles. He could not do it. But now even this unattained achievement would have been insufficient. With the addition of MIRVs and very much improved accuracy of Soviet "medium" missiles, only deep cuts in the number of *all* their ICBMs could impair the first-strike capability. It posed an enormous challenge, testing to the utmost the utility of arms control negotiations as a means to improve deterrence.

President Carter did not have much experience in international diplomacy; worse still, his bargaining chips were in extremely short supply. He had practically no political chips. The Russians were still very much interested in the legitimacy derived from being treated as equals by the Americans and from association with the United States in international ventures. But during the presidential campaign Governor Carter had attacked détente, and the Helsinki Treaty in particular, and voiced his regret about "our government's continuing failure to oppose the denial of freedom in Eastern Europe and in the Soviet Union."[13] President Carter's inaugural address included the statement: "Because we are free we can never be indifferent to the fate of freedom elsewhere. Our moral sense dictates a clear preference for those societies which share with us an abiding respect for individual human rights." In office he added symbolic acts to his rhetoric. He sent a letter to Andrei Sakharov, a prominent dissident intellectual in the Soviet Union, then received Vladimir Bukovsky, a prominent dissident in exile, in the Oval Office. The Soviet leadership found such activities provocative. They resented them as efforts to interfere with their internal affairs, which was bad enough. What hurt them more was the assertion of American moral superiority and the attempt to conduct international relations based on this moral superiority.[14]

President Carter had little more in the way of military bargaining chips. In SALT I we had sacrificed our strategic defensive weapons; since then we had held our strategic offensive weapons at a plateau. All we had were new weapons in research and development. A new nuclear submarine (Trident) could carry more missiles with larger and more accurate warheads, but their range and their accuracy would still not be sufficient to pose a threat to hardened Soviet ICBM silos. A new bomber (B–1) would be faster and its capability to penetrate Soviet airspace might be greater, but it was still too slow to pose the threat of a surprise attack. New systems of cruise missiles (ground launched, sea launched, or air launched) also could penetrate and conceivably surprise the defense, but they are not accurate enough to destroy hard targets.[15] In short, none of these new weapons were designed to be, or were particularly suitable for, a first strike. The Minuteman III could deliver a surprise attack, and we did have almost ready for deployment a new guidance system (INS–20) and a new warhead (Mark 12A) that would improve its prospects of destroying a Soviet silo to 88 percent. Moreover, we were developing a new missile (MX) that would "increase confidence to a comfortable 99.9 percent."[16] But even when all the improvements had been made and when the MX was deployed, the United States would still not have a first-strike capability. All the "time-urgent hard target capable" missiles would still have too few warheads to destroy all Soviet ICBMs, let alone all Soviet strategic retaliatory vehicles. To contemplate a surprise attack on the Soviet Union, knowing full well that its retaliation would certainly produce altogether unacceptable costs for us, is not a first-strike capability but a qualification for the Pennsylvania Home for the Bewildered.

Soon after he took office, President Carter decided to open negotiations in the first high-level contact with the Soviet Union with a "comprehensive" proposal. It would cut deeply into the Vladivostok ceilings, reducing the total strategic launchers of each side from 2,400 to 1,800 or at most to 2,000, limiting all the strategic launchers with MIRVs to 1,100 or not more than 1,200, all the ICBMs with MIRVs to 550, and all the heavy ICBMs to 150. All these reductions would have represented major Soviet sacrifices. Existing Soviet arsenals would drop below the minimum level necessary to cripple our land-based strategic missiles.

In turn, President Carter offered to sacrifice the development of U.S. "hard target killers." The development, testing, and deployment of any new ICBMs would be banned, and flight testing of existing missiles severely curtailed. In short, President Carter offered to return to the theory and conditions of the 1960s. Mutual assured destruction could once again become mutual assured deterrence: neither side would have a chance to launch a successful first strike; both would possess a survivable second-strike capability.

The Soviet leadership turned him down flat. President Leonid Brezhnev opened the first meeting with a "diatribe in which he catalogued alleged human rights abuses in the United States." He also was quoted as saying that "the constructive development of relations was impossible . . . if the U.S. did not respect the principles of equality, non-interference in each other's internal affairs and mutual benefit." At the meeting President Brezhnev called the U.S. proposal "unconstructive and one-sided" and "harmful to Soviet security." Afterward, in a press conference Foreign Minister Andrei Gromyko denounced it as a "cheap and shady maneuver" aimed at achieving "unilateral advantages."[17] The Secretary of State was shocked, President Carter was surprised. Henry Kissinger himself, it was explained, thought that the Soviet Union might welcome their proposal. Now it was rejected, and rejected brutally. There seemed to be no alternative but to rely once again on our strategic offensive weapons for deterrence of a nuclear attack.

To be sure, the President canceled the B–1 strategic bomber program, but his decision was made on cost-effectiveness grounds. The B–52, modernized, loaded with sophisticated electronic equipment, and armed with cruise missiles, would perform just as well at very much less cost. Either approach, moreover, would have only been a stopgap measure until the ultramodern Stealth bomber could be developed and deployed in the 1990s.[18] The deployment of the new Trident submarine, however, was now within sight. The modernization of the Minuteman with a much improved guidance system and a more powerful warhead was moving ahead. So was the testing of cruise missiles. And so was the development of the MX.

Negotiations toward a SALT II treaty continued, but with a fundamental difference. Any expectations that the Soviet Union might be prepared to trade away its emerging first-strike capability fell victim to realism. When SALT II was signed in 1979, it did project (into 1981) a reduction in the aggregate number of missiles from 2,400 to 2,250 and a limit of ICBMs with MIRVs of 820, but it did not significantly affect the rapidly expanding Soviet arsenal of warheads. At the time they possessed some 5,500 warheads, but under the treaty these could quite legitimately expand to more than double this number. Indeed, by 1985 the total of Soviet ICBM and SLBM reentry vehicles passed the 8,800 mark,[19] which would allow a combination of SS–18s and SS–19s capable of raining some 5,500 highly accurate 550–kiloton warheads (the Minuteman's most advanced 12A warhead has a yield of 335 kilotons) on 1,000 missile silos and perhaps a few hundred command and communications centers. There would still be 600 warheads left, many of them in the megaton range, to devastate American cities and the countryside. Under the treaty the United States also could build enough warheads to destroy most of the Soviet Union several times over and build the MX, which could destroy Soviet missile sites. In fact, SALT II did impose a constraint on the factor of overkill. Possibly with its limits, Americans could not be destroyed ten times over, only three or four times. Quite evidently SALT II was not an instrument of the "real arms control" President Carter and most Americans fervently sought. It contributed little to our strategic deterrence. In any case, for that and a variety of other reasons SALT II was never ratified. After all the effort we had reached an impasse.

THE SECOND STRATEGIC DEFENSE INITIATIVE

Upon taking office, President Ronald Reagan pushed through Congress a massive military program. The defense budget, at $89.6 billion in 1976 and at $134 billion in 1980, jumped to $237.5 billion by 1984. Much of it went to the "modernization" of strategic offensive weapons, which now included the reinstated B–1 bomber.

Negotiations with the Soviet Union continued, but they made little progress. Critics blamed the President's ignorance and inattention as well as conflict and anarchy among his advisers.[20] Actually, it may have been due mostly to the fact that the times were simply inauspicious. During his first term President Reagan's attention was absorbed in turning around a domestic environment marked by high unemployment, ruinous inflation, and sagging public morale. At the same time the top Soviet leadership was undergoing a period of instability. The aging President Brezhnev, who had outlasted four U.S. presidents, died and was followed in quick succession by no less than three Soviet party chiefs (Yuri Andropov, Konstantine Chernenko, and Mikhail Gorbachev). And, of course, the United States was still woefully short of bargaining chips. The modernization of our strategic offense was barely under way; new weapons and new capabilities were still in the future. No longer in the distant future, but in the future nevertheless. Add to this that the President had always taken a dim view of Communism and Soviet power. "Their leaders," the President explained in his very first news conference, "openly and publicly declared that the only morality they recognize is what furthers their cause . . . meaning they reserve unto themselves the right to commit any crime, to lie, to cheat in order to attain that. . . ."[21] He was not in the least inclined to accept suggestions that there was no moral difference between our democracy and their "evil empire." Nor was he attracted to any arrangement that would imply any U.S.-Soviet partnership in the conduct of international relations.

In any case, President Reagan ordered substantive changes in the American negotiating position. The United States remained interested in diplomatic benefits, and the President himself was quite aware of the popular appeal of "nuclear disarmament," but clearly the transcendent criterion for the negotiations had become their contribution to strategic deterrence. The President's main concern was "real arms reduction" or, more precisely, real reduction in Soviet first-strike capability. To make sure that no one missed the point, the title of the negotiations was changed to Strategic Arms Reduction Talks (START). The "consensus option" approved by the President in a National Security Council meeting on May 3, 1982, set the goal of much more drastic cuts in the Soviet arsenal than had President Carter's "comprehensive proposal" five years before. While "protecting" the MX, the cruise missiles, and the rapid advance of American strategic forces' modernization, it required the Soviet Union to sacrifice most of its recent gains: to reduce ICBM warheads from 6,000 to 2,500, its total launchers from more than 2,300 to 850, its SS–18 "heavies" from 303 to 110, its SS–19 "mediums" from 300 to 100, and to eliminate its SS–17 "mediums" (some 150 missiles) altogether. Had the Soviet Union agreed to these terms—and there is some question whether anyone thought it might—it would have meant real arms reduction, a sacrifice of cherished first-strike capability, and the restoration of the "stability" of mutual assured destruction.

President Reagan also ordered changes in negotiating posture. The American delegations in the past tended to be activist, at times almost compulsively so. They were always anxious to advance "negotiable" positions; thus, throughout their preparations much time and thought went into finding some incentives for the other side. Indeed, the Soviet negotiators have become accustomed to the United States leading the way with concrete concessions. They could then react or not, but remain comfortably certain that the Americans, either through their formal delegations or through a "back channel," would come up with new ideas, at times offering further concessions. President Reagan was not in any great hurry; he was quite prepared to let the Soviet Union take the negotiating initiative, and then *he* would think about it. His chief negotiator, General Edward Rowny, "knew how to say 'no' as firmly and as frequently as the Soviets knew how to say 'nyet.' Rowny could out-stonewall the master stonewallers."

The absence of progress was punctuated when, on December 8, 1983, the Soviet chief delegate, Viktor Karpov, ended the fifth round of START and declined to set a date for the resumption of talks. Strobe Talbott, the diplomatic correspondent of *Time*, thought he knew why: "If talks did resume, the agenda would be more complicated, and the Americans' expectations would have to be far more modest."[22]

The keystone of President Reagan's approach, however, turned out to be the Strategic Defense Initiative (SDI), which he formally announced on March 23, 1983. Few remembered that it was actually the second such initiative, following President Kennedy's program by about two decades. He and President Johnson (who was rather less interested) were not successful. The psychological costs of an effective passive defense (civil defense) proved to be exorbitant, and the political costs of an ABM (active defense) system proved to be too much for Presidents Johnson and Nixon while they were deeply engaged in Vietnam. The ABM, it may be recalled, also had several technical problems, the most fundamental being that under the best of circumstances a successful interception would require the detonation of its nuclear warhead over Canadian or U.S. territory.

The situation, however, was changing. Longer-range radar (perimeter acquisition radar) and longer-range interceptors (Spartan) had become available. Thus the point of interception could be pushed further out into space and further away from North American targets. These advances, however, were largely counteracted by the development of missiles with MIRVs and a catalog of penetration aids—all kinds of decoys, balloons, and chaff—that are relatively cheap to produce and easy to release during the flight but enormously complicate the identification and tracking of hostile missiles. Other technological advances include a family of airborne warning and control systems (AWACS) featuring radar, fast-reaction computers, and reliable communications. They are very useful in defense against planes and cruise missiles, but less so against ICBMs. The most far-reaching technological advance, however, was in the development of satellites. By the mid 1970s they were used for communication and intelligence; they were reporting missile launches and could be used for warning of an impending missile attack. The question invariably arose: Could space be used for strategic defense? Could a combination of developments in space technology and directed energy (laser or particle beam) technology wholly overcome the two most serious ABM flaws and achieve interception with nonnuclear means *and* over the territory of the aggressor rather than of its victim?

Looking once again at the course of a missile, this time from the perspective of the attacker, four stages can be identified. The first is generally called the booster stage. It starts when the missile is ejected from its protective silo and its rocket engines are ignited; it lasts for five minutes or less, until the missile is boosted into orbit and the main rockets stop burning. The second stage is often called the bus stage. The missile is now in orbit. One by one it releases its warheads. These are independently targeted, which means that they are released with slightly different trajectories. Also released are penetration aids, all kinds of decoys and chaff designed to confuse radar and overload defenses. By the third stage, the midcourse, all the warheads and the penetration aids are traveling separately through space in descending arcs. They soon enter the atmosphere. Decoys and chaff are quickly burned up, but the warheads in this fourth, the terminal, stage plunge to their targets.

It is, of course, easier for the defense if it does not have to sort out warheads, decoys, and chaff. It is very much easier if it does not have to intercept the six, eight, or ten warheads of a missile but can destroy the missile itself before it can release any of those warheads and any of its decoys.

The logic of interception in the booster stage was always theoretically sound but appeared practically beyond reach. Still, if American ingenuity combined with American technology could actually accomplish this, it would in a single stroke eliminate the Soviet advantage of missiles with MIRVs. In fact, it would cripple Soviet first-strike capability and very much improve the survivability

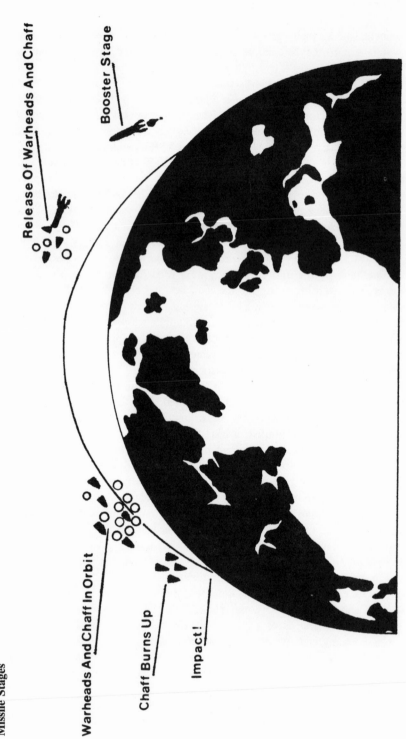

Figure 3
Missile Stages

(and credibility) of U.S. second-strike capability. It would be a decisive contribution to our strategic deterrence and our national security. President Reagan was convinced that it should be tried, and committed the country to making the effort.

The technological problems are formidable. Perhaps each could be solved, but not without creating a new set of problems no less formidable. One possibility seemed to be to place laser guns on space vehicles from which, on command, we would beam intense light energy upon a rising ICBM and (as a lens concentrating sunlight on a piece of paper) disable it by burning a hole in its "skin." The missiles that could lift the laser guns into orbit, however, would have to be enormous, requiring boosters far, far more powerful than anything we have; and, once in space, for operation the laser guns would need a space-based power supply of fantastic magnitude. It would be easier to place into orbit space guns that instead of light energy (laser) would use electronic (particle beam) energy. But if the particle beam is charged (electron), it will be bent by the earth's electromagnetic field; if the particle beam is neutral (neutron), it will work well in a vacuum but will deteriorate in the atmosphere.

Alternatively, instead of very heavy "active" space vehicles we could rely on "passive" ones. We could place into orbit space mirrors that could reflect beams from ground-based laser guns upon enemy missiles. This would solve the problem of lifting colossal weights into space, but the space mirrors (if they could be built of perfect quality, of sufficient size, and in sufficient quantity, and could be placed in various, closely coordinated orbits) would be extremely vulnerable. The Soviet Union could place in close proximity to our mirrors its own "escorts," which it could detonate at will and make the space mirrors useless at the very time we would need them. If, instead of being in regular orbit, space mirrors are "popped" into space at our command, this problem may be solvable, but it could leave us practically no decision time. The booster stage of the SS–18 is about 300 seconds (that of the MX is just 180 seconds); it would perhaps be possible to pop up a mirror in about 120 seconds, leaving 3 minutes to make the decision and to communicate it to the forward bases (probably submarines) for execution. This is really too fast for a human decision process. Quite probably the process would have to be turned over to computers, a course that, given the unimaginable stakes, would probably be undesirable in a democratic system and, given the experience of most Americans with occasional computer errors, politically unsupportable. And, of course, by increasing the power of the booster at relatively modest cost in payload, the available decision time could be reduced further and further until it might disappear altogether.[23]

There are also problems in terms of international treaties. The Treaty on Principles Governing the Activities of States in the Exploration and Use of Outer Space, Including the Moon and Other Celestial Bodies, signed by the United States on January 27, 1967, obligates us (among other things) "not to place in orbit around the earth any object carrying nuclear weapons of mass destruction, install such weapons on celestial bodies, or station such weapons in outer space in any other manner. . . . The establishment of military bases, installations and fortifications, the testing of any type of weapons and the conduct of military maneuvers on celestial bodies shall be forbidden." The ABM Treaty in 1972 was even more specific. Article V states: "Each Party undertakes not to develop, test or deploy ABM systems or components which are sea-based, air based, space-based or mobile land based."[24]

A Philadelphia lawyer with a determined effort no doubt could find a loophole somewhere. During the final days of negotiations the U.S. chief negotiator made a unilateral statement that: "If an agreement providing for more complete strategic offensive arms limitations were not achieved within five years, U.S. supreme interests could be jeopardized. Should that occur, it would constitute a basis for withdrawal from the ABM Treaty."[25] In any case the treaty provided for regular reviews every five years. All the same, to break or to terminate a treaty signed by the President and ratified by the Senate is very unattractive behavior. Americans would not like it at all, and partisan opposition would be easily mobilized. Thus, quite apart from the international repercussions, it is highly questionable whether it is domestically do-able.

Perhaps most difficult and most dangerous, however, is the strategic problem. The fact is that any U.S. capability to intercept SS–18s and SS–19s launched in a first strike necessarily carries with it the capability to intercept these missiles if they are launched in a second strike. Since the Soviet strategic force structure is based primarily on ICBMs, it follows that any space based defense shield protecting the United States from Soviet surprise attack necessarily means a deterioration in Soviet credibility of deterrence. Ultimately a total U.S. defense would (under these circumstances) produce a total loss of Soviet strategic deterrence. Forty years of massive effort would be wiped out. The Soviet Union would find itself back in the 1950s, when the only protection it had from U.S. nuclear attack or nuclear blackmail was our traditional reluctance to use force as an instrument of foreign policy.

It would be an enormously unsettling experience. Even contemplating the possibility may intensify Soviet anxieties. If they ever suspect that we had reached the threshold of such a breakthrough, they may in desperation seek to preempt by taking a chance of a first strike against us. Actually, there is no need for so gloomy a scenario. The Soviet Union has other options. Concerned about the possible success of SDI, it could use the period of American research and development to engage in negotiations that would lead to "real" arms control. It could use the time for diversifying its strategic forces, placing more emphasis on manned bombers and submarines. (It is already doing this with the development of the Blackjack [SU–27] bomber and perhaps has been doing it with the Typhoon, a very large, quiet missile submarine.) The Soviet Union may have to trade some of its "hard target" capabilities for the survivability of its strategic system. Either alternative would enhance U.S. deterrence but could also be in the best long-term interest of the Soviet Union. Alternatively, the Soviet Union could choose to concentrate on defeating our defense initiative by developing effective antisatellite weapons. And it could try to match the SDI program, resulting in an intense and specialized arms race. If perchance both countries could succeed, at roughly the same time, in building a space defense, it would enormously reinforce mutual deterrence.

Our concern for the perils of our successes, however, should not distract us from the perils of their successes. It is no secret that the Soviet Union has been working on space-based strategic weapons.[26] So, in the final analysis, it all comes down to this: Can we be certain that if we stop, they will stop? Can we be certain that if they do not stop (for all the reasons our scientists tell us), they will fail? Can we be certain that if they do not fail, they will be kind to us and not confront us with Soviet global hegemony, in which case everything we hold dear—our lives, our values, not to mention our material possessions—will depend entirely upon their mood and generosity?

By the end of the Reagan administration support for SDI was deteriorating. Most prominent scientists were opposed, many campaigning against it (albeit at times on ideological, political, or strategic grounds on which their qualifications were unestablished). Congress was still in favor, but the positive margins were shrinking, the divisions more sharply drawn. The electorate remained attracted to the idea of a defensive shield but was beginning to wonder just what this, as a practical matter, would mean and require.

It soon became apparent that a perfect defensive shield, if at all possible, would demand a sustained effort well into the next century. The best we can accomplish in the foreseeable future is a partial shield, a capability to destroy some of the missiles launched against us. This would still be an asset for deterrence. An aggressor could never be sure just which of its missiles would be shot down. As it is, there presumably are entire sets of warheads targeted on each of our silos, just to make sure that one will get through and score a direct hit (redundancy). Conceivably our SDI weapons would intercept one or two in each set, but the remainder would reach the target and destroy our ICBMs. No problem for them. But it would also be possible that our SDI weapons would intercept some entire sets, not all by any means but quite a few, leaving some of our missiles safe to deliver destruction in retaliation. A big problem for them.

The logic for SDI was still there, but it required much more explanation. This was somewhat of a setback. What made it worse was the increased confusion about our specific purpose. When it was first announced, SDI was generally seen as a booster-stage intercept.[27] Soon the idea was extended to other sectors of the trajectory. In January 1985 Zbigniew Brzezinski, Robert Jastrow, and Max M. Kampelman argued that with development and some additional research, we could construct and deploy a two-layer or double-screen defense. It could be in place by the early 1990s at a cost of about $60 billion. A conservative estimate of the effectiveness of each layer, they argued, would be 70 percent. The combined effectiveness of the two layers would be more than 90 percent: less than one Soviet warhead in ten would reach its target—more than sufficient to discourage Soviet leaders from any thought of achieving a successful first strike.[28] Later that same year *Discover* (September 1985) and *Science* (December 1985) carried drawings of a whole arsenal of exotic weapons and space vehicles: early warning satellites, imaging radar, laser battle mirrors, relay mirrors, electromagnetic rail guns, pop-up X-ray lasers, chemical lasers, eximer and free-electron lasers, neutral particle-beam weapons, kinetic kill vehicles, and so forth.

A report by the George C. Marshall Institute (December 15, 1986) proposed a "3–layer defense" and calculated its effectiveness to be "approximately 93 percent." It would mean that an aggressor would have to "expend 42 warheads on each target to be confident that 2 . . . will penetrate U.S. defenses and reach that target . . . [or] 42,000 warheads to achieve that destruction of 1,000 U.S. targets." Most of the equipment would still have to be developed, but we could (and should, the report urged) deploy kinetic killer vehicles by the early 1990s. Fired from a "porcupine" in space, these small, high-speed rockets of varying range could collide with and destroy Soviet missiles.

Two and a half years later the *Washington Post* reported (April 29, 1989) the view of Secretary of Defense Richard Cheney that the future of SDI funding depended on the successful development of "brilliant pebbles," swarms of new mini-missiles designed to detect, track, and pulverize incoming missiles in flight. Shortly thereafter (July 18, 1989) a successful test of a neutral-particle-beam weapon was announced. All very interesting, no doubt, but these were all essentially "bus" stage, midcourse, and terminal stage weapons. The prospect of booster-stage intercept was fading fast. The suspicion was growing: Did the Pentagon and the administration conclude that booster-stage intercept in the 1990s, very much like the ABM in the 1960s, was well beyond the state of the art in any foreseeable future? Were they just keeping the notion alive because it worried the Soviets, a purpose not without merit, and because it was good business, an enterprise not without profit?

Meanwhile, startling changes seemed to be occurring in the Soviet Union. To be sure, the Soviets were developing two new strategic missiles, but these did not aggravate the menace. The SS–24 is comparable in size with the MX and can carry ten warheads. It is expected to be fully deployed in the early 1990s. Like conventional ICBMs it can be placed in a heavily reinforced shelter (silo). But possibly it could be made mobile by mounting it, just as we are trying to do with the MX, on a railroad car. The SS–25, which has been deployed since 1985, is a fully mobile missile and carries one warhead. That these missiles are (can be) mobile clearly increases the survivability of land-based missiles, but their deployment does not enhance Soviet first-strike capability. Indeed, it may be construed as a retreat from such intentions. Both are solid-fuel missiles. Their mobility somewhat decreases their accuracy:yield ratio, and with it their utility as "silo busters." Finally, the SS–25 with its single warhead reduces the "MIRV temptation," that is, the advantage in a surprise attack of trading warheads for missiles. With double-targeting, conceivably it would have taken just 240 SS–18s to destroy our entire ICBM force, but it would take more than 2,000 SS–25s! Could it be that we were moving back to deterrence condition I, that is, to the relatively stable position where mutual assured destruction produces mutually assured deterrence?[29]

After the reelection of President Reagan the Soviets were visibly anxious to return to Geneva. So anxious, in fact, that not even the death of Chernenko would keep them from the opening session scheduled for March 12, 1985. They were met by the new head of the U.S. delegation. Max Kampelman could say no as often as General Rowny, but his main skill was bargaining.

Soviet leaders missed no chance to let the world know that they quite understood that a nuclear war could not be won. The implication was clear: they wanted to assure the United States that they planned no first strike. Indeed, they sincerely wished to get an agreement for a massive cut in strategic offensive forces. Suddenly it rained Soviet arms reduction proposals. The Americans could hardly catch their breath, let alone say no, before a new one was coming. At the hastily arranged Reykjavik summit (October 1986) Gorbachev caught the President unprepared. Going far beyond President Carter's "comprehensive proposal" and Reagan's "consensus option," and far beyond Brezhnev's position, Gorbachev offered a mutual 50 percent reduction of all strategic missiles and aircraft. All he wanted in return was a U.S. commitment not to develop, test, or deploy SDI for ten years. It was a stunning suggestion. The Defense Department had no inkling that it was coming, having been more or less kept out of the preparations. Our allies were not consulted. The President made a counterproposal: a ten-year delay in the deployment of SDI in exchange for the complete elimination of all ballistic missiles from the arsenals of both nations. Nuclear disarmament of the superpowers—the conversation was assuming fabulous proportions.

The summit meeting broke down. It was damage control time. "The President's performance was magnificent. and I have never been so proud of my President as I have been in these sessions, and particularly this afternoon,"[30] exhausted Secretary of State George Shultz proclaimed an hour later. Back home, the President assured Americans: "The door is open and the opportunity to begin eliminating the nuclear threat is within reach."[31]

Thus Reykjavik, more clearly than ever before, linked negotiation for arms reduction with SDI and our nuclear retaliatory capabilities. Thus, it signified a new era in which our strategic deterrence, *our vital national interest*, rests on a Grand Strategic Triad: diplomatic negotiations on limiting (and reducing) arms levels, the maintenance of survivable strategic offensive capabilities, and the continued development of strategic defense. As was true in the conventional concept of the Triad, each leg has its vulnerabilities, but together they are strong enough to assure that we may live in peace.

NOTES

1. Sir John Slessor, *Strategy for the West* (New York: William Morrow, 1954), p. 120.

2. Quoted in Harland Moulton, *From Superiority to Parity* (Greenwich, Conn.: Greenwood Press, 1973), p. 82.

3. *New York Times*, July 26, 1961, p. 10.

4. Arthur M. Schlesinger, Jr., *A Thousand Days* (Boston: Houghton, Mifflin, 1965), pp. 747–48.

5. Ibid., p. 747.

6. Moulton, *From Superiority to Parity*, pp. 214–15, 235–41.

7. See, for example, Abram Chayes and Jerome B. Wiesner, eds., *ABM: An Evaluation of the Decision to Deploy an Anti-Ballistic Missile System* (New York: Harper and Row, 1969); J. I. Coffee, "The ABM Debate," *Foreign Affairs*, 45 (April 1967), 403–13; R. L. Rothestein, "The ABM: Proliferation and International Stability," *Foreign Affairs*, 46 (April 1968), 487–502. See also Kissinger, *A Thousand Days*, pp. 204–10.

8. Richard L. Garwin and Hans A. Bethe, "Anti-Ballistic-Missile Systems," *Scientific American*, 218, no. 3 (March 1968), 21–31.

9. Moulton, *From Superiority to Parity*, pp. 207, 208.

10. Schlesinger, *A Thousand Days*, pp. 132, 137–38, 403–04, 811.

11. Ibid., p. 150. With hindsight the reasons became obvious. They were preparing to add MIRVs as well, and with many more warheads than we could.

12. It was actually two treaties: one restricting anti-ballistic missile (ABM) defenses and the other limiting strategic offensive arms.

13. Speech before B'nai B'rith Convention, Washington, D.C., September 8, 1976. Quoted in Jimmy Carter, *A Government as Good as the People* (New York: Simon and Schuster, 1977), p. 167.

14. Zbigniew Brzezinski, *Power and Principle: Memoirs of the National Security Adviser, 1977–1981* (New York: Straus and Giroux, 1983), p. 154. In a letter to President Brezhnev, Carter tried to put a softer gloss on his position: "It is not our intention to interfere in the internal affairs of other nations. We do not wish to create problems for the Soviet Union. But it will be necessary for our government to express publicly on occasion the sincere and deep feelings of myself and our people." Brezhnev responded in a "chilling manner," recorded Brzezinski.

15. In the final stages of its flight the cruise missile is dependent on guidance by terrain contour matching, that is, a comparison between a map programmed into its computer and the topographic characteristics of the terrain over which it is cruising. The missile may be misled not only by dummy structures erected a short while before, but also by fog and even snow.

16. John M. Collins, *U.S.–Soviet Military Balance* (New York: McGraw-Hill, 1980), p. 136.

17. Cyrus Vance, *Hard Choices* (New York: Simon and Schuster, 1983), pp. 53–54; Talbott, *Deadly Gambits*, pp. 70, 74.

18. Vance, *Hard Choices*, pp. 57–58.

19. United States, Department of Defense, *Soviet Military Power, 1985* (Washington, D.C.: U.S. Government Printing Office, 1985), pp. 30, 33.

20. See for example, Talbott, *Deadly Gambits*, pp. 224, 250, 263, 273–74. Reporters, columnists, and academics like to consider Ronald Reagan an actor who may learn his lines expertly, who may be a nice and decent guy, but who is essentially a naive, simpleminded, and rash fellow. Just what their subject may think of it all may be suggested by the following. The night before he was sworn in as fortieth President of the United States, the Inaugural Gala organized and attended by his supporters included a sketch by

Rich Little. "Gentlemen," announced the comedian, impersonating Ronald Reagan speaking to his close advisers, "I have the solution to the energy problem. We shall build a pipeline to the sun. Now, I know what you are thinking. You are thinking that as we are approaching the sun, it will be all too hot to build. I have the answer to that: we shall build at night." Ronald Reagan and the audience roared with laughter.

21. Presidential news conference, January 29, 1981, in *Weekly Compilation of Presidential Documents* (Washington, D.C.: Office of the Federal Register, 1981), vol. 17, p. 67. A year later White House humor described President Brezhnev on his deathbed giving advice to his successor, KGB chief Andropov. "Be sure," he said, "that the people follow you." "Don't worry," Andropov replied, "If they won't follow me, they will follow you."

22. Talbott, *Deadly Gambits*, p. 314.

23. See Ashton B. Carter, *Directed Energy Missile Defense in Space* (Washington, D.C.: Office of Technology Assessment, April 1984); Hans Bethe, Richard L. Garwin, Kurt Gottfried, and Henry W. Kendall, "Space-based Ballistic-Missile Defense," *Scientific American*, 251, no. 4 (October, 1984), 39–49; and United States Congress, Office of Technology Assessment, *Strategic Defenses, Ballistic Missile Defense Technologies, Anti-Satellite Weapons, Countermeasures and Arms Control* (Princeton: Princeton University Press, 1986).

24. United States, *Treaties and Other International Agreements* (Washington, D.C.: U.S. Government Printing Office, 1973), vol. 23, pt. 4, p. 3441.

25. Ibid., p. 3460.

26. "We have our own space defense program and our research is making progress in different ways than yours is," Gorbachev insisted to Nixon. Memorandum on conversation with General Secretary Gorbachev at the Kremlin, July 18, 1986, from former President Nixon to President Reagan.

27. Carter, *Directed Energy Missile Defense*, saw it as such; Bethe et al., "Space-based Ballistic-Missile Defense," concentrated on it.

28. *New York Times Magazine*, January 27, 1985, p. 29.

29. Another advantage of the single-warhead missile is in the verification of arms control agreements. Curiously, though, until September 1989 the U.S. negotiating position in START included the elimination of mobile, single-warhead missiles. The explanation suggested was that if the Soviets keep building mobile single-warhead missiles, we shall have to match them. (We are already developing the Midgetman.) But these missiles are very expensive, and with only one warhead they radically reduce the number of Soviet targets that could be imperiled. Thus, for example, 900 Minuteman plus 100 MXs with their 3,700 warheads could credibly threaten all Soviet ICBM launchers, but 1,000 Midgetmen could not possibly do so. This is true enough, except that if we have to absorb a first strike, many of our fixed-base ICBMs with all their warheads will be destroyed, and those left may be targeted on Soviet silos from which the missiles have already been launched. It is not at all clear that the retaliatory capability of our Minutemen and MXs will exceed that of an admittedly much smaller number of warheads mounted on much more survivable mobile missiles. Moreover, we could look at this equation differently. If all Soviet ICBMs (through an arms control treaty) could be changed to single-warhead missiles, the Soviets could not credibly threaten our land-based missiles, and thus any prospect of a Soviet first strike would recede into insignificant probability. There is, however, another, more theoretical argument so far not publicly articulated. Radically reducing the warheads may drop strategic capabilities below overkill, and thus enormously

increase uncertainty and the risk of strategic confrontation. The possibility that our second strike could not assure wholly unacceptable cost for an aggressor would seriously degrade deterrence.

30. *New York Times*, October 13, 1986, p. A–10.

31. Ibid., October 14, 1986, p. 1.

4

OUR SPECIAL INTEREST: FRIENDS AND ALLIES

We do not want to be attacked; nobody does. We must be eternally vigilant; we should be willing to make every effort to deter aggression against our national territory. At the same time we ought to be careful to avoid making our national existence the sole concern of our foreign relations, or reducing all other concerns to this single common denominator. Our interests do not end at our borders; our lives are not defined by sheer existence. Our military security and our quality of life need the support and friendship of some special foreign countries.

As a military matter, special interests may indeed be potentially of vital interest. Think just for the moment of the unthinkable: our deterrence fails, we become victims of aggression, and we choose to defend ourselves. No one can win a nuclear war in any sense of a potential gain, no question about it. Even so, there may be a difference in the fate of the combatants. Bad as a choice may be between awful and worst, we would rather not be worst.

We can, when we must do so, think of nuclear war as an engagement of possibly three stages. In the first stage, the (sneak) attack, the aggressor has the enormous advantage of determining the time, place, and manner of the attack. Its advantage can be decisive, and that is that: a lightning exchange of nuclear weapons followed by strategic surrender. Still, it is conceivable that the aggressor, with all its successes, could not quite force a surrender. The defender, though badly wounded, would still resist, and thus the conflict would enter the second stage. And here is an interesting point: While the advantage in the first stage is clearly with the aggressor, in the second stage it may well pass to the defender. The explanation is found in the circumstances. The aggressor, invariably pleased by its gains, will be greatly tempted to repeat in new attacks its original, almost successful plan. The defender, on the other hand, its forces shattered, its plans disrupted, is likely to have no choice but to innovate: to build new, perhaps better, weapons and to resort to new, perhaps better, strategies. The precarious balance of stage two may then be resolved in favor of the defender, leading to the defeat of the aggressor in the final stage.

The two world wars in this century followed approximately this pattern. Admittedly, the course of a third world war, quite unimaginable, may be very different. Still, if there is any merit in this model, it focuses on the crucial second stage. We know that we will not strike first, and we are determined not to surrender. Whether we can turn the aggressor's advantages around so as to come out of the conflagration in an awful rather than a worst condition will depend on a number of domestic conditions: our resources surviving the sneak attack, our organizational skills, and our will to resist. It also may depend upon key foreign countries. If they help us, we have a good chance; if not—well, we do not have to belabor the point. Whether they would help us, and whether *we* could be special to them, would depend upon their estimate of final outcome. Surely they cannot be expected to commit suicide for us. But it also may depend on their past experience with us. Were we friendly in peacetime? Were we supportive when they needed us? Were *they* special to us?

Actually we need not conjure up the horrors of a third world war to find military reasons for special relationships. We are fortunate that the rimlands of Eurasia are in the hands of friendly states. It is in our interest that they remain friendly and secure. We do not want hostile forces gaining control over areas that could serve as staging areas and jumping-off points against us. Mostly, though, the reasons for our special interests are not security concerns; they are those of economics and culture. Americans want to live in peace. More than that, they want to live in peace in their own way.

We enjoy a very high standard of living, we want to continue to enjoy a high standard of living, and, what is more, we want to improve upon it. The United States is rich in resources; Americans are highly skilled and talented. Their propensity for innovation is legendary. We have done, and can do, much with our own resources. Much, but not quite all. We need to import some raw materials for strategic (national security) purposes; we are dependent on imports to satisfy our consumer demands. And in order to pay for our imports, we need access to foreign markets where we can sell our goods.[1]

To be sure, Americans are willing to make sacrifices in their standard of living for the sake of national security or, as was the case in the 1974 oil embargo, to resist foreign countries blackmailing our foreign policy—but they'd rather not. They prefer giving special attention to countries where our economic interests lie.

The U.S. way of life, however, is not only notable for the pleasures of material affluence, but also for its intangible values. One of these is a commitment to a democratic polity. Americans cannot imagine living without basic constitutional rights that would be upheld, if necessary, by the courts—even against the government. They have become very much accustomed to electing their public officials and to holding them accountable for their actions. Indeed, they take it for granted that those are the terms of the only proper relationship between citizens and their government. Looking beyond their borders, they feel a measure of solidarity with people and governments that share these values. They dislike authoritarian, and especially totalitarian, governments,[2] feel sure that they are up to no good internationally, consider their rule immoral, and have sympathy for the people who must serve under them.

The other basic American value is a preference for a pluralist society, a devotion to diversity: diversity in values, opinions, tastes, and, most to the point here, in national origins. This was not always so. At the time of Independence we were primarily a homogeneous nation. We treated Indians as foreigners. We negotiated with the tribes and regularly fought wars with them. We treated blacks even worse, as inferior creatures worth three-fifths of a human being. But from the very beginning this was a country of immigrants. Five delegates to the Constitutional Convention had been born abroad.

At first people came from Western Europe, later from Southern and Eastern Europe, and then from practically every part of the globe. By the end of the nineteenth century the inscription on the Statute of Liberty proudly proclaimed: "Give us your tired, your poor, your huddled masses yearning to breathe free." Our ancestors came, attracted by political freedom and economic opportunities. They helped develop the land, build the railroads, construct vast industrial plants, establish great universities. They helped to build the United States.

Gradually the attitude toward racial and ethnic diversity changed. It was still cautious. Laws were passed to limit the number of immigrants and favored them according to country of origin. Still, diversity was beginning to be accepted—as a temporary, transitional condition. Newcomers with different racial and cultural backgrounds were welcome to live with us, share in the wealth, learn our language, assimilate into our way of life, and then in a generation or so to be accepted as Americans. Our favorite symbol for the country was the melting pot, in which the additives to native iron would produce the steely alloy of our nation.

More recently, however, public attitude has been changing further. Diversity, many now argue—and at times the Supreme Court appears to agree with them—is not just a useful temporary inconvenience. On the contrary, it is a subject of national pride. Surely one can see that immigrants should not be stripped of their heritage. Without it people lose their balance, like a fiddler on the roof. Surely one can see that the United States is enriched by the variety of cultures. They keep us from becoming smug and stagnant. Never mind the melting pot; never mind the assimilation of diversity. Perhaps the tossed salad is a better metaphor. Bring the tomatoes, the cucumbers, the radishes, the lettuce together. Do not homogenize them. If you process them through a blender, all you get is a dull, insipid, mess. Let this be a nation of minorities working together, each bringing its own unique contributions, and all being held together by one common belief: that America is the greatest.

The ties of ethnic heritage, however, are not entirely devoid of political overtones. Indeed, in some cases these are rather pronounced. Being a minority is always a stressful experience, even in the land of minorities. Relatively recent arrivals and other vulnerable groups are in dire need of reassurance, both personal and collective. In their relationship to their former countrymen they wish to exhibit pride at having become Americans; in their relationship to their fellow citizens they need the dignity of their foreign origin. They need their "mother country" to be secure and respected, and they are often quite intense about the United States (*their* fellow citizens and *their* government) visibly demonstrating its support. In short, individual and group pressures for special interest in particular foreign countries in our pluralist democracy are not an indication of separatism or disloyalty; indeed, they are part of the dynamics of integration. Our foreign policy should recognize this reality; it can neglect it only at exorbitant costs to our national cohesion.

SPECIAL OBLIGATIONS

It follows from our special needs that good relations with some governments and the friendship of some peoples are especially desirable for us, and that we should try to build special relationships with them. These may be ceremoniously proclaimed in treaties of alliance or may be the products of less formal diplomatic "understandings," but they are far from easy.

Two conditions make our special relations particularly strenuous. First, since they are based on our specific needs, they are ephemeral. George Washington knew this and most earnestly advised: "It is our true policy to steer clear of permanent alliances with any portion of the foreign world. . . . The nation which indulges toward another an habitual hatred or an habitual fondness is in some degree a slave." Our friends and allies must know this, and are not comforted. We have looked with friendship on the countries of Western Europe and Latin America for quite a long time, but even there our relations have had their ups and downs: with Great Britain, with Germany, with Mexico, with Argentina, or Cuba, for example. We had a special relationship with Japan during the second half of the nineteenth century that turned into hostility and a bitter, bloody war, but was renewed in the second half of the twentieth century. Our newer ties in Asia with Turkey, Israel, (Iran), Pakistan, and the Philippines cannot be expected to be firmer.

The second problem is that "special interest" is so imprecise: it means something between total commitment and no interest at all. It offers a wide range of intensity and a fertile field for misunderstanding by friend and foe alike. The fact is that since our special relations are based on our special needs, they usually conceal a disparity between what is expected of us and what we can actually deliver. Foreign countries turn to us for many reasons. From time to time they may need diplomatic support; some may need economic aid. They are pleased with our friendship, our expressions of respect and support, but usually at the heart of it all is their vital need for assurance that the United States will protect them. The United States, for its part, may need the support and value the friendship of allies. It may even give the impression that its loyalty is total, that it would consider an attack upon them as an attack upon itself. The harsh reality is, however, that our commitments must be limited. We all know that when their vital interests come in conflict with our vital interest—they may not, but just possibly they might—theirs will be sacrificed. Actually, it is even worse than that. Even if our vital interests are not at stake, our government and/or our people may consider the cost of protection excessive. Such, for example, was the fate of our ally Pakistan when India invaded its East Wing in 1971.

Moreover, as a superpower the United States has global responsibilities. At times the interest of an ally may conflict with our geopolitical strategy. Then we have to make a choice, and possibly our ally will lose. Ask the Republic of China (Taiwan). Add to this that as a superpower, the United States has special relations with a variety of countries throughout the globe. The interests of our friends may conflict with each other, and then we may have to make a choice. We could explain that our choice was made quite fairly and was based purely on merit, but inevitably one side would feel let down. Such was the fate of our hemispheric partner Argentina during the Falkland (Malvinas) war in 1982. There is no denying that some of our special relationships seem to be more special than others.

Our friends and allies may become targets of aggression due to some local conflict or some traditional hostility. They may become targets because of their assets, assets that are valuable to us and may be coveted by others. And they may become targets of external predatory designs precisely because of their special relations with us.

As a matter of fact, most of our friends do not want to be saved by U.S. military intervention. They much prefer to be protected by U.S. deterrence of attack against them. The problem is that when we seek to extend our deterrence from the protection of our own existence to that of others, we have to meet the requirements of a different dimension of credibility. Deterrence of aggression against our vital interests rests almost wholly on visible evidence of our military capabilities, but deterrence of aggression in the areas of our special interests depends heavily on more elusive indicators of the political will to project force. Few would doubt that we would defend ourselves with everything we had, but many might wonder whether we would resort to nuclear retaliation in case of a subnuclear attack on one of our friends. If the aggressor is a nonnuclear power, Americans would be repelled by the prospect of raining mass devastation on a defenseless people even though their government is guilty of aggression. If the aggressor were the Soviet Union, Americans would be most unenthusiastic about the prospect of its raining mass devastation upon us. There is, of course, the possibility that the United States would come to the aid of its allies with conventional forces. The question is, how much of a possibility. Some might doubt that our conventional forces could be effectively projected into distant places to help repel local aggression. Many more wonder whether Americans, after their unhappy experience in Vietnam, would consider risking the lives of their fellow citizens for anything abroad. They do not know that we would not, but they wonder.

Ambiguity, of course, has its uses in foreign policy. When predators are unsure of our response, they may be restrained because they do not want to take a chance that we would do nothing. They have, after all, miscalculated before—in Korea, for instance. All the same, ambiguity has a serious negative consequence: it invites testing. As a matter of fact, there have always been doubts about the steadfastness of democracies. The Europeans remember Munich well. Europe knows the awesome military power of the United States. But the question lingers on: Does America (Congress, for example) have the will to use it?

Indeed, even when our threat to use force was only thinly veiled, we were tested. At his press conference on September 13, 1962, President Kennedy made it "clear once again" that " . . . if Cuba should ever . . . become an offensive military base of significant capacity for the Soviet Union, then this country will do whatever must be done to protect its own security and that of its allies."[3] In six weeks he had to use the Navy to impose a "quarantine." In June 1973, during a late night session at his home in San Clemente, California, President Nixon made it perfectly clear to President Brezhnev that the United States will not abandon Israel. Four months later, after the Syrian and Egyptian invasion of Israel, the President had to order a gigantic airlift to counter the Soviet resupply of Syria, and, a few days later, a global alert of U.S. forces in response to Soviet threats to intervene (unilaterally) in the war.[4] Actions speak louder than words.

The actions of President Kennedy and President Nixon were salutary—because they were successful. But action speaks louder than words in failure as well, and words followed by a failure to honor them are disastrous. They undermine deterrence and invite hostile forces to gamble on aggression. They raise doubts among our friends about the value of special relations with us (is America after all just a paper tiger?) and tempt them to appease our adversaries. In 1966 Secretary of State Dean Rusk tried to explain it to the Senate Foreign Relations Committee:

I cannot tell you how important it was to the peace of the world that the President of the United States . . . be believed when . . . [he says] to the other side: "Gentlemen, this you must not do." Because if we ever get to a point where that simple statement is not believed, then I don't know where the future and the safety of this country is, or that the possibility of general peace would exist.[5]

We cannot, of course, assure that no failure would ever follow the words of our president, but our national interest mandates that whenever our government decides to threaten or actually to project force, the prospects of success should be most favorable. And that fundamentally depends on a consensus on the proper uses of U.S. forces in support of our special interests. Indeed, the outline of such a consensus on rules is already discernible.

First, it is fairly clear that Americans will not support the use of military force except in response to an essentially military challenge. They *will not* support force to prevent others from gaining economic advantages or to assure our access to markets and nonstrategic raw materials, or for the collection of foreign debts. And they will not support the use of force to prevent (punish) human rights abuses or to impose a democratic political system. Second, they probably *will* support the use of force in case of *direct* aggression against an ally or friend under special circumstances. In case our special relationship is based on our security needs, we may use force that does not risk a nuclear retaliation on the United States. In those instances where our special relationship is based on "quality of life" criteria, we may use force that accomplishes its purpose quickly and cheaply.

If in fact a consensus is emerging on military responses to direct aggression, it signals notable progress. But on *indirect* aggression (externally supported insurgency) no consensus is in sight. The problem is, there are countries and people who are of special interest to us but whose governments are not legitimatized by democratic processes. We may need them very much; all the same, Americans have profound doubts about such arrangements. They suspect that these governments are oppressive and that they stay in power (and can oppress their people) because they purchase U.S. support with their subservience to our foreign policy interests. While people do not doubt the short-run value of such services, they do deplore the "corrupt bargain" and are uneasy about its long-term consequences. Consequently, when revolutionary forces aided and abetted from abroad become ascendant in a friendly country with an authoritarian system, there is a domestic predisposition to be sympathetic toward the insurgents.

Surely it is absurd to deliver a people to Communism in the name of human rights, but on the other hand, how can it serve our national interest to perpetuate a fascist regime? Moreover, within these extremes, how can the electorate deal with all the various nuances? Intermediate positions are so difficult to define by government and to make credible by a State Department widely suspected of vested interest; and intermediate positions are so easy (and useful) to simplify and radicalize by the mass media upon which we depend for information (and some of us for judgment). Faced with all kinds of complexities, it is quite normal for perplexed Americans to revert to their instincts of distrusting nondemocratic governments and sympathizing with their challengers—however violent they may be and however anti-American they are likely to become.

So on the issue of force projection in case of indirect attack (insurgency) of a partner in special relations, we have a high degree of uncertainty. The American people might possibly support the use of force in case of indirect aggression (subversion or infiltration), provided (a) our special relationship is based on our security needs and (b) its purposes could be achieved quickly and cheaply. They are unlikely to support our use of force if the aggression is indirect and the basis of our special relations is a "quality of life" criterion. And when it comes to the aftermath of a successful Communist takeover in a country that is of special

interest to us, the debate over whether to accept it or try to reverse it by intervention goes on and on. President Kennedy did not know what to do about Cuba
before, during, or after the Bay of Pigs fiasco. President Reagan, in spite of his
outstanding communications skills and prodigious popularity, could not build a
consensus on Nicaragua.

SPECIAL PERILS: THE LESSONS OF IRAN

If special relations hold risks for our friends and allies, they are not without
peril to us. All too easily they lead us into excessive entanglements. Special
interest groups, of course, will push. No camel is ever satisfied with only its
nose in the tent. Corporations will find opportunities to expand contact; they
will make profits and want to increase them. And government bureaucracies will
develop a vested interest in policies and will vigorously defend them.

It is extraordinarily difficult to hold a steady course. Little by little, almost
imperceptibly, a special relationship may become more and more special until,
with the best intentions, it begins to dominate, and perhaps drag us into policies
and situations we did not want and should avoid. This point is well illustrated
by a recent practical experience.

An American Adventure

Late in the morning of June 25, 1953, senior American officials were meeting
in the office of the Secretary of State. In addition to the Secretary they included
the Under Secretary of State, the Assistant Secretary of State for the Near East,
Africa, and South Asia, the Director of Policy Planning, the Secretary of Defense,
and the Director of the Central Intelligence Agency. Secretary John Foster Dulles
opened the meeting:

First, you gentlemen do know, I assume, where Iran is and what it is. Persia, as it used
to be named, has been throughout history the bridge between Far Eastern Asia and the
lands of the Mediterranean and Europe. Although her importance as a trade route declined
after the construction of the Suez Canal in the 1860's, her strategic location has made
her a bone of contention among great powers—always Russia, often France and Germany,
now Great Britain and, by association, the United States.[6]

A rather elementary introduction that reflected the Secretary's judgment that his
high-level audience knew little about Iran. Certainly most Americans knew less,
and cared not at all.

American interests in Iran were minimal. When the United States began granting aid for economic development under the Point Four program, Iran's share,
in the view of the Shah, was "a small fraction of the minimum necessary to
rehabilitate our occupation devastated economy. . . . The American economic
development advisers left for home."[7]

There remained American interest "in association" with Great Britain, and just then the British had their trouble with Iran. In March 1951 Iran nationalized the Anglo-Iranian Oil Company, a large, strategically important corporation. Shortly thereafter Dr. Mohammed Mossadegh, a wily demagogue who had been rousing the population against the oil company and Britain, was named prime minister. He rejected all comprises, forced the closing of all British consulates, and in October 1952 broke diplomatic relations with Britain. Always moving, always on the offensive, he soon expanded his horizons. By 1953 he matched his anti-British harangues with attacks on Iranian political institutions. He abolished the Senate, dissolved the highest court, eliminated the National Assembly, and set his sights on the Shah.

With the Soviet Union so close by and with the Communist-controlled Tudeh Party apparently gaining popularity, U.S. concern was aroused. The Anglo-Iranian Oil Company proposed a plan for a U.S. covert operation (AJAX), the British government supported it, and on June 25, 1953, the U.S. government approved it. "Mr. Secretary," said the American ambassador toward the end of the meeting, "I don't like this kind of business at all. You know that. But we are confronted by a desperate, a dangerous situation and a madman who would ally himself with the Russians. We have no choice but to proceed with this undertaking. May God grant us success." "Sir," added Kermit Roosevelt, the CIA agent to be in charge of the operation, "I think this simply has to be done. It is impossible to be sure, but for some reason I *am* sure. We can do it." The secretary rose with a quick grin. "That's that, then: let's get going!" he ordered.[8]

So the United States intervened in Iran and secretly managed a countercoup that removed Dr. Mossadegh from office and restored the young Shah, His Imperial Majesty Reza Pahlavi, to full powers. It was a quick, effective, almost festive, nearly bloodless operation.[9] No fuss, no muss; a team of five U.S. agents and a half dozen Iranians, and an expense of less than $100,000 worth of rials.[10] President Eisenhower promptly authorized $45 million in emergency grants, and for the next three years monthly U.S. economic aid averaged $5 million.

Soon American interest waned. Iran did join the Baghdad Pact (1955), renamed Central Treaty Organization after the Iraqi withdrawal, but neither the alliance nor Iran's contributions were particularly significant for Western security.[11] Economic aid (though fluctuating) dropped from $51.9 million in 1958 to $21.2 million in 1966.[12] The only notable remnant of the 1953 intervention was the role of the CIA in organizing and training SAVAK, the Iranian State Intelligence and Security Organization. At first this agency was very much like a Western intelligence and counterintelligence agency, but by the mid 1960s it had become more like the Gestapo. The CIA liaison nevertheless was continued.

Special Relationship

The 1960s saw the continued withdrawal of Britain from its imperial positions east of Suez. There could no longer be a question of American interests "in

association." In 1967 the Arab-Israeli war left the United States with few friends
and the Soviet Union with growing influence just west of the world's richest oil
fields. Four years later, just east of this region, India emerged from its ostensible
nonalignment and signed a treaty of peace, friendship, and cooperation with the
Soviet Union, then defeated and dismembered U.S. ally Pakistan. The need for
special relations with some fairly friendly, at least potentially powerful, state in
the area became a pressing need.

There were no very suitable candidates, but through the lenses of necessity
Iran appeared to offer a possibility. The Shah was grateful to Kermit Roosevelt—
he gave him a gold cigarette case—and seemed to like Americans. Iran had good
relations with Israel and maintained them in the face of Arab pressure. Above
all the Shah obviously disliked and distrusted the Russians. He had had bad
experiences with them in 1945–46 when they did not want to withdraw from
the Iranian territory they occupied as a temporary measure during World War
II. In fact, they conspired with their agents in the Tudeh Party to detach the
"Azerbaijani Republic." Worse still, investigations after the unpleasantness with
Mossadegh revealed deep penetration by Soviet agents of the Iranian political
system, even into the Imperial Guard. It was discovered, to the shah's utter
consternation, that the commander of his most trusted battalion was a hard-core
Communist.[13]

The Shah was widely applauded as a modernizer. He disposed of the crown
estates, some 2,000 villages, then urged other large (mostly absentee) landlords
to follow his example, and finally through land reform legislation compelled
them to do so. He did more than that. His "white revolution" included programs
for political equality (and increased visibility) of women, massive improvements
in health and education, and rapid industrialization with employee ownership of
the new plants.

The Iranian political system, moreover, was considered to be stable. "Iran is
the calmest country in the troubled Middle East today," reported the *New York
Times*.[14] The Shah knew the risks he was taking. "Especially in a country with
such venerable traditions as ours, rapid change naturally brings its strains and
stresses. These are the price we must pay for Westernization and modernization."[15] He was prepared to pay the price. And when, in December 1962 and
June 1963, riots broke out in the streets, security forces soon restored order.

Finally, according to most reports, the Shah was impressive as a monarch and
a really nice guy, shy perhaps and melancholy at times, but a really nice guy.
"I could never escape the impression," wrote Henry Kissinger, "that he was a
gentle, even sentimental man who had schooled himself in the maxim that the
ruler must be aloof and hard, but had never succeeded in making it come
naturally."[16]

These assessments were essentially accurate but not quite complete. They
missed, perhaps ignored, other realities—for instance, in the Shah's personality.
Every since childhood he had had intimations of divine protection.

Soon after my investiture as crown Prince, I had fallen ill with typhoid fever, and for weeks I had hovered between life and death. . . . I then had a dream about Ali, who in our faith was the chief lieutenant of Mohammed. . . . He was sitting on his heels on the floor, and in his hands he held a bowl containing a liquid. He told me to drink, which I did. The next day, the crisis of my fever was over and I was on the road to rapid recovery. . . .

Almost every summer my family and I made an excursion to Emamzadeh-Dawood, a lovely spot in the mountains above Teheran. . . . Some way up the trail, the horse slipped, and I was plunged head first on to a jagged rock. I fainted. When I regained consciousness, the members of the party were expressing astonishment that I had not even a scratch. I told them that as I fell, I had clearly seen one of our saints, named Abbas, and that I had felt him holding me and preventing me from crashing my head against the rock. . . .

The third event occurred while I was walking with my guardian near the royal palace in Shimran. . . . Suddenly I clearly saw before me a man with a halo around his head. . . . As we passed one another, I knew him at once. He was the Imam or descendent of Mohammed who, according to our faith, disappeared but is expected to come again to save the world.[17]

Children, especially children with a high fever, do have dreams and occasionally even visions. That the Shah should have had them is not particularly remarkable. What is remarkable, however, is that after he grew up, he recounted them. He told them to Kermit Roosevelt with follow-up stories about manifestations of divine protection in his adult life,[18] and he declared them to the world in his autobiography.

Something else seems to have been missed about the Shah's personality. While time and again he demonstrated personal courage when facing imminent physical danger, when there was time to think and reflect, his vacillating disposition asserted itself. He was unsure when faced with major decisions—especially in times of crisis; in fact the American ambassador already reported this back in 1954.[19]

Some realities also were missed or ignored regarding the stability of the Shah's position. The title "king of kings" was impressive enough, but, in fact, he was not exactly a scion of ancient royal lineage. His father was a semiliterate officer of a Persian cossack brigade who through ability, determination, and intrigue overthrew the reigning Qajar dynasty. After a short flirtation with the idea of proclaiming a republic (in the manner of his Turkish neighbor Kemal Pasha), he decided in 1925 to have himself crowned shah. This, of course, did not make his son any less of a man, but it did make him a ruler not altogether established by traditional norms, a vulnerability exacerbated by his determined efforts at modernization.

To be sure, traditional norms had been losing some of their hold, but now, insofar as they were still respected by Iranians, they were increasingly becoming political instruments of the unfriendly fundamentalist (Shiite) clergy. What made this especially significant was that while the Shah may have tried to build many things, he never attempted to build modern political institutions to serve as a basis of his (modern) legitimacy. Benevolent as it was, his was a personal rule. Elections were managed; legislators were manipulated. Cabinet members and senior administrators were appointed by His Imperial Majesty; all officials served at his pleasure and acted accordingly. Originality was not visibly promoted; dissent was forcefully discouraged.

Most dangerous, however, was the uncritical acceptance of some conclusions about the consequences of modernization. "The Shah," explained Henry Kissinger, "was applying axioms of all the more 'advanced' literature of the West. ... Political stability was supposed to follow from economic advance."[20] The Shah believed them; worse still, so did American policymakers.

It was poor scholarship and a shaky foundation for policy. For centuries Iranians had been buffeted by the great powers. They were imposed upon, dominated, and invaded. They did not like it—nothing could make them like it—but at least, they felt with pride, their cultural heritage remained intact. "Modernization," however, presented a new dimension. It promised advancement to a new, foreign way of life—new values, new methods—better in every respect. Material benefits, comforts, and vanities, powerful though gross temptations, were luring Persians away from their cherished traditions. Thoroughly alarmed, by the early 1960s Iranian intellectuals began to mobilize against "Westoxication."[21] Then in 1963 "an obscure individual who claimed to be a religious leader, Ruhollah Khomeini,"[22] pointed a finger at the source of temptation: the United States, the patron of Israel, the enemy of Islam. American presence at the time was perfunctory; the picture of the Great Satan was still blurred. But it could be—and here lurked the danger—brought quickly into focus.

In any case, as we moved into the 1970s U.S. decision makers struggling with a chaotic and volatile international environment became very much attracted to Iran and to the shah (not necessarily in that order). In the Middle East, "an area essential for the security, even more the prosperity, of all industrial democracies appeared in grave jeopardy."[23] Iran could provide one of the "two pillars" (the other being Saudi Arabia) of stability. Finally the decisive factor was added. The superpowers were engaged in important arms control negotiations. They had a chance to succeed only if compliance could be verified. We had some listening posts in Pakistan, but these had recently been closed down. Almost by accident we suddenly discovered that Iran could provide the most suitable monitoring installations for us. So realities were missed or ignored. Our special relationship was established.

Excessive Entanglement

Since it was to play the role of a regional power, Iran would have to have the might to do it. Military grants and sales hovering around $50 million annually in the late 1960s jumped to $97.9 million in 1969 and to $128.2 million in 1970.

And then they went through the roof: $648.8 million in 1974, $1 billion in 1975, almost $2 billion in 1976, and $2.4 billion in 1977.[24]

A fiftyfold quantitative increase in less than a decade was spectacular by itself; its composition made it phenomenal. After his visit to Teheran in May 1972, President Nixon overruled the objections of the Defense Department (placing U.S. technological secrets into unsafe hands) and the State Department (provocative action) and approved the sale of F–14 and F–15 aircraft and associated equipment to Iran, then added a proviso that in the future Iranian requests should not be second-guessed.[25] Now all restraints were off. The U.S. Military Assistance Advisory Group (MAAG) was happy to acquaint the Shah with all the latest weapons and to facilitate his orders. Private businessmen descended in droves, offering their wares. Retired U.S. generals reappeared in Teheran, eager to be helpful. "It was a salesman's dream for a while," General Ellis Williamson, chief of the MAAG, was quoted as saying. "About thirty-five corporate visitors a week dropped in at MAAG headquarters, and this was only a portion of the total."[26] Naturally nothing but the latest and most sophisticated weapons were acceptable. At times even they would not do. At the Shah's insistence Spruance class destroyers to be delivered to Iran were equipped with more electronic gear and more creature comforts than those used by the U.S. Navy.[27] The F–18L light bomber was still on the drawing board, and the U.S. Air Force had not ordered a single one, when Northrop President Thomas Jones met with the Shah. Within days he received an Iranian contract for 250 of the planes plus equipment and services, a $2.5 billion package.[28]

As a pillar of American foreign policy in the region, the Shah received backing for flexing his military muscle. When he sent troops to fight a Marxist insurgency in Oman, when he seized three strategic islands belonging to Arab sheiks that guarded the Straits of Hormuz, he had U.S. diplomatic support; when he needed to provide arms for the Kurdish rebels in Iraq, the United States obliged; and when he abandoned them a few years later, so did the United States.

Moreover, as a close friend the Shah received plenty of support within the United States. Prominent Americans were ready to serve on the board of the Pahlavi Foundation. Mrs. Marion Javits, wife of New York Senator Jacob Javits, a senior member of the Foreign Relations Committee, accepted a $67,500-a-year job to conduct a pro-Iranian information campaign.[29] In Washington influential people flocked to the Iranian embassy. Ambassador Zahedi was charming, simply charming. His receptions and dinners were the talk of the town. The food was excellent, the decor was lavish, and the guests, carefully selected from the various sectors of the capital, were important.[30] Major U.S. universities (including Harvard, Columbia, and Georgetown) accepted grants to help plan educational facilities in Iran or to conduct educational exchange programs.

The U.S. government was ready to go to great lengths to protect the reputation of Iran and its ruler whenever and wherever they needed it. And they soon needed it. Doubts began to surface about our good friend who nationalized oil companies and then kept jacking up oil prices, one who was not loath to remind us: "Can the United States, can the non-Communist world, afford to lose Iran? Do you have any choice?''[31] Or to threaten us: "We have ten other markets to provide us with what we need. There are people just waiting for that moment. [Iran] can hurt you as badly if not more so than you can hurt us.''[32]

Doubts about Iran's capability to use all the military hardware it purchased soon arose. New equipment arriving at its harbors had to wait months for unloading, then sat around for many months more. Maintenance was another problem. All weapons need care, complex modern weapons all the more so. But Iran had few with the technological skill to perform these tasks, and because they were low-prestige jobs, few wanted to learn. In the end it seemed advisable to hire U.S. firms to keep the planes of the Iranian Air Force flying. The position of a pilot did have prestige, and Iranians did manage to learn. It took time and instruction by Americans, but then the Shah bought new and different planes and they had to start learning all over again from more and other American instructors.[33]

There were also doubts about the integrity of the Shah's rule. Rumors of widespread corruption were rampant. Soon they were followed by more than rumors. There was evidence of payoffs by American companies: $2.9 million by Textron and $700,000 by Northrop. There were convictions: two senior officials of the Iran Trading Company, the commander of the Iranian Navy, 10 other naval officers, and 19 army engineers. An "anti-profiteering campaign" found some 10,000 merchants guilty and closed about 600 shops.[34] Worse still, people were convinced that these revelations touched only the surface of corruption and touched the royal family, where much of the heavy action took place, not at all. Their wealth was rapidly and visible rising—like a bunch of upstarts, they could not resist ostentation.

Corruption, however, was not the worst problem of the Iranian government's (the Shah's) reputation. Just exactly what SAVAK learned about external espionage from the CIA is not entirely clear, but as far as internal subversion was concerned, it was a failure. SAVAK could not reliably identify, let alone apprehend, terrorists and insurgents. Unable to cope with persons who were organizing to overthrow the government, it attacked people who disagreed with any of its policies—a very different group. Late in 1978, "on the advice of international lawyers," defense attorneys were permitted to participate in custodial interrogation; until then SAVAK had done all the interrogating by itself. It was invariably a very forceful interrogation. The shah indignantly denied rumors that tens of thousands were arrested for political reasons and quoted with some pride an opposition source that set the number (1968–77) at "exactly 3,164." He explained: "Our Prime Minister was directly responsible for the day-to-day operations of SAVAK. . . . However, when I learned that torture and abuse existed, as a matter of policy I ordered it stopped.''[35] Actually SAVAK did not mind inflated numbers of prisoners or reports of its brutality. Incompetent as it was, it hoped to cope with any insurgency problem by an "all pervasive, constant intimidation" of the entire population.[36]

All of this raised doubts about the stability of the political system (the Shah's rule) as early as 1973; doubts by academics, a year later doubts by reporters and businessmen.[37] There also were doubts in the Defense Department and doubts in Congress. A Senate Foreign Relations Committee staff report concluded that with all the arms buildup Iran would still be unable to engage in major combat operations in five to ten years, and worried about the possibility that the United States might become entangled in a war at a time and place of the Shah's choosing. But official support did not waver. When Israel's representative in Teheran suggested deep political troubles, U.S. Embassy personnel ridiculed the idea. From Washington came a personal message from President Ford: "I have let it be known to all the senior officials of my administration who deal with these issues, that they should keep constantly in mind the very great importance which I attach to the special relationship that we enjoy with Iran."[38] A Defense Department request for reconsideration of policy toward Iran was successfully managed by the State Department. Regarding SAVAK, Assistant Secretary of State Alfred Atherton assured Congress: "I believe that the advances which have been made in improving the human rights of the broad majority of Iran's population under considerable adversity far outweigh such abuses as have occurred in an attempt to control the violent challenges to the government."[39]

Our entanglement, however, went beyond massive arms shipments and statements of support. While the Shah sought CIA advice and training, he definitely did not want promiscuous information gathering in Iran by Americans. The United States apparently obliged. Political officers assigned to the Teheran embassy whose responsibility was to report on domestic developments found their numbers dwindling noticeably: from 21 in 1963 to just 6 in 1973. The number of economic officers declined only from 9 to 8, but by 1973, 3 of them were completely tied up in servicing the onrush of U.S. sales agents.[40] Just what the CIA was doing all this time is, of course, classified, but in terms of results it was not very impressive. It did not know, or it did not tell the President of the United States, the dimensions of the growing political opposition to the Shah. And it did not know, or did not tell the President of the United States, that in 1974 the Shah had been diagnosed by French doctors as having cancer.[41]

More than that, our entanglement had incredible domestic consequences. SAVAK was permitted to operate in the United States. Iranian students were approached and urged to inform on other (Iranian) students; those engaged in political activity were threatened. Information on a naturalized U.S. citizen, the editor of the Virginia-based *Iran Free Press*, was requested by the Foreign Ministry in Teheran and reportedly was supplied by the State Department. The story (if true) then grew weird.

Some time in 1975 or 1976, SAVAK decided to assassinate Afshar [the editor]. They requested a complete file on [him] from the CIA, without apprising them of their final intentions. The agency went to the FBI, obtained a file on Afshar and turned it over to SAVAK. In the meantime, the CIA obtained word that SAVAK had been training a non-

Iranian assassin, though it did not know for what purpose. Some months later, the man in question contacted the CIA, told them that he had been ordered to carry out the murder, but had refused to go through with it.[42]

In any case, U.S. entanglement with Iran continued during the Carter administration. The new ambassador, William H. Sullivan, had some concerns of his own. He thought that whatever advanced literature Henry Kissinger had been reading, rapid industrialization would necessarily have adverse political ramifications. During his preparation to assume his post, the ambassador met in New York with some 30 senior executives of corporations with interests in Iran. While "all these indicated that their Iranian business was highly profitable . . . [he] detected a common feature, however: very few of them made any significant equity investment in Iran."[43]

Ambassador Sullivan knew, of course, that Jimmy Carter had campaigned hard against the United States becoming an "arms merchant" and for basic human rights everywhere in the world. Consequently, during his first meeting with the President, he raised three issues.[44] First, how would projected arms sales restrictions apply to Iran? "His answer was quick and specific. He wished to be quite generous with the Iranians, and there was nothing currently on their shopping list under consideration that he felt it necessary to deny them."[45] Second, what was the U.S. position on the Iranian determination to acquire late-model U.S. nuclear reactors? "Again the president was precise and affirmative. He saw no problems, he said, in providing nuclear power plants to the Iranians on the condition that they accept appropriate international safeguards concerning their use and the disposition of spent fuel."[46] And third: Did the President wish to continue collaboration with SAVAK?

The President again answered promptly, indicating that he had examined this issue and had reached the conclusion that the intelligence which we received, particularly from our listening stations focused on the Soviet Union, was of such importance that we should continue the collaboration between our two intelligence agencies. He qualified this general endorsement only by indicating that he expected me to try to persuade the shah to improve the human-rights performance of his government in all its aspects.[47]

Once in Teheran the ambassador moved to test his doubts. At a dinner with ten prominent Iranians (including the Minister for Economic Affairs and the head of the National Planning Organization) he raised the problems of rapid industrialization.

When I finished, there was general silence and all the Iranians turned toward the minister for economic affairs.

The minister, in a rather impassioned defense of the shah's wisdom, rejected all my observations and defended the industrial program in its entirety. He denied the existence of corruption, except for petty bribe taking by minor officials, assured me that all bottlenecks were in the process of being resolved, and defended the competitive nature of the Iranian projects. After he finished there were two or three comments supporting his remarks from other senior officials in attendance, but by and large it was clear that most of them wished not to pursue the subject further. . . .

However, as the evening broke up and the guests left, I walked with each of them to the front door, beginning with the economic minister. To my astonishment he pulled me aside as he was retrieving his coat from the cloakroom and told me that my remarks were absolutely well founded and that he agreed with everything I said. He confided, however, that he could not, in that company, afford to be critical of the shah or the shah's program.

One by one, as each of my Iranian guests left, he made substantially the same remarks, . . . Jack Miklos, my deputy, shook his head and said that the performance was inevitable. Not one of those around the table knew who among them might be a SAVAK agent.[48]

The ambassador did not quite give up. During a visit to Washington he

tried to encourage the Department of State and CIA to continue and elaborate the examination of the Iranian economy that they had halfheartedly begun a year earlier. Once again this bogged down in the miasma of Washington bureaucracy. I could not seem to get a group that was willing to invest the time necessary to undertake a serious examination of the issue. On the other hand, I found some who were all too eager to turn such a review into a broader examination of the entire Iranian political system, introducing subjective factors [sic] that would have made the basic economic review meaningless.[49]

In the middle of November 1977 the Shah visited Washington. Clashes between rival student groups were broken up by the police. The tear gas was carried by the light wind to the White House grounds, bringing tears to the eyes of the president and the shah at the official reception. At the end of December, President Carter visited Teheran. During this flight his staff was given a briefing on the "extreme security measures." The instructions were stern: "Do not plan to leave the hotel unless absolutely necessary or on official business."[50] Even so, at the state dinner the President, ignoring the State Department draft for his toast, declared: "Iran is an island of stability in one of the more troubled areas of the world. This is a great tribute to you, your Majesty, and to your leadership and to the respect, admiration and love which your people give you."[51]

Just a week later riots broke out in the streets. Disorders spread quickly; nevertheless, during the spring, summer, and into the fall of 1978 both State Department and CIA reporting assured political continuity. Specifically, in August a CIA study declared: "Iran is not in a revolutionary or even a 'prerevolutionary' situation." A message from Ambassador Sullivan on October 27, 1978, included the assertion that "our destiny is to work with the Shah." And on November 22 a CIA analyst "concluded that the shah 'was not paralyzed with indecision.' . . . His vacillation . . . probably meant that he was 'continuing to cope with problems of his regime.' "[52] This was just three months before the whole "system" collapsed and the shah departed into exile, leaving behind an Iran in utter turmoil and full of hatred for the Great Satan, America. Very unpleasant facts, to be sure, yet without disastrous consequences for our global strategic position.[53]

The lesson, of course, is not that the United States should have no special relations. For military, economic, political, and cultural reasons some countries and some people on this globe are of special interest to us. But our experiences in Iran do suggest that we should learn to be careful about which governments we select for special relationships, and that we should be very alert to the prospect that such relationships will undermine our objectivity (after all, anyone will tell you that you cannot be objective with a friend). By shading evidence, shifting emphasis, overvaluing rationales, and overlooking realities, almost imperceptibly and with the best of intentions we can easily become entangled in a special relationship that is detrimental to our national interest.

NOTES

1. U.S. imports (in billions of current dollars) amounted to 15.0 in 1960, 40.0 in 1970, 244.9 in 1980, and 325.7 in 1984—respectively, 3.0 percent, 4.0 percent, 9.3 percent, and 8.9 percent of gross national product. In the same years U.S. exports amounted to 19.6, 42.7, 220.6, and 217.9 billion (current) dollars and 3.9, 4.3, 8.4, and 5.9 percent of gross national product, respectively. United States, Department of Commerce, *Statistical Abstract of the United States*, 1986 (Washington, D.C.: U.S. Government Printing Office, 1986), pp. 431, 807.

2. Authoritarian governments are selected by means other than free elections and are not accountable to the electorate. Totalitarian governments do not concede any rights to the individual (any civil liberties); they insist that they have the right to control and regulate all aspects of human behavior, even thought.

3. *New York Times*, September 14, 1962, p. 12.

4. Richard Nixon, *RN, the Memoirs of Richard Nixon* (New York: Grosset and Dunlap, 1978), pp. 885, 922, 939.

5. Testimony before the Senate Foreign Relations Committee, February 18, 1966.

6. Kermit Roosevelt, *Countercoup, the Struggle for the Control of Iran* (New York: McGraw-Hill, 1979), pp. 10–11.

7. Mohammed Reza Shah Pahlavi, *Mission for My Country* (New York: McGraw-Hill, 1962), p. 89. Actually U.S. aid in 1950 amounted to $500,000; in 1951 it was $1.6 million; it jumped in 1952 to $23.4 million; and in 1953 it fell to $22.1 million.

8. Kermit Roosevelt, *Countercoup*, p. 18. Interestingly U.S. documents released in late 1989 include only one item implying U.S. covert involvement. It is a record of a telephone conversation between the secretary of state (John Foster Dulles) and the director of Central Intelligence (Allen Dulles) about a month before the operation (July 24, 1953): "The Secretary called and said in your talk about Iran yesterday at the meeting you did not mention the other matter, is it off? AWD said he doesn't talk about it, it was cleared directly with the President, and is still active. . . . " United States, Department of State, *Foreign Relations of the United States, 1952–1954*, vol. 10 *Iran* (Washington, D.C.: U.S. Government Printing Office, 1989), p. 737.

9. One notable victim was Foreign Minister Hossain Fatemi. After a trial (of sorts) he was executed. Dr. Mossadegh was sentenced to three years in prison.

10. Roosevelt, *Countercoup*, p. 166. The British government and the Anglo-Iranian Oil Company may have spent much more. Nikki R. Keddie, *Roots of Revolution, an Interpretive History of Modern Iran* (New Haven: Yale University Press, 1981), p. 140.

11. Indeed, Secretary of State Dulles tried to keep Iran from joining the pact because it was "too soon after their troubles." Barry Rubin, *Paved with Good Intentions, the American Experience and Iran* (Dallas, Pa.: Penguin Books, 1981), p. 97.

12. John D. Stempel, *Inside the Iranian Revolution* (Bloomington: Indiana University Press, 1981), p. 65.

13. Pahlavi, *Mission*, p. 105.

14. December 2, 1956, p. 31.

15. Pahlavi, *Mission*, p. 160.

16. Henry Kissinger, *White House Years* (Boston: Little, Brown, 1979), p. 1259.

17. Pahlavi, *Mission*, p. 160.

18. Roosevelt, *Countercoup*, pp. 73–74.

19. United States, Department of State, *Foreign Relations of the United States, 1952–1954*, p. 762.

20. Kissinger, *White House Years*, p. 1259.

21. Keddie, *Roots*, pp. 203–05.

22. Mohammed Reza Shah Pahlavi, *Answer to History* (New York: Stein and Day, 1980), p. 104.

23. Kissinger, *White House Years*, p. 1263.

24. Stempel, *Inside the Iranian Revolution*, p. 69.

25. Kissinger, *White House Years*, p. 1264. The president's instructions were confirmed by a memorandum from the National Security Council to all the departments and agencies involved. Stempel, *Inside the Iranian Revolution*, p. 73.

26. Rubin, *Paved with Good Intentions*, p. 135.

27. Actually they were never delivered; the revolution intervened. To the delight of U.S. officers they are now used by the Navy and are generally referred to as belonging to the Ayatollah class.

28. Rubin, *Paved with Good Intentions*, p. 175. They were not delivered either.

29. Ibid., p. 151. She was forced to resign.

30. "Over 1,000 presents were delivered each Christmas, including 150 cans of caviar, 90 bottles of Dom Perignon champagne, and 600 to 700 books." Ibid., p. 153.

31. *Washington Post*, August 7, 1976, p. A–10.

32. Rubin, *Paved with Good Intentions*, p. 173.

33. There were 9,087 Americans living in Iran in 1972. Six years later this number was 53,941. Stempel, *Inside the Iranian Revolution*, p. 74.

34. Rubin, *Paved with Good Intentions*, p. 76.

35. Pahlavi, *Answer to History*, pp. 157–58.

36. Rubin, *Paved with Good Intentions*, pp. 178–80.

37. The series in the *Washington Post* by Louis Simons and discussions with an Exxon executive, two friends whose judgment I learned to respect, induced me to visit Teheran in August 1975. The terror of SAVAK was apparent at the airport. Popular hostility to foreigners was palpable even in tourist hotels. In my discussions with a very senior Finance Ministry official, I was describing the highly complex relationships between economic development and political stability, and more specifically the pressures of political destabilization produced by rapid economic growth. He was totally unimpressed. "Professor," he explained, "we are not worried by such matters. When we have such questions we just ask His Majesty."

38. Rubin, *Paved with Good Intentions*, p. 154.

39. Ibid., p. 186.

40. Stempel, *Inside the Iranian Revolution*, pp. 70–71. Even at the height of the crisis the State Department's Bureau of Intelligence and Research did not have a single Iranian analyst. Gary Sick, *All Fall Down: America's Tragic Encounter with Iran* (New York: Viking Penguin, 1986), p. 107.

41. There is still some controversy, however, over whether the Shah was told and/or understood that he had cancer.

42. Rubin, *Paved with Good Intentions*, p. 181.

43. William H. Sullivan, *Mission to Iran* (New York: W. W. Norton, 1981), p. 31.

44. Ibid., pp. 20–22.

45. Presidential Directive no. 13, dated May 13, 1977, specified that all arms sales would have to be approved by the President personally. In July 1977 the President approved seven AWACS planes (reduced from ten requested) for Iran and in the face of vigorous opposition fought it through Congress. Sick, *All Fall Down*, pp. 29–31.

46. Sullivan, *Mission to Iran*, p. 21.

47. Ibid., pp. 21–22.

48. Ibid., pp. 69–70.

49. Ibid., p. 151.

50. *Washington Post*, January 1, 1978, p. A–4.

51. Sullivan, *Mission to Iran*, p. 134; Rubin, *Paved with Good Intentions*, p. 201.

52. Zbigniew Brzezinski, *Power and Principle* (New York: Straus and Giroux, 1983), pp. 358–59; Sick, *All Fall Down*, pp. 107–08.

53. Brzezinski thought that had the Shah not fallen, the Soviet Union would not have moved into Afghanistan so openly, but that was about all. *Power and Principle*, p. 356.

5

THE NORTH ATLANTIC TREATY ORGANIZATION

The security of Western Europe, and by extension that of Northern and Southern Europe, is of special interest to the United States. Their civilization formed the foundation of our own; their people provided a large share of immigrants who settled and developed this country. Their values are very much like ours; their commitment to human rights and the democratic form of government is no less profound. We have been friends for a long time and comrades at arms with most of them in two great wars. Economically Western Europe offers important markets for our industry and commerce. Militarily it denies valuable jumping-off points for aggression against us.

After World War II, Western Europe became vulnerable. Soviet forces stationed in Eastern European countries were close by; the Soviet Union itself was not far away. Western European countries, each by itself or even all together, were no match for Soviet military might. To be reasonably secure from predatory initiatives they needed U.S. support, and the United States was quite willing to give it. In April 1949 Western Europe and North America joined in the North Atlantic Treaty Organization (NATO). The signatories proposed to establish an integrated military command structure and called for the assignment of forces to NATO by each of the member states. Perhaps most important was Article 5 of the Treaty:

The Parties agree that an armed attack against one or more of them in Europe or North America shall be considered an attack against them all, and consequently agree that if such an armed attack occurs, each of them . . . will assist the Party or Parties so attacked forthwith, individually, and in concert with the other Parties, with such action as it deems necessary, including the use of armed force, to restore and maintain the security of the North Atlantic area.[1]

As unambiguously as its constitutional provisions permitted, the United States let it be known that any military superiority that the Soviet Union might have against any Western European country (or all Western European countries together) would be more than offset by adding U.S. military resources to the Western European side of the scale. In consequence any Soviet attack would suffer defeat, or at least the Soviet homeland would suffer enormous (unacceptable) devastation.

It was a relatively simple matter—during the first decade of the treaty. The United States had a nuclear monopoly or at least was safe from nuclear attack. Credibly and without much cost it could "extend" its own strategic deterrence by a written commitment. Our allies could feel safe under a U.S. nuclear umbrella. As the Soviet Union deployed its own nuclear weapons and long-range delivery systems, however, the situation changed radically. The question arose: Were there holes in the umbrella? Europeans began to doubt that, treaty or no treaty, Americans would actually use their strategic nuclear weapons in order to punish aggression in Western Europe, since this might trigger a Soviet nuclear retaliation on their homeland, especially if this aggression were carried out by conventional (nonnuclear) weapons. Once the doubts that the United States would risk its own territory to save Western Europe were shared by the Soviet leadership, the credibility of "extended deterrence" was very much in peril.

IN SEARCH OF DETERRENCE

Faced with the fundamentally changed strategic circumstances, three alternatives seemed indicated. First, it was still possible to believe that the United States would risk its own territory for Western Europe. The strange combination of idealism and pragmatism that is so characteristic of Americans and has marked their foreign policy is rather unpredictable. In the two world wars this country invested its wealth and risked the lives of its young men for its ideals—and for Western Europe. The Soviet Union cannot be sure that it will not do so again. All the same, it was a high-risk option. Europeans with their long diplomatic experience and historical memory (Munich was not so long ago) could hardly believe in a security based on the treaty commitment of an ally. President Charles de Gaulle could not believe in it at all. "Despite its power," he confided shortly after his retirement, "I don't believe the United States has a long-term policy. Its desire, and it will satisfy it one day, is to desert Europe. You will see."[2]

A second possible approach was for the major European powers to build their own independent strategic nuclear capabilities. Britain already had one. President de Gaulle was determined that France, too, should get one. The Soviet Union must be left with no illusions. Any attack on France would cost it quite a lot, way out of proportion to any possible gain. Even if the Americans let her down, France would still have the strategic force of its own to punish the Soviet homeland. But there were problems. Even the largest of the European powers was, in modern global terms, relatively small in territory. All of France could easily fit into Nevada and New Mexico; Britain could fit into either with room to spare. How could strategic weapons become survivable in such limited space? How could a relatively small strategic nuclear force deter a very much larger one? Worst of all, what about West Germany, the closest and most vulnerable country? Would Britain and France be comfortable with strategic nuclear weapons under German control? Would the Soviet Union, at the slightest clue that Germany was developing them, preempt?

Then there was the third, very different, approach. Instead of relying on assured strategic punishment, a conventional attack on Western Europe could conceivably be deterred by the prospect of defeat in the field. In 1955 West Germany was admitted to NATO. Its forces, when added to those of France and Britain reinforced by U.S. units, would present a formidable combination. Surely, so ran the argument, the Soviet Army is not invincible. It has problems of leadership and morale; some of its equipment is flawed, and its maintenance is spotty; and the supply lines of an attack on Western Europe would have to run through satellite countries whose people would not be wholly supportive. The Soviet Army could be defeated.

In the event, all three options were combined. Britain maintained, and France built, their own strategic (nuclear) forces. Meanwhile, NATO collectively would develop a system of "flexible response,"[3] that is, deter each level of aggression by symmetric capabilities. The U.S. commitment of Article 5 of NATO stands; public assurance never wavered. The United States would not accept the Communist conquest of Europe; the Soviet Union should entertain no doubts. The deterrence of an attack upon us would remain coupled to the deterrence of an attack on Western Europe. If everything else failed, the United States would use its full strategic retaliatory capacity to punish the aggressor. But it may not come to that. For the aggressor may well be deterred by the knowledge that we could, with our joint conventional forces, defeat a subnuclear attack. Indeed, as we moved through the 1960s and 1970s, this prospect was expected to carry the weight of NATO deterrence.

A deterrence strategy based on the prospect of the aggressor's defeat in the field, however, had its own problems. First of all, for it to have credibility, the *possibility* of defeat is not sufficient. What is required is, at a minimum, a *high probability* of defeat that can be sustained into the future. Optimistic estimates soon received a sharp setback when President de Gaulle withdrew French forces from the unified NATO command and forced NATO headquarters to leave his country and relocate in Brussels, Belgium.

What made deterrence by the prospect of defeat in the field especially problematic, however, were our long-term systemic handicaps in trained manpower and military spending. The fact is that authoritarian systems can maintain large standing armies much more easily and much longer than democratic systems. For example, the Soviet Union, Poland, and Czechoslovakia conscript their young men for 24 months of military service. Total Soviet military manpower is close to 5 million; if its ready reserve of another 9 million is added, that force would amount to over 5 percent of the population.[4] Western Europeans and North Americans, on the other hand, actively resist any prospect of becoming garrison states. France and West Germany use conscription for 12 months and 15 months, respectively. The United States, Canada, and Britain all have volunteer armies. Total U.S. military manpower (2,041,000) plus ready reserves (1,222,000) add up to less than 1.5 percent of our population.

Similarly, authoritarian governments can maintain massive military budgets much more easily and much longer. All through the 1970s the Soviet Union sustained a steady 3 percent annual increase in its defense budgets. Democratic governments find it a constant struggle to support any increase in military spending when they would much rather appropriate funds for social welfare and justice. Indeed, total U.S. defense expenditures (at constant prices) remained about the same throughout the 1970s. Defense share of GNP declined steadily from 7.4 percent in 1971 to 4.9 percent in 1980. In May 1979 the NATO Defense Planning Committee agreed to an annual increase of 3 percent in spending through 1985. Within a year and a half West Germany announced that it would not be meeting this commitment.[5]

U.S. defense spending increased in the early 1980s. Even so, it was not until the middle of the decade that appropriations (in constant dollars) reached 1967 levels, and then once again they began declining. In any case, the Soviet Union and its allies continue to hold a numerical superiority over NATO forces in troops and most conventional arms. Recently the ratio of total military forces (including naval units) was 1.5:1 against NATO; that of battle tanks 2:1 against NATO, artillery 1.8:1 against NATO, attack helicopters 2:1 against NATO, armored personnel carriers 1.6:1 against NATO, fighter bombers 1.2:1 against NATO, and interceptor aircraft 5:1 against NATO. The depressing monotony was broken only by the 1.5:1 NATO advantage in transport helicopters.[6]

The quantitative gap in weapons, moreover, was exacerbated by a continued disparity in areas of production. For example, from 1983 to 1989 annual Soviet tank production increased from 2,600 to 3,500, while ours dropped from 1,200 to 775. The ratios in the annual output of other weapons were similarly heavily in their favor: specifically, in armored vehicles, 1,500 to 1,000; in fighters and fighter bombers, 700 to 550; in submarines, 10 to 5; and in surface warships, 9 to 3. In fact, during the first four years of Mikhail Gorbachev's rule (1985–89), the Soviet Union produced 450 ICBMs, the United States only 56.

To be sure, democracies seek to compensate for their enemies' quantitative edge through advanced technology and its qualitative advantages. Unfortunately, qualitative differences are not as telling and not as readily convertible into credible deterrence as quantitative indicators. And in any case the weapons, if not the soldiers, of the Soviet Union generally are not qualitatively inferior.

There is another problem as well. High probability of Soviet defeat under *some* circumstances is not enough. For purposes of deterrence, high probability of Soviet defeat *over the full spectrum of military contingencies* is required. A Soviet invasion, whatever its initial form, must be stopped.

Figure 4
Forward Defense

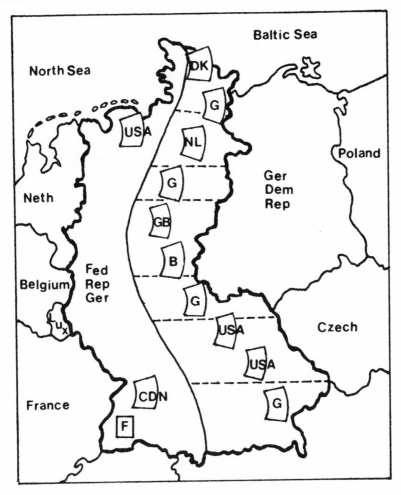

First, NATO must be able to stop a surprise attack. Stationed close to the West German border are 6 East German and 20 of the best Soviet divisions. In a short time and with only a modest risk of discovery they could be concentrated for a sudden breakthrough. Facing them are 20 good NATO divisions. Their most fundamental dilemma is this: On the one hand, "forward defense" at the point of contact is very difficult in a surprise attack. Unless it can know ahead of time where the Soviets are massing their troops, NATO has to spread its forces thinly all along the border, which makes them vulnerable to a breakthrough. On the other hand, a defense in depth is nearly impossible. Politically, the problem is that German units, the bulk of NATO forces, would not be inclined to concede, for the sake of mobility, much, let alone most, of German territory to the enemy. When Germans sang of the *Wacht am Rhein* (watch on the Rhine) they did not have in mind a defense on the left bank of the river against an attack from the east. Militarily, the problem is that there is little room to maneuver. West Germany's "waist" is now barely 130 miles wide, the distance between Philadelphia and Washington; but with the exception of the narrow strip of Holland and Belgium, that is all the room there is (all there might be) ever since President de Gaulle evicted NATO in 1967.[7]

Second, NATO should also have a good chance of defeating a more massive assault. Soviet forces in Poland and in western Russia could participate in the attack, thus raising the initial force to about 80 divisions. There could be no strategic surprise in this case. Preparations would take about 30 days. Our intelligence is too good; our military leaders would soon know about the massive movement of troops and equipment. The quality of the additional forces, moreover, is estimated to be lower. The most fundamental problem for NATO here is reinforcement. The *estimate* of NATO planners is that we should have 22 days (hence the designation of 30:22 scenario), but would we? It is difficult to imagine that NATO would respond quickly, since Soviet preparations, it can safely be assumed, would be camouflaged by the use of peacetime military exercises and by a massive effort of disinformation. The people in (democratic) NATO countries would wish to believe that military intelligence could be in error; their (democratic) governments would wish to avoid any action that might be misrepresented as provocative. We would temporize and hope until the very last minute, if not longer. Would West German mobilization have enough time to field massive reinforcements? Would the Dutch and Belgian governments interpret intelligence reports differently? How would France respond? How much reinforcement could be brought on short notice from the United States? Two divisions? Three divisions? The quantitative ratios on the day of aggression would probably be even more unfavorable to NATO than in case of a surprise attack.[8]

Finally, NATO must be able to stop a massive invasion launched by the fully mobilized forces of the Soviet Union and its allies. Such an event would be the culmination of an extended period (six months or more) of steadily deteriorating relations punctuated by regular and escalating acts of provocation. Some 200 divisions supported by planes and attack helicopters and the massed firepower of tanks, artillery, and armored vehicles, but without recourse to nuclear weapons, would invade Western Europe. Even if NATO used the time for full reinforcement and France added its forces, Soviet quantitative superiority would still be awesome.

There are, of course, many variations of the basic Soviet attack scenarios, with widely differing assumptions. Most of them are useful primarily for military officers and defense analysts considering and/or preparing for contingencies in war-fighting. Europeans understandably are very much more interested in deterrence than in war-fighting; keeping that perspective in mind, it is enormously significant that while some of these scenarios end with NATO conventional forces stopping a Soviet conventional attack, not many, not most, and certainly not all do.[9]

Yet even if the invasion could be stopped, that is only half the task. Credible deterrence requires sustained resistance over time. On this, too, NATO is at a disadvantage. While fresh Soviet supplies can be moved over a few hundred miles of roads, ours must be shipped across several thousand miles of ocean. Although some of our equipment and material is stored in Europe, even after the buildup of the early 1980s (as an optimistic estimate), NATO forces had only about 30 days of supplies and in some procurement items and in "war-risk kits" (such as spare parts) had even less. To quote a subcommittee of the House of Representatives:

In general, the very high degree of professionalism and dedication of the staff of the 21st SUPCOM [Support Command] was evident. Unfortunately, this professionalism and dedication cannot make up for the dearth of support received in terms of personnel and force structure and as the CG [Commanding General] stated, their "magic act" could only last a few days.[10]

The Supreme Allied Commander Europe did not mince any words: NATO's "conventional capabilities today," he said, "are clearly inadequate to meet the growing Warsaw Pact conventional threat."[11]

It is, of course, conceivable that the Soviet Union has no designs on Western Europe, that it would find no profit in possessing the territory after a war had devastated its resources, and that (as in the times of Stalin) it would fear exposing its people to the quality of life there if it were captured intact. If so, at least until the mid 1980s the Soviets were sending the wrong signals. For 40 years after Soviet tanks rolled into Berlin and Marshal Georgi Zhukov presided over the unconditional surrender of Germany, consistently, without any interruption, the Soviet Union was building up its forces facing Western Europe. During the 1950s, perhaps even the 1960s, it could be argued that the Soviet Union needed "the threat of massive attack that could overrun Western Europe . . . [to] deter the Americans from exploiting their overwhelming advantages in [strategic] nuclear forces."[12] In other words, the Soviet Union could feel safe only if it held Western Europe hostage. But whatever plausibility this argument had then was lost by the time of mutual assured destruction in the mid 1970s. What had become plausible was that the Soviet Union was seeking in Europe a deterrence of a different kind. Not a deterrence of an attack upon itself but a deterrence of NATO defense if it should choose to attack. A deterrence not to prevent aggression but to safeguard aggression!

It is also conceivable that the Soviet Union may be deterred by any risk (not just a high probability) of defeat. We all know that military operations are not like mathematical equations; uncertainly is their constant feature. Given the enormous stakes, and with the awful devastations of World War II still vivid in many a Russian memory, it is possible that the Soviets would be most reluctant to take any risks at all; but for us to rely on their being so deterred is a very different matter. Deterrence is credible enough as long as any potential aggressor knows it cannot win; it is seriously degraded when a potential aggressor begins to believe that it might win and begins calculating risks. In the former case deterrence rests on stable, objective conditions created by the defender; in the latter it depends on the variable subjective conditions of the aggressor.

EUROPEAN THEATER NUCLEAR FORCES

The objective conditions of a successful NATO defense against a Soviet conventional attack, it appeared for a while, would be vastly improved if the NATO command quickly escalated or, better still, resorted immediately to nuclear weapons. The existence of tactical nuclear weapons would complicate the task of a buildup for a surprise attack and would help offset Soviet advantages in quantitative ratios. In case of larger-scale invasions they would give NATO the capacity to fight a "deep battle," hitting second- and third-echelon forces in their staging areas and during their approach to the front. That is the reason for what superficially appears to be a contradiction: while firmly committed to *no first strike*, the United States has never pledged to forgo the *first use* of nuclear weapons in case of aggression.

Actually, ever since the early years of NATO, U.S. forces in Europe have been equipped with tactical nuclear weapons. At first these were artillery pieces (howitzers) capable of firing nuclear shells. They were followed by short-range nuclear-tipped surface-to-surface and air-to-ground missiles.[13] There were, however, always reservations about them. One was the consequence of severe civilian casualties and collateral damage from blast and heat that seemed unavoidable. Another was the difficulty of using them against moving targets. But a mobile, massed armored attack was a Soviet tradition, and without an effective defense against it there could be no prospect of checking or defeating "conventional" Soviet attack.

During the Ford administration the need to modernize NATO's tactical nuclear arsenal became acute. Its last budget included a new artillery shell and a new missile warhead. Their special feature: they were enhanced radiation weapons (ERWs). They were more accurate against moving targets (Soviet massed armor) than their predecessors. They would destroy crews by "enhanced radiation," but significant reduction in explosive yield would minimize civilian casualties and civilian property damage in the vicinity, at least in the short run. (The long-run equation between civilian deaths by blast and heat and civilian costs from enhanced radiation was less clear.) Five months into the Carter administration, the *Washington Post* spotted their presence in the Carter budget. In its report the newspaper reduced all ERW weapons to a single category, renamed them "the neutron bomb," and characterized them as the weapon that kills people while it protects property.[14] In a follow-up editorial the newspaper compared them with chemical warfare weapons, described the argument in their favor as "devilishly seductive—and dead wrong," then urged the President to reject them.[15]

The story and the designation were a great success among Europeans. The State Department had enormous difficulties enlisting their governments' support for the new defensive weapon. It did have some success until President Carter, in what was described as a very personal decision (overruling all his advisers), decided against the production of ERWs.[16]

The Soviet Union, however, was not similarly constrained. It already had fighters and short-range bombers that could deliver small nuclear bombs. It also had nuclear-capable artillery and kept building better artillery pieces and more of them. Indeed, "the number of their nuclear-capable artillery tubes had gone from less than 800 to over 7,700 in about ten years."[17] The time was passing when NATO disadvantages in case of aggression by conventional forces could be overcome (and deterred) by escalation to tactical nuclear weapons.

Clearly the strategy of "flexible response" was going bankrupt. The prospects that NATO had a high probability of defeating aggression at symmetric levels— that is, defeat a conventional attack with conventional forces, or defeat an attack if both sides escalated to tactical nuclear weapons—had become perilously slim. NATO deterrence could still work provided, and only provided, (1) the Soviet Union believed that in case of adversity on the battlefield, American leadership would act *irrationally*: it would escalate, escalate even to the point of a global nuclear holocaust; and (2) the Soviet leadership knew that in case of adversity they themselves would act *rationally*: they would not escalate but accept failure.

Still not satisfied, the Soviet Union went one step further. It deployed a new offensive weapon: the SS–20, an intermediate-range missile.[18] It was a secure weapon. Mobile and deployed far to the east in the Soviet Union, it was beyond any NATO capability to take it out. MIRVed with three warheads, the SS–20 had a range of 2,700 miles. Once fired, it would take only a few minutes to reach NATO forces and facilities so heavily concentrated in West Germany. By radically improving the prospects of a Soviet surprise, preemptive strike, it presented a formidable challenge to deterrence.

The SS–20 forced Europeans to think of the unthinkable: the breakdown of deterrence. And that contingency places them in a frightful dilemma. Understandably they wish fervently that deterrence be successful and they be spared Soviet attack. To have any chance of credible deterrence they need and want the Americans: their military forces and their nuclear power. No less understandably, they want very much, in case deterrence fails, to be spared becoming a nuclear battlefield. It would be quite all right if, as a consequence of Soviet aggression against Western Europe, the United States incinerated Russia. It would be very regrettable, but still bearable, if in turn the Soviet Union devastated the United States. It would be just manageable if a Soviet attack were hurled back after a short, intense battle. The people and the countryside along the West German border admittedly would suffer badly, but the rest of Western Europe would remain safe. What would not be all right would be a deep, wide-ranging battle all across the western part of the continent; it would be altogether unacceptable if this battle were fought with nuclear weapons, leaving Western Europe—win or lose—a radioactive ash heap.[19] To put it simply, if deterrence fails and the Soviet Union does invade Western Europe, most Europeans would find it in their vital interest to surrender. But they are not sure about the Americans. They might be quite willing to fight it out—on European soil. Contemplating that contingency, Europeans do not want the Americans: not their military forces and especially not their nuclear power.

SEARCH FOR DETERRENCE RENEWED

All things considered, it was an unsatisfactory situation. Something had to be done. The Western Europeans knew it; the Americans knew it. The negotiations had their ups and downs, and President Carter's personal relations with Helmut Schmidt, the West German Chancellor, deteriorated; but by December 1979 an agreement was hammered out. It called for a dual approach. First, to appease European public opinion, President Carter agreed to enter into arms control negotiations in order to try to persuade the Soviet Union to eliminate its SS–20s or at least to stop deploying them. Second, a military countermove. The plan called for the deployment of 464 new ground-launched cruise missiles and, most important, 108 new Pershing II missiles.[20]

The Pershing IIs could not help much in stopping any Soviet invasion; for that the Pershing Ib would have been much better. The Ib had all the technical improvements hoped for in the Pershing II, including the "radar-homing terminal guidance" that improved accuracy enormously. Its range of 500–plus miles could have effectively supported any deep battle reaching far into the rear echelons. What the Pershing II had (or was promised to have), however, was more than twice the range. In less than ten minutes' flight time it could reach well into the Soviet Union itself (probably not quite as far as Moscow). Moreover, its accuracy (within 60–120 feet of the designated target) gave it some hard-target capability. In short, while it could be used as a tactical weapon affecting the outcome of a battle, it could also serve as a strategic weapon.

From the point of view of deterrence, therefore, the Pershing II made an enormous difference. By adding a new dimension it restored credibility. The prospect that the cost of aggression against NATO could be limited to Western European battlefields was practically eliminated. As in the case of strategic attack against the United States, an aggression against NATO risked the Motherland itself—part of it to the Pershing II, all of it in case of possible (probable) escalation.[21]

Following the "dual-track" approach he inherited, President Reagan was willing (albeit much less enthusiastically) to engage the Soviet Union in negotiations on the reduction of intermediate-range nuclear forces (INF). Just over two months in office, he made the commitment during a National Security Council meeting on March 30, 1981; in another eight months he revealed the

U.S. position before the Press Club. As his first of four proposals he urged the zero-zero option in intermediate-range ballistic missiles. "The United States is prepared," the President declared, "to cancel its deployment of the Pershing II and ground launched missiles if the Soviets dismantle their SS–20, SS–4 and SS–5 missiles."[22]

The zero-zero option was essentially politically motivated. As President Nixon explained:

When the United States proposed in November 1981, the zero option . . . it did so not because policy makers thought that such a solution served Western interests but because it expected the Russians to reject the idea and suffer politically for doing so. It was assumed that the proposal would score political points in Europe and enable the United States to station intermediate range nuclear forces in NATO countries.[23]

That is not to say, however, that it did not have any military rationale. Pentagon studies had "concluded that there were 250 to 300 vital military installations in Western Europe—air bases, nuclear storage sites and ports."[24] They had been somewhat vulnerable to Soviet SS–5s and SS–4s, old, large-yield missiles of low accuracy. With the SS–20 missiles they became very much more so. By the time of the NATO dual-track decision there were 140 SS–20s; by the time of President Reagan's proposal there were over 250, and their number was growing at the rate of one new launcher a week. The 140 in December 1979 would have been more than enough to cover all appropriate NATO targets; after that it meant building redundancy. During the negotiating year of 1982 the Soviet Union had well over 300 SS–20s. Had it as a "great concession," and presumably at a great cost to us, reduced the SS–20s by a full two-thirds, to just 100 (with the three warheads each), it would still have not reduced the vulnerability of the vital NATO targets one iota. "Only as you approach zero," Richard Perle, Assistant Secretary of Defense argued, "do you reduce the Soviet threat to those targets."[25]

The Soviet leadership liked half of the President's proposal: the U.S. zero, especially the Pershing II zero. "Whatever else they accomplished in INF, the Soviets were bent on stopping the NATO modernization program in its entirety," concluded the diplomatic correspondent of *Time* magazine.[26] Their counterproposal, "Statement of [or Accord on] Intentions," advocated a ceiling of 300 for all intermediate-range nuclear weapons on each side; the total of all British, French, and U.S. weapons, the total of all aircraft and missiles. By Soviet count there were already 250 French and British intermediate-range nuclear weapons in place. For the United States this meant zero Pershing IIs and zero Tomahawk cruise missiles, but we would be permitted to keep 50 planes! In turn the Soviet Union could retain its 100 Backfire bombers and 200 SS–20 missiles. It was an offer the Americans could not *but* refuse.

The President stood firm. A National Security Decision Directive made it quite clear. Zero-zero was the U.S. position. Any alternative that would permit the

Soviet Union to keep SS–20 missiles must also permit the United States to keep Pershing missiles in Europe. The American delegation, while authorized to listen to Soviet ideas, should not take the initiative or propose any new compromises of its own.

Indeed, the Soviet Union had other ideas, and as the deployment of U.S. missiles was approaching, it proposed them with increased frequency. None of them permitted the deployment of any Pershing IIs, and none dropped the permitted SS–20 level below 140. None of them could be acceptable to the United States. In November 1983 the deployment of cruise missiles in Britain and Pershing IIs in Germany commenced, and the Soviet Union walked out of the negotiations.

They did come back. Negotiating sessions were scheduled, delegations met and discussed a wide range of technical details, but the initiative had passed to the highest political levels. And on the highest political level fundamental changes were in progress. The Soviet Union had a new, very different leader. Mikhail Gorbachev wasted no time. Even before his predecessor was quite dead he flew to London for talks with the United States' closest ally. Accompanied by his elegant, charming, and intelligent wife, Raisa, he arrived with "a smile and a shoeshine." Very different from the dour Brezhnev or the crude Khrushchev, he exuded goodwill and reason. He spoke of peace; he appealed to "our common" civilization. He impressed Prime Minister Margaret Thatcher, a close friend of President Reagan. The message was flashed to Washington: We can do business with this man. So on December 8, 1987, at the Washington summit the treaty on the elimination of medium- and short-range missiles was formally signed.[27] In it each party pledged (1) that it would eliminate all its intermediate-range launchers, missiles, and their support structure and support equipment within three years;[28] (2) that it would eliminate all shorter-range missiles and launchers and their support structures and support equipment;[29] and (3) that it would not in the future produce or flight-test any intermediate- or shorter-range missiles or produce any stages or launchers of such missiles.

For us there was not much choice but to ratify the treaty. It was clearly a major political breakthrough in superpower relations. The treaty eliminated an entire class of nuclear-armed missiles, and it may have been the first successful move to start a momentum for reductions in strategic missiles. Moreover, had it not been ratified, it would have discredited not just the Administration but also our decision processes. If a popular Republican President, supported by the Democratic leadership in the Senate, cannot make a binding commitment for our country, what foreign state would want to negotiate with us? All the same, the treaty deserves a close and dispassionate look to see whether it meets the most elementary criterion of national interest: Are we better off with it?

Those many who supported the treaty focused on the military balance sheet. They organized their arguments generally along these lines.[30] First, we are no worse off than we were before the Soviet Union deployed the SS–20s. Indeed, we have gained because the Soviet Union must remove missiles with four times as many warheads as ours.[31] We have gained because the elimination of the SS–20 significantly reduces the chances of a surprise attack on vital NATO installations.

No one raised the point that the "elimination" of an entire category of missiles was actually limited to the two superpowers, leaving only them bare of these weapons.[32] Britain, France, and China kept their intermediate-range missiles. Some, such as India or South Africa, could develop them; others could acquire them. Indeed, within three months of the signing of the treaty, Saudi Arabia acquired Chinese missiles (CSS–2) with an estimated range of 1,800 miles.

The relatively few who opposed the treaty concentrated on two points. First, we were taking an enormous risk, because we cannot trust the Soviets to keep their word and the methods of verification provided by the treaty could be circumvented. That is true enough, up to a point. We can have no absolute assurance that the Soviets would not cheat and later would not clandestinely break out. But if we require such absolute certainty, we can never have any arms limitation or arms reduction treaty. Of all verifications the zero level is the easiest, and surely this treaty has the most stringent verification provisions.

The second point the opponents made was that we traded a special capability (hitting Soviet targets with U.S. ballistic missiles based in Europe) for a reduction in redundancy (fewer and shorter-range Soviet missiles hitting Western Europe). The Secretary of State disputed this assertion and assured the Senate Foreign Relations Committee[33] that after the treaty was implemented, we would still have some 8,000 nuclear warheads under NATO control, of which only about half would be limited to short (less than 500 km) range. The implication was left that the others could be delivered against Soviet territory. That was a somewhat close point. Tactical aircraft launching cruise missiles could come close to matching the range of the Pershing II, but they are much slower. Submarines with SLBMs can be made available to NATO command, but they are part of our strategic triad, and in terms of deterrence they are not readily distinguishable from its other legs, the B–52 (B–1) and the Minuteman (MX). There was not much of a chance that if NATO had fired Pershing IIs against Soviet targets, the Soviets would not have retaliated with a nuclear attack on the United States; but if they were hit by SLBMs launched from U.S. Tridents (under whatever command), the chances would quickly reach zero. So while substitutes for Pershing II capabilities continue to exist, after the implementation of the treaty they are substitutes of less than equal value.

For Europeans it marked a significant turning point. From their perspective the crucial question was how the INF treaty affected deterrence. They (especially the West Germans) were concerned that the removal of the Pershing II could mean a return to the earlier, unsatisfactory strategy of "flexible response": extension of the U.S. strategic deterrence plus deterrence by the prospect of defeat in the field. The United States sought to reassure them. To give the first some credibility, President Reagan solemnly pledged that an attack on Munich was the same as an attack on Chicago.[34] To give the second a chance, congressional leaders demanded a follow-up of unilateral (asymmetric) reduction in Soviet conventional forces.[35] The Administration in turn spoke of the need to modernize our own forces.[36]

American reassurance did not altogether allay Western European worries about the credibility of NATO deterrence. Worse still, American calls for "modernization" produced new anxieties. Exactly what did the United States mean by it? Did the Americans have in mind the modernization of NATO tactical nuclear forces, and more specifically the short-range Lance missile? In economic terms this would not be too costly. But the INF treaty has radically reduced the range of permissible missiles, and as anyone could see, "the shorter the range, the more dead Germans." Statesmen at the 1988 NATO summit in Brussels solemnly rejected any notion of "singularity," that is, any member bearing an extravagant burden. Still, as a practical matter, in case of war short-range U.S. nuclear missiles would massacre East Germans while Soviet nuclear missiles would massacre West Germans. Not an attractive prospect to Germans, but not necessarily a distressing contingency for the Soviet Union. In any case, as an increment in deterrence one could not heavily count on it.[37]

Alternatively, did the Americans urge the qualitative improvement of conventional forces (troops and weapons)? It would require enormous expenditures. (Few appreciate how very much cheaper in purely economic terms nuclear weapons are.) Given the substantial reductions in the U.S. defense budget, many Europeans wondered whether this was the overture to a campaign of "burden sharing," that is, a demand for more European contributions. Britain was doing fairly well, but new military spending after all the Conservative belt-tightening would be politically hazardous. The West German budget was already stretched to the utmost. New defense expenditures would conflict with the heavy cost of social programs; and social programs, some insist, are the mainstay of German democracy. No government wants to choose between guns or butter.

Indeed, Western Europeans felt keenly that they were already bearing their share of the burden—at the very least. By their count of the standing NATO forces, the Europeans provide 90 percent of the manpower, 95 percent of the divisions, 85 percent of the tanks, 95 percent of the artillery, and 80 percent of the combat aircraft. The West Germans were especially annoyed. For decades they patiently put up with two, three, and more major military exercises per year: the damage to the roads and the fields, the infernal clanking of tanks, the deafening thunder of low-flying jets (*Tiefflieger*), day and night, day and night. Too much noise, too much trouble. The cows would give no milk, the chickens laid no eggs, even the rabbits were reluctant to multiply. And, just as they were becoming sick and tired of it all, two unrelated, spectacular accidents catalyzed a massive public resentment.

Late in August 1988 the U.S. base of Ramstein (at Kaiserslautern) was host to an international airshow. The mood was festive but relaxed as the audience visited the exhibits and watched the aerobatics. Suddenly, during the performance of the Italian precision team, disaster struck. Three planes collided in the air, then exploded, showering the helpless guests with flaming debris. Television covered the event. Over and over it played its own tapes and some especially dramatic footage from a spectator's videocamera. Germans, their eyes glued to their TV sets, watched (in color) the stark horror of human mayhem, people in panic, twisted, burning bodies, and heard in the background the plaintive cry of a distraught, searching mother: "Anje, wo bist du?" (Annie, where are you?) The casualties included some 46 dead and 500 injured. It was one of those media spectacles that, as we saw in Vietnam, shape the mood of a people.

Then, before the mood of the people could regain its equilibrium, on December 8, 1988, a U.S. jet fighter on a training mission plunged into a row of homes at Remscheid, killing at least five people and wiping out a section of the town. A new set of distressing television pictures and a new tone by the commentators. They reported that this was actually the twenty-second NATO crash of the year and quoted German official complaints that the Americans had hindered rescue efforts, presumably because they were more anxious to protect the military secrets in the plane than to save lives. The question arose: Was it possible that deterrence (through preparedness) was getting to be too expensive?

While these issues were still being pondered and debated in Europe and America, General Secretary (now also President) Gorbachev resumed the initiative. Speaking to the United Nations on December 7, 1988, he announced the unilateral reduction of the Soviet armed forces by 500,000 men. As far as Europe was concerned:

By agreement with the Warsaw Treaty allies, we have decided to withdraw by 1991 six tank divisions from East Germany, Czechoslovakia and Hungary and to disband them.

Assault landing troops and several other formations and units, including assault crossing units with their weapons and combat equipment, will also be withdrawn and the groups of Soviet forces stationed in those countries will be reduced by 50,000 men and their armaments by 5,000 tanks.[38]

Americans quickly pointed out that even if the plan were actually implemented in two years, it would still leave Warsaw Part forces with an advantage in men and equipment. And, it was added, the Soviets could choose to withdraw their worst units and obsolete weapons. That was true enough, but somewhat irrelevant. For if and when the plan is implemented (with assault crossing units relegated to the rear echelons), Soviet capability of a surprise attack will be severely impaired, and (with reductions in total force and especially in tank units) Soviet prospects of a conventional victory in the field will be substantially reduced. Indeed, that a commitment of specific and unilateral cuts was made by President Gorbachev gave credence to the claim that the Soviet Union has given up aggressive designs and was taking a "clearly defensive" stand. The momentum had shifted. The question arose: Is deterrence really necessary?

The Soviet Union moved to exploit the new atmosphere. It pushed the bilateral negotiations on conventional force reductions by new proposals from the highest levels. On March 6, 1989 Foreign Minister Shevardnadze offered a three-stage program. On May 11 President Gorbachev proposed weapons ceilings that approached the limits advocated by the West. Finally, at the end of May, during NATO's fortieth anniversary summit, President Bush responded with his own set of numbers. He proposed that the Soviet Union top its unilateral military cuts announced the previous December by further, highly asymmetric reductions. It should cut troop levels by 325,000 in return for a U.S. reduction of 30,000. Regarding armaments, he urged the Warsaw Pact to accept the proposed Western ceiling on tanks, armored personnel carriers, and artillery pieces. Attack helicopters and land-based aircraft would be reduced 15 percent below the existing NATO levels. All of this would be accomplished not in the six-to-ten-year time span suggested by the Soviet Union but much sooner, very much sooner: in six months to a year. Surely by 1992.[39] It was a fair offer, the President said, that would "increase the stability on the continent and transform the military map of Europe."

It was somewhat of a media event. President Bush was bubbling: "Here we go now, on the offense with a proposal that is bold and tests whether the Soviet Union will move toward balance." The American press cheered him on. NATO leaders emphasized unity and went along. "The President needs a victory," a "key British official" was quoted by the *New York Times*. The German chancellor was mostly interested in negotiations on short-range missiles. He was willing to accept obfuscation—and that was what he got. President François Mitterand and Prime Minister Margaret Thatcher were not so sure that the reduction of NATO planes and helicopters would increase stability on the continent, and maintained their reservations. The Dutch prime minister admitted: "The experts may not be happy with this, but as a politician, I think it is the right thing to do."

The proposal certainly created a splash in the press, but what it meant was another matter. Quite apart from a basket of problems of verification, there were questions about the definitions of the categories of weapons. Just what could be included in "artillery pieces," "armored vehicles," or "land-based aircraft"? There were questions about the geographical area affected. Would the ceiling refer only to the "central front," or would it include all of Europe from the Atlantic to the Urals? What about Turkey?

Even more difficult are wide disagreements about baselines. For example, we say that we have 14,458 "artillery pieces" and suggest a maximum limit of 16,500, leaving us room for an additional 2,000. The way they count, we have 57,060 and propose a limit of 24,000 which means we would have to destroy some 23,060 "artillery pieces." Similarly, we say that NATO currently has 22,224 tanks. Given the agreed limit of 20,000 we would have to destroy 2,224 (probably obsolescent). The Soviets insist we have 30,690 and hence would have to destroy 10,690. Quite a difference. Incidentally, just whose NATO tanks were we planning to blow up? Our own, or are we considering French, Spanish, or Turkish tanks as well?

Public opinion in Western Europe was supportive—more for the idea of arms reduction than for U.S. leadership. Scholars and media pundits recognized that Bush was testing Gorbachev's true intentions, but they were also struck by two features: the enormous disparity against the Soviet Union in the proposed reductions, and all the public relations hoopla in which the proposals were embedded. It might have been more judicious, some suggested, had the offer been made privately. It would not have had quite the implication that the Americans were less interested in arms reductions than in putting the Soviet leader on the spot. And, many thought, it may not be necessary to be quite so meticulous about a balance. Though not sympathetic, Europeans understand that the Red Army is not just an instrument of war but also a means of political control at home and in the satellites. The new "openness" and democratization (as is evident in China) are not without risks. With such radical cuts Soviet security forces may feel vulnerable and become inadequate, while the emerging forces may become more militant and uncompromising in their push for power. So if the Soviets were to reject the offer, most Europeans would not blame them for it. Many would blame the Americans for demanding the unreasonable. If, however, Gorbachev should accept, he would get the credit for going the extra mile for peace, and we would be torn by all kinds of internal struggles (within NATO and within the United States) about implementation.

Negotiations continue for the reduction of conventional forces in Europe (CFE). Most of the movement is on the part of the Soviet Union. By October 1989 it had made major concessions in practically every category of negotiations. It has been willing to accept our figures on NATO weapons and has been remarkably forthcoming in admitting the size of its own stocks—some of them even higher than our intelligence reported. And it has offered practically anything we wanted to assure verification. The mood in Europe is bordering on the euphoric. No one debates what weapons should be modernized. The talk is about the peace dividend. Our NATO allies are already spending it with gusto.

There still remain some difficult technical problems, but we seem to be moving toward a treaty and massive arms reduction in Europe by 1992. Alternatively we may now be on the road where incremental unilateral moves are made by both sides. They on their own reduce their military forces; then sometime later NATO on its own (not just the United States) may reduce its forces somewhat; then the Soviet Union on its own may withdraw its forces far within its borders, and the United States on its own may withdraw some of its forces from Europe. No exact equivalence, no clear quid pro quo, but gradually their capability of aggression in Europe may become mitigated, and their capability for a surprise attack will disappear altogether. We may go a long way without arguments about actual numbers of troops and weapons that each side has and that each side must eliminate. We may go a long way without cumbersome and incredibly complicated verification procedures and without formal agreements until anxieties are soothed and a treaty would become superfluous, and hence could be easily signed.

Clearly the original rationale of NATO is fast becoming obsolete. If the Soviet Union would actually carry out the enormous, nonsymmetric cuts urged by the

President, and would do so by 1992, when Western Europe will become unified into the second largest economy in the world, the questions will inevitably arise on the Continent: Do we need the Americans? Whatever for? The answers could not come from U.S. economic power; they would not come from U.S. military might. They could come only from the political interest of the North Atlantic community.

NOTES

1. United States, *Treaties and Other International Agreements of the United States of America 1776–1949*, Department of State Publication no. 8521 (Washington, D.C.: U.S. Government Printing Office, 1970), vol. 4, p. 829. NATO was later joined by Greece and Turkey (1952), West Germany (1955), and Spain (1982).

2. André Malraux, *Felled Oaks: Conversation with de Gaulle* (New York: Holt, Rinehart and Winston, 1971), p. 30.

3. John Lewis Gaddis, *Strategies of Containment, a Critical Appraisal of Postwar American National Security Policy* (New York: Oxford University Press, 1982), pp. 213–20. More recently "flexible response" was referred to as "gain denial." J. J. Martin, "Nuclear Weapons in NATO's Deterrent Strategy," *ORBIS*, 22 (Winter 1979), p. 878.

4. John M. Collins, *U.S.–Soviet Military Balance* (New York: McGraw-Hill, 1980), p. 88.

5. Zbigniew Brzezinski, *Power and Principle* (New York: Straus and Giroux, 1983), pp. 293, 311.

6. United States, Department of Defense, *Soviet Military Power, 1985* (Washington, D.C.: U.S. Government Printing Office, 1985), pp. 77, 88. The ratios are even more unfavorable, according to a congressional report. United States, House of Representatives, Subcommittee of the Committee on Appropriations, *Readiness of the U.S. Military* (Washington, D.C.: U.S. Government Printing Office, 1983). These ratios assume special significance when we read in the official U.S. Army combat manual that a 1.5:1 overall (theater) advantage is necessary and possibly is sufficient for a successful attack. United States, Department of the Army, *Army Field Manual 100–5* (July 1976), p. 53.

7. The dilemma is currently handled through a compromise. Three German and two U.S. corps are deployed forward close to the East German and Czechoslovak border, with provisions for one British, one Belgian, and one Dutch corps. Some NATO forces are held back to block Soviet advance and to protect the mobilization of Danish, Dutch, and Belgian forces as well as the cross-Channel reinforcement by Britain.

8. Carnegie Endowment for International Peace, *Challenges for U.S. National Security* (Washington, D.C.: Carnegie Endowment, 1981), pp. 77–79.

9. Collins, *U.S.–Soviet Military Balance*, pp. 308–16; Carnegie Endowment for International Peace, *Challenges for U.S. National Security*, pp. 74–80; United States, House of Representatives, Subcommittee of the Committee on Appropriations, *Readiness of the U.S. Military* (Washington, D.C.: U.S. Government Printing Office, 1983), vol. 1, pp. 725–28; United States, Department of Defense, *Soviet Military Power, 1985*, pp. 75–76.

10. United States, House of Representatives, Subcommittee of the Committee on Appropriations, *Readiness of the U.S. Military*, vol. 1, p. 730.

11. General Bernard W. Rogers, "The Atlantic Alliance: Prescription for a Difficult Decade," *Foreign Affairs*, 60, no. 5 (Summer 1982), p. 1152.

12. James Schlesinger, "The Eagle and the Bear: Ruminations on Forty Years of Superpower Relations," *Foreign Affairs*, 63, no. 65 (Summer 1985), p. 942.

13. The 155mm. gun can fire a 0.1–kiloton shell about 11 miles; the 203mm. gun can fire a 12–kiloton one over a range of about 15 miles. The Lance missile has a range of nearly 70 miles with a 10–kiloton blast.

14. It just omitted the crucial modifiers. The weapon would kill *their* people (the aggressor's troops) and protect *our* property (the homes and possessions of the victim).

15. *Washington Post*, June 7, 1977, p. A–5; and June 8, 1977, p. A–22.

16. Cyrus Vance, *Hard Choices* (New York: Simon and Schuster, 1983), pp. 68–69; and Brzezinski, *Power and Principle*, pp. 302–06. In the view of former Secretary of Defense James Schlesinger, it was "a capital blunder from which he never wholly recovered." Schlesinger, "The Eagle and the Bear," p. 955.

17. United States, House of Representatives, Subcommittee of the Committee on Appropriations, *Soviet Military Power, 1985*, pp. 39, 68. Their short-range nuclear missiles were estimated at 700 in 1983.

18. By 1979, 120 were deployed; by 1985, 400, two-thirds opposite NATO. Collins, *U.S.–Soviet Military Balance*, p. 461; United States, House of Representatives, Subcommittee of the Committee on Appropriations, *Soviet Military Power, 1985*, p. 36.

19. In June 1955 NATO held an exercise to find out what casualties might result from tactical nuclear warfare. In less than three days, it was found, 1.5 to 1.7 million people would be killed and 3.5 million wounded if only 268 bombs fell on German soil. The rate of German casualties would be five times that suffered in World War II as a whole. In 1960 NATO maneuvers in Schleswig-Holstein showed that between 300,000 and 400,000 civilian deaths could be expected within 48 hours of the initiation of tactical nuclear warfare. These figures did not take into account the effects of radiation and ensuing diseases. Theodore Draper, "Nuclear Temptations: Doctrinal Issues in the Nuclear Debate," in Charles W. Kegley, Jr., and Eugene Wittkopf, eds., *The Nuclear Reader: Strategy, Weapons, War* (New York: St. Martin's Press, 1985), p. 28. It does not take much imagination to conclude that by the 1980s potential casualties have multiplied many times over.

20. To reassure public opinion that NATO was not expanding its reliance on nuclear missiles, however, 1,000 nuclear warheads already in Western Europe were to be withdrawn. Brzezinski, *Power and Principle*, p. 309.

21. In 1981 President Reagan explained our response to the SS–20. "Now the only answer to these systems," he said, "is a comparable threat to Soviet threats, to Soviet targets. In other words, a deterrent preventing the use of these Soviet weapons by a counter-threat of a like response against their own country." *New York Times*, November 19, 1981, p. A–17. Some two years later, shortly before the deployment of the Pershing II, the Director of the State Department's Bureau of Political-Military Affairs left no doubt. At a staff meeting where the technical difficulties that plagued the missile were once again pointed out, Richard Burt exclaimed: "We don't care if the goddam things work or not. After all, that doesn't matter unless there's a war. What we care about is getting them." Strobe Talbott, *Deadly Gambits, the Reagan Administration and the Stalemate in Nuclear Arms Control* (New York: Alfred A. Knopf, 1985), p. 187.

22. *New York Times*, November 19, 1985, p. A–17.

23. *New York Times Magazine*, March 13, 1988, p. 79.

24. Talbott, *Deadly Gambits*, p. 59.

25. Quoted in ibid., p. 60.

26. Ibid., p. 90.

27. *New York Times*, December 9, 1987, pp. A–24–A–25.

28. For the United States this meant its Pershing II and its ground-launched cruise missiles. For the Soviet Union this meant the SS–20, SS–4, and SS–5.

29. For the United States this meant the Pershing IA, and for the Soviet Union it meant the SS–12 and SS–23.

30. Testimony by the secretary of state before the Senate Foreign Relations Committee, January 25, 1988.

31. Only the missiles are to be destroyed, not the warheads.

32. It is practically impossible to see from the outside whether a missile carries a nuclear or a conventional warhead, so the treaty eliminated all intermediate range missiles. Most countries do not yet have the capacity to arm them with nuclear warheads, but are not prevented from doing so in the future, and may continue to produce them with conventional warheads.

33. Testimony on March 14, 1988.

34. A few days later, after the Brussels summit, the president repeated his pledge but substituted Amsterdam for Munich.

35. When, in March 1988, Secretary of Defense Frank Carlucci asked Soviet Defense Minister Dmitri Yazov whether Gorbachev's statements on "reasonable sufficiency" in military forces meant reduction in the conventional forces facing NATO, Yazov responded, "You have nothing to worry about, the threat is over." But when Carlucci pressed the point, it turned out that the answer was actually no. "We are already in a defensive position," insisted Yazov.

36. *New York Times*, March 3, 1988, p. A–3.

37. The NATO summit could agree only on an "appropriate mix of adequate and effective nuclear and conventional forces which will continue to be kept up to date." *New York Times*, March 4, 1988, p. A–6. The German translation was weaker still.

38. Ibid., December 8, 1988, p. A–16.

39. Ibid., May 30, 1989, p. A–13.

6

THE NORTH ATLANTIC
COMMUNITY

Troublesome as the military problems of NATO are, the political challenges of the North Atlantic community are even more demanding. The fact is that in the late 1980s, four decades after World War II, we have much rhetoric and considerable symbolic practice, but have not yet developed the optimal terms for the relationship.

Part of the problem may have been the peculiar conditions of the point of departure. For Americans the war in Europe and its aftermath were rather exhilarating experiences. Our homeland was never in danger, and our casualties were modest. To the people stunned by the Great Depression, the war restored self-confidence. It demonstrated the heroism and self-reliance of our young men, our immense industrial capacity, our irresistible military power, and our decency and generosity. The greatness of our people and our country, we had no doubt, was there for all to see. We knew what was right; we knew what to do.

To Western Europeans, however, the war was a very different experience. It was just dreadful.[1] Without exception they were victims of a total war that brought uninterrupted horrors to all, to combatants and civilians alike. When it was over, Germany was on its knees, but the cost to Britain, France, Belgium, and Holland was monstrous. Towns everywhere were in shambles; their inhabitants were hungry, cold, and often homeless. Their ties to their families and friends were shattered; their confidence in government was at best severely strained. The economies had collapsed. People everywhere were disoriented. Everything had a price; nothing was holy any more. In Germany, American cigarettes and chocolate bars could, and did, buy anything and almost every human being. Indeed, Western Europeans, victors and vanquished, were very much in the same boat—and a very leaky boat at that.

WASHINGTON TAKES CHARGE

The United States did a number of things to help. It gave a large loan to Britain, accepted hundreds of thousands of displaced persons, and financed the massive and comprehensive European Recovery Program (Marshall Plan). Between 1948 and 1952 the United States gave away more than $12 billion of goods (more than half of it to Britain, France, and West Germany), a fabulous sum in times when even a single million was highly respected. By 1952 Western European production had increased to 200 percent of prewar levels. Obviously the United States knew what to do and was willing to do it.

Prompt, short-run rehabilitation was not all. The United States had very special ideas for long-range solutions as well. First, economic integration. The Economic Cooperation Act of 1948 made it clear that Americans were "mindful of the advantage which the United States has enjoyed through the existence of a large-scale domestic market with no internal trade barriers and [believed] that similar advantages can accrue to the countries of Europe."[2] Second, political unification. Many in government hoped that political integration would be a natural (and necessary) consequence of economic integration. But in any case, political unity would be compelled by common sense. Surely Western Europeans had learned the lessons of war. Had it not been for intense national divisions and rivalries, all the misery could have been avoided. Look, just look, at the example of the United States. Thirteen rather insignificant sovereign states united; together they spread across a whole continent and grew into a world power. *E pluribus unum.* Europe, especially Western Europe, could surely follow the example: the United States of Europe.

The Europeans were pleased with their recovery and were willing to credit the heavy (and free) inflow of U.S. goods. They were not nearly as sanguine about the long-range solutions "Made in the USA." They went along with economic integration. The Organization for European Economic Cooperation (the counterpart of our European Recovery Program) pledged that its members would "cooperate with one another and with other like-minded countries in reducing tariffs and other barriers to trade."[3] Soon a sharp reduction of import quotas was achieved, and the European Payments Union was established in July 1950. At about the same time French Foreign Minister Robert Schuman proposed the intertwining of heavy industries through the European Coal and Steel Community. Within 24 hours President Truman expressed his support. American lawyers helped draft the treaty, and the U.S. High Commissioner in Bonn helped sell it. It was approved and became operational in 1953. Economic integration was further expanded when the European Atomic Community and especially the European Economic Community (Common Market) came into force on January 1, 1958. According to plan, all trade barriers should be removed by 1992.

These were remarkable advances in economic integration. It should be noted, however, that they were made possible not by a European zeal for transnational ideals but by the practical persistence of strictly national anxieties and ambitions.

France wanted to control German power and keep Britain off the continent. West Germany wanted the end of military occupation and was prepared to pay any price for an opportunity to reenter the Western community. And Britain desperately sought to protect its empire. It stubbornly resisted becoming involved in any "economic integration" schemes until the empire was gone and the survival of the British economy compelled it to seek admission. Even then it wanted to enjoy special privileges.[4]

When it came to a political union, however, the pièce de résistance of the American design was getting nowhere fast. The Western European Union, even a common parliament, was organized; but as the economies recovered, as the Soviet threat appeared to be checked, notwithstanding U.S. threats of "agonizing reappraisal," the momentum turned away from regional integration. Traditional solidarities reasserted themselves. Consultations and cooperations would continue, even improve in cordiality; alliances would remain desirable, but their fundamental and increasingly explicit assumption was the sovereignty of the nation-state, the right of each, independently of each other and of the United States, to determine its own national interest. General Charles de Gaulle, since 1958 once again President of France, spelled out the position:

I have already said, and I repeat, that at the present time there cannot be any other Europe than a Europe of States, apart, of course, from myths, stories, and parades.[5]

The states are, in truth, certainly very different from one another, each of which has its own spirit, its own history, its own language, its own misfortune, glories, and ambitions; but these states are the only entities that have the right to order and the authority to act.[6]

Facing so clear a challenge, the Americans would not back down; they would not abandon their design for the United States of Europe: " . . . the technology of effective power has outstripped the scale of the old states of Europe," declared the Chairman of the State Department's Policy Planning Council.[7] Shortly thereafter, in Germany, President Kennedy reiterated the point:

It is only a fully cohesive Europe that can protect us all against fragmentation of the alliance. Only such a Europe will permit full reciprocity of treatment across the ocean, in facing the Atlantic agenda. With only such a Europe can we have a full give-and-take between equals, an equal sharing of responsibilities, and an equal level of sacrifice.[8]

So it went. Behind the debate over the political organization of Western Europe, however, lurked a much more fundamental issue: the role of the United States in the Atlantic community. Times had changed. Such descriptions as patron-client or doctor-patient relationships may have been fairly realistic in the 1940s, though not much appreciated by Europeans. By the 1960s these descriptions were inappropriate and deeply resented by them.[9] All the same, the undeniable political reality of Europe was the preeminence of bipolar power. On one side was Soviet might augmented by a belt of satellites; on the other side were militarily vulnerable Western European states protected by U.S. might. For a political community of the North Atlantic to persist, the United States would have to be its leader. For the community to prosper, however, a new, more satisfactory mode of American leadership would have to be developed.

TROUBLED PARTNERSHIP

Perhaps it would have been easier if President Kennedy's wishes had been realized and a partnership between the United States of America and the United States of Europe could have been established. But apparently General de Gaulle was closer to the mark. The Europe of states more accurately reflected reality. The United States would have to learn to relate to a variety of nation-states, each jealous of its sovereignty. The United States could be first, but only first among equals.

It was an enormous challenge—at an inconvenient time. Henry Kissinger knew the problems, and as early as 1965 he publicly identified them.[10] But the United States was distracted by Vietnam. President Nixon and his adviser Henry Kissinger were busy engineering an honorable peace and building a "structure of peace" (détente). By the time they were ready to devote a year to Europe (1973), crises in the eastern Mediterranean kept interrupting, and then Watergate put an end to U.S. initiatives for nearly a decade.

The problem did not go away. The continued disparity in power did not help, but *what made it intractable was a disparity in perspectives*. One possibility favored by many Europeans was symmetric equality. The United States and Europe would assume principal responsibility for their own regions. With all their experience and local talent the Western Europeans were entitled to lead the North Atlantic community in its European business, while they would be quite willing to support U.S. regional initiatives in (Central and South) America. It would be a neat but unrealistic arrangement. The United States is not just a regional power, it is a superpower and as such has global responsibilities. It must deal with problems—some regional problems of Europe, even some regional problems of America—with a global perspective.

An alternative would be symmetric equality on the global scale: a full partnership for all, or at least the larger, Western European countries with North America in the conduct of global relations. It, too, would be neat; it, too, is impractical. Western Europeans cannot manage it. They may have diplomats and economic interests all over the globe, but they do not have the capability of force projection to back them up. Britain had great difficulty coping by itself with a rather weak and incompetently led Argentina in the Falkland Islands war. France did somewhat better in its African interventions. West Germany is constitutionally prohibited from moving troops abroad except as part of a collective NATO operation. In any case, Americans do not want this kind of partnership. They are prepared to consult their allies—sometimes, but not always—and when they do, they do not want all to participate in the shaping of a joint policy. They do not want low- or middle-level discussions where a freewheeling, idea-generating interaction by all could explore the full range of options and carefully blend diverse interests. When they "consult," they actually inform their allies of the already developed U.S. position, leaving to others the choice of adapting or confronting the president of the United States. To the Europeans this is not a very satisfactory approach.

This leaves patterns of asymmetric equality for the North Atlantic community: Western European countries to concentrate on their region and the day-to-day diplomatic "footwork" and the United States to lead in world affairs and in matters of grand strategy. The problem with such a specialization of functions is that most Europeans do not have much confidence in U.S. leadership. The world, they believe, has become enormously complicated, but they see our foreign policy as a captive of simplistic dichotomies. Ever since President Nixon, and especially under President Reagan, the United States appears to have subsumed every international issue into the Soviet–U.S. conflict (competition). No problem is worthy of American attention unless it can be related to a Soviet threat. But if such a relationship is discovered, even if the relationship is minor and peripheral, it soon becomes the dominant consideration for Americans.

Worse still, most Europeans profoundly doubt that the United States has a global strategy—indeed, many are convinced that the United States is inherently incapable of formulating and implementing any strategy at all. They see Americans as too self-centered and too impatient to persist in any larger purpose. They see a constant turnover in political leadership. Every four years, possibly even every two years, the diplomatic corps in Washington is forced to acquaint itself and learn to work with a group of newcomers from who knows where who are determined to demonstrate that they have different and better ideas than their predecessors. In any case, Europeans complain, American foreign policy is not carefully crafted according to what is reasonable and feasible in the international environment, but reflects partisan advantages of the domestic government. All too often it is shaped by the noisiest pressure group of the moment. A case in point is the U.S. position in the Middle East. Most Europeans doubt the soundness (not to mention the justice) of what appears to them to be a single-minded support of Israel. Many sympathize with the Palestinians, who, some 40 years after the independence of Israel, are reduced to despair about their political future. Frankly, Western Europeans are fearful to trust the fate of mankind (let alone their own fate) in the nuclear age to the people across the Atlantic and their leaders in their capital along the Potomac.

In fact, whether they were characterized as symmetric or asymmetric, and however often they were lauded publicly, the political arrangements did not work very well. When it came to their global responsibilities, Americans almost by habit looked for support to their allies in the North Atlantic community. They were astonished when they received little help when the rulers of Iran blatantly violated the most elementary rules of international law and held U.S. diplomats as hostages. They were disappointed when they were told that such matters were "out of area." They were very much annoyed when they found European airspace denied to them when they tried to get emergency aid to Israel in peril (1973) or when they sought to punish Libyan terrorism against Americans in Europe.[11]

More recently Americans were shocked by new evidence of a blatant double standard in Western European conduct. While their governments sanctimoniously harangued us when U.S. Navy jets shot down two aggressive Libyan planes over the Mediterranean, their private firms aided and abetted the construction of a Libyan chemical weapons plant. In turn, Western Europeans wished that the Americans would accept that (a) in their economic and political relations with their eastern neighbors they knew what they were doing and (b) in matters of regional security they preferred collective negotiations under their own management (Helsinki, 1975; Stockholm, 1986). They were irked by U.S.–Soviet bilateral talks and summits regarding their region, and they became indignant when the United States tried to prevent them from carrying out agreements they had signed for building gas pipelines between Western Europe and the Soviet Union.

Disparity in perspectives between the United States and the states of Europe is probably inevitable and, hopefully, need not be a barrier to a successful partnership based on equality. But it has been a source of tensions that require tender and carefully considered attention. We may have missed an opportunity in 1960–85 to solidify the political ties of the North Atlantic community and to develop a stable decision process.

THE PASSING OF BIPOLARITY

Western European attitudes are now changing. A new generation of men and women is moving into policymaking (and opinion-leading) positions. Born after the great European holocaust, they learned about it from history books, just as they learned about the U.S. Civil War, the Russo-Japanese War (1905), or, for that matter, that quaint movement which once claimed a Communist world revolution to be inevitable.

The new generation is self-confident; it takes opulence for granted and prides itself in Western civilization and its heritage. It is aware of the existence of external predatory forces and is still concerned about becoming the victim of aggression, but it considers the dangers to be receding. It still feels some solidarity with the United States and looks at the Soviet Union with some suspicion, but it is not prone to simple and crass dichotomies. If Western Europeans ever saw the Soviet Union as evil incarnate, they now regard it as a sinner capable of redemption. If they ever saw the United States as the epitome of good, they are now inclined to regard it as a sinner who keeps trying to do good. A difference in shades: dark gray, not black; light gray, not white—shades that in recent years have been approaching each other.

The fact is that the bipolar model has become obsolete. Time and events have torn the Iron Curtain. We can no longer usefully think of Europe as two separate spheres: the Soviet Union and its satellites, and Western Europe and its U.S. protector. We are witnessing the growing independence of Soviet satellites. No member has withdrawn from the Warsaw Pact, but as a military alliance it is practically dead. While the Soviet Union stood by idly (helplessly), one Eastern European state after another turned to the West for economic aid and ideological inspiration. Mass demonstrations unceremoniously removed Kremlin henchmen from their accustomed positions of power. Constitutions were quickly amended to strip the communist parties of their guaranteed monopolies. Democratic elections were called, then held. And that is only the beginning. On our side, France has always been quite independent. Our closest ally, Britain, is busy building special relations with the Soviet Union. The Queen is preparing for her state visit to Moscow. The British government is preparing for a joint space venture with the Soviet Union. The first Englishman in space will get there on a Soviet vehicle commanded by a Soviet officer. Most important, however, Germany is about to be reunified. Most Germans want very much to be part of the North Atlantic community (even NATO) and especially to maintain close ties with the United States, but new economic ties to Eastern Europe and the Soviet Union will present constant and easy temptations. Soon we shall see in the center of Europe a powerful Germany which cannot be taken for granted or dominated.

A new wind is blowing in Europe: a warm breeze from the East carrying songs of peace and friendship. Their words promise military security; they speak regularly of the common house of Europe. By culture and tradition, they intone, the place of France and Germany, perhaps even Britain, is in Europe. The European community, not some recent marriage of convenience with a transatlantic upstart, should be their focus of solidarity. The appeal is subtle but persistent. It presents the most formidable challenge to the integrity of the North Atlantic community. Are the British, French, Dutch, Belgians, Norwegians, Danes, Icelanders, and Germans fundamentally tied to North America, or are they essentially Europeans, with the continent from the Channel to the Urals providing the natural boundaries of their community?

To be sure, the Soviet Union has pressing problems—problems that may offer a favorable opportunity to Western Europe. Except for its military power (possibly because of it), the Communist state is not in very good shape. President Gorbachev's approach seems to be to safeguard the European (more specifically Russian) hegemony of the Soviet Union. Our NATO allies have noticed this, and it has occurred to them that to be credible at all, Gorbachev needs at least their symbolic support.

Meanwhile, Soviet economic problems continue to fester. After 70 years of Communism the Soviet people are still among the poorest in Europe. Nothing, not even a return of terror, could make them believe that they are better off than "the exploited masses of capitalism." After 60 years of state planning the economy is marked by chronic inefficiency, mismanagement, and shortages in consumer goods. It needs a firm internal reorganization and substantial foreign credit. Western Europeans are confident that this means that the Soviet Union needs their money. Gorbachev knows he cannot get it through intimidation; they expect him to try ingratiation.

So for at least the remainder of the twentieth century, change will be the dominant reality of Europe—dynamic change. We can expect all kinds of moves by Western European countries toward the Soviet Union and the United States, and all kinds of moves by Western European countries toward each other. We are on the threshold of prolonged, multiple-set adjustments with outcomes far from predictable.

A big question mark is 1992, the year that may see the full implementation of the European Common Market and the removal of all economic barriers. Although most Europeans are sanguine, success cannot be taken for granted. And in the case of success, what will be its consequences? Will the Western European economy, the second most powerful in the world, work well together with our own? Will it become a vigorous competitor, finding a close association with the more complementary Soviet economy more congenial?

Then there is another big question: Will the states of Europe revert to their traditional unbridled nationalism? France flirted with such a course under de Gaulle. Will it do so again? Even more important, will our two closest allies, West Germany and Britain, with their troubled national identities, succumb?

Indeed, the national identity of West Germany is deeply troubled. To begin with, while there may be a German nation, for almost half a century there was no such thing as Germany. There was the Federal Republic separated from the Democratic Republic by barbed wire and shoot-on-sight no man's land, and the vast eastern territories lost to Poland and to the Soviet Union. There is, of course, a flag of the same color (although the East Germans placed their special insignia in its center) and on official holidays it was displayed on public buildings, but citizens have little pride in or affection for it—nothing remotely akin to an American's attitude to the Stars and Stripes.

Indeed, national dignity relies heavily on the past; people must be able to recall with pride the glories of their ancestors and the collective achievements of their community. But the recent past is very troublesome for Germans. Thinking about it brings back memories of World War II. They cannot help but know that in 1939 Germany was guilty of aggression, and remember quite well that six years later the country was in ruins, decisively defeated. Yet they can also recall some extraordinary acts of heroism by Germans, not just by the few men of character who plotted the overthrow of Hitler, but by many average persons, by men and women, by civilian and soldiers, perhaps even by individual members of the Waffen S.S. A nation needs heroes, and Germany assuredly had a goodly share, but how can they be recognized and honored when their exemplary acts of integrity, courage, and self-sacrifice occurred during an immoral war than ended in utter defeat?

Thinking about the past also brings back memories of the Nazi period. Germans pride themselves on correct behavior. They are really a very decent, if not always lovable, people. There is no facet of human development to which they have not contributed heavily. And yet the Nazi regime in Germany was among the most barbaric in human history. Not just because many (though not all) of its members were monstrous brutes—and that they were—but also because it systematically abused and subverted all the fine human qualities with which man is endowed, and systematically catered to his primitive (animal) urges. It is a source of wonderment how civilized people could be ruled by such evil barbarians and remain loyal to them to the bitter end.

It is a question Germans wanting self-respect and a German nation seeking to resume its proper position in our civilization must face. They owe an honest answer, if not to the world, at least to themselves and to their children. Ah, but there's the rub. For, seeking an honest answer, Germans come face to face with a horrendous truth. Almost to the end most of them actually enjoyed the Nazi period. Indeed, it felt good to have a job again, to be able to buy decent food and clothing, to go on a vacation. It felt good to watch grand parades with colorful flags and fanfare—indeed, to march together in a solid phalanx. It felt good that Germany was no longer a pathetic pariah but could dominate, conquer, and rule foreign countries. It felt good not to feel ashamed of being German but to be proud of it. It felt very good.

Yes, yes, but what about the Jews? Well, of course, Jews had been living in Germany for centuries. The relationship had its ups and downs, but for most of the time it was good to tolerable. Some Jews were successful in industry, some married into the officers' corps, some were knighted by Kaiser Wilhelm II. Most Germans had Jewish friends or acquaintances and dealt with Jewish tradesmen. They were all right; they were German Jews—more accurately, Jewish Germans.

The defeat in World War I brought much misery to Germany. It brought confusion and distress. Patriotic Germans who had marched off to defend their country, women who had exchanged their gold wedding bands for rings of some gray alloy to finance the war, could not understand what had gone wrong, how virtue had not been rewarded, why they should be punished—indeed, why they should be treated as pariahs. They yearned for an explanation; soon they could use a scapegoat.

It was the time for movements. Actually there were some good causes: a few earnest men speaking of reason, moderation, and democracy, followed by a handful of individuals, always thoughtful, always cautious—worried that their involvement might hurt their loved ones. Mostly there were evil causes: demagogues appealing to the baser human instincts: envy, hatred, violence. Soon they were followed by desperate masses, who by now cared not a whit whom and how many they would hurt. Erich Maria Remarque described the sickness most perceptively:

On the platform was a powerful, stocky fellow, talking. He had . . . a voice that carried conviction without one's hearing much what it said. And what it did say was easy to understand. . . . suddenly he stood still, turned full on the audience, and in a . . . shrill voice whipped out sentence after sentence, truths that everybody knew of misery, starvation, unemployment, climbing all the time higher and higher, sweeping his hearers along with him till in a furioso he smashed out "This cannot go on! This must be changed!"

The audience roared applause, . . . And then it came—broad, persuasive, irresistible—promise after promise; it simply rained promises; a paradise was built up over the assembled heads; . . . it was a lottery where every loser was a winner, and in which every man found his private happiness, his private right and his private revenge.

I looked at the audience. They were people of every calling—clerks, little business people, civil servants, a sprinkling of workers and lots of women. . . . It was curious—different as they all were, the faces had all the same absent expression, a sleepy yearning look into the remoteness of some misty [mirage]; there was vacancy in it, and at the same time a supreme expectancy that obliterated everything—criticism, doubt, contradictions and questions, the obvious, the present, reality. He, up there, knew everything—had an answer for every question, a help for every need. It was good to trust oneself to him. It was good to have someone think for one. It was good to believe.[12]

As it happened, the end of World War I brought a massive influx of immigrants from the east, Poland and Russia, many of whom were Jewish; quite a few were Hasidic Jews. Ideal scapegoat material, they were people different in culture and style. They wore different clothes; they had beards and sideburns. On top of it all, they apparently parlayed their ethnic solidarity into an advantage in the German economy. A mass of immigrants distinguishable and quite noticeable appeared to manage quite well (live very much above their conditions in the East) when everyone else in the country was miserable because they were impoverished and because they were German. So Jews became the easy targets of frustration: immigrants from the east and, since frustration and fanaticism do not differentiate, Germans committed to their country who confessed the Jewish faith. Economic conditions were improving. The Nazis claimed credit. All along they kept spreading their venom, pointing their fingers at the Jews, the Jews, and the Jews as the source of all of Germany's troubles. Spellbound, honest, decent people watched when Stormtroopers abused their neighbors, seized their property, and brutally herded them into concentration camps. They shrugged their shoulders and thought: This does not concern me; I am not a Jew.

There is no excuse, but there are explanations; more to the point, there are lessons for us. Fascism is not a special German affliction but a human disease. A virulent form infected Germans for two decades, not because they were German but because they were human. It infected others as well; no nation is immune. That which feels good is not necessarily good; it may be evil. We have our reason to tell us the difference. But civilization is still a thin veneer. There is evil in men, and there are still evil men. Modern mass society, one that caters to emotion and promotes the subjectivity of values, may be especially vulnerable. Though fascism is utterly repugnant to Americans, we are not immune. We must never forget that the price of our democracy is eternal vigilance.

Germans haunted by their past, however, cannot offer this explanation. Only America can do so meaningfully. It made a deep impression in West Germany that when, ten years after their unconditional surrender, Chancellor Adenauer visited the White House, the Marine Corps band played their national anthem and President Dwight David Eisenhower, the Supreme Commander of "the Crusade in Europe," stood at respectful attention. President Kennedy was enormously popular, and especially after his visit to Berlin, the capital city of the Third Reich, the very place from which, two decades earlier, external aggressions and internal outrages had emanated. Dramatically he proclaimed his conclusion that most Germans were decent and some were heroic, then declared himself to be "ein Berliner." Germans also were grateful to President Reagan for his demonstration of empathy when he visited Bitburg military cemetery and honored Germans who had given their lives for their country in World War II. But Americans are an idealistic people; they have some difficulty understanding the "human" explanation. They are also an optimistic people; they have some difficulty becoming concerned about a potential fascist peril. So Germans continue to avoid addressing the Nazi past,[13] and remain ambivalent about the United States. They want very much to be aligned with the American people and their government. Any tension in relations will produce deep anxieties. At the same time Germans are pleased to credit stories about "American diseases"—gangsters, illicit sex, and widespread drug abuse—and they are not distressed to have American military action equated with aggression and American reverses with defeat.

Meanwhile, a new generation has been growing up, raised by parents unsure of themselves and of moral imperatives. They delight in an exceptionally high standard of living, in physical comfort, in electronic gadgets, in entertainment, and in vacation travel, not to mention racing down the *Autobahn*, routinely at 120 miles per hour. They also enjoy the collective rewards of belonging to social organizations and professional associations. Some think hopefully that it will be enough. The West Germans will be satisfied without national pride and will not need any of the satisfactions of nationalism. Presumably because of their tragic experiences of the past, they will focus on local loyalties and be inspired by such causes as a clean and safe environment. Such optimists cited as evidence the difference in national consciousness on the two sides of the Elbe River. National consciousness was very high in East Germany, where the standard of living was much lower. In West Germany, people seemed to be much less concerned about ethnic solidarity. They were reluctant to accept ethnic Germans (*Volksdeutsche*) from the East. Indeed, most appeared far from enthusiastic about German unification, which might jeopardize the very generous pensions and other social and economic benefits of the *Bundesrepublik*. Then came the surprising news of East Germany's opening its borders. Masses of Germans flooded to the West—some as refugees, some as visitors. Young people in blue-jeans danced on "the Wall." Miles and miles of cars crept through border points. It became a colossal media event. Excitement swept throughout the Western world. American networks sent their top reporters and anchormen to Berlin. They ran the story over and over. The past did not matter. For the first time in many decades the American people were elated by and almost universally cheered a German achievement. Suddenly once again it felt good to be a German.

Ah, but what does it, what will it, mean? For more than four decades West Germany has been a successful democracy and a faithful ally. Conceivably, Germans will be satisfied with being just Europeans, but not while the French insist that they are French, and the British that they are English. Probably, Germans will find a national identity that is confident but not arrogant, one that serves as a source of dignity, not as a driving force of aggression. But there is volatility there; it would be hazardous to ignore it.

Our closest ally too faces an identity problem. Britain has little trouble with its past. It was the first country in history to achieve a global empire, which it managed, on the whole, quite well. Britain was also the cradle of modern democracies, with its emphasis on human rights, its temper of moderation, its willingness to compromise and its approach of gradual and incremental advance in politics. And, of course, Britain has not lost a war since the Lord knows when. The British have much to be proud of.

National dignity, however, also requires satisfaction in the present and confidence in the future. And here Britain's troubles lie. For the sun has set on the British Empire, and Britannia no longer rules the waves. Indeed, it is barely a major power any more. Its position in international politics is awkward. As part of the British Commonwealth it has special ties to practically every region of the globe, but the Commonwealth has become more and more a symbolic aggregate. It is still important, but not very much so. Britain is also a very special friend of the United States, and for some time after World War II it tried to make a significant role out of that. But conditions necessitated its entry into the European Common Market, and the continental states resent any British position that would carry with it a privileged status with the United States. So just what is Britain's role? Charles, the Prince of Wales, offered a suggestion at Harvard's 350th anniversary: Britain, ideally placed between America and Europe, could provide the vital political, economic, and cultural links between the two continents. The trouble is that France, West Germany, and the continental states in general do not want an intermediary. They want direct access to Washington. Washington, in turn, thinks that it does not need an intermediary. It prefers to deal directly with all members of the North Atlantic community. So the questions remain: Just what is Britain's proper place in the world? What will it be in the twenty-first century?

These developments have necessarily caused some distress, some loss of self-confidence, some loss of pride. The British elite, a blend of aristocracy and oligopoly so successful in managing the Empire, is still present—all dressed up with no place to go. Worse still, national identity has become ambiguous. To be British always has a very specific meaning, clearly and narrowly defined in terms of culture and ethnic origin. At the height of the British Empire, noble sons of India, wallowing in British culture, doing very well indeed at Oxford or Cambridge, were treated with respect and courtesy in British society (and by the British government). But they remained "worthy oriental gentlemen." They could not become British; they could not be born British.

Conditions have changed. Masses of people from former colonial territories have come to Britain, not just to study or be entertained by British society but to settle down. They have had children born and raised in Britain whose skin is not white and whose ancestors in India, Pakistan, or Jamaica had not the remotest kinship with Normans, Saxons, or Celts. Consider the story of Astel Parkinson, a devoted Jamaican-born youth worker who spends his life walking the troubled streets of Brixton, trying to understand the young. "I took my son back to Jamaica recently as a present for his seventeenth birthday. He had never been to Jamaica before. Everything went fine for two weeks. Then during dinner our third week there, my son said to me, 'By the way, when are we going home?' "[14] Britain is the young man's home; he was born there. But is he British? Can he feel British? Can he believe that the British soil on which he was born, the British air he breathes, do in fact link him to the rich but particular traditions of his fellow citizens? No less important, will his fellow citizens consider him British, not as a more or less worthy West Indian gentleman? Will they ever? Few do so now.

There is nothing the United States can do. Our own integration of racial, ethnic, and cultural diversity has its own stresses and strains. Our economic, political, and social conditions are different. Our experience may be revealing; to offer advice, however, would be highly presumptuous, and to suggest our approach as a model would be inappropriate. But the British themselves do not seem to have any perceptible program or plan for dealing with the problem, and appear to look on the entire matter with traditional equanimity. They may, of course, be right. Britain might just muddle through, as she has done for centuries. But meanwhile, below the surface the tension is building.

There is still a sound basis for the Atlantic community. Western Europe and North America have much in common: very similar values and traditions, shared economic interests, and compatible political goals. We did not want Soviet domination of Western Europe; none of us did. We do not want a reversion to the unbridled nationalism of the past; none of us do. For four decades the Cold War put a lid on historical hostilities and rivalries. Now that the lid has been at least partially lifted, they may once again bubble forth. The French and the British see the U.S. presence as reassuring against any possible German intransigence. West Germans consider it helpful to their legitimacy, and possibly an asset in the process of reunification. There is another reason as well. Our particular form of mass culture has stirred the imagination of people throughout the world. For better or worse, the center of gravity of Western civilization has moved to the United States.

We cannot control (or even predict) the future course of events, but that does not mean that we should just sit around and wait until the Europeans themselves sort things out. We can no longer afford the reactive posture. If we value the North Atlantic community, it would be wise to try to guide the developments. It would be wise to try to develop a U.S. leadership that is acknowledged and appreciated on both sides of the Atlantic. It would be wise to abandon the comfortable notion that America knows best, and learn to listen. When we speak for the community, our positions should not be made in Washington with the tacit acquiescence of its other (major) members, but should be the result of a collective effort: genuine consultation and compromise. Since inevitably we shall be faced by surprise moves, it would be wise for our decision makers to learn to improvise—within a framework of a consensus.

As the cement of our relationship, we must keep our nuclear umbrella in good repair. We have to do more. We must take the initiative. In cultural matters, for example, 1992 is a year with significance apart from the full implementation of the European Common Market. It will be 500 years since Columbus discovered America. The opportunities for celebrating the event and our common ties are practically endless and, if properly used, could be enormously beneficial. We also should take the initiative in economic matters. However unpredictable and difficult our future relations with the Common Market may be, we should not assume that they have to be detrimental to us. It was, after all, our idea, which we pressed vigorously—often against European inertia. Why should we now assume the inevitability of tariff wars or darkly suspect that the Common Market was designed to replace America in Western Europe? Indeed, at least in the past, the most suitable and profitable trade partnerships were among highly industrialized countries. Western Europe may offer us a much larger market than the Pacific Rim and will remain quite probably more accessible to us than Japan. We could do much with a positive attitude.

Most important, however, we need to reclaim the political initiative from Gorbachev.[15] It is not wise to concede to others a monopoly of idealism and a vision for the future. Effective leadership needs to offer more than pragmatism and prudence, and more than the regular repetition of this claim. It will take special moves on the Presidential level, moves not made at a superpower summit but within the broader (Helsinki-type) European framework. It will take much more than proposals about numbers of missiles, tanks, armored vehicles, or even troops. It will require initiatives very different from media events, fabricated by special consultants to improve the image of President Bush among American television viewers. Europeans must feel that the President has their interest at heart as well. He needs to project a vision of what we can do together. The common house of the North Atlantic community has rooms connected by open doors and windows facing the global environment. It is a house which offers common challenges and common opportunities. It is a house built on common aspirations for the future and a common desire to advance civilization and human development.[16] Toward it we need to develop a common strategy—in fact, we do not have one now—that can identify the incremental steps along the way. Together we need to spell out the proper role of the Soviet Union in Europe; together we need to design our changing relations with the former Soviet satellites, and together we ought to plan the gradual and orderly process through which Germany could be unified and play a constructive and leading role on the continent. Most difficult of all, we need to recognize and learn to live with the new multi-polar reality. It is unwise to indulge in nostalgia about the simpler, bi-polar past or dream about its returning in the future with the United States of Europe. Several of the states of Europe have acquired significant power themselves. They are major players in the international arena. They have their own interests and will maintain some of their own relationships without guidance, let alone approval, from Washington. But that will not have to mean that they are unfriendly or disloyal to us. International diplomacy actually may be a lot of fun if we, the people and the media, would learn to appreciate its complexities and Congress and the executive branch could develop a competence in coping with them.

In turn, if Western Europe values the Atlantic community, it ought to recognize and learn to understand the fact that the United States as a superpower must be guided by its global perspective, which may lead to conclusions at variance with their regional interests, and they ought to recognize and learn to cope with the changing internal realities in America. Our civilization is no longer entirely Western. Increasingly, our values and our ethnic composition are becoming a much broader, global mix. Citizens with Western European ancestors are becoming a smaller and smaller minority. WASPs are becoming an endangered species. In terms of economic relations we have begun to reinforce the North American market with the U.S.-Canada Free Trade Treaty (1988). And American eyes have been turning to Asia. In our daily lives we have become accustomed to rely on imports from the Pacific Rim. Since 1978 the majority of our trade has shifted to that region. Hyundai has replaced Volkswagen. Japan, Korea, and Taiwan are now the principal ($100 billion) surplus countries. And Americans' eyes may be turning south to Latin America with its intense and ambivalent attitudes toward the United States, its population explosion, its chronic economic problems, its fascist perils, and perhaps its new democratic opportunities.

NOTES

1. For the Soviet Union it was worse in the cost of lives and physical destruction; it was also better—the glory gained by the Communist state far outshone anything the Russians had ever accomplished under the czars.

2. John Spanier, *American Foreign Policy Since World War II*, 9th ed. (New York: Holt, Rinehart and Winston, 1983), p. 38.

3. Ibid., p. 39.

4. Britain finally was admitted into the Common Market in 1973.

5. Press conference, May 15, 1962. *Major Addresses, Statements and Press Conferences of General Charles de Gaulle, May 19, 1958–January 31, 1964* (New York: French Embassy, Press and Information Division, 1964), p. 176.

6. Press conference, September 5, 1960. Ibid., pp. 92–93.

7. W. W. Rostow, "The Atlantic Community: An American View," speech to Belgo-American Association, Brussels, May 9, 1963, *Department of State Bulletin*, 48, no. 1249 (June 3, 1963), p. 856.

8. John F. Kennedy, address at Frankfurt, Germany, June 25, 1963, *ibid.*, 49, no. 1256 (July 22, 1963), p. 122.

9. "Three decades . . . [after World War II] the United States was sharing its pre-eminent economic and monetary position with Western Europe and Japan, was compelled to acknowledge the Soviet Union as its equal in nuclear capabilities, and had suffered a decline in prestige and influence because of mismanagement of foreign and domestic affairs." Wolfram F. Hanrieder, "German-American Relations in the Post-war Decades," in Frank Trommler and Joseph McVeigh, eds., *America and the Germans: An Assessment of a Three Hundred Year History* (Philadelphia: University of Pennsylvania Press, 1985), vol. 2, p. 105.

10. Henry A. Kissinger, *The Troubled Partnership, a Re-appraisal of the Atlantic Alliance* (New York: McGraw-Hill, 1965).

11. In 1973 only Turkey permitted overflight, and in 1986 only Britain approved U.S. planes taking off from and flying over British territory in their raid on Tripoli and Benghazi. Just a few months earlier, when the U.S. Navy intercepted the plane carrying the terrorists who had hijacked an Italian-flag cruise ship and murdered a U.S. citizen, Italian armed forces prevented their U.S. allies from transporting the terrorists to the United States; then, while the Justice Department was preparing extradition papers, they secretly released the mastermind of the atrocity!

12. *Three Comrades* (Boston: Little, Brown, 1936), pp. 399–400.

13. Recently German historians have engaged in a vigorous and extremely bitter debate on the issue of the Nazi period. Some have argued that it was just one of those things that tend to appear regularly in human history. Indeed, according to Ernst Nolte, "The United States was after all putting into practice in Vietnam its essentially crueler version of Auschwitz." Others have suggested that it was one man's fault. In Andreas Hillgruber's view, Hitler parted company with his fellow Nazis in the extremity of his anti-Semitism. The final solution was his alone. Some have suggested that it was the Prussians; others have built social science models from the uniqueness of German "national character," or a process of industrialization that supposedly lacked the bourgeois base. And so on. The heat produced has far exceeded the amount of light generated. The judgment of Richard Evans that "the whole debate ultimately has little to offer anyone with a serious scholarly interest in the German past" is right on target. "The New Nationalism and the Old History: Perspectives on the West German *Historikerstreit*," *Journal of Modern History*, 59 (December 1987), pp. 761–97.

14. Caracas, *The Daily Journal*, January 14, 1986, p. 13.

15. On June 10, 1989, less than two weeks after President Bush's "triumph" at NATO, poll results were published. To the question "Which statesman do you trust most?" by far the largest number of West Germans replied, Gorbachev. Two days later the Federal Republic and the Soviet Union signed cultural, economic, and political treaties to strive for disarmament, broadly intensify their bilateral cooperation, and respect people's rights of self-determination, with the overall aim of "overcoming the division of Europe."

16. At his press conference in Brussels (May 30, 1989) President Bush explained the U.S. position by highlighting the following purposes: (1) to overcome the division in Europe, (2) to place primary emphasis on basic freedoms for the people of Eastern Europe, (3) to tear down the walls that prevent the free exchange of persons, (4) to let people decide through their elected authorities what form of relations they wish to have with other countries, (5) to expand economic and trade relations with Eastern European countries, and (6) to integrate Eastern European countries into cooperative strategies in such

areas as the environment, terrorism, and drugs. *New York Times*, May 31, 1989, p. A–15. The words (though too general) were all right, but the media-oriented approach was not. Western European leaders were annoyed when the President's media handlers sought to use them as backdrops for his diplomatic spectacular and when in Paris, during the bicentennial celebration of the French Revolution, they encountered efforts to make the U.S. president the center of attention, they had had enough. As diplomatically as possible they cut short the "Economic Summit."

7

HEMISPHERIC SOLIDARITY

Much of Latin America is further from us than is Europe (or Africa, for that matter), but we have always taken our special relationship for granted. Physical contiguity may have contributed to this attitude, but the foundation of our common bond was intangible: the heritage of a shared venture.

When Columbus landed on the island of San Salvador, he took the first steps toward a historic enterprise: the New World. It offered much more than an opportunity to explore vast, previously (to Europeans) unknown territories. It offered to the people of the Old World an inspiring vision: the promise of a new beginning. The dichotomy was established by the Monroe Doctrine. In 1823 President James Monroe foreswore any U.S. interest in Europe but committed us to hemisphere solidarity. "We should consider any attempt on their [European] part to extend their system to any portion of this hemisphere as dangerous to our peace and security," he warned in his State of the Union message.[1] As far as we were concerned, the Old World and the New World were clearly divided and should remain an ocean apart.

This attitude of solidarity continued. At the end of the nineteenth century, the United States took an active role in promoting the establishment of a permanent secretariat, soon called the Pan American Union, to coordinate inter-American interests. More recently, President Franklin D. Roosevelt defined our relationship as that of a "Good Neighbor" (1933) and President Kennedy launched the Alliance for Progress (1961).

All along U.S. diplomacy was ready to offer its good offices to help settle disputes. It contributed, for example, to the resolution of the Tacna-Arica controversy between Chile and Peru. President Grover Cleveland arbitrated a boundary dispute between Brazil and Argentina; and the U.S. minister to Argentina served as the umpire for the Chilean-Argentine commission that defined the long, hotly disputed mountainous boundary line between the two countries. Indeed, at times the United States intervened to support Latin American countries under pressure from European powers. In the 1890s, for example, which were hard times for Venezuela, Britain tried to advance British Guiana's border well into Venezuelan territory. Britain could have done it except for U.S. insistence that the matter be submitted to arbitration. And in 1902 the United States prevailed upon the Europeans to suspend their naval blockade imposed to collect Venezuela's debts.

SHADOWS OF THE PAST

Even so, we should keep in mind that there were enormous differences between the people of North and South America. The colonists in Boston or Philadelphia, and to some extent those in Charleston as well, came to live in their own way, to be free of repressive religious orthodoxy, to be free of a social and economic order set firmly by tradition, or even to be free to make their own political choices. They were pioneers, bold, brave, and adventurous. They were extraordinarily optimistic people with inordinate faith in themselves and a determination to improve. Their eyes were on the future. The British government issued charters and imposed some economic restrictions (for instance, the Hat Act, the Iron Act, the Navigation Acts), but in general it let the colonists handle their own affairs.

In contrast the Spanish crown tried to exercise full power over the colonies. Laws were passed interfering with practically everything in daily life. For example, the Law of Indies specified how much meat must be provided to each Indian servant. More than that, the Spanish crown screened the migrants to the colonies. Only Catholics, and at first only Castilians need apply. Protestants, Jews, and aliens were prohibited. Thus, the settlers were essentially products of the past. They were inbued with the crusading spirit, the continuation of the spirit that sustained 700 years of struggle against the Arabs (Moors). They brought a vision of the medieval world, one that was later reinforced by Spanish isolation. Simply put, Latins who came to the New World were transplants from a kind of culture and society that by 1500 was dead in almost all of Europe.

Nor should we miss the fact that our positive attitude to Latin America was something of an on-and-off affair. The Monroe Doctrine was not yet two years old when the United States was invited to a conference at Panama arranged by Simon Bolivar. President John Quincy Adams accepted and was ready to send two delegates. When he sought Senate approval for his appointees and a congressional appropriation for their expenses, however, he found little support and less interest. Although in the end the legislators reluctantly gave their consent, no U.S. delegates ever reached Panama. One delegate, poor fellow, died en route, and the other started too late. He soon concluded that he could not reach his destination in time and gave up trying.

In 1881 the United States itself set out to organize the Inter-American Conference. Secretary of State James G. Blaine sent out the invitations, but three weeks later (for domestic partisan reasons) decided to leave office. Latin American leaders were preparing to attend. Never mind, Blaine's successor peremptorily canceled the meeting. Indeed, for much of the time the U.S. government and especially Congress treated the rest of the hemisphere with skepticism, even disdain, and the American people preferred to ignore it altogether.

And we should not forget that quite a number of times North American special interest did not have happy consequences for Latin American countries. In the middle of the nineteenth century the United States became quite interested in Mexico. It led to a war, more or less instigated by the U.S. government, that ended by our southern neighbor's being compelled to cede to us about half of her territory.[2] In 1892 our attention was focused on the other end of the hemisphere. After an incident in which unarmed U.S. sailors on shore leave were attacked, Chile was compelled to apologize publicly, show public respect for the Stars and Stripes, and pay $75,000 in reparations. We may have been right,[3] but the Chileans felt humiliated. Eating humble pie did not improve their appetite for a special relationship with the United States.

Soon our special interest shifted to Cuba. Since the Civil War, U.S. investments in the island had been substantial, even exceeding those of Spain. Meanwhile, as Caribbean commerce expanded, we were concerned about control of that sea. At an opportune moment (1898) we went to war with Spain to gain Cuba's independence. After the colonial power was forced to withdraw, the U.S. government compelled the newly independent state (through the Platt Amendment) to lease part of its territory to us for naval and coaling stations and to include in its constitution a provision granting us the right to intervene militarily. In 1902 U.S. forces that had liberated Cuba withdrew; in 1906 U.S. forces returned "to restore order." Our special interest then moved to Central America. The United States was determined to build a canal linking the Atlantic and Pacific oceans, so Colombia was forced to stand by while one of its provinces (Panama) was severed.

Indeed, throughout the twentieth century our special interest often has had the consequence of intervention. Political and economic intervention in South America has regularly been augmented by military intervention in Central America and the Caribbean: the Dominican Republic, Haiti, Cuba, Grenada, Nicaragua, Honduras, Guatemala, and Mexico. U.S. reasons included helping to collect customs duties, restoring internal order, and blocking Communism. It may have been a logical and necessary consequence of the United States' assuming global responsibilities, but Latin Americans were unsympathetic to this kind of geopolitical rationale.

What made these unhappy episodes of the past especially memorable to Latin Americans was that they perceived them as symptoms of their own general fiasco. Conditions, they could not help recalling, had been very different just two and a half centuries earlier. The British colonies in North America did not amount to much. They occupied a narrow strip of land along the Atlantic between

Canada and (Spanish) Florida. Boston and Philadelphia were fair-sized towns, but most people lived in rural settlements. Their existence, exposed to inclement weather and often to hostile Indian tribes, was precarious. The vast Spanish American empire to the south was far more powerful and incomparably richer. It had more than a dozen flourishing cities. Mexico City and Lima were the foremost centers of civilization in the New World. But all this was in the past. Since then the history of the United States had been one of continuous success. In contrast, "going to the heart of the matter . . . the history of Latin America, to the present day, is a story of failure."[4]

Anyone can see the political disparity. Independence in Latin America did not bring unity; it reinforced division. Simon Bolivar, the Liberator, after a twenty-year futile struggle to bind together Venezuela, Colombia, and Peru, confessed, "I consider that for us, [Latin] America is ungovernable."[5] In fact, all through the nineteenth century and into the twentieth, while in North America the hard-pressed thirteen British colonies joined together, integrated into their union territories across a whole continent, then built the most powerful country in the world, Latin Americans fiercely fought interminable border wars and extremely costly civil wars between conservatives and liberals, federalists and centralists, republicans and monarchists, anti-clericals and pro-clericals, all of which left them politically fragmented.

Anyone can see the economic disparity. While the United States developed the richest economy and a standard of living that is the envy of the world, Latin Americans could not manage a takeoff into self-sustained growth. They remained faithful to traditional processes lacking impetus for capital formation. As a generalization it is fair to say that Latin America contributed no technological interventions nor any innovations in the modes of production.

This does not mean that the national product remained constant. It rose, but it did so mostly as the result of foreign credits and investment, and occasionally by a fortunate coincidence in circumstances, such as windfall export earnings due to temporary price increases in rubber, oil, meat, or coffee. Thus, for example, during the latest rush of North American investment and Latin American borrowing (1970–80) the gross domestic product of Argentina increased at an average annual rate of 2.9 percent; of Brazil, 13 percent; of Mexico, at 9 percent; and of Venezuela, 5 percent. As soon as raw material prices began to decline and credit started drying up (1980–85), this figure changed radically: − 2.1 percent for Argentina, 1.8 percent for Brazil, 1.7 percent for Mexico, and − 1.2 percent for Venezuela.[6] Although new plants have been built and manufacturing has visibly increased in most Latin American countries, they generally reflect foreign entrepreneurship. They produce models (under license) developed in North America or Europe. One major exception is the Bandeirante, a 20–passenger plane designed and built by Brazilians. Such exceptions, however, are rare—all too rare for a takeoff into self-sustained growth. Latin America, which in the past was recognized to be in the First World, is now inclined to classify itself as part of the Third World.

Failure is really too harsh a verdict, but the idea is firmly embraced by Latin American leaders. With the ''colossus of the North'' so close and so very visible, this may not be surprising. Their way to deal with it, however, exacerbates the problem. One method is the assertion of superiority. North Americans, alas, suffer from a primitive culture. Stories of their gaucheries, recounted with glee, provide a constant source of amusement. Political leaders forced into exile might find Philadelphia congenial, but until recently parents looking abroad for desirable educational opportunities or suitable honeymoon trips for their children looked to Spain, France, or England. Consider this quote from Jose Enrique Rodo, writing in 1900, just about the time the United States appeared on the world scene as a major power:

North Americans have no ear for the right note, the note of good taste. In such a setting, true art can come into being only in the form of individual revolt. . . . The idea of beauty has no appeal for North Americans, any more than the idea of truth. To them any intellectual activity that has no immediate practical application appears vain and sterile, is an object of contempt. . . .

[The educational system of the United States] has resulted in a generalized half-culture and an actual retardation of genuine culture. As illiteracy disappears, so do superior culture and genius.[7]

Then there is the seeking of a haven in the world of fantasy. Octavio Paz, another prominent Latin American intellectual, concluded:

. . . we tell lies for the mere pleasure of it. . . . Lying plays a decisive role in our daily lives, our politics, our love affairs and our friendships, and since we attempt to deceive ourselves as well as others, our lies are brilliant and futile, not like the gross inventions of other peoples. . . . The Mexican tells lies because he delights in fantasy, because he is desperate, or because he wants to rise above the sordid facts of his life.[8]

Added Carlos Rangel:

In our most far-sighted beliefs, in our most serious actions, there is invariably and inevitably, a measure of distortion, some compromise with our need to see Latin America come out well in comparison with the rest of the world—and particularly in comparison with the United States.[9]

Related is the reaction of grievance. Latin Americans in different countries, of different social status, economic position, or political persuasion, all emphatically agree on this: the United States is to blame. Borrowing a page from Lenin's book, most believe, and many proclaim vociferously, that the reason the United States could develop was because it successfully exploited Latin America. By force and trickery it created a condition of dependency. Latin American governments were intimidated by intervention (and threats of intervention); Latin American markets were dominated from the north. U.S. firms decided what would be produced and consumed south of the Rio Grande. Indeed, the current "debt crisis" is an example of this pattern. U.S. banks enticed Latin American governments to borrow, borrow, borrow. Most of the money was spent on the purchase of U.S. goods and irresistibly tempted Latin appetites to buy more and more "made in the USA." In fact, for all these years Latin America has been a victim of Yankee imperialism.

This attitude of feeling aggrieved was somewhat softened when the Organization of American States (OAS) was formally established in 1947. Its charter contained the solemn declaration: "No State or group of States has a right to intervene, directly or indirectly, for any reason whatever, in the internal or external affairs of any other State." More than that, its Governing Council was composed of one representative from each member: 20 from Latin America and 1 from the United States. This is a very favorable voting ratio requiring constant attention and tender loving care by Washington.

More recently, however, the situation has changed significantly. New Caribbean countries, former British colonies, had to be admitted into the OAS (which had carefully excluded Canada)—four, five, six, ten, eleven with Surinam. Not only are they not Latin countries, but they have shown a predisposition to vote with the United States. Washington still has to be careful to avoid an adverse majority vote, but now it can, with relative ease, block a two-thirds vote necessary on important issues. The OAS has changed too much, Latin American leaders now keep lamenting; it is no longer very useful. Perhaps as a consequence they have begun to assume their own initiatives. The Contadora Group (Colombia, Mexico, Panama, and Venezuela) has taken a lead toward a political settlement in Nicaragua. President Arias of Costa Rica offered his own plan. More recently the Group of Eight (Argentina, Brazil, Colombia, Mexico, Peru, Uruguay, Venezuela, and at times Panama) has been meeting regularly to plan joint strategy on Central America, on the "debt problem," and occasionally on foreign policy issues not limited to the Western Hemisphere—all without U.S. participation.

It all adds up to this: When we consider the utility of special relations, we have to recognize that Latin American attitudes toward us are loaded with heavy emotional baggage accumulated in the past. Spontaneous responses may have favorable elements: the élan of the New World, and memories of helpful initiatives by the United States or of friendly and generous acts by individual Americans, but often these are weighted down by anxiety and suspicion, by grievances of past real or imagined harm by the United States. And perhaps more fundamentally, as one of Latin America's foremost social scientists, Dr. Mauricio Baez, put it: because "little people like to humiliate a big one. This is part of human nature." Moreover, such calculations of utility are complicated by evidence of changes in strategic realities, economic relations, and political conditions, but continued uncertainty of the extent and direction of those changes.

NEW STRATEGIC REALITIES

Nowhere are the changes in our relationship with Latin America more pronounced than in strategic realities. Until recently we saw ourselves as the protectors of the Latin American republics from European imperialism, but we ourselves felt safe enough. Now, the Monroe Doctrine notwithstanding, a European power has established a foothold in the Caribbean and could pose a threat not just to the area but to the United States as well. Thus the strategic component heightened our special interest in Latin America considerably. In fact, Central America is now potentially of vital interest to us.

It makes good sense for us to deny the Soviet Union forward bases in this hemisphere. Specifically, this means a successful response to three kinds of challenges. First, there is the contingency that the Soviet Union, in conspiracy with a Central American country, in time of peace could *deploy strategic weapons* within a few hundred miles of the United States. Our vulnerability to surprise attack would be extreme. We are almost "blind" to the south. The eyes of our early warning system, including our satellites in the sky, are trained toward the north. At enormous costs we could improve our early warning system, but the flight time of Soviet missiles, even bombers launched from Cuba for example, would still be too short even for an alert, not to mention a successful response. In 1962 President Kennedy made it clear that we would not tolerate such an eventuality. We would prevent it, by force, if necessary.

Another contingency to consider is the *construction of support facilities for strategic weapons* that, in case of war, could be deployed and used against us: extra-long runways at airfields or submarine pens, for example. We would have some difficulty preventing such a development by the use of (overt or covert) force. Domestic opposition would be fierce and prone to argue that such support facilities did not present a clear and present danger. Indeed, many would argue that there could be valid peaceful uses for such facilities and a perfectly innocent explanation. We must not be paranoid; we must not overreact. This contingency is an example of those "worst case scenarios" for which the Pentagon is so famous (and which is their duty) but that rarely ever came true.

Of course, the completion of such facilities would not serve our interest, but the potential danger would be manageable. Our intelligence is too good—the Soviet Union cannot sneak in strategic forces and present us with a fait accompli. And, thinking of the unthinkable again just for a moment, in case of World War III, no Central American country would be anxious to become a target of U.S. retaliatory force. In any case, in such an extreme national emergency, frankly, we would almost certainly deliver an immediate ultimatum to all unfriendly countries in the area: destroy all facilities with any possible use to enemy strategic forces, destroy all naval and air force equipment capable of disrupting Caribbean commerce and the Panama Canal, and do so within hours and so that we can verify it—or we shall do it for you. It is inconceivable that the Atlantic Fleet would permit itself to become tied down patrolling the Caribbean while its enormous power would be sorely needed in the main conflict, or that it would move north against Soviet bases and leave its back uncovered.

The third strategic challenge is *a Communist revolution* fomented by the Soviet Union. It poses a danger only in a Latin American country whose political regime, social order, and/or economic system has become vulnerable to Communist agitation, but then it places us in an awkward position. A successful response requires early diagnosis, while the clues are still subtle. If government analysts do not overlook them, Congress will be reluctant to follow through. And it requires carefully crafted long-range responses, mostly of a political and economic nature, in which the U.S. electorate (and Congress) is not greatly interested. By the time the problem is recognizable to everyone, by the time opposition has grown into insurgency, economic and political help is usually too late. By 1978 it was too late for Nicaragua. Whether 1983 was in time for El Salvador and Honduras remains to be seen; and it remains to be seen whether the approximately $500 million we have been pumping into them annually since then is being invested wisely. The persistence of the insurgency in El Salvador and the serious anti-U.S. riots in Honduras (1988) may or may not give us a clue. One thing is certain, though: if economic and political measures fail, our military options are not too good.

Indeed, there are at least three reasons for a heavy presumption against U.S. military intervention in Latin America. First, it usually cannot help. Even if it is successful, we are left with two choices. We may restore, and help maintain, a widely discredited system—not a happy task for the United States, and in the long run probably a futile effort in any case. Alternatively, we can try to install a new system. We are not very good at such political engineering, and in Latin America such a system, in spite of all our good intentions, would have to carry the heavy burden of the stamp "Made in the U.S.A." It could survive for some time with the help of our military force, but how it could legitimize itself is difficult to see.[10]

The second reason against our military intervention is that our armed forces are not well suited for so highly specialized a warfare as counterinsurgency. When the insurgents declare their struggle to be a "people's war," they may be engaging in propaganda, but they are also entirely accurate. Their objectives are not territorial but human gains. Their prime concern is not the military (and police) forces of the government. What they want, what they fight for, is the loyalty and support of the civilian population. And in this they have an unmatchable advantage. The insurgents speak their language, they are part of their history and tradition, they know how to talk to their fellow countrymen. Against them our troops have little chance in a psychological campaign. They are foreigners. They do not speak their language, and have little cultural sensitivity and less knowledge. They have little training in the values of political philosophy or in the skills of dialogue and persuasion.

Against insurgents, moreover, our troops are at a considerable handicap in an armed conflict. We may find an explanation for this in our secular democratic values. We believe deeply in the sanctity of human life, and especially of American lives. Projected into military affairs, this adds a constant caveat to the rules of engagement: no casualties. We must fight not with men but with weapons. Indeed, our whole defense posture, not just our nuclear deterrence, is based on destroying enemy forces not by risking the lives of our men but by maximizing our firepower. That view may be sound enough for most military tasks, but not for all.

Faced with insurgency, for example, we do not deal with large, clearly identified enemy formations, but with small, elusive, irregular cadres. Their great strength lies in their ability to blend into the general population. It is crucial to our success to pick out the insurgents accurately. But, if the past is any indication, we may easily miss them, leaving them safe to pursue their guerrilla attacks. Worse still, in our anxiety not to miss them, our forces may sweep too broadly and also hit uncommitted and friendly civilians. It could be a small mistake, but given our reliance on firepower, it is likely to be a big one.

The fact is that the only way to target insurgents accurately is through old-fashioned, personal, hand-to-hand combat with primitive weapons—a knife, a wire, perhaps a handgun—man against man, where personal strength and skill matter most. But we prefer artillery, helicopter gunships, and aerial bombardment. Even the basic rifle of an infantryman (M–16) is designed to kill not by marksmen aiming at a specific target but by anyone spraying bullets all over the field of fire. Under the circumstances the prospect of hitting insurgents is good; unintentionally killing anyone around, much better. Understandably, once innocent people are killed, their relatives and friends rarely remain uncommitted, and remain friendly more rarely still. If the past is any guide, our counterinsurgency efforts will soon degenerate into a highly unsatisfactory process. We would simultaneously inflict casualties upon the insurgents *and* recruit volunteers for them with the arithmetic turned against us: recruiting at a higher rate than imposing casualties. That is no way of getting ahead.[11]

The third reason—perhaps the most controversial one—against U.S. military intervention to defeat insurgency in Latin America is that it imposes severe, perhaps unendurable strain on Latin American democracies. They are still frail and are vulnerable to any emotional eruption by the masses. The governments are managing to keep always volatile domestic issues from taking over the streets. Could they do so with the deep resentment and public outcry that would probably follow the use of U.S. military force in any Latin republic? The risk is enormous. Is the overthrow of a Communist-dominated government in Nicaragua or the defeat of Communist insurgency in El Salvador strategically worth the destabilization of Venezuela, Colombia, or Costa Rica, the proponents of the argument keep asking. Would it not be very much better to see Communism thwarted by Latin American democracies that could offer the example of a far preferable way of life? In this the United States could really be helpful by refraining from conduct that provokes Latin pride. It could be most helpful by investing in the prosperity of Latin American democracies. It sounds idealistic; in practice it could be the road to success—a long and tortuous road.

ECONOMIC RELATIONS

Turning to economic considerations, we find that reasons for our special interest in Latin America do exist, but they are changing and are somewhat ambiguous. The facts are these. For some time the region's share in our international trade has been significant but not commanding. Recently it has been declining. It accounted for 13.6 percent of our exports in 1965, well behind Europe (32.2 percent), Canada (20.3 percent), and Asia (16.5 percent). In 1975 it rose to 14.6 percent, then dropped to 12.8 percent in 1986, always behind Europe, Canada, and Asia.[12] Concurrently Latin America's share in U.S. imports moved downward steadily: 17.8 percent in 1965, 12.2 percent in 1975, and 10.7 percent in 1986. Indeed, we are now importing some four times the value of goods from Asia.[13]

Meanwhile, the composition of our trade has changed. Traditionally we have gained because the Caribbean area offered us easy and cheap access to its agricultural products (such as tropical fruit, sugar, coffee, and rum) and industrial raw materials (such as oil and iron ore). We have gained because the rest of the continent (with the possible exception of Argentina) provided us with easy access to uncompetitive markets for our manufactured goods. Such convenient, mercantile trade patterns, however, have become obsolete.

Growing industrialization has changed the Latin American market. It has become much broader, providing new opportunities for export of U.S. capital goods (heavy machinery and farm equipment) and for the export of agricultural products. That is the good news. But, at the same time, Latin American countries have built some manufacturing capacity of their own, which has linked them to the world economy. U.S. exports now face competition, indigenous and international. In addition, Latin American governments have imposed greater control over U.S. imports. They have established government monopolies. They regulate and restrict trade. Mexico, for example, has limited its oil exports to its northern neighbor to 50 percent of its production and offers the rest to distant places throughout the world. Clearly we no longer have easy access and our imports are no longer cheap.

Add to this a new and very troubling phenomenon: narcotics. More than a dozen of our southern neighbors are involved in the chain of illicit activity that floods the United States with drugs.

Cocaine earnings in Bolivia are estimated to be three times the value of all the country's other exports. Repatriated drug profits are said to account for about 20 percent of Peru's export earnings. A similar share of Colombia's foreign exchange is earned from the drug trade, and drug income has also become a major source of dollars in Mexico. During the 1980's, when debt service obligations have been rising and the prices of Latin America's legal exports have been falling, drugs have been the only significant regional export increasing in value.[14]

That is not how most Americans see the benefits of free trade.

Apart from trade, we are involved in Latin America through private sector investment. Its range has expanded from natural resource extraction and utilities to include substantial investment in manufacturing and services. Its dimensions are still significant but have been declining, from 38 percent of our total foreign investment in 1950 to 13 percent in 1985.

United States firms now have almost twice as much invested in Canada than in all of Latin America and the Caribbean; they have as much invested in the United Kingdom and Ireland as in all of South America; and more invested in Denmark than in all of Central America.[15]

This, however, is only part of the story—the less important part. For while U.S. investment in the Latin American private sector was declining, suddenly, U.S. private credit to Latin American governments (government corporations) rose sharply. Indeed, in the mid 1970s U.S. banks were prepared to lend money for almost any project for which a Latin American government had an appetite. In 1975 Latin America and the Caribbean owed private creditors, about two-thirds of them American, $34.8 billion in long-term loans. Five years later this figure had more than tripled ($111 billion), and in 1985 it hit $222.7 billion and was still rising! If one added the long-term loans owed to "official creditors" and the short-term loans, the total exceeded $387 billion.[16] In the case of Brazil, for example, this meant that its external debt, which stood at 17 percent of gross national product in 1975, jumped to 46 percent in 1984. Panama's debt exceeded 75 percent, and Costa Rica's 140 percent, of gross domestic product.[17]

Obviously this could not go on. Hundreds of U.S. banks were involved. By 1982 the nine largest of them had considerably more than 100 percent of their stockholders' equity exposed in Latin America.[18] To be sure, default is a technical term made even more elusive by various practical applications, and in any case is a designation devoutly to be avoided. Still, whatever they would call it, very soon Latin American debtors—Costa Rica, Peru, Mexico, Brazil—found it impossible to pay on the principal and were even forced to suspend interest payments. Argentina required two "bridge" loans; Bolivia was permitted to pay off its debt at eight cents on the dollar. By 1984 foreign investment was drying up, and U.S. banks were desperately seeking formulas to avoid admitting and absorbing colossal losses. Nevertheless, in the second quarter of that year the profits of Manufacturers Hanover Trust dropped 23 percent due to "nonperforming" loans in Argentina. In the first quarter of 1985 First National Bank of Chicago registered no net profits due to its problems with Brazil. In the first quarter of 1987 Citicorp's net income dropped $264 million. Thereupon it decided upon a bold move; in the next quarter it wrote off $2.5 billion of its Latin American loans. Some other major banks followed—just once. They would go to great lengths of negotiating and restructuring the debt to avoid admitting default, but anxiety over price:earnings ratios, reduction of assets, and the prospect of having to sell shares soon halted any inclination to continue to write off debts.

Thus, the problem festers. The previously contracted debt is still out there, and payments on interest (one way or another) are more or less regularly made.

The banks pay lip service to the prospects of eventual repayment; they continue the status quo month by month, year by year, in the hope that sooner or later help will come. If the problem persists long enough, even becomes exacerbated by short-term patching, a point could be reached when the U.S. government would have no choice but to bail the banks out, just as it is doing now with the savings and loan associations. And the American taxpayer of course would have to pay for it.

POLITICAL CONDITIONS

The most intriguing change in Latin America is political. In the past, even as recently as the late 1970s, we would have had to deal with mostly authoritarian governments: dictators, presidents for life, or military juntas. Some were friendly; other, persuadable. In the 1980s, however, we seem to be witnessing the resurgence of democracy in Latin America. To be sure, Cuba is still a Communist state but Nicaragua is no longer one, and seven other countries have replaced authoritarian rule with more or less democratically elected governments. Paraguay is moving in that direction, and Chile has completed its transition to civilian rule. Meanwhile, the ailing Mexican political system, given the last rites by foreign observers just a few years ago, seems to be recovering. Thus, if the current trend continues, by the early 1990s all Latin American governments except Cuba (not to mention Haiti) will have elected chief executives and legislatures.[19] Lest we become too confident in the prospect, however, we should consider several reasons for caution.

First, we do not know the depth of the new commitment to democratic institutions and processes. As it was sometimes in the past, democracy may be their choice only by default. Indeed, the period since the late 1970s has been hard on alternatives. Military rulers have proven incompetent, unable to cope with the complexities of modern government, all too prone to brutal repression. And the socialist option has lost most of its appeal. The big Communist powers (the Soviet Union and China) had a falling out, and both are struggling to adjust their ways to modern realities. The little Communist power, Cuba, successfully defied the United States, which was admirable, but even with massive Soviet aid it cannot provide anything but an unenviable way of life. Meanwhile, with U.S. credit streaming down, "capitalism" seemed to deserve a try.

Second, we do know that Latin American political values are different from ours. For example, we habitually pride ourselves on the assertion that the basic building blocks of our system are the individual citizens enjoying equal votes. Indeed, we are regularly concerned about the excessive influence of "special interest" groups. Latin Americans, on the other hand, feel quite comfortable in a *corporate state*, where decision making is based on such groups: the Church, the landed gentry (*latafundistas*), labor unions, business organizations, professional associations, and so on. Similarly, while we believe that government should be limited in scope, that we should look to it for remedy only as a last resort, Latin Americans are accustomed to a more comprehensive, *paternalistic* arrangement. People take it for granted that the state should, and will, take care of their problems. In the past such predispositions have supported authoritarian regimes. What kind of democratic institutions, if any, can comfortably rest upon them remains to be seen.

This leads us to the third point. We do not know just how viable the nascent democratic institutions in Latin America are. They may be vulnerable to an attack from the Left. Marxist doctrine points to proletarian unrest as the principal source of political instability. Among tourists it is a common observation that while expensive homes and comfortable apartments are being built in large numbers, shantytowns (*barrios, favelas*) are springing up close by. Impressed by the contrast, the conclusion promptly follows that income disparities between the rich and the poor are widening, or to put it in the conventional, ideological form, the rich are getting richer and the poor are getting poorer. Indeed, the Kissinger Commission lists as its second principle that "the encroachments of poverty must be stopped."

Poverty undoubtedly is widespread in Latin America. Clearly, it is a serious moral problem. But the assumption of its "encroachment" is very much more tenuous. A closer look at the *barrios* and *favelas* reveals these additional observations: (1) the people living in these places came there from rural areas and enjoy a significant increment of amenities over their existence in the countryside (which is the reason they came);[20] (2) the *barrios* or *favelas* are different from our slums in that their inhabitants take care of homes, however ramshackle— indeed, have pride in them; and (3) for many the *barrios* or *favelas* represent a transitional stage from which, once they have adjusted to their way of life, they move on to better quarters. During the 1970s per capita gross domestic product gained an impressive 40.9%.[21] There are indications that some of it did "trickle down." The governments are certainly aware of and concerned about the political perils posed by poverty. They invest heavily in health care;[22] they heavily subsidize basic consumer goods and services.[23] And then there is the safety valve: emigration, legal and illegal, to Latin American neighbors and to the United States. Thus a class-conscious urban proletariat does not yet exist. It may emerge in the future if the subsidies of basic consumer goods and services, under pressure from the World Bank or some other external lending source, are seriously curtailed; and the danger of Communist insurgency may emerge if economic and physical mobility is lost, when people stuck in their *barrios* or *favelas* for two or more generations look out and see their fellow citizens enjoying extravagant luxuries.

Actually, in the short run an attack from the Right presents more of a danger to the new Latin American democracies. It is not often recognized, but middle classes in Latin America are very different from the European bourgeoisie or the North American middle classes, which provide the backbone of democratic stability. The reason is that the traditional bourgeoisie emerged slowly and gradually. People entered the middle classes through some form of objective individual achievement: the accumulation of wealth by a tradesman (industrialist), the special skill of a professional (physician, lawyer), or the intellectual distinction of a teacher (scientist). Each had to pass through a highly competitive selection process; success was rewarded by earned increments in material benefits and also, for the bourgeoisie no less important, by intangible rewards of earned status. Indeed, it was the intangible rewards that were so reassuring and made the position so secure.

In contrast, the emergence of the middle classes in Latin America was extraordinarily rapid—often a giant leap in only one generation. Moreover, Latin Americans seem to be convinced that a steady improvement in their quality of life is a collective entitlement, not something to be earned through individual merit. Competition is seen as uncivilized, pitting one human being against another. Advance in schools and on the job is almost automatic. Children of the old elite can still draw upon the reputation of their families, but those of the new middle classes find their status strictly linked to their job title or to the wealth they can affect. In their search for prestige, their appetite for consumer goods is practically insatiable; their conspicuous consumption is legendary.

It is not a very stable and reassuring condition. In times of prosperity the new middle classes seem to enjoy themselves. They pretend a lot, but deep down there remains a gnawing anxiety that they may lose it all. Any economic setback is viewed with alarm and pessimism. A serious recession would trigger a search for a scapegoat. The United States is a favorite—but a close runner-up is their own, much more accessible, democratic government.

In the current period of economic stringency the new middle classes bear the brunt of the burden. Their special tastes for imports and foreign travel (study) have been noticeably curtailed. Their middle-class economic margins have been eroded by inflation. Their quality of life has suffered,[24] and their mood is becoming tense. With the recent examples of Germany and Italy (possibly Argentina and Brazil) we cannot easily dismiss the possibility of coups fomented by economically depressed middle classes. Latin American democracies do not yet appear to be in peril, although in Argentina, Peru, and El Salvador their position has become precarious. The danger of fascism will remain until on their own, or with external help, economic growth is resumed.

Finally, there is another problem that urges caution. We do not know just how a firm foothold of democracy in Latin America would affect those nations' foreign policy. Would a shared ideology rekindle the solidarity of the New World and foster closer ties with the United States? Or would democratic governments be all the more prone to appease the popular addiction of "gringo bashing"? Would they be more than ever inclined to take international positions hostile, even harmful, to our interests? We hope that the former would be the case, but we must consider the latter as at least possible.

So let us be clear about this. Our traditional relations with Latin America are due for a fundamental overhaul. The old ties of shared Western culture and tradition may need some repair, but are still in place. We do have some pleasant memories. Clearly, most Americans have more in common with our neighbors to the south than with our new business associates across the Pacific. Add to this our short-run needs for hemisphere cooperation. We need Latin American cooperation to help contain the flow of dangerous drugs into our country, to help control the flood of illegal immigrants, and to help get at least some of our loans repaid. However, whether it is in our long-term interest to underwrite a special relationship, and on what terms, is not entirely clear. We ought to make an effort. Politically stable conditions and the prevalence of democratic governments throughout the hemisphere are worthy goals, but the governments and people of Latin America will have to make their own contributions. They have to realize that much depends on them. They may need help and understanding—who does not?—but only they can build prosperous economies and viable political structures in their own countries. And they have to realize that perpetual adversary postures do not build solidarity. The United States will have to make its contributions to a viable partnership, but Latin America must want to be friends and learn to meet us halfway.

NOTES

1. Thomas A. Bailey, *A Diplomatic History of the American People*, 3d ed. (New York: Appleton-Century-Crofts, 1946), p. 185.

2. The Mexican title to the land was based on the principles of "discovery" and "occupation" (fewer than a dozen missions in California), accepted at the time but already obsolescent. On the U.S. side apart of victory in war was the emerging principle of self-determination.

3. Two sailors were killed, 17 were injured, and the rest were beaten and imprisoned. The local police reportedly joined in the mob attack. A month passed without any visible Chilean regret, then another, and yet another before a U.S. ultimatum had its effect.

4. Carlos Rangel, *The Latin Americans, Their Love-Hate Relationship with the United States* (New York: Harcourt Brace Jovanovich, 1976), p. 6.

5. Quoted at ibid.

6. Inter-American Development Bank, *Economic and Social Progress in Latin America* (1987 Report) (Washington, D.C.: Inter-American Development Bank, n.d.), p. 426.

7. Rangel, *The Latin Americans*, p. 97.

8. Ibid., pp. 67–68.

9. Ibid., p. 67.

10. Conditions are somewhat different in the former British and French colonies of the Caribbean (such as Grenada) with a different cultural and historical background.

11. The U.S. Army has been searching somewhat casually for a "doctrine" on counterinsurgency. It has been experimenting off and on with the Green Berets and with the "Light Division." The U.S. Marine Corps seems to have even less interest. Until recently an officer could successfully move through the ranks to General without being exposed to any training in counterinsurgency. Only recently has the subject entered the curriculum (one or two classes) at the Staff and Command School (majors and lieutenant colonels).

12. By 1986 Asia had risen to the number one spot.

13. United States, Department of Commerce, Bureau of the Census, *Statistical Abstract of the United States, 1967* (Washington, D.C.: U.S. Government Printing Office, 1967), pp. 838–39; and *Abstract, 1988*, p. 770.

14. Abraham F. Lowenthal, *Partners in Conflict, the United States and Latin America* (Baltimore: Johns Hopkins University Press, 1987), p. 190.

15. Ibid., p. 54.

16. World Bank, *World Debt Tables 1987–1988*, 1st supp. (Washington, D.C.: World Bank, 1988), p. 18.

17. Celso L. Martone, *Macroeconomic Policies, Debt Accumulation, and Adjustment in Brazil, 1965–84*, World Bank Discussion Papers (Washington, D.C.: World Bank, 1986), p. 10; United States, *Report of the National Bipartisan Commission on Central America* (Washington, D.C.: National Bipartisan Commission, January 1984), p. 44.

18. Lowenthal, *Partners in Conflict*, p. 57.

19. The Kissinger Commission listed as the "first principle . . . democratic self determination." United States, *Report of the National Bipartisan Commission on Central America*, p. 13.

20. In Mexico, for example, in 1960 the urban population grew to twice the size of the rural. Inter-American Development Bank, *Economic and Social Progress in Latin America*, p. 191.

21. Ibid., p. 2.

22. Between 1960 and 1978 life expectancy in Mexico rose from 58 to 65 years; in Honduras, from 46 to 57 years; in El Salvador, from 50 to 63 years; in Guatemala, from 47 to 57 years; and in Costa Rica from 62 to 70 years. Meanwhile the infant mortality rate dropped from 78 to 60 per 1,000 live births in Mexico, from 130 to 118 in Honduras, and from 80 to 28 in Costa Rica. World Bank, *Poverty and Human Development* (New York: Oxford University Press, 1980), pp. 78–79.

23. In Mexico City, for example, the fare on public transportation until recently was one peso, about a nickel. Rampant inflation has forced an increase in the fare, but it is still the equivalent of only a few cents. One problem with the intervention (support?) of the International Monetary Fund is its relentless pressure to eliminate direct and indirect subsidies.

24. During the last five years consumption throughout Latin America declined steadily, rolling back all gains to the level of the late 1960s.

8

OUR GENERAL INTEREST: INTERNATIONAL ORDER

Not so long ago we could think of our national interest in just two categories: (1) what will protect us from attack an (2) what will gain and maintain the cooperation of countries that are strategically or economically useful to us. It was, of course, never really quite as simple as that. What happened in other parts of the world did touch our interest; that we knew little and cared less about it did not change that. But we could afford to ignore other countries as long as they did not threaten us or hamper our commerce. Countries on distant continents could suffer turmoil, fight wars, or kill each other in revolutions. It was their problem. Our particular world could go on in its splendid isolation; our peace was secure. We kept our own order.

This will no longer do. Like it or not, our national interest now includes a third general component: a stable international order. One reason is that our domestic reality will no longer permit a policy of splendid isolation. During the last decades our racial, ethnic, and cultural diversity has continued to expand. As President Reagan so vividly put it to the United Nations General Assembly in 1985: "The blood of each nation courses through the American vein, and feeds the spirit that compels us to involve ourselves in the fate of this good Earth." Americans want peace for themselves, but they also wish peace for their (distant) relatives everywhere on earth.

Another reason is that our international environment can no longer be limited in any way we choose. We have reached the age of global interdependence. Unlike our parents and grandparents, we can no longer live comfortably in our own small communities, in our towns; our horizons cannot end at the shores of the Atlantic and the Pacific. Our world, simply put, is the planet Earth. Our fortunes, even our lives, now regularly depend on conditions, events, and people in distant—for all too many of us, unknown—lands. Conflicts abound in them;

hatred and suspicion are rampant. Remote tensions are regularly forced upon us. Adversaries scheme to get us involved. Terrorists plot to intimidate us into supporting their side. Weapons are cheap and accessible; any fanatic can take them anywhere and use them on anyone. Local quarrels can get out of hand, explode into a peril to our friends and allies, even escalate into superpower confrontation. Prudence urges us that we know what is going on everywhere, that we try to prevent armed conflict, or that at the very least we quarantine violence. All these are good reasons, but what mandates our interest in international order is more than pragmatism. It is, in a word, civilization.

If we take just a little time to reflect, we can soon realize that history is not merely a catalog of past events but the record of the unfolding of human development. All living beings change. They are born, they grow, and they die. When subjected to radical changes in their environment, species try to adapt. Some manage, while others become extinct. Man is very special. He alone can take the initiative. She alone can through her intellect and will change her environment, can even change herself. Birds are still building the same kinds of nests they did thousands of years ago; bees are still confined to the same "social and economic organization": the queen, the drones, and masses of workers. Dogs may be trained, elephants may be domesticated—by man. But just look and see how man has modified nature itself, and how he has changed himself. Our homes, where we are safe from the elements and control the temperature by setting a thermostat, are a long way from caves, or even the houses of our fathers, where coal furnaces had to be banked each winter night. In our schools we can learn the intricacies of the universe and how to manage them for our benefit. We have come a long way since we believed that Earth was flat and the sun circled it daily. In our hospitals physicians are performing organ transplants and experimenting with genetic codes. We have come a long way since medicine meant reciting mysterious incantations and applying leeches. And in our societies we are learning tolerance, even the value of diversity. We have come a long way since any stranger was seen as an enemy to be suspected, feared, and, if possible, harmed—better still, killed.

If people have the unique capacity to develop, it stands to reason that they should have the opportunity to do so. No political system can be just unless it provides a favorable environment for human development. And if human development is a discernible historical process, we are part of it. We can try to retard, arrest, even reverse it, but we ought to help advance it. *Let us be very clear about this. We must understand it fully. For this is the moral foundation of our secular society.*[1]

Human development has many expressions, but politically it is recognizably marked by an expanding scale of integrated diversity—the family, the clan, the tribe; starting from the smallest scale, it has been moving toward the unity of all humanity. Thus some 200 years ago, after a long struggle, human interaction had reached the global scale. For a century and a half (European) great powers struggled with the problem of designing some minimally stable pattern that could manage so wide a range of diversity. They did have considerable successes but ultimately could not quite cope with it, and the blood of two world wars washed away their achievements. It is now America's turn. We are a superpower, possibly the foremost superpower. We may have rights, probably have advantages, and surely have obligations. Quite possibly history will judge us on how we use this opportunity.

This does not mean that Americans have the sole responsibility to assure that each and every person on earth has an opportunity to develop. Nor does it mean that the United States has a right (not to mention the capability) to impose a set of rules or a pattern of order upon other countries. But it does mean that the U.S. government should actively participate in, perhaps even lead, the efforts toward a stable international order. The task is enormous; it is hopeless in our democratized domestic environment without the support of the American people. And that will not be forthcoming without a major reorientation. Not in our values but in our attention to them. Not in our appreciation of education and knowledge but in their principal focuses.

Our people, especially the younger generation, would benefit greatly from a clear understanding of where we are: some 240 million of us amid 5 billion human beings, most of whom speak a different language, have different traditions, and pursue different interests. We are a small minority (less than 5 percent) in humanity, enormously fortunate and highly privileged. And we would benefit greatly from a clear understanding of where we came from: a slow and tortuous advance marked by continuous struggle: struggle with nature, with predatory beasts, with hostile neighbors; a struggle marked by humanity's singular blend of genius for creativity and idealism, and its propensity for savagery. Our progress was not steady, smooth, or gradual. It had its dramatic, at times almost fatal, reverses as well as "quantum advances." Moreover, our advance is not the property or privilege of any group; it belongs to all. All races and ethnic communities in practically every region of the globe have made critical contributions to our human heritage.

Such a reorientation, with its new perspectives and its new sensitivity to the uses of the past, is quite probably the most daunting challenge to our foreign policy and to our democratic institutions. It will not be easy to focus attention on events of long ago and in distant places. We are too absorbed in our daily lives. But at least we ought to try.

Actually, we need not go back to Adam and Eve. We should credit the contributions of Africa, where quite probably the human race had its origin and where it took its first precarious steps for survival and development. And we should credit the riparian states of Egypt, Israel, and Mesopotamia, which served as the cradles of some great civilizations. From the perspective of international order, however, we can pick up the story of human development when it was approaching the scale of regional empires.

CHINA

Some 3,000 years ago China was a loose aggregate of 1,800 feudal states. Three centuries later, at the beginning of the Spring and Autumn period (722–481 B.C.) the number was reduced to 124. Humanity had already come a long way on its road to civilization. Standards for proper conduct (*li*) in peace and war had already been developed. The report on the famous battle of Hung in 638 B.C. is worth repeating. The old-fashioned Duke Hsiang of Sung personally directed his forces. The enemy army had to cross a river to form its lines. Seeing this as a favorable opportunity, his general urged immediate attack. The duke refused because he had qualms about assaulting an unprepared foe. The result was a disastrous defeat of the Sung army, and the duke was wounded. Even so, he defended his original decision. It was a matter of civilization. For a "superior" (civilized) man, he insisted, there were rules of conduct that superseded expedience.[2] A century later Confucius taught: "The Superior Man is informed in what is right (*i*). The inferior man is informed in what is profitable." He elaborated: "The Superior Man . . . takes righteousness (*i*) as his 'basic stuff'; brings it forth with modesty; and renders it complete with sincerity: such is a Superior Man."[3] Can we put it much better 2,500 years later? But as a practical matter "righteousness" was not the standard; success in battle was. Kindness was an exception; brutality was common. By the end of the Spring and Autumn period, the total of Chinese states had been forcibly reduced to seven.

During the next period, that of the Contending States (403–222 B.C.), the six most civilized states saw the flowering of law and literature. In philosophy it was the brilliant time of the "hundred schools." Lao-tzu warned:

The more restrictions and prohibitions there are in the world, the poorer the people will be. The more sharp weapons the people have, the more troubled will be the country. The more cunning craftsmen there are, the more pernicious contrivances will appear. The more laws are promulgated, the more thieves and bandits there will be.[4]

Mo Tzu identified the most important calamities:

I say that the attack on the small states by the large ones, disturbances of the small houses by the large ones, oppression of the weak by the strong, misuse of the few [minority] by the many [majority], deception of the simple by the cunning, disdain toward the humble by the honored: these are the misfortunes of the world.[5]

And increasingly pressing was a yearning for political unification. "How may the world be at peace?" asked King Hui of Liang. "When there is unity, there will be peace," Mencius the philosopher replied. "But who can unify the world?" the king continued. "He who does not delight in killing men can unify it," was the answer.[6]

Mencius was sadly mistaken about the real world. The achievement of unification did not come from the six civilized states, and it was not the product of the gentle yearning for peace. In the far west of China, bordering on the barbarians, was the kingdom of Ch'in. It was for a long time the smallest and most insignificant of the seven states. Indeed, for centuries it was treated by the other states as something apart from the rest of China, with customs of the barbarians.[7] Soon, though, the social savoir faire of the Ch'in was improving, and so was the reputation of their public officials. "They are high minded," Hsun Tzu, an eminent Confucian philosopher, testified after a visit in about 264 B.C., "and there are none who do not have understanding of the common welfare. They are worthy of great prefects."[8]

In diplomatic relations with the other six Chinese states, however, the Ch'in were ruthless. Trickery and deceit were their stock in trade. And in war they were relentless and merciless.

In 318 B.C., according to historical records, the states of Han, Chao, Wei, Yen and Ch'i were defeated by Ch'in with a loss of 82,000 men; in 312, Ch'i was defeated with a loss of 80,000; in 293, Han and Wei were defeated with a loss of 240,000; and in 274, Wei suffered defeat, with a loss of 150,000. The grimmest touch of all came in 260 B.C., when no less than 400,000 soldiers of the state of Chao, who had surrendered to Ch'in on a promise of safety, were ruthlessly executed.[9]

Although these figures, enormous even in terms of our times, probably were considerably exaggerated, they do not include those killed in the last 40 years of the ascendancy of Ch'in during which, through Machiavellian intrigue and relentless warfare, it annihilated the last opposing state and its Chou rulers. In 221 B.C. the king of Ch'in became China's first emperor, Ch'in Shih-huang-ti, and China was united.

The new empire was founded on exclusionary Chinese solidarity. China was the Middle Kingdom, the center of the universe. "The world" meant China, and everyone in the world knew that there were three kinds of living beings: the Chinese, the barbarians, and the beasts. It went without saying that the gap between the Chinese and the barbarians was much wider than that between the barbarians and the beasts.

The new empire naturally required a new structure. Feudalism was abolished and replaced by an imperial bureaucracy recruited through competitive examinations. It needed more. Grand Councilor Li Ssǔ launched a program of "unification of writing." All characters were to be "made uniform according to [the standards of] Ch'in," and the others abolished. Still more was needed: "the unification of thought." The Grand Councilor submitted a memorial to the emperor (213 B.C.):

At present your Majesty possesses a unified empire, has laid down the distinctions of right and wrong, and has consolidated for himself a single [position of] eminence. Yet there are those who with their private teaching mutually abet each other, and who discredit the decrees (chih) of laws and instructions. When they hear orders promulgated they criticize them in the light of their own teachings. Within [the court] they mutually discredit them, and outside they criticize them upon the streets. To cast disrepute on their ruler they regard as a thing worthy of fame; to accept different views they regard as high [conduct]; and they lead the people to create slander. If such conditions are not prohibited, the imperial power will decline above, and partisanships will form below. It is expedient that these be prohibited.

Your servant requests that all persons possessing works of literature, the Shih, the Shuh [collections of poems and historical documents], and the discussions of the various philosophers, should destroy them with remission of all penalty. Those who have not destroyed them within thirty days after the issuing of the order, are to be branded and sent to do forced labor. . . . As for persons who wish to study, let them take the officials as their teachers.[10]

The emperor approved the recommendations. Books were burned throughout China.

The Ch'in dynasty did not last long. The emperor died suddenly in 209 B.C. A conspiracy between the Grand Councilor and Chao Kuo, the Keeper of the Chariots (the person in charge of imperial communications), suppressed the Emperor's letter naming his eldest son, a man who was "firm, resolute, warlike and courageous," as his successor. Instead, with the help of forged communications, they placed the youngest son, impressionable and dissolute, on the throne. The new emperor, Erh Shih-Huang-ti, forced the suicide of the rightful heir and then had all his other brothers executed. Within two years he also condemned his grand councilor to the five punishments.[11] As a matter of course he added the extermination of Li Ssŭ's kindred to the third degree. Within another year, however, Erh Shih-Huang-ti himself was betrayed by Chao Kuo and forced (tricked?) into suicide.

After a short civil war in 202 B.C., Liu Pang, the King of Han, gained control of the empire and resumed the policy of the Ch'in. He and his successors retained—indeed, developed—the new bureaucratic system. They claimed a "mandate from heaven" and were less blatantly violent, but force remained the mainstay of their power. They were less determined to reduce education to the utterings of officials but continued to pursue the unification of thought. In 136 B.C., Emperor Wu-ti announced that henceforth Confucianism would be the official state teaching.[12] It became the basis of the competitive examinations for the bureaucracy. The Han dynasty stayed in power until A.D. 219. Since then China has had its periodic ups and downs. It could claim to be the first regional empire and set the model for it: *hegemony* based on force plus orthodoxy. Perhaps because of its firm exclusionary (ethnocentric) orientation, however, it never transcended that level.

INDIA

At about the time of the Ch'in final push for Chinese unification, the Indian subcontinent witnessed a similar attempt with very different results. Chandragupta Maurya, after successfully defeating an invasion of his relatively small northeastern state, set out on a course of conquest in 312 B.C. His son Bindusara persisted; his grandson Asoka almost succeeded in unifying India. Asoka's last campaign led to the conquest of Kalinga and his conversion to Buddhism. According to one of his most important inscriptions:

Directly after the annexation of the Kalingas began his Sacred Majesty's zealous protection of the Law of Piety, his love for that Law, and his inculcation of the Law (dharma). Thus arose His Sacred Majesty's remorse for having conquered the Kalingas, because the conquest of a country previously unconquered involves the slaughter, death and carrying away captive of the people. That is a matter of profound sorrow and regret to His Sacred Majesty.[13]

Although Asoka was ardent in the advocacy of the Buddhist "Way," he never sought to establish it as a state religion or "official state teaching." And now military force ceased to be an instrument of public policy. Upon his death the Mauryan empire was once again fragmented, and the subcontinent soon receded into a state of historical semidarkness. If there is a lesson to be found in there somewhere, it may be that empires cannot be built on the kindness and love of a king.

GREECE

More relevant were the developments in the Mediterranean region. It was an area where commerce prospered, but commerce could be secure only through military protection. The city-state of Athens was favorably located, and when, in 594 B.C., Solon was granted dictatorial powers, its course was set, for Solon concluded that he could not rest his city's fate on agriculture. The thin soil of Attica was really not suitable for growing grain. Let the farmers plant olive and other fruit trees, or else take up a craft or trade.

By the time of Confucius in China, the city-state of Athens had prospered well in the Mediterranean. It had established numerous trade centers and colonies along the coastline of Southern Europe, Asia Minor, and North Africa. Through the Delian League, a loose alliance of some 200 city-states, it dominated most of the commerce in the area. Athens was also a phenomenal center of culture. Socrates taught there and died for its laws. Plato and other great philosophers wrote about justice, virtue, duty, and human kindness. In the streets people could be amused by the fables of Aesop; in the theaters they could watch tragedies by Sophocles and Aeschylus or the comedies of Aristophanes. And for some time they could enjoy the benefits of a democratic government. In his most famous oration Pericles declared with pride: "Our constitution . . . favours the many instead of the few; this is why it is called a democracy. If we look to the laws, they afford equal justice to all in their private differences."[14]

To advance their interests, however, the Athenians did not hesitate to use

force. For instance, in 410 B.C., Athens sent 30 ships to Melos because the
Melians "were unwilling to obey the Athenians like the rest of the islanders [in
paying tribute]." Faced with the invasion, the Melians requested a conference.
At the meeting their ambassadors sought to reason with the Athenian general.
They offered their friendship. "No," said the general, "for your hostility cannot
so much hurt us as your friendship will be an argument to our subjects of our
weakness."[15] They appealed to justice. No, again: "Since you know as well as
we do that *right, as the world goes, is only in question between equals in power,
while the strong do what they can and the weak suffer what they must.*"[16] Being
religious men, the Melians claimed divine protection. No, once again.

When you speak of the *favour of the gods, we may as fairly hope for that as yourselves;
of the gods we believe, and of men we know, that by a necessary law of their nature
they rule wherever they can.* And it is not as if we were the first to make this law, or to
act upon it when made: we found it existing before us, and shall leave it to exist for ever
after us; all we do is to make use of it knowing that you and everybody else, having the
same power as we have, would do the same as we do.[17]

The conference broke up. The Melians fought valiantly, but after additional
Athenian forces landed and some treachery within Melian ranks, they were forced
to surrender. "The Athenians put to death all the grown men . . . and sold the
women and children for slaves, and subsequently sent out five hundred colonists
and inhabited the place themselves."[18]

Significantly, Athenian conquests were not reinforced by a common belief
system. The Athenians themselves did share a measure of political orthodoxy—
Socrates died in obedience to it—and Greeks in general believed in the same
primitive religion. (Human sacrifice was still an accepted practice during the
great Greek centuries.) But their values, as those of the Chinese, were essentially
exclusionary. They assumed a radical discontinuity between Greeks and all other
human beings, the barbarians. The big difference was this: while Chinese interests
were dominated by the political, which roughly coincided with ethnic boundaries,
Athenian interests were primarily commercial, which went far beyond the limits
of their community. There were many markets throughout the Mediterranean
that were not Greek. The Chinese were quite content with their ethnocentric
isolation. They could not care less about the barbarians; the Athenians needed
them. Greek merchant communities, reinforced by military power, would for a
time dominate them. But Hellenism could offer them no common solidarity,
only mercantile ties. Athens never succeeded in increasing the scale of integrated
diversity.

Perhaps it never tried. But another state, Macedon, did. Not unlike Ch'in, it
was a state on the periphery. Its people combined a mixture of Greek and primitive
characteristics. Until the fourth century Macedon was not much more than an
insignificant arena for the petty squabbles of trivial local "aristocrats." In 359
B.C. the great King Philip changed all that. He repressed all the bickering and

made himself the master of the country. He developed its economy and built a first-class army. He moved into Greece and won a great victory at Chaeronea in 338 B.C. Although he did not annex all the city-states, they could retain only nominal control over their own affairs. Philip of Macedon was master of the Greek peninsula.

In 336 B.C. he was assassinated. His son Alexander, a lad of twenty, handsome, strong, determined, and well educated (Aristotle was his tutor), promptly took control.[19] His father had united Greece; he would unite the world. Soon Alexander led his Macedonian and Greek forces into Asia Minor and faced Persian forces that were said to have numbered "ten hundred thousand fighting men." The Macedonian captains were deeply affected and, like the commander of the Duke of Sung's army, sought to gain an edge.

Thereupon they went unto Alexander . . . and did counsel him to give battle by night, because the darkness thereof should help to keep all fear from his men, which the sight of their enemies would bring them into. But then he gave them this notable answer, 'I will not steal victory,' quoth he.[20]

Alexander did indeed win. He moved deeper into Asia, deeper still, and then, just barely 30 years of age, he entered India.

The world had never seen anything like it—neither the dimensions of his conquest nor the manner of his rule. For the first time in history an empire was built on inclusionary ideas and ideals. Alexander did not admit radical discontinuities among human beings, not between Macedonians and Greeks and not between Greeks and Persians. He was the first to stress those precious qualities that all human beings share, rather than the differences that separate the peoples of the world.

The people he conquered were puzzled by his conduct. Alexander was not just magnanimous toward his defeated foes. He treated them as equals. He encouraged his soldiers to marry Persian women; he himself married Roxana, a Persian princess. He was not just tolerant toward their religion and customs, which would have been startling in itself; he recognized them as worthy. While in Persia he often wore Persian garb; whenever he found people devoted to a divinity, he added their god to the Greek pantheon.

His own troops were utterly astonished. They wondered just what evil possessed him, which sorcerer had cast a spell over him. They were astonished, then resentful. Even though Alexander continued to set a splendid example of personal courage and strategic acumen, even though he was uncommonly generous with his own possessions, not to mention in the distribution of war booty, his officers and men began to grumble. Worse still, a few began to plot against him; some even rebelled. When they reached the Ganges River, the troops refused Alexander's order to cross it and move further into India. They would follow him only if he would lead them home. It was on his return from India that, under somewhat mysterious circumstances, Alexander died at age 33. Very soon his empire fell apart, leaving behind many plaques and stone memorials to his military conquests.

The lesson may be that political integration is essentially a gradual, incremental process. People's absorptive capacity for change imposes very real limits on the inspired leaps of their leaders. Alexander's empire was ephemeral indeed—his vision of the unity of the human race was not.

ROME

This vision was soon to be given its first practical test. While the Athenians were building their commercial empire and while, somewhat later, Alexander was roaming through Asia, a new power in the Mediterranean was approaching its rendezvous with history.

There are no reliable historical records about the origins of the Roman people or the name "Rome." Of fables and tales, however, there is no shortage. One of the most popular is Virgil's *Aeneid*, which tells of a group of Trojan warriors who, upon their defeat, sought to save their lives (and those of their families) by escaping in some boats they found (had stolen or captured). Eventually the winds brought them to the river Tiber. It was a difficult journey, and their wives, who, "being so sore seasick that possibly they could not any more endure the boisterous surges of the seas," under the leadership of a lady called Roma decided to terminate the voyage by setting all the vessels afire. Their husbands at first were "marvelously offended" but soon were appeased when they found the soil fertile and the natives friendly. It also helped that they found their own wives especially obliging. According to Plutarch (writing at the end of the first century A.D.), it was they who started the popular custom, "continuing yet to this day at Rome," of ladies pleasing their husbands by kissing them on the mouth.[21]

Rome was not built in a day; it took much longer than Alexander's 13 years. Well over a century passed before its territory reached nine square miles, another three centuries before it gained preeminence on the Italian peninsula (265 B.C.), two more centuries before it dominated the Mediterranean (44 B.C.), and another two centuries before it reached its furthest expansion (A.D. 180). Nor was Rome built by one man or even a single dynasty. In its earliest history it was ruled by kings (including some foreign kings). Then (from 509 B.C.) followed more than four centuries of the Roman Republic, several decades of turbulence, and (from 27 B.C.) more than three centuries of the Roman Empire. Throughout its thousand years many men led Rome, but in a most fundamental sense a vastly larger number of men and women from Asia, Africa, and Europe built Rome.

Unquestionably one important instrument of its expansion was the Roman army, which was largely a citizen army. Not unlike the modern Israeli Defense Forces, most of its officers responded when called up in time of danger or at the beginning of a campaign, but otherwise were engaged in their civilian professions.[22] Many of Rome's wars were fought in self-defense or in support of imperiled allies, but, of course, by no means all.

Remarkably, the Roman expansion in scale was not reinforced by a religious thrust. Their religion, similar to that of the Greeks, was polytheistic. Jupiter (Zeus), to be sure, ruled in heaven, but he did not have much to teach about universal moral principles. Other gods, deeply involved in human affairs for various and sundry subjective reasons, would regularly side with mortals not only against other mortals but also against fellow divinities. Romans, as well as the Greeks (and the Chinese and the Indians), took the existence of supernatural beings for granted. They feared their anger, sought clues about their wishes, and curried their favor. Above all, they were fascinated by stories about the goings-on—the more scandalous the better—in heaven. Their gods never asked them to launch a holy war or a crusade, and it never occurred to the Romans that they should.

Nor was Roman expansion consolidated by attempts at unifying thought. The fact is that there was not much Roman thought to unify. Intelligent men gathered in Rome at one time or another or were brought there as slaves. But the Romans themselves never founded any great schools or produced any great philosophers. Their only political theorist of any note, Cicero, was an indifferent philosopher. Unlike the Greeks (and the Chinese), Romans were not attracted by ideas of great generality, nor were they especially concerned about long-term ramifications. They were practical men who addressed problems as they arose; Romans sought pragmatic solutions, not eternal truths or transcendental principles.

In support of their expansion in scale, Romans had one formidable asset: Roman law, a remarkable innovation. Political systems of the sixth century B.C. were marked by hierarchy and privilege. Law everywhere was the formal expression of the will of the ruler. Rome at the time was a monarchy; its hierarchy had its privileges. But even then, law in Rome was already more a method of government than an instrument of rule. A subtle difference, perhaps recognizable mostly by hindsight. Still, at least by hindsight the signs were unmistakable: egalitarian features in public processes and concern for human rights as well as responsibilities. There was never any notion about the divinity of the Roman king; the people knew quite well that he was a human being. Noble birth or royal ancestry was a recommendation, not a requirement, for office. Any citizen could be selected. Moreover, there was never any question of a Mandate from Heaven. The source of his authority was the civil community. The law ruled; the king could only implement it. If he sought to deviate from it or change it, he needed the consent of the popular Assembly or the Council of Elders. There were, of course, cases when the kings of Rome (especially those who were foreigners) violated this principle and actually made laws; but when they did, although obeyed, they ceased to be perceived as kings and were viewed as tyrants.[23]

Within the community the citizens were equal before the law, which prohibited the authorities to use torture in order to obtain a confession and assured the right of bail for the accused. After the last Etruscan king was deposed (509 B.C.) and the Republic was established, these directions of Roman law were accentuated. Indeed, about 449 B.C. a special commission drew up a written statement, engraved on twelve wooden tablets, specifying the rights of citizens so that they would know what they were and could rely upon them.

Admittedly in Rome (as everywhere else) the community was based not on individual human beings but on special human beings, the citizens. It was the citizen who had rights; it was the citizen who was equal before the law. But in Rome (unlike most communities at the time) citizenship, which radically divided human beings, remained a special class privilege for only a short time and was limited by race or culture for not much longer. Even under the kings the plebeians (lower-class persons) had important citizenship rights and were members of the popular Assembly; under the Republic they became full members of the community. As Roman conquests expanded across Italy, Roman citizenship was gradually extended throughout the peninsula. That is probably the explanation for the remarkable fact that when Hannibal, at the head of Carthaginian forces, decisively defeated the Roman army at Cannae (216 B.C.) and Rome lost some 70,000 of its 80,000 soldiers—when the cause of Rome seemed irretrievably lost—the people previously conquered by Rome remained loyal. Clearly not by force alone was the territory of Rome held together. Later, as Roman conquests expanded over much larger areas, over racially and culturally more varied people, Roman citizenship was gradually extended to them as well. The Roman community continued to grow. By the time of the Empire (after 27 B.C.), from Britain to Egypt, from Mauretania to Armenia, no prouder statement could be made than the simple "Civis Romanus sum" (I am a Roman citizen).

Roman law made the Roman citizen. As the community became larger and the citizens more diverse, they in turn developed Roman law. It became a powerful *inclusionary* force. The twelve tablets remained the basis; indeed, it was not until much later, by the time the Empire had begun to decline, that new codifications were undertaken. But through legislation or through judicial interpretation the law continued to grow, adjusting to changing conditions and differing circumstances, steadily widening its scope and broadening its range of relevance.

As Roman rule extended into Asia, Africa, and Europe, however, the question arose of how to adjudicate local conflicts. If they were between two Roman citizens, the answer was simple: by Roman law. If one was a Roman citizen, the answer was still "by Roman law." But what about a dispute in which neither party was Roman? To handle such cases, which by the second century B.C. had become more numerous and diverse, Rome decided to codify the rules and customs of all its various subject peoples. It took some time, but as the effort proceeded, it produced the most astonishing discovery: the basic rules of all the various local communities of Asia, Africa, and Europe, which varied widely in race, culture, and historical experience, were almost identical. Quite evidently mankind had much in common. Cicero expressed it this way:

There is in fact a true law . . . it will not lay down one rule at Rome and another at Athens, nor will it be one rule today and another tomorrow. But there will be one law, eternal and unchangeable, building at all times upon all peoples.[24]

Cicero wrote this in 51 B.C. The Republic was already in turmoil. Rome, in terms of human development, had reached its zenith. Soon followed the time of Caesar, then of Augustus and the Empire. For 200 years the Empire administered regional order at the western end of the Eurasian continent. It was the time of the Pax Romana. Some of the times were brilliant. Rome continued to expand, reaching far into Europe, Asia, and Africa. But Rome no longer grew. It neglected the military foundation of its system, the army. Its forces and strategies were becoming obsolete. Worse still, the Empire, through extravagance and excesses, corrupted the dynamic core of Roman law. The rule of the Emperor (*Imperator Rex*) was very different from the government of the early Roman kings, more akin to his Chinese counterpart. He claimed to be a god, and he proclaimed his legitimacy by divine authority. The citizen, too, had become very different. He flaunted his wealth, of which he had much; he enjoyed pomp and circumstance, of which he had much; and he did not miss his human and civil rights, of which he had none. Nothing was holy anymore; everything had a price. By A.D. 378 Rome was quite definitely dead, ignominiously and brutally destroyed by barbarian hordes.

The night had descended on human development. The fifth and sixth centuries were bad times for mankind. There were, to be sure, a few spots of stability and a few enclaves of prosperity, but these were small units or, as was the case with Byzantium, the remnant of the Roman Empire that proved to have no capacity for any lasting expansion in scale. Europe had sunk into the night of the Dark Ages. China, after the collapse of the Han dynasty, was once again divided, much of its territory (north) under foreign occupation. Political control passed into the hands of palace eunuchs; intrigue and corruption were rampant. Eurasia was at the mercy of a variety of barbarian leaders who roamed freely across its vast plains and regularly crossed its mountains and rivers. They struck quickly, pillaging and burning. They had no concept of the human race; their attitude was exclusionary in the extreme. They fiercely protected their own kin; they tortured, raped, mutilated, and murdered all others.

It was a severe setback to human development, but it was only a temporary one. The time was approaching when two great civilizations, moved by two great religions, Christianity and Islam, would emerge, vastly expand the scale of human interaction, and bring humanity into the modern age. As a religion Christianity came first, but as an instrument of political integration Islam had precedence.

ISLAM

Arabia in the sixth century was an altogether unattractive place. The land was poor; most people were poor; and those who were not were vulgar and depraved. They buried their daughters alive to avoid having sons-in-law who might challenge them. The oldest son, upon the death of his father, inherited and used his father's wives. They took pleasure in adultery, gambling, and drinking, or—better still—in plunder, arson, rape, and murder. They worshiped stones, trees, idols, stars and spirits. They had no government; each tribe was autonomous, and they were often at war with each other. They had no law; life, honor, and property were constantly in peril.

Mecca, like the other towns of Arabia, was a commercial center. It was not on the main routes and was not large enough to be a worthwhile prize for conquerors, but it was large enough and close enough to the flow of commerce to enjoy some prosperity. It had also the special distinction of being the home of the Ka'ba, a great black stone (probably a meterorite) that had fallen from the sky and was the object of many pilgrimages. The town was controlled by the Quraysh tribe and ruled by an oligopoly of clans. Two clans, that of Hashim and its rival, the Omayads, contested for the honor of being the guardians of the Ka'ba, with the former gaining the advantage during the sixth century. This in itself was quite an achievement for the Hashimites, but nothing compared with what was about to unfold. Probably in 571 a son, Muhammad, was born into the clan. His father had died before his birth, his mother died a few years afterward, and his grandfather eight years later. From then on, Muhammad was reared by his uncle. He soon learned various trades, and at the age of 25 he married a wealthy and influential widow. He seemed to settle down to the more or less routine life of a man of local prominence.

But Muhammad was a sensitive and thoughtful young man. Periodically he withdrew to fast and meditate. He became much concerned about the state of the world, which he considered deplorable, and about the state of morality in Arabia, which he considered abominable. According to tradition, at age 40, while in the solemn solitude of a cavern on Mount Hira, he had his first revelation. The angel Gabriel appeared to him with two messages: first, that there is but one God, and His name is Allah, and second, that Muhammad was chosen as His prophet.[25] Soon other revelations followed, some in the form of messages delivered by Gabriel and some in the form of dreams; according to tradition, one night Gabriel took him on an aerial journey to Jerusalem and to heaven.

Muhammad accepted his mission and set out to declare the unity of God to all he could reach. His (first) wife was quickly converted, but most men, even his closest relatives, remained doubtful. Yet progress was made, sufficient progress to make enemies and to worry the ruling oligopoly. They did not mind his theological tenets so much; it was all the constant haranguing about morals and virtue that unsettled the community. They fought him with fair means and foul, but Muhammad persisted. They ostracized his family; even so Muhammad kept insisting to all who would listen: "There is no god but one God, and Muhammad is His Prophet." Prominent people began to listen; some, then more, converted. The rulers of Mecca plotted against him; they even hired assassins. To quote the Holy Qur'an:

> Remember how the Unbelievers
> Plotted against thee, to keep
> Thee in bonds, or slay thee

Or get thee out [of thy home].
They plot and plan
And God too plans,
But the best of planners
Is God.[26]

In A.D. 622 Muhammad successfully escaped to Yathrib, an agricultural community some 200 miles to the north, whose leaders had been converted earlier and had solemnly vowed "to defend the Prophet from his enemies and to guard him against all perils."

Until he reached Yathrib, Muhammad was essentially a preacher with a mission, a moral reformer. He taught, he persuaded. He had "companions" and some followers. Once in Yathrib, however, he became the head of a community. He deftly resolved innumerable civil disputes; he successfully managed the day-to-day routine. More important, he brought together in harmony two different groups, the people of Yathrib and the fairly sizable number of refugees from Mecca. Soon Yathrib became known as "The City of the Prophet" or Medinat al-Nabi, Medina for short.

In spite of his new and heavy burden, however, for Muhammad his religious mission remained paramount. Indefatigably, he taught the unity of God. Over and over he repeated and had others repeat: "There is no god but one God." To ensure that they would not forget, he required prayers five times a day, devotional services once a week, and fasting and the special contemplation of God for one full month each year.

Muhammad also taught the unity of morality. He had a very sharply defined idea of right and wrong. Polytheism was the bane of morality: a person could do anything he pleased, even the most dastardly acts, and still be comfortable in knowing that, if pressed, he could find some god who would grant approval. But in fact there was only one God, and He was neither confused nor a relativist. Murder, rape, theft, adultery, deception, to name just a few of the contemporary diversions, were plain evil. Morality, like truth (and Cicero's true law), was the same in Medina and Mecca, or Rome or Athens or Damascus. It would be the same a thousand years after the Prophet's death, as it was while he lived and taught in Medina. God, who through His prophets had revealed to man what was right and wrong, will judge everyone's conduct. He will severely punish those who ignore or disobey Him, but for the righteous there will be marvelous prospects on Earth and in heaven.

Most directly relevant to the consideration of human development, however, Muhammad taught the unity of man. To quote the Holy Qur'an:

O mankind! reverence
Your guardian-Lord,
Who created you
From a single Person,
Created of like nature,

His mate, and from them twain
Scattered (like seeds)
Countless men and women; . . . [27]

Indeed, as a concept our human community had come a long way. The "we" had expanded beyond the ascriptive constraints of kinship and of racial and ethnic solidarity. In Rome it had expanded beyond social class and become synonymous with citizenship. Barbarians and slaves were still ineligible, but all others, *with the approval of the state*, could be included. Islam expanded the concept further still. Barbarians and slaves were no longer ineligible. No person needed the permission of any mundane authority or public official. He *and she* were part of the "us" by their own will alone, by their faith.

An enormous conceptual advance, but in reality the acceptance of the concept a year and a half after Muhammad's escape from Mecca was still limited mostly to that microscopic speck on the globe, Medina. It was time for a new revelation. Permission was granted to use force.[28] War could be fought in defense, in retaliation, and in the holy causes of Islam. Moreover, the champions of Islam who gave their lives in such wars were assured by God Himself that they would be transported directly to heaven.

Then Muhammad, the great religious teacher, the able manager of the civil affairs of his city, proved to be a brave soldier and above all an outstanding general. His tactical skill was excellent, his strategic sense uncanny, his judgment in selecting military commanders exceptional and his luck extremely good. Within a year (A.D. 624) at Bedr he defeated a force of "Meccan infidels" three times the size of his own. During the next four years he repelled a siege of his city, fought guerrilla skirmishes against Meccan trade routes, and subdued a number of Jewish communities. The reputation of his military prowess swept across Arabia. Not quite ten years after he had to flee, Muhammad, the Prophet, returned to Mecca. When some surrounding tribes united against him, he defeated them decisively at Hunayn. He then returned to Medina, received Arab delegations from various tribes, sent missions to foreign rulers urging them to accept the true faith, and planned expeditions in practically every direction.

In A.D. 632 Muhammad died, but Islam did not die with him. Far from it. As a religion it retained its vitality and appeal; as an armed force, its power and thrust. Indeed, the combination produced a veritable explosion of Islam across the globe. Within years of the Holy Prophet's death expeditions to the north and northwest, then east, led to the conquest of Damascus and Jerusalem (A.D. 635 and 639), the occupation of the Persian capital near Baghdad (A.D. 637), the final defeat of the Persian armies (A.D. 651), and the occupation of Sind in northwestern India (A.D. 713). At the same time Muslim power swept westward, capturing Alexandria (A.D. 642), then across North Africa and into Europe. By 714 practically all of Spain and Portugal was in its control. Islam's conquests took longer than Alexander's but much less time than Rome's—and they were only the beginning.

Still while this spectacular expansion in scale was taking place, Islam struggled with two serious handicaps. One was quickly apparent. The death of the Holy Prophet brought great consternation and greater confusion to Medina. Since Muhammad did not (clearly?) designate a successor, the question arose: Who should it be? More important for the long run: Could the authority of Muhammad be passed on? The first, after some animated, at times violent, discussion was promptly settled. The second plagued the world of Islam throughout the centuries. During his stay in Medina, Muhammad acted as the governor of the city and later assumed the role of the military Commander of the Faithful, but his authority rested primarily on his claim of being the Holy Prophet, and the people's acceptance of his claim. But it was (and is) a cardinal tenet of the Muslim faith that Muhammad was the *last* of the prophets. No one could ever succeed him as Messenger of God. So where would the legitimacy of his successors come from? It did not take long for authority to move with the point of the sword.

It was a very unsatisfactory arrangement, for authority based on force invites challenges by violence, the violence of a rival's army and the violence of the assassin's dagger. Indeed, the turnover rate in caliphs was almost faster than the eye could behold: two years, one year, even less. Invariably it was violent. The overthrown caliph, if not murdered, was blinded and reduced to penury.[29] The new caliph quickly set out to eliminate all the potential rivals he could reach.

The struggle went on and on. The further Islam expanded, the further the centrifugal force moved its power centers from the holy cities of Mecca and Medina: to Damascus and Baghdad, then further still to Egypt, Spain, and India. United in faith, Muslims remained hopelessly fragmented. They never developed a unified religious hierarchy or a centralized administrative structure. That is, perhaps, why Islam never managed to convert its successes into an integrated political system.

Most important, though, in terms of human development, was its other handicap. The Muslim faith has an altogether extramundane focus. No human being, no king, not even the Holy Prophet himself deserved adulation, not even a little bit.[30] As a special precaution, pictures and paintings of persons, especially those who were dead, were forbidden. All idols of any kind had to be destroyed. Man must always concentrate his mind on God. He may be able to make decisions of some private significance. He may even plan ahead, but he must know that his fate depends entirely on the essentially unfathomable will of Allah. (I still have a strange feeling whenever, on approach to Karachi Airport, the Pakistan International Airlines pilot announces that "Inshallah" [if Allah wills it] our plane will land shortly.) He must accept it and obey it unquestioningly. Thus the Muslim faith, so intensely focused on God Almighty missed the special quality of a human being, his or her unique capacity to develop. It did not recognize that each individual is not only part of the process but also is potentially, and hence may become in fact, an instrument of human development. That may explain why Islam, having produced a quantum jump in integrated diversity, held at a plateau and could not sustain further advance.

THE HOLY ROMAN EMPIRE

While Muslim zeal and military enterprise rolled across Asia and North Africa, another historic thrust of human development was in the making in Western Europe. For some time Teutonic and Asian tribes had been roaming across its northern plains. They marauded into Central Europe, then, emboldened, challenged the Roman Empire. Their focus of orientation was the tribe; their ideals were military. They were nomadic barbarians: fierce, brutal, and highly mobile. They raided Roman territory, then confronted Roman might. In A.D. 378 at Adrianople, the Visigoths decisively defeated the Roman emperor and his army. They moved into Italy and in A.D. 410 reached Rome. The city quite probably could have resisted successfully, but some of its civilized leaders, hoping for peace, wanting to trust the solemn assurances of the barbarian chieftains, betrayed it. Rome was sacked for three days, its people subjected to all the brutalities the minds of barbarians could imagine. The only peace they found was in death—and often not even then, as dead bodies were frequently abused and mutilated. The Visigoths withdrew but were followed by the Vandals, who sacked Rome in A.D. 455, and the Ostrogoths, who in A.D. 476 ousted the last of the Roman Emperors, the figurehead Romulus Augustulus, and formally put an "end" to the Empire in the West.

Other tribes, larger and smaller, Teutonic and Asian, were marauding throughout the western regions of the continent. They sacked cities and towns, they pillaged and ravaged, they fought each other, and, after leaving a legacy of new synonyms for barbarism, they disappeared. Later, though, there were some exceptions to this spectacle of human regression. The Burgundians and the Langobards (Lombards) stopped their marauding, settled down, and later played important roles in France and Italy. Another group of Teutonic tribes, the Angles, Saxons, and Jutes, moved into Britain, eliminated Roman colonial rule, settled down with the native Britons, organized politically, and began the slow return to civilization. The most important exception in that melee of travesties, however, was the Franks.

They were first noticed by history in the twilight of the Roman empire, when they were around the lower Rhine. Like other tribes they moved around, but much more slowly and cautiously. Unlike the other tribes, they never deserted their home base. They pushed southward in their wars and raids but kept returning to their capital at Aachen. By the beginning of the sixth century they had consolidated their hold over most of the land north of the Pyrenees. Then their king Clovis (probably through his wife) was converted to Christianity. And this was not just a personal act of faith. His tribe (more or less voluntarily) followed his example, and so did (rather less voluntarily) the increasing number of people conquered by them. It marked the beginning of an alliance between the Kings of the Franks and the Popes of Rome, an alliance carefully nurtured by Clovis' successors and solemnized on Christmas Day A.D. 800 when Charles, King of the Franks, was crowned Holy Roman Emperor by Pope Leo III.

Islam and Christianity have much in common. Both religions teach the unity of God, the unity of truth, and the unity of man. There is one highly relevant difference, however. In Christianity there is no radical discontinuity between God and man. On the contrary: Adam was not only the first man created by God (and the first Prophet); Christianity accepted the Hebrew version that Adam was created in the image of God and that his spirit was breathed into him by God himself. The linkage became vital and dramatically revealed through Christ, the Son of God, in nature both man and God. So the individual human being was a value in him/herself and life on Earth in itself is a meaningful experience.

Similarly, while Muslim regimes and the Holy Roman Empire had much in common, they were different in one fundamental characteristic. The Holy Roman Empire had a strong, hierarchical structure. In fact, it had two (parallel) strong hierarchical structures. The spiritual one ran from priest, bishop, and archbishop to the Pope; and the temporal one from baron, lord, prince, and king to the Emperor. It was a partnership of two more or less equal, powerful forces. During those dark centuries that separated the fall of the Roman Empire and the birth of the Holy Roman Empire, the Papacy had grown too powerful in the West for the kind of caesaropapist takeover that plagued the Eastern church. In turn, the Emperor was too independent, and his military power base too distant, to be subverted into a theocracy. It was a reality recognized in doctrine as well. The Pope was the Vicar of Christ. In all spiritual matters his authority was supreme. The Emperor's power, however, also came directly from God, and in temporal matters *he* was supreme. It was emphasized that Christ had ordained that man should "render . . . to Caesar the things that are Caesar's: and to God the things that are God's."[31] St. Paul had explained: "There is no power but from God: and those that are, are ordained of God."[32] Thus submission to civil authority was a Christian's religious duty.

It was of historic significance that the partnership did more than legitimize the secular authority of the emperor. It also legitimized the secular concerns of his subjects. To be sure, life in this world was a time of testing, but it need not be a period of misery. Human suffering was not ordained by the will of God; indeed, much of it was due to the ignorance of man. Human intellect, which informs of the difference between right and wrong, may legitimately be used for experimenting and exploring. By learning about the human and physical environment, human beings could ward off or mitigate adversity.

Man's free will, which enables him to earn salvation in Heaven, may legitimately be used to choose (within reason) the course of comfort and happiness on earth. In good times, when technological advances and/or agricultural innovations produced a surplus, Western Europeans built great cathedrals and great universities, but no less diligently they sought to accumulate personal property.

The partnership prospered while it was outward oriented; it soon turned inward and then became troubled. On Charlemagne's death his empire began to fragment, at first into three parts (Treaty of Verdun, A.D. 843), then during the next 100 years into many more. The title of Emperor[33] was revived when Otto

I, a great Saxon king, succeeded in reunifying most of the area that is now Germany and Italy, and the Pope placed a crown on his head in A.D. 962. In theory he was the ultimate secular ruler of all Christians, if not all men, but in fact the Emperor's authority extended over only a portion of them. The kings of Poland, Lithuania, and Hungary, significant rulers at the time, were very much on their own; the King of France paid little attention to him; and the King of England, none at all. The secular realm of Christianity was never actually united, nor was the spiritual realm. The Bishop of Rome emerged as the dominant figure, but his supreme authority was regularly challenged in Eastern (Byzantine) Christendom and frequently in Western Christendom as well.

Worse still, at the apex of the system the Emperor and the Pope soon came into conflict and then sought to incite discord in each other's hierarchy. The Emperor insisted on deciding who could serve as bishops, thus undermining the Pope's authority; in turn the Pope conspired with Kings ("the King is Emperor in his own domain"), thus undermining the Emperor's authority. And regularly they attacked each other. Emperors were excommunicated; Popes were deposed and captured. Each side had its coterie of apologists who regularly turned out legal, philosophical, and theological tracts demonstrating the supremacy of the spiritual or of the temporal head of Christendom. By the sixteenth century the prospect of a united Christian empire, to say nothing of an empire on a global scale, sank beyond the horizon.

Still, withstanding all the contradictions and struggles of the Holy Roman Empire was the legitimacy of secular orientation; it not only survived but also built its momentum into a new impetus for human development. Medieval man feared the power of the Almighty; he prayed to God and sought salvation in Heaven. He also wanted to know about this world and thought he could find out. He could, he believed, learn much through his faith in the Church and its priests. He could do more. He could *learn on his own*, through his own special tool, his senses and his unique endowment: reason. Whenever he had the chance, he erected splendid cathedrals and castles, but he also built universities.

The secular momentum was building toward the art of the Renaissance, toward the exploration of distant places and the discovery of the New World. It drove Western Europe to science. St. Thomas Aquinas (1225–1274) set out to demonstrate that human reason, applied properly, will come to the same conclusions as the teachings of the Church, which are based on divine revelation. When many of his contemporaries thought he succeeded, he also demonstrated that truth can be known not only through the Word of God, as proclaimed by theologians and priests, but also can be discovered by the mind of any human being. Sir Francis Bacon (1561–1626), Lord Chancellor of England, openly stated that while the human mind may seek truth to better understand the will of God, and see the path of virtue more clearly, through a scientific approach it may also develop "a line and race of inventions that may in some degree subdue and overcome the necessities and miseries of humanity."[34]

Western Europe was on its way to René Descartes's (1596–1650) method, the method that had as its irreducible foundation man with his mind seeking to grasp, perhaps even to master, his world: *Cogito, ergo sum* (I think, therefore I am). And Western Europe was on its way to Sir Issac Newton's (1642–1727) principles, which demystified the physical laws of the universe by converting them into formulas of measurements.

And all along, the secular momentum was building toward democracy.[35] In Germany important commercial centers became Free Imperial Cities, usually governed by a coalition of guilds. The three most important cities in northern Italy—Milan, Venice, and Florence—for a while experimented with the republican form of government. But the issue was most clearly joined in England.

When James I ascended the English throne, he united the crowns of Scotland and England, a definite plus. A few years later, when the "Authorized Version of the Bible" was produced by the King's printer and copies could be bought for as little as five shillings, it was an even greater plus for His Majesty. Even so, James's reign was fraught with turbulence. The problem was that by the time the King began his leisurely journey from Holyrood to London, "the country gentlemen on whom the Tudors relied to maintain a balance against the old nobility and on whom they had devolved the whole business of local government, were beginning to feel their strength. England was secure, free to attend her own concerns, and a powerful class was now eager to take hand in their management."[36] Their instrument was Parliament, both houses: the House of Commons and the House of Lords.

The days of absolute rulers were long gone, certainly since the Magna Carta (1215), but James held the traditional view that kings were kings by divine right. In the exercise of their royal privileges they were accountable only to God in heaven and to their own consciences on Earth. He was quite adamant, an immovable object faced by what was growing to be an irresistible force. When in 1625 his son succeeded him, the force had indeed become irresistible. The new King was not quite as immovable as his father, but when he resisted, he was forcibly removed.[37] After the dozen years of the Reign of Terror and Virtue, the monarchy was restored—but it was a very different kind of monarchy. Some royal prerogatives were accepted by Parliament, but gone was any talk about divine rights. Indeed, within a generation a new king and queen succeeded to the throne, not because of the traditional order of events but because Parliament put them there. And Parliament would not put them there until William and Mary accepted the Declaration of Rights and made their commitment under oath to "govern" according to the statutes Parliament agreed on. The democratic momentum accelerated further when in 1701 Parliament once again determined royal succession and through the Act of Settlement made it perfectly clear that England had a monarch depending on a parliamentary title and a constitution based on law.

As it happened, the phenomenal scientific breakthroughs of seventeenth-century Europe and the spectacular advance toward democracy, especially in England, were accompanied by achievements in technology and industrial organization as well as by a burst of vigor that led to a quantum jump in the scale of human interaction and interdependence. In the middle of the eighteenth century, some 2,000 years after Chinese unification, Alexander's empire, and Rome's republic, two battles were fought by European powers far from home. In 1757 in Bengal, India (Plassey), British forces defeated the French. Two years later, on the other side of the globe in North America (Quebec), British forces also defeated the French. The Treaty of Paris (1763) was intercontinental in scope. After so many years mankind had finally reached the global scale. The question arose: Could we manage it successfully?

NOTES

1. Human development provides the moral foundation of a modern state. On this all ideologies agree. The difference is this: Communism and fascism look to the collective as the prime instrument of human development. The state, through specially selected persons and all others assigned by it to their proper places, would advance mankind. In direct contrast, democracies rely on the human individual as the prime instrument. Any person, any common man working by himself/herself or through a political system whose officials he or she may help select and who are accountable to him or her, we believe may move us ahead.

2. Fung Yu-lan, *A Short History of Chinese Philosophy*, edited by Derk Bodde (New York: The Free Press, 1966), p. 179.

3. Fung Yu-lan, *A History of Chinese Philosophy*, translated by Derk Bodde (Princeton: Princeton University Press, 1952), vol. 1. pp. 66, 75.

4. Ibid., p. 186.

5. Ibid., p. 91.

6. Fung, *A Short History of Chinese Philosophy*, p. 180.

7. Edouard Chavannes, "Les Mémoires historiques de Se-ma Ts'ien," in Derk Bodde, *China's First Unifier: A Study of the Ch'in Dynasty as Seen in the Life of Li Ssŭ* (Leiden: E. J. Brill, 1938), p. 3.

8. Bodde, *China's First Unifier*, pp. 19–20.

9. Chavannes, "Mémoires historiques," pp. 4–5.

10. Quoted in Bodde, *China's First Unifier*, pp. 23–24.

11. The five punishments were branding the forehead, cutting off the nose, cutting off the feet, death by flogging, and exposure of the head and corpse in the marketplace.

12. Fung, *A Short History of Chinese Philosophy*, pp. 205–6.

13. Vincent A. Smith, *The Oxford History of India* (Oxford: Clarendon Press, 1923), p. 95.

14. Thucydides, *The History of the Peloponnesian War*, translated by Richard Crawley (New York: Dutton, 1974), p. 93.

15. Ibid., p. 301.

16. Ibid., p. 302. Emphasis added.

17. Ibid., p. 303. Emphasis added.

18. Ibid., p. 306.

19. Remarkably, he was a mamma's boy, somewhat like Churchill and FDR.

20. Plutarch of Chaeronea, *The Lives of Noble Grecians and Romans*, translated from

Greek into French by James Amyot and from French into English by Thomas North (New York: Heritage Press, 1941), vol,. 2, p. 1291.

21. Ibid., vol. 1, p. 55.

22. Cincinnatus twice led Rome to victory during the middle decades of the fifth century B.C. On both occasions he was plowing his fields when he was summoned to command the Roman army.

23. Theodor Mommsen, *Römische Geschichte* (Berlin: Weidmannsche Buchhandlung, 1868), pp. 66–67.

24. Marcus Tullius Cicero, *On the Commonwealth*, translated by George Holland Sabine and Stanley Barney Smith (New York: Bobbs-Merrill, 1929), pp. 215–16.

25. *The Holy Qur'an*, text, translation, and commentary by A. Yusef Ali (Brentwood, Md.: Amana Corp., 1983), p. 1760.

26. Sura VIII:30, *The Holy Qur'an*, p. 422.

27. Sura IV:1, *The Holy Qur'an*, p. 178. He adopted the idea that all of mankind is descended from common parents from the Hebrew tradition.

28. Sura II:190, *The Holy Qur'an*, p. 75.

29. At one time no less than three blinded former caliphs were begging in the streets of Baghdad.

30. Thus, to call his followers Muhammadans is at best an act of grave ignorance.

31. Luke 20:25.

32. Romans, 13:1.

33. It was changed to Holy Roman Emperor of the German Nation.

34. Sir Francis Bacon, *The Great Instauration and New Atlantis*, edited by J. Weinberger (Arlington Heights, Ill.: AHM Publishing Corp., 1980), p. 26.

35. "It is impossible really to understand the growth of Western Constitutional thought unless we consider constantly, side by side, ecclesiology and political theory, ideas about the church and ideas about the state. . . . It is hardly possible to understand unless we consider the whole period from 1150 to 1650 as a single era of essentially continuous development." Brian Tierney, *Religion, Law and the Growth of Constitutional Thought, 1150–1650* (Cambridge: Cambridge University Press, 1982), p. 1.

36. Winston S. Churchill, *A History of the English-Speaking Peoples* (New York: Dodd, Mead, 1956), vol. 2, p. 280. The king in preparation for his execution put on an extra shirt. He thought it might be cold outside and did not want his shivering to be mistaken for fear by the masses.

37. Geoffrey Holmes, ed. *Britain After the Glorious Revolution, 1689–1714* (London: Macmillan, 1969), p. 41.

9

ORDER BY MAJOR POWERS

For a while in the early 1760s it seemed that the traditional method of regional consolidation could be applied to the largest human scale. The British Empire, its power projected to all the inhabited continents, appeared to be on its way to *hegemony*. Democracy, with its potential for universal appeal, could provide the common belief system. In less than a generation, however, it became apparent that the impact of democracy in international relations was rather ambivalent. Its basic axiom of human equality could be a force for unity, but its normative focus on the human individual could drive and legitimize political diversity and separatism. And in less than a generation it became apparent that all the military power of the British Empire was still not sufficient for hegemony.

The first clue came from North America. Settlers, mostly from Britain, established their own communities, insisted upon their (democratic) right to govern themselves, and, when it became necessary, by force of arms won their independence from Britain (1783). Then more followed. The French monarchy, the foremost continental power in Europe and competitor in global aspirations, was overthrown (1789) and the Republic was proclaimed. It soon became apparent that its commitment to popular sovereignty did not restrain the French Republic from jeopardizing British vital interests. At the earliest opportunity it occupied Belgium and opened the Scheldt estuary. The first act placed powerful French forces just across the Channel, posing a grave military threat to Britain; the second offered the port of Antwerp, with its vast continental Hinterland, as an alternative to London, presenting a bold challenge to the commercial structure of the British Empire. Nor did the common commitment to popular sovereignty mitigate Britain's response. With bulldog determination it moved to eliminate these threats at all costs—even at the cost of an alliance with the absolute (divine right) rulers of Austria, Russia, and Prussia.

It took 20 years of more or less continuous warfare to defeat the French (the Republic, then Napoleon's Empire). When, at the end of hostilities (1814–1815), the statesmen gathered in Vienna to negotiate the peace treaty, there was little room for doubt (1) that international relations had reached the global scale—the war was certainly fought on the global scale; (2) that no single power had established or could be expected to establish global hegemony–clearly the British could not do so; and (3) that no belief system, ideology, or religion could serve as a common orthodoxy—democracy was still only the theory of some intellectuals and the practice of only the important but peculiar British and the much less important and possibly more peculiar Americans. Thus the question remained: how to manage on the global scale through some new reasonably stable processes.

THE FIRST TRY: VIENNA, 1815

It was a brilliant affair. Emperors, kings, princes, all with large and splendid retinues, were present. It was a fascinating affair: a summit meeting on the grandest scale. For months the rulers of Europe met in Vienna, the capital of the Holy Roman Empire that Napoleon just recently had formally abolished, to end the war and to build a lasting peace. Indeed, they negotiated, bargained, and compromised, as Henry Kissinger's Ph.D. dissertation documented, to restore the world.

The first question was relatively simple: What to do about the loser? Emperor Napoleon would have to go, of course. He was transported first to the island of Elba, off the coast of Tuscany, and later to the more remote island of St. Helena. France, however, would not be ostracized. Its historic borders would be left largely intact.

Second question: What about new territorial boundaries? Prussia gained a small part of Poland, part of Saxony, and lands on the left bank of the Rhine. Austria also gained a part of Poland, Venice, and the Adriatic coastal area of Dalmatia. Russia gained most of Poland; the Czar would rule over it as king. Significantly, the settlement went beyond Europe. Britain, in addition to the island of Malta in the Mediterranean and the island of Helgoland in the North Sea, gained the island of Ceylon in the Indian Ocean and the Cape of Good Hope in South Africa.

All led to the third and most important question: How would peace in the world be preserved? Came the answer: in concert by the major powers of Europe. They had the right and the responsibility to determine international order. If in the future disputes should arise anywhere in the world, they would have the duty to meet in a congress (in our jargon, hold a summit) and would have the right to determine (and impose) the proper settlement.

A formula based on the concert of the most powerful countries on Earth was an enormous leap from the conventional pattern of the hegemony of a single power in the region. It could serve as a stable arrangement, however, only if it was, and remained, in tune with the prevailing international environment and only when political leaders recognized and respected certain basic rules.

Circumstances seemed favorable at Vienna. While there, the leaders of the great powers had a chance to get to know each other quite well and developed a good working relationship. They were, moreover, sophisticated, cosmopolitan statesmen who pursued national interest but also cared about international order. And they were leaders of powerful countries with an exportable surplus in resources of control. Through coercion and/or persuasion each was busily building his colonial empire; together they could implement any decision on the global scale.

Whether or not the statesmen were aware of the necessary rules of the arrangement (Concert of Europe) is a moot point. At least in the beginning they tended to follow them. With hindsight we can indentify the most important ones.[1] First, all major powers must be part of the system. Any such power excluded would naturally form a counterpole and, by constantly enticing members, would gradually tear the system apart. Second, the major powers should be roughly equal in strength. One that was much smaller or significantly declining in power would soon lose its independent position; one that was much greater or disproportionately rising in power would soon seek to dominate. Among equal and independent powers a flexible balance would emerge, providing security and stability. Third, although ideologically diverse, the major powers should share in a minimal consensus. At the very least they should agree that the concert system was worth preserving even at the cost of sacrifices of national aspirations. No major power should perceive it as oppressive and hence seek to overthrow it.

Three corollaries accompany the third requirement. First, no major power should threaten the vital interests of its partners in the concert. Each must remain confident (a) that all the conflicts among the partners would be held at the levels of lesser interests and hence be negotiable, and (b) that national aspirations remain incremental (not revolutionary) and preferably would be directed toward distant, less salient, and uncontested areas of the world. Added to this was a second corollary: the symmetry of norms. A difficult principle, but it is a normative cornerstone of the global scale of human interaction. For most of history people acted as if the moral value of behavior depended on the actors: Who did it to whom. If we did it to them, it was good, even virtuous, but if they did the very same thing to us, it was bad, even evil. By the principle of the symmetry of norms the value of an act is the same, regardless who does it. Thus, for example, the moral value of the Cuban government's conspiring to assassinate the President of the United States is no better and no worse than that of the U.S. government's conspiring to assassinate the Cuban president. Finally, the third corollary: the reliability of commitments. Once a major power has given a pledge, others must be able to depend upon it. Changing conditions might warrant renegotiations, but obligations could be revised only by mutual consent, not by arbitrary unilateral terminations, and certainly not by deception and double dealing.

Formally, the Concert of Europe lasted for about a century. To be sure, there were conflicts and some wars. But the wars were not global in scope; they were localized and not too costly in life and treasure, and the conflicts were often settled through agreements by the major powers worked out at congresses.[2]

All the same, the arrangement was precarious. The close working relationship of the British, Austrian, and Russian leaders so carefully nurtured during the wars against Napoleon and the Congress of Vienna, was soon terminated by events. An unsuccessful assassination plot against Czar Alexander I turned this already moody monarch, bent on religious causes and horrified by the prospect of revolution, into an arch-conservative zealot until his death in 1825. And in 1822 Robert Castlereagh died by his own hand. Of the Big Three only Clemens von Metternich remained. His diplomatic skills were formidable and his personality towering, but with Austrian power visibly on the decline he could accomplish no more than a (brilliant) holding operation.

Not just personalities changed. With Napoleon gone and peace restored, foreign policy returned to secondary importance. The demands of the domestic environment resumed their dominance of public interest and government priorities. The Russian monarchy rested heavily on the church, and the army was under constant pressure for causes and conquest. Austria, which dominated Germany, had become an ethnic goulash trying desperately to keep its various nationalities under control. Prussia was confused and vacillating. The army so effectively built by the Great Elector and so well employed by Frederick the Great performed pathetically against Napoleon and had become very unsure of its sovereign. The nobility and the emergent middle classes were beginning to mix, with very uncertain results. In France the Revolution was over, but the country was badly divided. The monarchists dreamed about the past and intrigued about royal succession. The bourgeoisie, now in power, feared the masses but could not quite decide whether they preferred the pomp and glitter of an empire or the participation of the republic. They knew, though, that they wanted "la gloire."

Great Britain was in the midst of the industrial revolution, with all its phenomenal economic accomplishments and distressing social strains. It was still struggling with the question of just what elements of its population should be qualified to vote in parliamentary elections. As far as foreign policy was concerned, Britain was interested in the peace of Europe, primarily to keep its back secure. Mostly it looked beyond the seas to the colonies, principally to India. In short, the glimmer of international order through the concert of (European) major powers was fading fast. Absorbed as they were in their own particular domestic concerns, their foreign policy reflected their national focus of orientation. Diplomatic activity in the chancelleries of the great powers remained brisk, but there were no more summits (congresses) for quite a while.

That was not all. Circumstances were never too favorable for an international order enforced by the (European) major powers in America. The United States would have none of it, and after 1823 (Monroe Doctrine) it declared the entire Western Hemisphere off limits to Europe. Moreover, conditions were turning unfavorable in Asia and Africa as well. The nineteenth century saw the European powers penetrate deeper and deeper into these continents. All the same, their imperial control was never very sturdy. They never had enough to govern the people in their colonies directly. The best they could manage was "indirect rule." The "natives" remained leaders; in turn the native leaders (through manipulation of succession, bribes, and coercion) were controlled by European administrators (and advisers).[3] The further colonial powers expanded their rule, the thinner they had to spread their exportable surplus of control. Worse still, the further they penetrated into Asia and Africa, the greater the prospect that colonizers from different "mother countries" would rub against each other. And so European attention to Asia and Africa, which could in theory serve as a safety valve to reduce major power rivalries within Europe, boomeranged. When serious conflicts arose in Asia and Africa—and they soon did—they were reflected back and further exacerbated (European) major power rivalries.

As mankind entered the twentieth century it was no longer the time when, in pursuit of international order, European major powers in concert could export their resources of control to various parts of the globe. On the contrary, it was the time when some of them were becoming increasingly dependent for their prosperity upon the economic resources of their colonies and for their security upon troops recruited in Asia and Africa. The flow of power was reversing itself. Major powers still asserted their special right to define international law and settle international disputes, but matters were getting out of hand. In East Africa, in the Near East, in India, resentment and resistance to the European design was on the rise. In China the Boxer Rebellion (1900) against foreign domination had to be repressed by force, a force that included participation by non-European powers: Japan and the United States. The crisis over Morocco was settled at Algeciras at a convention (congress) called by and influenced by Theodore Roosevelt, President of the United States.

The growing dissonance between the Vienna arrangement and the international environment was bad enough, but what really doomed the concert system was that as they passed the midpoint of the nineteenth century, the major powers no longer followed the rules. The struggle in the heartland of Europe reverted to a free-for-all.

Prussia was on the move. It's "Iron Chancellor," Otto von Bismarck, was determined to unite all the fragmented German principalities and lead the Second Reich. It required some skillful diplomacy, some deception, and several wars. Denmark was defeated (1864), then Austria (1866), and finally France (1870–71). When peace was restored, summit meetings were resumed, but the system had fundamentally changed. Goals were no longer limited and incremental, and they justified any means. For Bismarck saw the war with France not just as a final step in German unification but also as the first step in the struggle for hegemony on the European continent. After French armies were defeated in the field but the population still resisted, the Iron Chancellor insisted on the bombardment of Paris. As he recalled later:

I was tormented during sleepless nights by the apprehension that our political interests, after such great successes, might be severely injured through the hesitation and delay . . . [due] to personal and predominantly female influences with no historical justification, influences which owed their efficacy, not to political considerations but to feelings which the terms humanity and civilization, imported to us from England, still rouse in German natives.[4]

Bismarck prevailed, and Paris was bombarded by heavy artillery. The French surrendered and were forced to sign a harsh peace treaty. They were deprived of territory (Alsace-Lorraine) and had to pay a $1 billion indemnity and endure humiliation. Prussian troops paraded through Paris; the country would remain occupied until the indemnity was paid in full. That was not all. France was to be diplomatically isolated. The French hated it, and especially they hated the Germans. France was thirsting for revenge.

At first France could do little, but not for long. Bismarck's system was not five years old when (1875) Czar Alexander II indicated sympathy and support for France, and so did Queen Victoria.[5] For the time being French diplomacy remained low key, but France left no doubt that it had economic power that it would use for political purposes. Patriotism was sweeping the country. Social cleavages between the nobility and the bourgeoisie notwithstanding, all Frenchmen wanted the imposed war indemnity to be paid and the Germans out. They accomplished this in an astonishingly short time. The first government loan for this purpose (1871) was hardly announced when it was doubly oversubscribed. A similar loan the next year was quickly oversubscribed twelvefold![6] In a country where parsimony was legendary, money poured into the banks.[7] Then, under the guidance of the government, private investment was directed abroad.[8] Much of it went to Russia. The first of these loans, for 500 million francs, was listed on the Paris Bourse in December 1888, and proved a large success. The next year two more loans to Russia, one for 700 million francs and another for 1.2 billion francs, were equally successful.[9] Financially they were very risky, but politically the profits were enormous.

Bismarck saw the danger, and he tried to discourage and discredit French economic penetration of Russia. He attempted to exhibit goodwill toward France: French diplomats were treated with special courtesy and favor; French imperial designs in the Mediterranean and Africa were regularly and roundly encouraged. But Bismarck could not erase bitter memories and could not return Alsace-Lorraine. So the spirit of revanche and the urge to break up the existing European "order" remained the dominant mood. A nation suffering dismemberment, wrote the French ambassador in Berlin, "ought to never pardon anything, never forget anything."[10] Besides, the internally frail French Republic could always benefit from the solidarity produced by nationalism, especially an angry, aggrieved nationalism.

All along, Bismarck was very careful to keep his dominant coalition in good repair. With Austria, Hungary, and Russia there were formal treaties; with their foreign ministers, regular conferences; and with their rulers, regular summit meetings. And he was especially careful not to offend Great Britain. All of this was something of a magic act (ein *Kunststück*), as Austrian and Russian interests clashed in the Balkans and British and Russian interests clashed in much of Asia. But Bismarck, the master juggler, managed it; just barely he kept all four balls in the air.

In 1888, Kaiser Wilhelm II ascended the German throne. He yearned to conduct his own foreign policy, and soon balls were rolling all over the floor. No more consideration, no more encouragement for imperial expansions by France. Indeed, Germany by ultimatum forced the resignation of her foreign minister (Théophile Delcassé) and challenged her in North Africa. No more strenuous efforts to maintain close relations with Russia; the treaty with her was unceremoniously allowed to lapse. And gone was any deference to Britain; Germany challenged her by building a high seas fleet to rival the Royal Navy and by building a Berlin–Baghdad railroad to bring the German presence to the Middle East. While Britain was engaged in a struggle with the Boers in South Africa, the Kaiser sent a gratuitous personal telegram congratulating the Boer leader on a British defeat. When British Colonial Secretary Joseph Chamberlain offered an alliance with Germany, Wilhelm II ordered a dilatory response, told the czar that he was importuned by the British, then put it to him straight: "Now I ask you, as my old and trusted friend, to tell me what you can offer me, and what you will do for me if I refuse the British offers."[11]

All of this tore the dominant (Bismarck) coalition apart and replaced it with a Europe of contending and increasingly hostile camps. France got through to Russia and signed an alliance in 1894. Ten years later it got through to Great Britain.[12] A British-Russian understanding in 1908 completed the triangle. France was no longer isolated but at the apex of a powerful coalition (Triple Entente). Germany was no longer secure. The possibility of "encirclement" was no longer just a bad dream but a very disturbing reality. Germany still had Austria-Hungary (plagued by nationality problems) and Italy (a very uncertain friend), but its position had become precarious. It was on the defensive and all the more arrogant. Two alliance systems were set on a collision course.

The crash came when, after a decade of crises among the major powers of Europe, the heir to the Austro-Hungarian thrones, Archduke Francis Ferdinand, and his wife were assassinated on June 28, 1914. In just over a month, in the words of the British foreign secretary, "the lights went out all over Europe" and mankind was plunged into its first world war.

THE SECOND TRY: VERSAILLES, 1919

Four years later, when all the horrible killing finally stopped, the war had clearly demonstrated the global scale of human interdependence. It left international order, however, in a shambles. Any prospect of mankind's being managed by a concert of European major powers was scuttled by chauvinism and washed away by streams of European blood.

As the victors gathered at the Palace of Versailles outside of Paris to settle the terms of peace, they paid little attention to the lessons of the century-long record of the Concert of Europe. They had no doubt that international order was the prerogative of the major powers even though conditions had become very unfavorable.

One problem was the attitude of the delegates. In a mood of vengeance each pursued his own national purpose with single-minded determination; each sought absolute security. Some were satisfied with massive territorial gains; others insisted on reducing their enemies to abject impotence. Perhaps it was not surprising; it was tragic all the same. Henry Kissinger's observations on the Congress of Vienna are directly to the point on Versailles.

An impotent enemy is a fact; a reconciled enemy is a conjecture. A territorial accretion represents the surety of possession; to integrate an opponent into the community of nations through self-restraint is an expression of faith. It is no accident that the advocates of "absolute security" always have popular support on their side. Theirs is the sanction of the present, but statemanship must deal with the future.[13]

Only David Lloyd George, the British Prime Minister, was (vaguely) interested in a scheme of international order, and only Woodrow Wilson, President of the United States, was devoted to it.[14] His preoccupation with a long-term arrangement to safeguard peace did produce a novel idea: the League of Nations. The task of settling international disputes was not left to future ad hoc arrangements, but assigned to a permanent organization with regular annual meetings. Problems disturbing peaceful relations need not fester until they reached sufficiently dire crisis proportions for a congress to be convened; they could be addressed before they became intractable.

The other contribution of President Wilson was his insistence on ideological orthodoxy. Bubbling forth from a profound American belief that aggression was the particular habit of authoritarian governments was his insistance that only democratic countries could be peace-loving and that the only legitimate basis for international boundaries was the self-determination of peoples. That suited France and Italy, intent upon the dismembering the Austro-Hungarian Empire.

Possibly the Treaty of Versailles never had a chance. Times were changing fast. Gone (or at least going) were the days when the human race could be structured into imperial systems. The colonial powers, which dominated at Versailles and whose dominance the League of Nations enshrined, could not export sufficient coercive capacity to assure their control even in the nineteenth century. And in the twentieth century, when traditional "native" leaders were losing their legitimacy among the "native" masses, the colonial powers needed much more.

Nor could they rely heavily on the capacity to persuade. In the nineteenth century "native" leaders were attracted to the imperial system—indeed, they wanted very much to be part of it. As a young man Mahatma Gandhi "dreamt continually of going to England," and when he had a chance, he took it even though he knew it was against the rule of his caste. The order went out promptly: "This boy shall be treated as an outcaste from today. Whoever helps him or goes to see him off at the dock shall be punishable with a fine of one rupee four annas."[15] While in England, Gandhi was meticulously "playing the English gentleman," wore English clothes, and after his studies was "called to the Bar"—and was treated as a "coolie barrister."[16] By the twentieth century it had become painfully clear that, however much they wished to assimilate, however loyal they would be, the people of the colonies could not become full members of the British Empire. The color of their skin would bar them forever. Versailles added insult to injury when it trumpeted the principle of self-determination all over Central Europe but would not dream of applying it to India or Algeria. Just about the time (April 1919) the Covenant of the League of Nations was adopted in Paris, serious riots broke out in India. At Amritsar troops firing into the demonstrators killed 376 and wounded 1,200. It was also the time when Gandhi led his first *hartal* (mass boycott). The movement toward independence was under way.

What made the failure of Versailles inevitable, however, was the stubbornness with which its European architects refused to learn from the lessons of the past: from the mistakes of Bismarck or even from the gross blunders of Wilhelm II. The terms imposed on Germany were nothing short of brutal. She had to assume the burden of colossal reparations while losing all her colonies and much territory along her eastern and western borders; she was reduced to military impotence; and, perhaps worst of all, she had to accept the moral stigma of war guilt. The peace of Versailles ignored the basic requirement of major power rule and followed blatantly exclusionary practices. Thus the League chose to manage without Germany. But although humiliated and almost disarmed, Germany remained a place where enormous economic and human resources were concentrated. It was also a place where, not unlike France in the 1870s, anger and righteous indignation united the people in ferocious determination. Their single-minded purpose: to overthrow the Treaty of Versailles, and if in the process the League were washed away, so be it.

Russia, too, was excluded. Its new Bolshevik rulers, guilty of the murder of the czar and his family, guilty of betraying the Allies in a separate peace with Germany, and guilty of fomenting world revolution, could hardly be permitted to participate in regulating international relations. Still, as almost anyone could see, the Russian state, renamed the Union of Soviet Socialist Republics, had formidable resources and potentially great power, a disdain for capitalist countries, and a deep resentment for being ostracized internationally. It should have been no surprise that Germany and the Soviet Union, the two outcast states, approached each other.[17] Their combination accounted for most of the Eurasian continent—no negligible loss.

There were other losses. President Wilson, swept along by his foreign policy quest, neglected the demands of his domestic environment. Rudely ignored in negotiations across the Atlantic, the U.S. electorate, and more specifically the Senate, made it clear that they were not ready to participate in global ventures. This being a constitutional democracy, the issue was settled. The League of Nations would have to manage without its principal pillar, the United States. In addition, Italy was disgruntled with the Versailles settlement and Japan rapidly became disenchanted with the League. In practically no time all that was left of the coalition of great powers was France and Great Britain—a very unenthusiastic Great Britain.

By the late 1920s Germany and the Soviet Union were admitted to the League of Nations, but that did not help much, for the League remained bound to Versailles. France and its associates in Central Europe would not have it otherwise. Unless the territorial settlement of Versailles remained wholly intact, thundered the French foreign minister in Geneva, it would mean war. Unless the territorial settlement of Versailles was radically revised, the German foreign minister shouted back, it would mean war. So, concluded Professor Quincy Wright of the University of Chicago, the U.S. observer, we shall have war.

With Adolf Hitler's coming to power (1933) the German assault took shape. It was, of course, substantially assisted by French intransigence (and weakness) and British discomfort about the harshness of the terms of Versailles. With its empire increasingly on the defensive in the face of nationalist demands in Asia and Africa, by 1935 Great Britain was ready to give the collective rule of great powers another chance—preferably with all the great powers present but certainly with all the great European powers participating: Great Britain, France, Germany, and Italy. (The Soviet Union fell somewhere in the cracks.) Naturally the League of Nations was hopeless, but if through the policy of appeasement German grievances could be allayed, and she and her Italian ally could be enlisted for a common effort, political stability on the global scale could perhaps be restored. The risk seemed worth taking.

It was a policy that stood by idly while Hitler overthrew the Treaty of Versailles, rearmed, and then intimidated and invaded Germany's neighbors. It was a policy that led to Munich—where the British Prime Minister believed he had bought "peace in our time." Czechoslovakia had to pay for it with much of her territory. It was also a policy of wishful thinking. In less than six months British illusions were shattered. On March 15, 1939, Dr. Emil Hacha, the decent and frail old president of the helpless remnant of Czechoslovakia, traveled to Berlin. In the evening he called on the German Führer to offer his fullest cooperation. To his utter amazement and consternation, Hitler informed him that he had decided to invade his country at 6:00 next morning. Any resistance would be brutally broken ("mit Brachialgewalt gebrochen"). If necessary, German heavy artillery and the Luftwaffe would devastate Czech cities. Hacha asked for time to consider, but it was denied to him. He had a heart attack. Revived, he accepted the inevitable. Hitler had his way: Czechoslovakia was now smashed (*zerschlagen*).[18] In Rome, Count Galeazzo Ciano, the Italian foreign minister, knew what it all meant. He confided in his *Diary*:

The thing is serious, especially since Hitler had assured everyone that he did not want to annex one single Czech. This German action does not destroy, at any rate, the Czechoslovakia of Versailles, but one that was constructed at Munich. . . . What weight can be given in the future to those declarations and promises which concern us more directly?[19]

Ciano's boss, Benito Mussolini, was distressed. He finally found solace in invading Albania.

Indeed, it was a very serious matter. Winston Churchill observed:

If Chamberlain failed to understand Hitler, Hitler completely underrated the nature of the British Prime Minister. He mistook his civilian aspect and passionate drive for peace for a complete explanation of his personality, and thought that his umbrella was his symbol. He did not realize that Neville Chamberlain had a very hard core, and that he did not like being cheated.[20]

Munich taught a valuable lesson: Cooperation with dictators is always a risky business. They tend to be impatient with the incremental approach and insensitive to anyone else's vital interests. And fanatics committed to revolutionary change will not be restrained by considerations of international order. There could be security for no one: there would be no peace on earth as long as Hitler ruled a powerful Germany. Humanity was on the threshold of World War II.

THE THIRD TRY: SAN FRANCISCO, 1945

It was much worse than the last time. World War II lasted longer (1939–1945), it directly involved more countries, and the carnage and devastation far surpassed anything even a sick mind could conjure up.

The Americans were slow getting involved in the conflict. When the war had been raging in Europe for almost two years, most Americans still wanted to stay out of it. Many in the U.S. Army were chalking the motto O.H.I.O. ("over the hill in October") on walls, the Neutrality Act of 1939 was still in force, and the extension of the draft law was passed by a single vote in the House of Representatives. Only a massive attack by Japan on our territory and our armed forces could produce a (congressional) declaration of war. Even then the question remained: Just how can we fight the far greater threat, Nazi Germany? Anxieties in the White House and the State Department were finally relieved when, four days after Pearl Harbor, for reasons that are still obsure, Hitler declared war on us.

Once in the war the United States had absolutely no doubt about the outcome. The German Army occupied Poland, Denmark, Norway, the Netherlands, Belgium, Luxembourg, France, Yugoslavia, and Greece, stood at the gates of Leningrad and Moscow, and was approaching the Suez Canal; the German Navy was sinking 300,000–400,000 tons of Allied shipping a month; and the Luftwaffe was regularly bombing British cities. Meanwhile, the Japanese were on the rampage in Southeast Asia, in the Philippines, in Malaya, in the Dutch East Indies, in Thailand, even in Burma. Never mind all that. The United States never doubted victory for a moment. It was only a matter of time—not too much time. The State Department was already at work on plans for the postwar international order.

There were economic questions. Under the leadership of Dean Acheson, Assistant Secretary of State for Economic Affairs, new approaches were generated. Plans and agreements were prepared for the relief of war-torn areas (U.N.R.R.A.). The United States would provide most of the funds, though Latin American countries also helped substantially. "Relief, we said with righteous fervor, must be kept free from politics. The idea amused Litvinov [the Soviet Ambassador]."[21] Then followed plans and agreements on food and agriculture (FAO). Finally, the most difficult: plans and agreements for new monetary arrangements (International Monetary Fund, International Bank of Reconstruction and Development).

Then there were political questions. On those the ideas were rather less original. At the Teheran summit (end of November 1943) President Roosevelt raised the matter of the postwar political order with Marshal Stalin. He proposed a peacekeeping organization very much like the League of Nations. It would have an Assembly of all members and an Executive Committee dominated by the major powers. The most important component, however, would be an enforcement agency: " 'The Four Policemen'—the U.S.S.R., U.S., U.K. and China . . . with power to deal immediately with any threat to the peace or any sudden emergency."[22]

Stalin's response had two parts. First he voiced his doubts that the smaller countries of Europe would like the idea of "four policemen," especially one that included China. Then he quickly moved to his major concern. The idea, he suggested, might require the overseas deployment of U.S. forces. The President sought to reassure the Soviet dictator. The United States would use only air and naval forces. It would rely for ground forces on Britain and the Soviet Union.

[Roosevelt] saw two possibile kinds of threat—one minor, and one major—to world peace. The minor threat might arise from a revolution or civil war in a small country . . . This could be met by application of the quarantine method, the closing of limited frontiers and the imposition of embargoes.

The major threat would be provided by a gesture of aggression on the part of a large power; in this case the Four Policemen would send an ultimatum to the threatening nation and, if the demands were not immediately met, they would subject that nation to bombardment and, if necessary, to invasion. (*There seems to be no evidence of any discussion of the possibility that the offending aggressor might be one of the Four Policemen.*)[23]

The conversation revealed quite clearly Stalin's anxiety about U.S. power, and the last parenthetical observation showed Roosevelt's position on the Soviet Union. Many at the time, and many more since, have thought the president was beguiled by the Soviet tyrant and "soft on Communism." A more accurate appraisal would find the following logic:

1. There has never been a way to compel a major power to act against its will except by war.

2. Lasting peace after World War II would need the cooperation of the Soviet Union.

3. The Soviet leadership is suspicious and fearful of U.S. power and intentions.

4. To give peace a chance, the United States should make every effort to help alleviate Soviet anxieties—in fact, bend over backward to build confidence in our integrity.

5. If, in a worst case scenario, after all this genuine effort the Soviet Union were to press on with its avowed goal of "world revolution" and threaten other countries, we could resist with a clear conscience and a united people, convinced that we have done everything possible, that it was all their fault.

This helps explain why in the allocation of U.S. munitions the Soviet Union (by the President's dictum) received preferential treatment over all other Allies *and even over the armed forces of the United States.*[24] It helps explain why General Eisenhower indirectly, and then directly, prevented U.S. forces from liberating Berlin and summarily stopped General Patton from marching on Prague.[25] And it helps explain why President Truman, when faced with the situation of U.S. troops deep in German territory previously assigned to the Soviet zone of occupation and Churchill's request for temporizing, concluded that "the only practical thing to do was to stick carefully to our agreement and to try our best to make the Russians carry out their agreements."[26]

Negotiations on the postwar political order continued. The Soviets, like the French 25 years earlier, insisted on absolute security through territorial aggrandizement, and the Americans, like the Americans 25 years earlier, insisted on peace through international organization. The Soviets did get everything they wanted: all of Eastern Europe and parts of Southeastern and Central Europe. After negotiations and compromises at Dumbarton Oaks, Yalta, and San Francisco (June 1945), the United States got the Charter of the United Nations.

It was very much like the Covenant of the League. If there were differences, they were mostly in reinforcing the great power domination of the institution. References to international law and justice were rarer. The smaller states could debate all they liked in the General Assembly, as long as it did not involve disputes under consideration by the Security Council. Only the Security Council could act in matters of international peace and security, and on it the great powers had permanent seats and the power of the veto. Only the great powers could act, but they could act only in concert.

With all its merits, the United Nations as the guardian of world order and peace was a fantasy. At Vienna all the major powers were present; at Versailles some of the major powers were excluded. It soon became clear that at San Francisco some of the major powers were such only by arbitrary definition. Stalin had profound doubts about China as an equal; everyone could see the weakness of its forces and the corruption of its leaders. France was in no better shape. Politically unstable, economically weak, it was pathetically trying to regain its self-respect, prestige, and empire. Britain, proud and indomitable, was barely holding on; its empire, terminally ill for decades, was ready for the last rites. In fact, it had become a bi-polar world, a world of two superpowers, each with enormous exportable surplus capacities of control, and each suspecting the other of hegemonic aspirations.

In concert they could impose their will any time, any place in the world. But they were not in concert, not for long at any rate. Quite the contrary.

NOTES

1. See Henry A. Kissinger, *A World Restored* (New York: Grosset and Dunlap, 1964), pp. 1–3.

2. At Troppau (1820), Laibach (1821), Verona (1822).

3. Britain had begun building a civil service structure in India down to the local Subdivisions, but at the turn of the century it was still in a rudimentary form.

4. Prince Otto von Bismarck, *Reflections and Reminiscences*, edited by Theodore S. Hamerow (New York: Harper and Row, 1968), pp. 144, 200, 203–04. The Crown Princess, the wife of the Chief of the General Staff (von Moltke), the wife of the Army chief of staff (von Blumenthal), and the wife of the staff officer next in influence (von Gottberg), lamented Bismarck, were all Englishwomen.

5. Sidney Bradshaw Fay, *The Origins of the World War*, 2d ed. (New York: Macmillan, 1930), vol. 1, pp. 96–97.

6. For a detailed account see Leon Say, *Les finances de la France sous la Troisième République* (Paris: Levy, 1898), vol. 1, pp. 363–422.

7. By 1874 the balance of gold and silver of the Bank of France had risen to 1.13 billion francs; five years later it was 2.12 billion francs. Bernhard Mehrens, *Entstehung und Entwicklung der grossen französischen Kreditinstitute* (Stuttgart: J. G. Cotta'sche Buchhandling Nachfolger, 1911), p. 164.

8. In 1881–1885 French private foreign investment was practically nil. Some 15 years later (1897–1902) it had skyrocketed to 1.16–1.26 billion francs. *Bulletin de l'Institute international de statistique*, 20, pt. 2 (1913), p. 1406.

9. Fay, *Origins of the World War*, vol. 1, p. 10.

10. Quoted ibid., p. 100.

11. Quoted ibid., p. 131.

12. While Germany was challenging Britain's global position, French ambitions in North Africa clashed with British interests in the Sudan. At Fashoda (1898) the French

yielded and hauled down their flag: a humiliation in a distant land, a cheap price for an understanding with Britain.

13. Kissinger, *A World Restored*, p. 180. At the request of the British Foreign Office, Sir Charles Webster prepared a study on the lessons of the Congress of Vienna for Versailles. In Kissinger's view: "Webster's conclusion that it was one of the errors of Vienna to permit France to negotiate and the acceptance of his advice not to repeat this mistake with respect to Germany turned out to be one of the banes of the Treaty of Versailles." Ibid., p. 342.

14. William E. Rappard, *The Quest for Peace Since the World War* (Cambridge, Mass.: Harvard University Press, 1940), pp. 99–102.

15. M. K. Gandhi, *The Story of My Experiments with Truth*, translated by Mahadev Desai (Washington, D.C.: Public Affairs Press, 1960), pp. 57, 58.

16. Ibid., pp. 136–38, 140–44, 161–64, 181–84. In 1962 the chief justice of Pakistan, Mohammad Shahabuddin, recounted to me an early experience in Madras, where he had served as District Magistrate. By tradition, upon arriving at a new post, the wives of junior officers called upon the wives of senior officers. There were instances when the wives of English junior officers excluded from this courtesy the wives of the "native" senior officers of the Indian Civil Service. His resentment of such racial affronts still rankled many years later.

17. As early as 1922, at Rapallo, Germany and the Soviet Union signed a treaty ostensibly of economic cooperation but with wide-ranging military ramifications.

18. Erwin Wickert, *Dramatische Tage in Hitlers Reich* (Stuttgart: Steingruber Verlag, 1952), pp. 226–32.

19. Count Galeazzo Ciano, *The Ciano Diaries 1939–1943*, edited by Hugh Gibson (Garden City, N.Y.: Doubleday, 1946), p. 42.

20. Sir Winston Churchill, *The Second World War: The Gathering Storm* (Boston: Houghton, Mifflin, 1948), p. 344.

21. Dean Acheson, *Present at the Creation: My Years in the State Department* (New York: W. W. Norton, 1969), p. 69.

22. Robert E. Sherwood, *Roosevelt and Hopkins: An Intimate History* (New York: Harper and Brothers, 1948), p. 785.

23. Ibid., p. 786. Emphasis added.

24. General John R. Deane, *The Strange Alliance: The Story of Our Efforts at Wartime Co-operation with Russia* (New York: Viking Press, 1948), pp. 87–103. From October 1941 to May 1945, 2,660 ships carrying 16,529,791 tons of supplies were sent to the Soviet Union.

25. David Eisenhower, *Eisenhower: At War, 1943–1945* (New York: Random House, 1986), pp. 727–33, 740–41.

26. Harry S. Truman, *Memoirs*, vol. 1 (Garden City, N.Y.: Doubleday, 1955), p. 214.

10

DECENTRALIZED WORLD ORDER

Barely six months after San Francisco (February 9, 1946) Stalin made a campaign speech. It was marked by the usual Communist rhetoric, assertions about Soviet preparedness at the time of the German invasion, gloating about victory, and at the end a humble bit: the expression of gratitude for being nominated to the Supreme Soviet and the promise "to try to justify this confidence." As the State Department read it, "he also stated with brutal clarity the Soviet Union's postwar policy. Finding the causes of the late war in the necessities of capitalist-imperialist monopoly and the same forces still in control abroad, he concluded that no peaceful international order was possible."[1] Promptly a call went out to the American Embassy in Moscow for the "elucidation of this startling speech."[2]

Just what the State Department expected is not quite clear. What it got was the "long telegram" of some 8,000 words by George F. Kennan.[3] The Chargé d'Affaires being in bed with a "cold, fever, sinus, tooth trouble, and finally the aftereffects of the sulpha drugs administered for the relief of these other miseries," Kennan saw his chance. Within a comprehensive pedagogical exercise he made his point: We cannot expect anything remotely resembling reason from the Soviet Union!

> . . . please note that premises on which this party line is based are for most part simply not true. . . .
>
> Nevertheless, all these theses, however baseless and disproven, are being boldly put forward again today. What does this indicate? It indicates that the Soviet party line is not based on any objective analysis of the situation beyond Russia's border; that it has, indeed, little to do with conditions outside of Russia; that it arises mainly from basic inner-Russian necessities which existed before recent war and exist today,[4]

In other words, however hard we may try to gain their confidence, "their neurotic view of world affairs" will abort any endeavor requiring Soviet cooperation. It was really a foolish waste of time to try at all.

The message was leaked and became an instant success. James Forrestal, secretary of the navy (soon to become the first secretary of defense), liked it very much. The State Department was more cautious, but Dean Acheson, who in the meantime had become under secretary of state and was a man President Truman trusted, agreed that "his [Kennan's] predictions and warnings could not have been better."[5] Since the president himself was developing profound doubts about the Russians, a consensus was forming in the government that in spite of all U.S. hopes and efforts, a concert with the Soviet Union, at least for some time to come, was a fantasy.

THE FOURTH TRY: A NEW BEGINNING

Events that followed are well known. What these events meant, however, is open to various interpretations. The orthodox version holds that U.S. foreign policy was captured by national security policy. We set out to dam the Communist tide, and became fully absorbed in building alliance systems along the Communist periphery. We designed and single-mindedly pursued the Cold War and called it the strategy of containment.[6] An alternative interpretation, one I think more closely reflects the truth, is that *the American government did not abandon its deeply felt commitment to international order*. It gave up the orthodox approach of Vienna, Versailles, and the "Four Policemen." It gave up the approach of international order through the Concert of great powers and tried something different, something new: *a decentralized world order*.

To be sure, anxiety about Communist expansion was quite real. The Soviets were aggressively active in Iran and Greece, and provocatively demanding to Turkey. They required a forceful U.S. response: a resolution in the United Nations (Iran), a presidential declaration (Truman Doctrine), and programs of military aid (Greece and Turkey). Western Europe was in dire economic straits, vulnerable to Communist subversion, and defenseless against direct Soviet attack. It required economic aid (the Marshall Plan) and a military alliance (NATO). But even in our response to these specific Communist challenges there is evidence of a discernible broader concern for international order. A case can be made that the government of the United States, and more specifically Dean Acheson, who masterminded our postwar foreign policy, knew that the American people (and the Congress), so recently committed to isolation, would not readily understand and support our *general interest* in international order. Since they did want popular support and needed congressional approval, they thought it necessary to resort to a ploy, to reformulate such general goals and publicly present them in terms of our *special interests* in helping our friends and allies, and even in terms of our *vital interests* to thwart a Communist threat to the United States.

As a case in point, at the first White House briefing of congressional leaders on Greek and Turkish aid, the Secretary of State, seeking to place the program in the context of our general national interest, "most unusually and unhappily, flubbed his opening statement." Dean Acheson, sitting next to General Marshall, in desperation asked permission (from the President and the Secretary) to speak.

In the past eighteen months, I said, Soviet pressure on the Straits, on Iran, and on northern Greece had brought the Balkans to the point where a highly possible Soviet breakthrough might open three continents to Soviet penetration. Like apples in a barrel infected by one rotten one, the corruption of Greece would infect Iran and all to the east. It would also carry infection to Africa through Asia Minor and Egypt, and to Europe through Italy and France, already threatened by the strongest domestic Communist parties in Western Europe. The Soviet Union was playing one of the greatest gambles in history at minimal costs. . . . We and we alone were in a position to break up the play. . . . A long silence followed. Then Arthur Vandenberg[7] said solemnly, "Mr. President, if you will say that to Congress and the country, I will support you and I believe that most members will do the same."[8]

It seemed to work, so the strategy was repeated, with the "rotten apples" eventually replaced by "falling dominoes."

A year later (1947), at Harvard's commencement the Secretary of State announced the Marshall Plan and justified it in terms of general international cooperation. His Under Secretary later recorded:

If General Marshall believed, which I am sure he did not, that the American people would be moved to so great an effort as he contemplated by as Platonic a purpose as combating "hunger, poverty, desperation, and chaos," he was mistaken. *But he was wholly right in stating this as the American governmental purpose.* I have probably made as many speeches and answered as many questions about the Marshall Plan as any man alive, . . . and what citizens and the representatives in Congress alike always wanted to learn in the last analysis was how Marshall aid operated to block the extension of Soviet power and the acceptance of Communist economic and political organization and alignment.[9]

While American aid to Europe was getting under way, historic events in other parts of the globe were moving along at an inexorable pace. In August 1947 India and Pakistan became independent, and that was just the beginning. New states based on the principle of self-determination were emerging all over the globe: a new reality, a phenomenal challenge to international order. The old colonial order was gone forever. The United States, with all its awesome power, had no interest whatever in gaining world hegemony but had not the slightest inclination to permit the Soviet Union to do so. In his inaugural address (1949) Harry S Truman, elected President in his own right, warned of the "false philosophy" of Communism, but went far beyond that. He pledged U.S. leadership for "a cooperative enterprise in which all nations work together . . . a worldwide effort for the achievement of peace, plenty and freedom." Afterward he explained to reporters in the Oval Office: "I spend most of my time going to that globe back there, trying to figure out ways to make peace in the world."[10]

Decentralized world order was indeed a radical departure from conventional wisdom. It was based on the novel proposition that the settlement of international conflict was not the private domain of the major powers but the right and responsibility of *all* states collectively. Insofar as any state would be given greater weight in such settlements, this was not the product of its power but the consequence of its regional proximity. Smaller states close by would be entitled to greater weight than large powers far off.

This, of course, did not mean that major powers would stop imposing their solutions on the disputes of others, let alone stop interfering in the business of smaller states. It did mean that they could not do so as a matter of course. They would have to have an excuse and would have to go to great lengths to justify themselves to a skeptical environment. This somewhat subtle point perhaps can be illustrated by two analogies. In one of his conversations the American Ambassador in Saigon mentioned to President Diem of South Vietnam that the latter had what might be called an "image problem" in the United States. The president thought about it, then inquired about the reasons. Tactfully the ambassador pointed out that the fact that the head of internal security was the president's brother did not make a good impression. President Diem was utterly surprised. That he should turn to a relative to serve in so vital a position was only natural. Anyone could see that. "But if I cannot trust my own brother," he exclaimed, "whom can I trust?" As it happened, just a few years earlier President-elect John F. Kennedy was selecting his cabinet. At a dinner party he confided to Ben Bradlee his decision to name his brother attorney general, the highest law-enforcement officer of the United States. Later that evening Bradlee inquired just how the announcement would be made. "Well, I think," said John Kennedy, "I'll open the front door [of his Georgetown house] some morning about 2 AM, look up and down the street, and if there is no one there, I'll whisper, 'It's Bobby.' " What Diem took for granted, Kennedy felt required explanation. The major powers had the *power* to intervene in the past—they still do. The major powers had the *right* to intervene in the past; now, when they intervened, they were obliged to offer some justification to the other members of the international community.

Decentralized world order, however, was still only a concept, at best a design. Formidable obstacles would have to be overcome before it could become a reality. To begin with, there was the basic theoretical problem: Its logic was too closely analogous to the American Wild West. There was not much law in Dodge City— or so the story went—about as little as in international relations. But there the similarity ended. In case of a threat to the peace of the City, the "bad guy" or the gang was hunted down by a posse of citizens. Since the posse heavily outnumbered the criminal(s), it could overwhelm and punish him (them). It could do so easily because there is relatively little difference in the physical power of human beings; hence a numerical superiority was decisive. But this is not true in the international arena where the basic units are states. In practically every region there is a state whose power vastly exceeds that of all its neighbors put together. The posse of the African "frontline" states can do little about South Africa. Pakistan, Burma, Sri Lanka, plus the Seychelle Islands together could not restrain India if she were to choose to become an aggressor, any more than the Arab states could restrain Israel.

There were practical problems as well. Some were quantitative. The system of great powers had four or five—at any rate, few—decisive components. It was difficult to get agreement, let alone a consensus, but it could be done. But decentralized world order, with the "sovereign equality" of all the various states, vastly inflated the decision-making number: 50, 100, 150. Agreement among so large a number, not to mention a consensus, was a very different, quite possibly unmanageable, task.

Worse still was a qualitative change. Many members of a decentralized world order actually lacked the minimal capacities of a modern state: they were not only economically underdeveloped but also politically unstable. While people would speak hopefully of "newly emerging states," the danger was quite real that in fact they would be submerging into primitive (tribal and communal) violence and chaos. How could an arrangement bring peace and order in the world when most of its "equal" members could not even maintain peace and order at home?

If decentralized world order was to have a chance at all, a special temporary transitional effort was needed by the United States. We would have to help build the political stability of the newly independent states of Asia and Africa. President Truman accepted the responsibility. As they emerged, American initiatives had a dual thrust: (1) to generate economic development and thus reduce the demands on government; and (2) to improve administrative skills and internal security forces, and thus increase the resources of government. The strategy had serious theoretical flaws,[11] but its most serious practical deficiency was its neglect of the possibility of external predatory initiatives. States with unstable political systems not only are vulnerable to internal revolution but also are magnets for external aggression. And, of course, the Soviet Union was not sitting idly by while world order "Made in the United States" was being established. It used its propaganda to discredit it, and its power and influence to challenge it. Sunday morning, June 25, 1950, the regular forces of Communist North Korea invaded the Republic of South Korea.

As a case of unprovoked aggression the North Korean attack was an affront to international order. It was also a Communist challenge, a Soviet challenge by proxy, to the United States. Dean Acheson, now the Secretary of State, explained: "to back away from this challenge, in view of our capacity for meeting it would be highly destructive of the power and prestige of the United States."[12] Accordingly, the American response was swift and decisive. U.S. air, naval, and ground forces were committed to repel the aggressor. Since at the time the Soviet Union was boycotting the Security Council, this could be done under United Nations auspices. All the same it was a very troubling matter. It was one thing to provide aid—economic or even military supplies and training—in order to build political stability in distant lands for the purpose of inernational order; to shed American blood for this purpose was something else again. We had never done so before. In the past, for so great a sacrifice we had needed a more direct and a more clearly perceived threat. Just three days after the invasion the Secretary of State warned that the administration "could not count on the continuance of enthusiastic support that our staunch attitude in Korea had worked in the country and in the world. Firm leadership would be less popular if it should involve casualties and taxes."[13]

Casualties were rising soon enough, but popular support remained enthusiastic. We were winning. Our troops destroyed the North Korean forces, captured their capital, and were on the verge of occupying practically all their country. Then Communist China intervened, and suddenly we came face to face with the full costs of a decentralized world order. We could, of course, withdraw, and abandon our cherished international design, but Americans do not easily accept defeat. Or we could escalate, and "shoot the works." General Douglas MacArthur, the Supreme Allied Commander in the Far East, was ready to do it, and the American public—while the option remained academic—was wildly for it. But the risks were enormous: the risk of a full-scale war with China, perhaps the Soviet Union, the risk of Soviet initiatives anywhere else on the globe (perhaps Western Europe), and the risk of scaring our allies (for example, British Prime Minister Clement Atlee) out of their wits.

All these risks might have been warranted in case of a threat to our vital interests, but surely were not justified by a challenge to our general interest in international order. What we needed was a limited response to a limited purpose. We needed firm leadership steering a moderate course, a president with careful judgment, a moderate temperament, and a feel for a delicate balance. And we needed an American electorate patient and understanding with a war in support of an Asian government perhaps friendly to us, but with not the slightest inclination to democratic values. We needed an American electorate patient and understanding with a war without glory, endlessly devouring American lives, money, and prestige. Possibly we had the necessary leadership; certainly we did not have public patience and understanding. President Truman managed a draw in Korea—at colossal political cost.

Dwight D. Eisenhower, his successor, had known for quite some time that international order had become an integral part of American national interest. As Supreme Allied Commander in Europe he had faithfully supported the contemporary view of a coalition of great powers and had gone to great lengths to build the confidence of the Soviet Union. As President he was no less determined to try to make decentralized world order work. He recognized the weakness that Korea exposed but, given a "new look," he believed a corrective could be developed. The problem, as everyone (including our enemies) could see, was that the American people had concluded that the price for the protection of vulnerable foreign states by U.S. arms was prohibitive. But did it have to be?

Quite possibly, as Eisenhower's Secretary of State, John Foster Dulles, suggested, the flaw in the Truman-Acheson approach was the commitment to a "symmetric response." It granted the aggressor the choice of place and weapons, a generosity even old-fashioned gentlemen duelers would not indulge in. Certainly Dulles would not. "The way to deter aggression," he said, "is for the free community to be willing and able to respond vigorously at places and with means of its own choosing."[14] And he wrote: "A would-be aggressor will hesitate to commit aggression if he knows in advance that he thereby not only exposes those particular forces which he chooses to use for his aggression, but also deprives his other assets of 'sanctuary' status." The Truman administration's self-restraint was counterproductive. With Eisenhower in charge, North Korea, China, the Soviet Union, and everyone else was on "public notice that if the Communists were to violate the armistice and renew the aggression the response of the United Nations Command would not necessarily be confined to Korea."[15]

Let them heed the warning: A country invading its neighbor will be punished by "instantaneous, massive retaliation." Then, sensing a new danger, the Secretary of State specifically warned China of "grave consequences which might not be confined to Indo-China" if it turned its aggression to the south. Through the "imaginative use of the deterrent capabilities of these new [nuclear] weapons," he explained, the United States would get more bang for the buck, actually the biggest gosh-darn bang anyone could imagine. Altogether, it was the most economical way to deter and punish aggressors anywhere in the world.

John Foster Dulles was close to the traditional power politics school. Even so, he was part of the continued American preoccupation with international order. "It is a fact, unfortunate though it be," he echoed Acheson, "that in promoting our programs in Congress we have to make evident the international communist menace. Otherwise such programs . . . would be decimated."[16] President Eisenhower himself regularly and dramatically demonstrated his own commitment to a new decentralized order. He had no faith in an international system linked to European colonial rule. He respected our "special" interest that tied us to our NATO allies—as a matter of regional security. On the global scale, however, he thought our general interest to be on the side of the newly independent Asian and African states. Preferably non-Communist, of course. In 1954, when France desperately needed U.S. military support in Indochina (Dien Bien Phu), he overruled his secretary of state and other senior advisers and refused to become involved in a scheme to restore the rule of a colonial power over subject peoples. Two years later, during the Suez crisis, he supported the sovereign equality of an unfriendly (even hostile) Egypt against the military action of Britain and France (not to mention Israel), our close World War II allies but former imperial powers.

Thus, with the Eisenhower-Dulles corrective of "massive retaliation," decentralized world order was given a new lease on life—but not for long. For "massive retaliation," or "asymmetric response," as the jargon went, rested on the pinpoint of American nuclear invulnerability. Though it was wildly unlikely, it was imaginable for some that the United States would bomb a country back into the Stone Age as an imposed penalty while she remained completely safe. But after October 1957 with Sputnik in the skies, revealing a vigorously pursued and rapidly advancing Soviet space program, the United States could not be completely safe much longer. That it should use its nuclear power against a Communist aggressor far beyond the seas, thereby risking a nuclear response from the Soviet Union, remained wildly unlikely but had become imaginable for hardly anyone.

Still, the American concept of decentralized world order was a very inspiring one, and to give up at all, let alone to give up easily, is not an American trait. It certainly was not part of the character of John Fitzgerald Kennedy. Understanding quite well all the new international realities, he proclaimed at his inauguration: "Let every nation know, whether it wishes us well or ill, that we shall pay any price, bear any burden, meet any hardship, support any friend, oppose any foe to assure the survival and success of liberty."[17]

It was a bold challenge. Just two weeks before, Nikita S. Khrushchev, the First Secretary of the Communist Party of the Soviet Union, had announced active Soviet support for "wars of liberation." Such wars, he said, "will continue to exist as long as imperialism exists, as long as colonialism exists. These are revolutionary wars. Such wars are not only admissible but inevitable. . . . "[18] Confronting the Dulles warning, he used as his principal example of revolutionary war "the armed struggle of the Vietnamese people." We were on a collision course, a course that led us to Vietnam and, as it turned out, to a historic test of decentralized world order.

BACKGROUND TO DANGER

Most Americans had never heard of the place. When, during World War II, the Japanese occupied French Indochina, our official position about its future was ambivalent. The United States wanted to support its French ally and hoped it would recover its lost prestige, but reconquering its colonies in Southeast Asia was another matter. Wrote President Roosevelt to his Secretary of State: "Each case must, of course, stand on its own feet, but the case of Indo-China is perfectly clear. France has milked it for one hundred years. The people of Indo-China are entitled to something better than that."[19] In war we carefully stayed away from the area; in the forthcoming peace, to use President Roosevelt's phrase, we "did not want to get mixed up in any Indo-China decision."

There soon appeared a complicating factor, however, growing steadily in salience: Ho Chi Minh. Born Nguyen Van Thanh on May 19, 1890, as a young man he attended Hue's Lycée Quoc-Hoc, a hotbed of nationalism; he dropped out; and just before World War I he found his way to Paris, where he joined anti-colonialist/Vietnam nationalist causes. Soon he became attracted by Lenin's writings. Later he recalled with pride: "By dint of reading it again and again, finally I could grasp the main part of it. What emotion, enthusiasm, clearsightedness, and confidence it instilled into me! I was overjoyed to tears."[20] In May

1920, Ho joined in the founding of the French Communist Party. The following years he spent in agitation, in revolutionary training in the Soviet Union, and intermittently in jail. By 1937 he had reached Communist bases in northern China, the next year he was reported in southern China, and in 1941 he crossed into Vietnam. With some American (O.S.S.) help he began disrupting the Japanese occupation, but most of all he spent his time and talents building Communist military and political cadres. By the time Japan surrendered, he controlled much of the countryside in the northern part of the country and was proclaimed president of the Democratic Republic of Vietnam. He was strong enough to negotiate an accord (March 6, 1946) with the returning French in which he agreed to "welcome amicably the French Army" but that had as its first point: "The French Government recognizes the Vietnamese Republic as a Free State having its own government. . . . "

Neither side, as events demonstrated, had the slightest intention of respecting the treaty; it was always a temporary expedient behind which to marshal forces. France gradually gained control of the major cities of Hanoi and Haiphong but made little headway in the countryside, then made no headway, and then lost much it had gained. Ho Chi Minh approached U.S. diplomatic representatives (the O.S.S. was sympathetic) for economic aid but received little support. State Department instructions to our representatives opened thus: "Keep in mind Ho's clear record as agent international communism, absence evidence recantation Moscow affiliations, confused political situation France and support Ho receiving French Communist Party. Least desirable eventuality would be establishment Communist-dominated Moscow oriented state Indochina."[21] Incidentally, the cable was signed "Acheson, Acting." Meanwhile the United States was giving some aid to France—not much—and kept pressing gently for progress toward self-determination in the area. The United States was still determined not to get mixed up in any Indochina decision.

Soon though there was another complication. The Communist forces of Mao Tse-tung gained control of China in 1949, and in the following year they intervened in Korea, causing heavy U.S. casualties. Both developments surprised our government; worse still, they enraged the American people. Soon the question arose: Who sold out China? The hunt was on—by Congress, by the media, and by the public. There were 57 card-carrying Communists in the State Department, shouted Joseph McCarthy, the junior senator from Wisconsin. Senior foreign service officers, "old China hands," were retired or removed. The newspapers were headlining wild charges, Congress was investigating, and the President issued executive orders establishing loyalty boards. The State Department was intimidated and demoralized. Who would dare risk the charge of being "soft on Communism"? Who would dare ignore the menace of the Red colossus of Asia? Who would dare doubt that it must be resisted everywhere and anywhere? In Indochina, for instance.

In Indochina the French were not doing well. Promises of progress toward self-government proved to be hollow. They turned to Bao Dai, a former Japanese puppet ruler, presumably in the hope that he would serve as their puppet ruler. The war against Ho Chi Minh's forces (Viet Minh) became overt, terribly costly in French lives and treasure, and increasingly hopeless. The situation had deteriorated badly, observed the American Joint Chiefs on April 5, 1950, who then concluded that "without United States assistance this deterioration will be accelerated."

President Truman approved $10 million in aid, but it did not help much. Warned Senator John F. Kennedy, "In Indochina we have allied ourselves to the desperate effort of the French regime to hang on to the remnants of an empire." All the same, in four years U.S. aid zoomed to $1.063 billion. In justification a National Security Council document proclaimed the "domino principle."

2. Communist domination, by whatever means, of all Southeast Asia would seriously endanger in the short term, and critically endanger in the longer term, United States security interests.

a. The loss of any of the countries of Southeast Asia to communist control as a consequence of overt or covert Chinese Communist aggression would have critical psychological, political and economic consequences. In the absence of effective and timely counteraction, the loss of any single country would probably lead to relatively swift submission to or an alignment with communism by the remaining countries of this group. Furthermore, an alignment with communism of the rest of Southwest Asia and India, and in the longer term, of the Middle East (with the probable exceptions of at least Pakistan and Turkey) would in all probability progressively follow. Such widespread alignment would endanger the stability and security of Europe.[22]

It did not help at all. The French position had become untenable, and the question of direct U.S. military intervention arose.

Its momentum was gaining. Some in the Pentagon were trying desperately to slow it down. Vice Admiral A. C. Davis, Director of the Office of Foreign Military Affairs, wrote:

Involvement of U.S. forces in the Indochina war should be avoided at all practical costs. If, then, National Policy determines no other alternative, the U.S. should not be self-duped into believing the possibility of partial involvement—such as "Naval and Air units only." One cannot go over Niagara Falls in a barrel only slightly.[23]

By April 1954 the French were in dire straits. Much of their forces were surrounded at Dien Bien Phu, with no prospect of relief. On the 4th they asked for our "immediate armed intervention . . . to save the situation." Secretary of State Dulles was ready to do so. A plan was drawn up (Operation Vulture) for a night raid on the Dien Bien Phu perimeter by about 60 B–29s accompanied by 150 fighters.

President Eisenhower would not be swayed. Having just recovered from an intervention in Korea, he would not jump into another one in Asia, especially one designed to preserve a vestige of the defunct colonial system. He never bought the "domino scenario" that explained why Vietnam was of special, let alone vital, interest to us. Moreover, he had read the U.S. Army position paper submitted to the National Security Council in early April, which left no doubt (and was uncannily prophetic):

1. U.S. intervention with combat forces in Indochina is not militarily desirable. . . .
2. A victory in Indochina cannot be assured by U.S. intervention with air and naval forces alone.
3. The use of atomic weapons in Indochina would not reduce the number of ground forces required to achieve a victory in Indochina.
4. Seven U.S. divisions or their equivalent, with appropriate naval and air support, would be required to win a victory in Indochina if the French withdraw and the Chinese Communists do not intervene. However, U.S intervention plans cannot be based on the assumption that the Chinese Communists will not intervene. . . . [24]

Eisenhower did not quite say no, but he set conditions (such as congressional support and united action with Britain and others) that he knew could not be met.

So the French had to surrender at Dien Bien Phu and negotiate terms with Ho Chi Minh at Geneva under the auspices of Britain and the Soviet Union. A very humiliating experience. And so the momentum of U.S. military involvement on the mainland of Asia was reversed. That was the end, at least for the moment, of the "domino theory." Said the Secretary of State: "Southeast Asia could be secured even without perhaps Vietnam, Laos and Cambodia."[25] Indochina had resumed its proper place in U.S. foreign policy: as a possible matter of international order of general interest, no more than that.

Unfortunately, it was not the end of the story. The General Accords of Geneva (1954) divided the former French colony into three successor states: Cambodia, Laos, and Vietnam. Vietnam itself was divided by a demilitarized zone into two zones, one in the north and one in the south. The northern zone, the Democratic Republic of Vietnam, was conceded to the control of Ho Chi Minh, but what about the south? Would it become the last visible vestige of the French empire in the area? Would it be absorbed, through the process of "unification," into the Communist power of the north? Or were there alternatives? The answer to the puzzle was partially dependent on a new personality rising in Saigon.

Ngo Dinh Diem was an independent, even stubborn, man. Very much like Ho Chi Minh he was extraordinarily able and a fierce nationalist. Unlike Ho Chi Minh, he was not a Communist—indeed, he was opposed to the system.[26] In short, Diem (as he became known in America)[27] had the very scarce qualifications that Americans sought to help build political stability in newly independent states so necessary for decentralized world order.

Just before the armistice of Geneva, Ngo Dinh Diem returned to his homeland and began organizing a government. In the past he had opposed the Japanese for occupying his country; now he had no intention of permiting the French to retain control. He missed no chance to reduce French power in the southern zone.[28] By February 1955 Prime Minister Faure, charging that "Diem is a bad choice, impossible solution, with no chance to succeed and no chance to improve the situation," agreed to French withdrawal from the area, and asked the United States to represent its interests. Nor did Diem intend to permit the Communists to gain control. He refused to implement the Geneva provisions for general elections as a step toward the unification of Vietnam. What he wanted was an independent state of South Vietnam.[29]

In the north Ho Chi Minh was busy consolidating his power—with the determination and efficiency of a modern Communist tyranny. He had a running start with a political structure organized through two wars and military forces just lately victorious over the French. "Land-reform" was his vehicle. "Beginning with punitive taxes, the Campaign matured [sic] terror, arrests, and public condemnations, trials, and executions." Each village was assigned a quota of one landlord death sentence. It was too little; their Chinese advisers felt that more exploiters should have been found. This was too much. Nearly a million North Vietnamese fled to the south; others resisted and rebelled. In November 1956

Thousands of peasants . . . swarmed over their local government offices, destroying land records, and blocking roads. Some militia deserted and joined the rebels, and attacks on nearby DRV troops were atttempted. . . . four columns of some 10,000 peasants [were] marching on the province capital, seizing arms from troops, and forcing party cadres to sign confessions of crimes. Two reinforced army divisions, some 20,000 strong, were committed to put down the uprising.[30]

In the south Ngo Dinh Diem also was quite active. He started with practically nothing. No bureaucracy, no political cadres, no police forces, no army. What he found was powerful sects and organized gangsters all pursuing, often by violence, their own sordid interests. He did have some friends, some supporters, and some skills. His approach was not unlike that of traditional Oriental despots. Avoiding mass executions, his secret police was busy rounding up some 50,000–100,000 political suspects and intimidating others. It was not enough. He needed help. He turned to America.

The Eisenhower administration was not unsympathetic. From time to time it provided diplomatic support against France, and it helped with the refugees. The U.S. Navy moved 310,848 persons in its "Operation Exodus"; U.S. government aid ($93 million) and massive donations by private charities helped them survive. Most important, perhaps (with about 70 percent of the total aid), the United States helped to build its security establishment: a regular army of about 150,000 men, a mobile civil guard of about 45,000, and local defense units to give protection on the village level. All the same President Eisenhower remained cautious. He did not want the United States to get involved.

Neither did Ngo Dinh Diem. Since his return he had made visible progress. The sect warlords (paid off by the Americans) were under control; the secret societies of river bandits and gangsters were effectively repressed. The country-side was supportive. A referendum in October 1955 gave Diem a dubiously overwhelming vote, but he plainly won nevertheless. Indeed, by 1956 there was actually emerging in Saigon a structure that was beginning to resemble a government.

One might speculate about Diem's chances of building a viable political system in South Vietnam had there been no external intervention. We shall never know, for there was at times very heavy external intervention. First came the attack of his Communist enemies. Ho Chi Minh was always committed to the unification of Vietnam. By 1959 his hold on the North had improved. Soviet and Chinese aid was forthcoming. He ordered the systematic infiltration of the South, where Communist cadres that after Geneva had gone underground[31] had become active again. Their preferred method was the assassination and kidnapping of public officials and village chiefs.

President Diem responded to violence with violence: he accelerated the buildup of the army, intensified police actions, controlled the press, and curtailed what we in the West call individual freedoms. In short, he acted very much in the traditions of the Orient. The struggle intensified. Insurgent losses were heavy but could be (and were) replaced from the outside. The strain on the social hierarchy and bureaucratic structure, targets of Communist violence, mounted. And so did the strain on the coercive capacities of the government. The army grew too quickly; it was too frequently assigned hazardous tasks against a better-trained and more deeply committed enemy. Internal security and political stability were not improving in South Vietnam, a fact that led to another form of intervention: the help of Diem's U.S. friends.

SOUTH VIETNAM BECOMES OUR SPECIAL INTEREST: FOREIGN POLICY LOSES CONTACT WITH INTERNATIONAL REALITY

By the spring of 1960 the U.S. Mission in Saigon was alarmed. It reported that internal security had once again become the primary problem. It offered a diagnosis: the insurgents were too tough and the government was too weak. In August a "Special National Intelligence Estimate" took the same position. In September the American Ambassador offered his recommendation: tell Diem what to do.

As a matter of fact, the President of South Vietnam did not ask us for any special help. Our aid, $377 million ($210 million economic plus $167 million military) in 1955–56, had dropped to $215 million ($150 million economic plus $65 million military) by 1960–61. And he certainly did not want any advice; he thought he knew what to do. President Eisenhower was quite content with the position. He was busy with (fruitless) negotiations with the Soviet Union and was concerned about the Communist takeover in Cuba. He saw nothing he wanted or needed to prove in South Vietnam. Soon, though, there was a new president in the White House. He was a man who cherished and radiated vigor, who promised to get the country "moving again," and who surrounded himself with men and women of firm convictions.

Conditions did not improve in South Vietnam. The assassination of rural leaders continued; worse still, hit-and-run attacks on military establishments and supply routes were becoming frequent. Occasionally Communist guerrillas seized a district or provincial capital, held it for a while, meted out revolutionary justice (massacred some people), and then, as government forces were approaching slowly and carefully—very slowly and very carefully—withdrew. The U.S. ambassador, though not the senior military representatives, became very nervous. In May 1961 Vice President Lyndon Johnson (carefully chaperoned by a presidential sister and brother-in-law) visited Saigon. During a discussion with Diem he offered American aid. Diem was very much impressed, "particularly because we have not become accustomed to being asked for our own views on our needs," and took him up on it. He asked for equipment to nearly double his army from 150,000 to 270,000 men and "a considerable expansion of the United States Military Advisory Group." Then, in three months (October 1), the South Vietnamese president surprised the American Ambassador by asking for a U.S.–South Vietnam defense treaty. Disturbed, President Kennedy sent General Maxwell Taylor, his personal adviser on military affairs, and Walt Rostow from the National Security Council on a fact-finding mission to Saigon. The question that had been lurking in the background for some time became increasingly visible: Just what did South Vietnam mean to us?

We might see it as it actually was: a place of international conflict in which we had a general interest. If we did so, our options were wide open. We could accept Vietnam as a test for a decentralized order. We might experiment a bit with various forms of aid. If they succeeded, we would teach a lesson; if not, who would care? Certainly most Americans would not. Alternatively, we could become impressed by the problems involved: the ambiguity of South Vietnam's international position (Geneva intended it as a transitional arrangement), the complexity of the conflict (the combination of external and internal elements of the "insurgency"), and the asymmetry of our long supply lines across the sea and their short supply lines on land. We could easily reject it as a suitable test case and could quite possibly leave it alone—as Eisenhower did. So sorry.

There was, however, another way of looking at South Vietnam, one that made it much more important to us. It saw North Vietnamese infiltration and insurgency as a move to cut across our global defensive chain that ran from Britain through Europe and Asia to Japan. It made quite a difference. For while the American people knew little and cared less about Vietnam, they would not take kindly to yet another country going Communist. Given such a perception, policy options were sharply limited. The Communists' march toward world revolution would have to be stopped; their drive toward hegemony had to be contained. It was a historic struggle between two giants, verily between good and evil. In that case intervention became a logical necessity. We had choices about its extent, perhaps even about its timing, but that was all. We could not just walk away.

President Kennedy was inclined to follow Eisenhower's lead. South Vietnam, as a test case of decentralized world order, did not appeal to him. The integrity and the prospects of a viable political system emerging there were far too uncertain. Personally he was willing to give it his sympathy, but as a policy he much preferred benign neglect.

All the same, President Kennedy was in a difficult position. He was steadily *pulled* into the conflict. With hindsight it seems most unlikely that the Communist powers would have let him experiment with a variety of minimal-to-moderate means. Ho Chi Minh was in fact prepared to pay any price, bear any burden for the success of his cause. China and the Soviet Union relished the prospect of haranguing throughout the world about our impotence and their successes. Meanwhile, the President was *pushed* into the conflict. The pressure of the political right was formidable. The outrages of the McCarthy era had become bad memories. Even so, the suspicion that the Democrats were "soft on Communism" lingered on. It did not help that his first 18 months in office were marked by a series of setbacks in foreign policy: the bungling into and at the Bay of Pigs, an indifferent performance at the Vienna summit with Khrushchev, indecision on Berlin and impotence at the Berlin Wall, persistent trouble in Laos. Voices were raised: Does he know anything? Can he do anything right? Pressure was building for bold "leadership." Another "loss to the Communists" could prove politically fatal.

Remarkably, the President also was pushed from the political Left. John F. Kennedy liked the company of distinguished academics, very intelligent men who had accumulated vast knowledge in their respective areas of specialization. Much like Franklin Roosevelt he brought along a large number to Washington in middle-level administrative positions. In their newfound political power an astonishing number of them soon asserted superior authority well beyond the limits of their expertise. Not for them a "let's give it a modest try: if it works; o.k.; if not; so what" approach. They wanted action. They saw the problem; they were ready to solve it; they knew what to do.

General Taylor, having returned from his mission to Saigon, had no doubt that U.S. military involvement was necessary to save South Vietnam. Still, he was cautious in his report. All he recommended was a very modest, primarily logistical support, a task force of "6–8000 troops . . . for the purpose of participating in flood relief." And he was especially cautious about American meddling in the political processes of the country. Taylor did not shrink from a candid estimate of the structural and moral deficiencies of the government or the political and administrative peculiarities of its President, but he rejected "his removal in favor of a military dictatorship . . . it would be dangerous for us to engineer a coup under present tense circumstances, since it is by no means certain that we could control its consequences and potentialities for Communist exploitation.'' Indeed, a main purpose of intervention was that ''of providing a U.S. military presence in VN capable of assuring Diem of our readiness to join him in a military showdown with the Viet Cong or Viet Minh.''

To be sure there was dissent, mostly by middle-level officials. They wanted more, not less, intervention. To be successful, the United States would have to overhaul the South Vietnamese government from top to bottom. John Kenneth Galbraith, Professor of Economics at Harvard and American Ambassador to India, visited Saigon. It was his first trip to the area, but after ''three intensive days'' he cabled his judgment to the President:

THE KEY AND INESCAPABLE POINT, THEN, IS THE INEFFECTUALITY (ABET-TED DEBATABLY BY THE UNPOPULARITY) OF THE DIEM GOVERNMENT. THIS IS THE STRATEGIC FACTOR. NOR CAN ANYONE ACCEPT THE STATE-MENT OF THOSE WHO HAVE BEEN EITHER TOO LONG OR TOO LITTLE IN ASIA THAT HIS IS THE INEVITABLE POSTURE OF THE ASIAN MANDARIN. FOR ONE THING IT ISN'T TRUE. BUT WERE IT SO THE ONLY POSSIBLE CON-CLUSION WOULD BE THAT THERE IS NO FUTURE FOR MANDARINS. THE COMMUNISTS DON'T FAVOR THEM.

''We are married to failure.'' Diem must go. '' . . . the only solution is to drop [him]. . . . He cannot be rehabilitated.'' Difficult problems require radical solutions. If necessary, the United States must instigate a coup against a man we had formally recognized as a head of state, his family, and his supporters. When we intervened, we must do so all the way. ''It is those of us,'' warned Ambassador Galbraith, ''who have worked in the political vineyard and who have committed our hearts most strongly to the political fortunes of the New Frontier who worry most about its bright promise being sunk under the rice fields.''[32]

On November 11, 1961, the Secretary of State and the Secretary of Defense were heard from.[33] Their top recommendation was that '' . . . We now take the decision to commit ourselves to the objective of preventing the fall of South Vietnam to Communism and that, in doing so, we recognize that the introduction of United States and other SEATO forces may be necessary to achieve this objective.'' Originally only a small number (8,000) of support personnel were to be committed for limited operations, but their number was expected ro rise and their functions to expand. It was ''the view of the Secretary of Defense and the Joint Chiefs of Staff'' however, that ''we [could] assume that the maximum United States forces required on the ground in Southeast Asia would not exceed six divisions, or about 205,000 men.'' Furthermore, it was their recommendation to use ''substantial United States forces to assist in suppressing Viet Cong insurgency . . . including relevant operations in North Viet-Nam.'' Clearly the President's senior advisers endorsed the posture of the middle-level administrators. Vietnam was not just a matter of our general interest in international order warranting tentative, limited responses. It was escalated into a special American national interest projecting a deep, unwavering involvement until Communism was thwarted.

John F. Kennedy still did not like the idea. He could not stop the momentum, only slow it down. He approved the aid, but any reference to a commitment "of preventing the fall of South Vietnam to Communism" was omitted from the formal decision paper (NSAM 111). Shortly before Christmas 1961 two U.S. helicopter companies (33 H–21Cs, 400 men) arrived in South Vietnam,[34] and we were in the war.

We set out to (help) build South Vietnam's armed forces. In two years the number of U.S. advisers rose from 900 to 16,000, South Vietnamese military strength was approaching 225,000 men, and their cost to us exceeded $250 million. We set out to (help) pacify the countryside. It meant moving the rural population into "strategic" and "defended" hamlets where the villagers could be protected from the intimidations of the insurgents (not to mention any inclination of their own to abet the insurgency). By September 1962, of the projected 11,316 such hamlets, 3,225 had been built (with a population of 4,322,034) and another 2,217 were under construction. Viet Cong-initiated incidents reportedly were declining sharply, and Viet Cong defections were steadily increasing.

There were still grumblings in Washington, and also sharply critical press reports (for instance, by Neil Sheehan and, after September, by David Halberstam) from Saigon, but the highest levels of our government exuded optimism. In October the President had handled the Cuban missile crisis skillfully, and at year's end he was making statistically validatable progress in Vietnam. On May 6, 1963, Secretary of Defense Robert McNamara explained at a briefing in Honolulu that in his view the South Vietnamese government would gain control of the insurgency by 1965 and that U.S. aid could be reduced. Accordingly, he announced, he had decided to withdraw about 1,000 U.S. military personnel by December 1963.

Two days later the troubles really began. At the celebration of Buddha's 2,525th birthday Thich Tri Quang, a Buddhist leader from the North, denounced the Diem government as anti-Buddhist, then led an aroused mass of people to the radio station, where they demanded that the tape of his speech be broadcast. When troops arrived, a riot broke out. There were explosions—set by the Viet Cong, the government insisted, a claim not believed by the American correspondents.[35] A month later (June 11) an aged Buddhist monk got out of a car in Saigon, assumed the lotus position, two associates poured gasoline over him, he lit a match, and he was engulfed in flames. Given advance warning, the Associated Press correspondent and his photographer were there. Next morning all of America heard about it and saw the pictures. Madame Nhu, President Diem's sister-in-law and officially South Vietnam's First Lady, explained the spectacular event on NBC News: " . . . [The Buddhist leaders] have done nothing but barbecue a monk, and, at that, not even with self-sufficient means, since they had to import gasoline." Americans were not amused.

The Administration was shocked. The policy settled in 1961 suddenly became an issue—just when it seemed to be working so well. The adversaries were still very much the same, but their relative influence had changed. Those who argued that we could not win with Diem now felt vindicated. Those who insisted that we must work with him, and especially those who claimed to be proven right by the progress of 1962, were losing credibility. Few knew what the conflagration was about, but the notion that South Vietnam was a Buddhist country and that the Buddhist demonstrations revealed the resentment of a popular majority brutally repressed by a small Christian (Catholic) clique was easily accepted. Something had to be done.

The two-prong approach that emerged got us in deeper. First, the United States would tell the South Vietnamese outright what we wanted them to do. Specifically, President Diem was warned "that unless drastic action was taken to meet Buddhist demands promptly, the U.S. would be forced to state publicly its disassociation from the GVN [Government of Vietnam] on the Buddhist issue." Second, just in case our tough line did not produce the desired results, we would prepare to remove the president of the country and install another government more to our liking.

On July 4 a meeting was held in the Oval Office. The Secretary of State was absent; and significantly, in terms of future developments, so was the Vice President. President Kennedy was briefed on Vietnam by middle-level officials and the instigation of a coup was raised. Within the month a new Ambassador to South Vietnam was appointed: Henry Cabot Lodge, a distinguished Republican statesman, a scion of one of the nation's oldest and most prominent families. Now our mandarin will take care of their mandarin, American journalists joked in Saigon.

President Diem was temporizing. He became even more withdrawn and suspicious. He relied heavily, some say exclusively, on his brother Nhu, a man of action when in 1962 he headed the strategic hamlet program, and still a man of action when in 1963 he headed the internal security (special military and police) forces. On August 21, before Ambassador Lodge had reached Saigon, government forces struck. They moved into the pagodas and arrested about 1,400 Buddhist monks.[36] Quickly, on American advice and with American support, the generals disclaimed culpability. Nhu and his wife, who considered the self-immolation of a monk an occasion for levity, became easy targets of righteous indignation.[37]

August 24 was a Saturday. The Secretary of State was in New York; the Secretary of Defense and the Director of the CIA were away on vacation. President Kennedy was relaxing at Hyannis Port. A draft of instructions to Ambassador Lodge was brought to him. It included the following unambiguous and far-reaching paragraphs:

U.S. Government cannot tolerate situation in which power lies in Nhu's hands. Diem must be given chance to rid himelf of Nhu and his coterie and replace them with best military and political personalities available.

If, in spite of all your efforts, Diem remains obdurate and refuses, then we must face the possibility that Diem himself cannot be preserved.[38]

The American Ambassador was, moreover, instructed to inform the key military leaders privately that

U.S. would find it impossible to continue support GVN militarily and economically unless above steps are taken immediately which we recognize requires removal of Nhus from the scene. We wish to give Diem reasonable opportunity to remove Nhus, but if he remains obdurate, then we are prepared to accept the obvious implication that we can no longer support Diem. *You must also tell appropriate military commanders we will give them direct support in any interim period of breakdown central government mechanism.*[39]

The President approved the message. Lodge in Saigon was ready to go straight to the generals with our demands, without informing Diem. He would tell them that we were prepared to have Diem without the Nhus but that it was up to them whether to keep him.

President Diem's fate was sealed; it was only a question of time. At first the generals were reluctant, but U.S. pressure was relentless. In Saigon, Lodge was plotting strategy. In Washington the National Security Council debated the best ways to induce a coup. Robert Kennedy spoke up:

As he understood it we were there to help the people resisting a Communist take-over. The first question was whether a Communist take-over could be successfully resisted with any government. If it could not, now was the time to get out of Vietnam entirely, rather than waiting. If the answer was that it could, but not with a Diem-Nhu government as it was now constituted, we owed it to the people resisting Communism in Vietnam to give Lodge enough sanctions to bring changes that would permit successful resistance.[40]

Geopolitically Vietnam was still a place of little consequence. The insurgency was still no more than one of the lesser disturbances of international order. U.S. military forces there were still few in number and assigned mostly to training functions. Americans still knew little about the place and cared less. And yet, in the National Security Council no one questioned the Attorney General's formulation of only two alternatives—to get in with both feet or to get out altogether—and no one suggested the latter, not even for the sake of argument. As far as our highest policymakers were concerned, Vietnam had become of major (special) interest to us. To the dismay of our friends and the glee of our enemies, the only consideration was how to assure that our involvement succeeded. They could think of no other answer than more and deeper involvement. We would call the shots—literally and figuratively.

Early in September the President declared on television: "I don't agree with those who say we should withdraw. That would be a great mistake." Lodge cabled: "We are launched on a course from which there is no respectable turning back: the overthrow of the Diem Government. There is no turning back in part because U.S. prestige is already publicly committed to this end in large measure and will become more so as facts leak out."

Indeed, we did not turn back. Finally, on November 1, the generals acted.

At 4:30 P.M. President Diem called the American Ambassador on the phone. "Some units have made a rebellion and I want to know what is the attitude of the U.S." The Ambassador feigned ignorance: "I do not feel well enough informed to tell you. I have heard the shooting, but am not acquainted with all the facts. Also it is 4:40 A.M. in Washington and the U.S. Government cannot possibly have a view. . . . " All Lodge would do was express concern for Diem's physical safety. The coup proceeded. Diem and Nhu fled the palace. The next morning they called the generals and, on the assurance of safe conduct, agreed to surrender and revealed their location. They expected to be taken to a U.S. air base and evacuated to the United States. A military convoy came for them; they climbed into an armored personnel carrier; the convoy roared off to military headquarters. When it arrived there, "both bodies were stretched out on the ground. . . . Diem had been shot in the back of the head, Nhu had been stabbed in the chest and numerous times in the back of the head and in the back. The hands of both victims were tied behind their backs."[41]

It was a case of "accidental suicides," our new protégés declared. President Kennedy did not believe a word of it. The news brought tears to his eyes. He was deeply distressed by the sordid end of this not very inspiring and not particularly sensible episode of his administration. Still, no official expression of sorrow or regret was forthcoming—only a pretense that it was all a Vietnamese idea. Of course, the government knew better. The judgment of the Pentagon Papers was not too harsh, and its conclusion was directly on target.

For the military coup d'etat against Ngo Dinh Diem, the U.S. must accept its full share of responsibility. Beginning in August of 1963 we variously authorized, sanctioned and encouraged the coup efforts of the Vietnamese generals and offered full support for a successor government. In October we cut off aid to Diem in a direct rebuff, giving a green light to the generals. We maintained clandestine contact with them throughout the planning and execution of the coup and sought to review their operational plans and proposed new government. Thus, as the nine-year rule of Diem came to a bloody end, our complicity in his overthrow *heightened our responsibilities and our commitment in an essentially leaderless Vietnam.*[42]

Indeed, by the time of the tragedy we already were deeply involved. Some 16,657 U.S. troops had been sent there; 69 of them had been killed. After the coup we were trapped. Other countries, whether they wished us well or ill, knew what had happened. We had made Vietnam a test of our determination and, by implication, a test of the viability of decentralized world order.

SOUTH VIETNAM IS LINKED TO OUR VITAL INTEREST: FOREIGN POLICY LOSES CONTACT WITH DOMESTIC REALITY

We had a tragedy at home as well, one that brought tears to most Americans' eyes. By the time Ambassador Lodge returned home, we had a new president.

Lyndon Johnson had many things on his mind: he wanted to do many things for Americans, but making decisions on Vietnam was not one of them. He did not know much about the country; his foreign policy experience was limited. He went along when his advisers wanted him to reiterate (NSAM 273) that "it remains the central objective of the United States in Vietnam to assist the people and government of that country to win their contest against the externally directed and supported communist conspiracy." "I was not going to be the President who saw Southeast Asia go the way China went," he explained.[43] But he had profound doubts about the events and the methods of the recent past.

I believed the assassination of President Diem had created more problems for the Vietnamese than it solved. I saw very little evidence that men of experience and ability were available in Vietnam, ready to help lead their country. I was deeply concerned that more political turmoil might lie ahead in Saigon. . . .

I told my advisors that I thought we had spent too much time and energy trying to shape other countries in our image. It was too much to expect young and underdeveloped countries to establish peace and order against well-trained and disciplined guerrillas, to create modern democratic political institutions, and to organize strong economies all at the same time. We would assist them with all three jobs, I said, but the main objective at present was to help them resist those using force against them. As for nation-building, I said that I thought the Vietnamese, Thai, and other peoples of Asia knew far better than we did what sort of nations they wanted to build. We should not be too critical if they did not become thriving, modern, twentieth-century democracies in a week.[44]

Senior officials quickly followed his lead. The activist middle-level group started leaving government within a month.

It was President Johnson's firm intention to concentrate on domestic matters. The Civil Rights movement was gaining steam. Confrontations had become frequent and violent. Extremists and demagogues were popping up all over. Fortunately for America, there were also responsible Black leaders. A voice of reason and peace, the voice of Martin Luther King, Jr., was heard over the land. He deserved help and recognition. Not by words but by action. President Johnson, the masterful parliamentarian, was guiding through Congress the first Civil Rights Act (1964) in almost a century and was preparing to follow it up with the Voting Rights Act (1965). It took practically all his time. He wished "that war" would go away; but it would not.

In fact, South Vietnam was not better off without Diem. It was a mess. The coup leaders lasted for less than three months. There followed another coup, then another, and another with distressing regularity. Progress in the struggle for the minds and hearts of the people, primarily statistical in the past, became largely illusory. The "strategic hamlets" were a failure. Time and again the President raised the option "to pack up and go home," only to be convinced (without much difficulty) by his advisers that

The American investment is very large, and American responsibility is a fact of life which is palpable in the atmosphere of Asia, and even elsewhere. The international prestige of the United States, and a substantial part of our influence are directly at risk in Vietnam. There is no way of unloading the burden on the Vietnamese themselves and there is no way of negotiating ourselves out of Vietnam which offers any serious promise at present.[45]

Whenever President Johnson hesitated or tried to insulate himself from events in Vietnam, the Communists escalated. Confrontation, getting the United States even more deeply involved, was evidently what they wanted. Just before the Democratic National Convention reports reached Washington that North Vietnamese torpedo boats had attacked U.S. destroyers in the Gulf of Tonkin. Subsequent investigations raised some doubts about whether the incident actually occurred, though not whether the U.S. Navy personnel on the spot believed they were under attack. And there are no doubts that two days before the presidential election Communist forces hit our airbase at Bien Hoa. Six planes were destroyed, 5 Americans were killed, and 76 were wounded. On Christmas Eve, U.S. officers' billets were bombed. In February 1965, while the President deliberated on our future course, they attacked American installations in Pleiku, destroying aircraft, killing 7 and wounding 109, and then assaulted the barracks in Qui Nhon, killing 23 and wounding 21 American soldiers.

Faced with such strategically timed dramatic challenges, President Johnson was left no choice but to respond. But foreign policy was a weak link in his broad range of political experience; he needed help. President Eisenhower, visiting the White House on February 17, 1965, urged a clear decision, one way or the other. If we decided to deny Southeast Asia to the Communists, he cautioned, we would have to share this purpose with other nations of the Western world, "and they should be brought to acknowledge and support this effort." We would have to engage in a massive information campaign in Vietnam and throughout the world. More than that, President Eisenhower "stressed strongly that the U.S. Government must tell our own people just what we are doing in the area, i.e., what our policy is, and what course of action we are following." In any case we must be firm. We cannot negotiate from weakness. We have learned that Munichs win nothing. Indeed, "the greatest danger in his judgement in the present situation is that the Chinese get the idea that we will go just so far and no further in terms of the level of war we would conduct. That would be the beginning of the end, since they would know all they had to do was go further than we do."[46]

President Johnson's official advisers counselled restraint and moderation. He himself did not feel sufficiently confident for clear-cut action. He felt much more confortable in the middle of the road. We should try to persuade Ho Chi Minh, he thought, to stop underwriting the insurrection. He waved the stick. In the South we would use forces in the field to demonstrate that a Communist victory was impossible. In the North we would use airpower to make the point that an aggressor can enjoy no sanctuary. But it would not be a very big stick. Just large enough to hold our own in the South and not large enough to cause crippling damage in the North. And he forever dangled a very large carrot. We would negotiate without preconditions, we would be satisfied with an independent and neutral South Vietnam, and we would be willing to contribute to the economic development of the area and have North Vietnam share in a billion-dollar program.[47]

One problem was that Ho Chi Minh was a devout believer in his cause. He was neither intimidated nor visibly tempted. The trouble also was that the cost of holding our own in the South was rising steadily and sharply. At first our troops were there for training purposes, then their mission was expanded to include guarding our facilities, and further expanded to permit "active and aggressive" patrolling. By June 1965 permission was granted to assist Vietnamese forces under attack when no other reserves were available. Toward the end of the month permission was granted to commit U.S. combat forces "independently" to search and destroy. As late as mid April 1965 there were 33,000 U.S. troops in South Vietnam. In July the President decided to "give our commanders in the field the men and supplies they say they need."[48] The massive buildup commenced. By October 1967, 480,000 men, 40 percent of our combat-ready divisions, half of our tactical air power, and a third of our naval strength were waging a counterinsurgency effort in a far distant country about which the American people knew nothing. Our casualties were running at 1,000 dead and 5,500 wounded per month. Meanwhile the annual dollar cost passed $25 billion.

Faced with such figures and a steady reporting in words and pictures from the field, the American people became interested. They wanted an explanation; they wanted assurance. It was too much for President Johnson (and perhaps for any president) to explain the sacrifices he asked in terms of the actual value of South Vietnam to us, that is, in terms of our general interest in international order. So he inflated the stakes. He justified the enormous American effort as a support of our special interests (a loyal ally), indeed, as a farsighted, long-term strategy to protect our vital interest. The domino theory once again became the rationale of our strategy. The Secretary of State warned:

Let me say as solemnly as I can that those who would place in question the credibility of the pledged word of the United States under our mutual security treaties would *subject this nation to mortal danger*. If any who would be our adversary should suppose that our treaties are a bluff, or will be abandoned if the going gets tough, the result could be catastrophe for all mankind.[49]

And the Administration, through announcements and pronouncements, offered reassurance. We were making continued military progress, declared the Secretary of Defense in June 1966. The first quarter's operations "exceeded our expectations."[50] In July the President himself reported that our troops were giving excellent account of themselves. As a result the enemy was losing ten men for every one of ours. Between 15 and 20 percent of their troops now were 12–to–16–year–old boys.[51] In August, General William Westmoreland, the U.S. military commander in South Vietnam, declared: "A Communist military take-over of

South Vietnam is no longer improbable. As long as the United States and our brave allies are in the field it is impossible.''[52] By November, General Earle Wheeler, Chairman of the Joint Chiefs of Staff, publicly reported a series of successful operations to the President. "The war," he concluded, "continues in a very favorable fashion. General Westmoreland retains the initiative and in every operation to date he has managed to defeat the enemy.''[53] And so the barrage of good news continued. A year later, things were better still. "I have never been more encouraged in my four years in Vietnam,''[54] announced General Westmoreland.

Behind the scenes, however, the administration was rent by doubts and incessant debates. There was, in truth, little confidence that progress was being made. Enemy losses were high, but their resupply seemed endless. Our losses were getting high, but few thought the patience of the people was endless. In the judgment of Alain Enthoven, the Pentagon's chief systems analyst, enemy (Viet Cong/North Vietnam Army) losses remained below their replacement capabilities. *"On the most optimistic basis,"* he warned the Secretary of Defense (May 1, 1967), 200,000 more Americans would raise their weekly losses to about 3,700, or about 400 a week more than they could stand, *In theory, we'd then wipe them out in ten years.*[55]

Widespread policy debates among presidential advisers are natural enough, even desirable. It was extraordinary, though, how long they lasted and how detailed they became. The bombing of North Vietnam was constantly under review, categories of bombing targets were argued endlessly. Should an airbase be bombed? Was it too far from the battlefield? Should POL (petroleum, oil, and lubricants) targets be bombed? Were they too close to the cities? Should a power plant be the target? Was it too close to China? Should a port be a target? Would Soviet ships be hit? On and on and on. The problem was, President Johnson wanted desperately to do the right thing for his country, but he did not know what that was.[56] He desperately sought a consensus of those he thought should know. And he found it—in appearance at formal meetings. But below the surface, not very much below the surface, disputes in every direction went on and on—and so did the President's uncertainty and helplessness.

Most Americans really wanted to believe their government, but their common sense was getting strained. They were unclear about why we were in Vietnam. They had never understood the application of the domino theory—it seemed like an unbelievably long row of distant countries would have to fall to Communism before it would come to one they could identify. They could not imagine how events in Vietnam could become a "mortal danger" to the United States. And Americans were dubious about just what we were doing. They were not reassured when official reports of progress were regularly accompanied by requests for additional young Americans being sent over there.

Their attitude toward the conflict in distant Southeast Asia, moreover, was complicated by fundamental political changes at home. The government, under the President's skillful and determined leadership, was steering through Congress civil rights legislation to right ancient wrongs. They were being righted, but not without turmoil in American society. About the same time television emerged as a major political actor. Coaxial cables now linked stations in every part of the country. Network news, and only network news, could bring pictures of events "live" into most homes. It was a heady experience of opportunites and power for the Media, not always led by the best and the brightest, but invariably attracted by the most dramatic, which it singled out and exaggerated. It was a welcome and somewhat bewildering experience for the people, who were not always able to put the emotionally evocative reports in their proper perspective. All along, the baby-boom generation was growing up, crowding and overloading our schools and trying hard to find its self-respect. Our young people had become afraid. Tens of thousands were sent to fight in a place called Vietnam, a place about which their teachers knew little and they knew less. Many of them—too many of them—had to die there. College students were deferred but could not help noticing that those who did have to go included a disproportionate number of Blacks. They were not too anxious to fight this particular "social injustice" by volunteering, but they felt guilty—all the more so. Gradually it all blended into a volatile brew that only needed a spark.

Actually, some progress was being made on the battlefield. The insurgents and the North Vietnamese infiltrators were suffering heavy casualties. Relations between China and the Soviet Union, North Vietnam's two great Communist friends, were becoming difficult. The President of the United States had dug in his heels. On the defensive, largely isolated by his advisers (especially by his National Security Adviser), he would not budge. At the current rate of attrition it would not take ten years before North Vietnam was exhausted; it would take much less. Sufficiently less for the American will to prevail? North Vietnam had to do something, something that might ignite U.S. public opinion. On January 31, 1968, during the Chinese New Year (Tet) celebrations, the Communists launched a dramatic broad-scale offensive. Some of the targets were military: they attacked U.S. bases. Most were political: they penetrated urban centers and captured some. They infiltrated Saigon, even invaded the American Embassy compound. When government forces were withdrawn from the rural areas to help out in the cities, Communist cadres quickly moved into the hamlets.

The American response was quick and fierce. Cities and towns were vigorously defended; within a month those which had fallen to the enemy were recaptured. Khe San (a Marine Corps base projected by propaganda as the American Dien Bien Phu) held and was relieved. The U.S. forces suffered heavy casualties— about 1,100 killed and 5,500 wounded. The cities suffered more. While the Communists held Hue, they summarily executed 300 local officials and prominent citizens and dumped their bodies into a mass grave. When the Americans fought their way back, their firepower devastated much of the ancient capital. It was the Communist insurgents, however, who suffered most. Estimates range from 33,000 to 45,000 killed. In any case, after the Tet offensive the Viet Cong ceased to play a significant military role. Thereafter the fighting was carried on primarily by North Vietnamese troops.[57]

Scholars may debate whether the Tet offensive was a military surprise to our government, and a good case can be made that for our armed forces the outcome was a military victory. What is abundantly clear, however, is that for most Americans, the Communist attack was a wholly unexpected shock, and for the Administration it was a major political explosion. All our domestic problems, all our international problems, suddenly converged into a common focus: Vietnam. In Congress and in classrooms old doubts were recounted with a heightened moral tone and with more resonance. Then Walter Cronkite, anchorman of "CBS Evening News," supplied the refrain. Not unlike Professor Galbraith some five years earlier, without any expertise in the subject after a short visit in the area, he solemnly pronounced his verdict on the air: "It is increasingly clear to this reporter that the only way out, then, will be to negotiate, not as victors, but as honorable people who lived up to their pledge to defend democracy, and did the best they could."[58] At Harvard, Professor Galbraith, so quick to demand that we get so deeply involved in South Vietnam as to conspire to overthrow its government, now was ready to leave it. To those who asked just how we could withdraw our troops in 30 days, he had a droll answer: "Some by sea and some by air."

The events in Vietnam and their consequences on the home front distressed the President. Even so, he was willing to hold the line. Just three days after it had begun, he pronounced the Tet offensive "a military failure for the enemy." He offered reassurance. When at a press conference he was asked about the possibility of additional deployment, he answered with confidence: "There is not *anything* in *any* of the developments that would justify the press in leaving the impression that any great new overall moves are going to be made that would involve substantial movements in that direction."[59] But then something incredible happened.

With the American people still in shock and the noise of opposition rising to crescendo, General Earle Wheeler, Chairman of the Joint Chiefs of Staff, a man who persistently and consistently filled the record with optimistic evaluations, just home from a post-Tet inspection trip, endorsed General Westmoreland's request for reinforcement: for about 200,000 more American men and who knows how many more American dollars! It was the straw that broke the camel's back. The President, beleaguered and distraught, was nobody's fool. He ordered an "A to Z reassessment." He wanted to know, and he used no tender euphemisms, not whether 200,000 more troops should be sent to Vietnam but whether the existing policy was actually tenable in the first place. And the President did more. He had already brought in a new Secretary of Defense, the politically savvy Clark Clifford. He now turned to Dean Acheson, the Secretary of State "present at the creation" of a new, decentralized world order. Acheson promptly assembled his own think tank and on March 15 gave the President his findings at a luncheon when the two men were completely alone.[60]

Acheson's advice remains top secret. We have some idea about Clifford's recommendations. He put it differently, but the implications were the same. As a test of American general interest in decentralized world order, the Vietnam involvement was a mistake. Its artificial inflation to the level of our special interest and then to our vital interest was a disaster: nothing short of a gross imposition upon our democratic system. In any case, whatever the prospects of ultimate military victory, there was no way to validate the President's position before the national elections in November, and certainly no way to do so before the Democratic National Convention three months earlier.

On Sunday, March 31, 1968, President Johnson addressed the nation on television. He had made his decision: no increase in U.S. forces in Vietnam. We would abandon the effort to gain military victory in the South and would no longer attempt to intimidate (through bombing) in the North. We would rely entirely on negotiation. Finally, he would forgo any further personal political ambition. "Accordingly, I shall not seek, and will not accept, the nomination of my Party for another term as your President."

Surely this was one of the most dramatic speeches on American television. It meant the tragic end to the political career of a great American, *a leader with a vision of the "Great Society"* and the effective champion of social justice. It also meant the end of our quest for a system of decentralized world order. For, in effect, it let every nation know, whether it wished us well or ill, that we shall *not* pay any price, we shall *not* bear any burden, we shall *not* meet any hardship, we shall *not* support any friend, we shall *not* oppose any foe to assure the survival and success of liberty.

NOTES

1. Dean Acheson, *Present at the Creation* (New York: W. W. Norton, 1969), p. 150.

2. *New York Times*, February 10, 1946, p. 30.

3. Kennan remembered the cause of his letter differently: as an inquiry about Soviet reluctance to join the World Bank and International Monetary Fund. George F. Kennan, *Memoirs, 1925–1950* (Boston: Little, Brown, 1967), p. 292.

4. Ibid., pp. 549–51.

5. Acheson, *Present at the Creation*, p. 151.

6. See, for example, Stanley Hoffmann, *Primacy or World Order: American Foreign Policy Since the Cold War* (New York: McGraw-Hill, 1978): John L. Gaddis, *Strategies of Containment* (New York: Oxford University Press, 1982).

7. Ranking Republican on the Senate Foreign Relations Committee.

8. Acheson, *Present at the Creation*, p. 219.

9. Ibid., p. 233. Emphasis added.

10. Harry Truman, *Memoirs*, vol. 2 (Garden City, N.Y.: Doubleday, 1956), pp. 226–27, 233.

11. For example, (a) technical administrative expertise plus police force does not add up to political legitimacy; or (b) economic growth does not necessarily produce political stability.

12. Acheson, *Present at the Creation*, p. 405.

13. Ibid., p. 411.

14. Speech to the Council on Foreign Relations, January 12, 1954, in *Department of State Bulletin* 30 (January 25, 1954), p. 108.

15. John Foster Dulles, "Policy for Security and Peace," *Foreign Affairs* 32, no. 3 (April 1954), p. 359.

16. Speech to the Associated Press, New York, April 23, 1956, in *Department of State Bulletin*, 34 (April 30, 1954), p. 708.

17. *New York Times*, January 21, 1961, p. 8.

18. Nikita S. Khrushchev, speech to the Higher Party School of the Institute of Marxism-Leninism of the Central Committee of the CPSU, January 6, 1961, quoted in Alvin Z. Rubinstein, *The Foreign Policy of the Soviet Union*, 3rd ed. (New York: Random House, 1972), p. 268.

19. Memorandum from President Roosevelt to Secretary of State Cordell Hull, January 24, 1944. Quoted in United States, House of Representatives, Committee on Armed Services, *United States-Vietnam Relations 1945–1967* (Washington, D.C.: U.S. Government Printing Office, 1971), vol. 1, p. A–14. Much of the data and analysis of our Vietnam involvement are based on the above source, popularly known as the Pentagon Papers. Therefore, unless otherwise indicated, all citations come from this elaborate study.

20. Ho Chi Minh, "The Path Which Led Me to Leninism," quoted in ibid., p. IC–33.

21. United States, House of Representatives, Committee on Armed Services, *United States-Vietnam Relations 1945–1967*, vol. 1, pp. IA-31.

22. Ibid., pp. IIA–48.

23. Ibid., pp. IIB–6.

24. Ibid., pp. IIB–10.

25. *New York Times*, May 12, 1954, p. 1.

26. At one point (1945) Ho offered him a cabinet post. Diem asked him just one question: "Why did you kill my brother?" It was a mistake, Ho admitted, but could not be avoided. Diem walked out. Russ Braley, *Bad News, the Foreign Policy of the New York Times* (Chicago: Regnery Gateway, 1984), p. 192.

27. This is an example of American ethnocentrism, and we should learn how to avoid it. President Ngo Dinh Diem's family name was *Ngo*. His generational name (shared by all the children of his parents) was *Dinh*. His first name was *Diem*. But because in the West we put family names last, he was referred to by our media, public officials, and even scholars as President Diem.

28. France, in turn, missed no chance to agitate against Diem in Washington. United States, House of Representatives, Committee on Armed Services, *United States-Vietnam Relations 1945–1967*, vol. i, p. IV.A-3.1.

29. The United States opposed elections because it feared a Ho Chi Minh victory. China and the Soviet Union did not press the matter. Indeed, in 1957 the Soviet Union proposed that both North and South Vietnam be admitted to the United Nations.

30. United States, House of Representatives, Committee on Armed Services, *United States-Vietnam Relations 1945–1967*, vol. 2, p. IVA–5, Table 3.13.

31. Estimated at 5,000 armed Viet Minh and 3,000 political cadres. Ibid., vol. 2, p. IVA–5, Table 13.7.

32. He did not receive the Galbraith cable until November 24.

33. United States, House of Representatives, Committee on Armed Services, *United States-Vietnam Relations 1945–1967*, vol. 2, pp. B–1.125–33.

34. *New York Times*, December 11, 1961, p. 21.

35. Braley, *Bad News*, p. 214.

36. But not the leader; Thich Tri Quang escaped and was given sanctuary in the U.S. Embassy.

37. Indeed, Nhu went to great lengths "to isolate the U.S. from an accurate assessment during the operation." He had the telephone lines to the Embassy and the homes of all senior U.S. personnel cut shortly after the raids got under way.

38. United States, House of Representatives, Committee on Armed Services, *United States-Vietnam Relations 1945–1967*, vol. 3, p. IVB–5.15.

39. Ibid. Emphasis added.

40. Ibid., p. IVB–5.25.

41. Marguerite Higgens, *Our Vietnam Nightmare* (New York: Harper and Row, 1965), pp. 218–19.

42. United States, House of Representatives, Committee on Armed Services, *United States-Vietnam Relations 1945–1967*, vol. 3, p. IVB–5.8. Emphasis added.

43. David Halberstam, *The Best and the Brightest* (New York: Random House, 1969), p. 298.

44. Lyndon Baines Johnson, *The Vantage Point, Perspectives of the Presidency 1963–1969* (New York: Holt, Rinehart and Winston, 1971), pp. 44–45. Richard Nixon held very similar views. It was, he said a week before the coup, a choice "not between President Diem and somebody better . . . [but] between Diem and somebody infinitely worse."

45. Report by "Mac Bundy and his specialists," quoted in Johnson, *The Vantage Point*, p. 126.

46. "Memorandum of Meeting with the President, 17 February 1965" by Lt. Gen. A. J. Goodpaster. Eisenhower Library, Abilene, Kansas.

47. President Johnson's speech at Johns Hopkins University on April 7, 1965. *New York Times*, April 8, 1965, p. 1.

48. Johnson, *The Vantage Point*, p. 149. A year later the president wanted to be sure that troop reinforcements were sufficiently accelerated "so that General Westmoreland can feel assured that he has all the men he needs as soon as possible." The secretary of defense checked with the joint chiefs, who (in their own jargon) reported that they were getting all they needed.

49. *New York Times*, October 13, 1967, p. 14. Emphasis added.

50. Ibid., June 12, 1966, p. 1.

51. Ibid., June 21, 1966, p. 18.

52. Ibid., August 15, 1966, p. 1.

53. Ibid., November 11, 1966, p. 18.

54. Ibid., November 16, 1966, p. 1.

55. United States, House of Representatives, Committee on Armed Services, *United States-Vietnam Relations 1945–1967*, vol. 5, p. IVC–6.122. Emphasis added.

56. All this time he was impressed by the dangers of "a Djakarta-Hanoi-Peking-Pyongyang axis." Johnson, *The Vantage Point*, p. 136.

57. Ibid., p. 382; Harry G. Summers, *On Strategy, A Critical Analysis of the Vietnam War* (Novato, Calif.: Presidio Press, 1982), p. 138; Townsend Hoopes, *The Limits of Intervention* (New York: David McKay, 1969), p. 142.

58. Some years later David Halberstam noted with some satisfaction: "It was the first time in American history that a war had been declared over by a commentator." Gary Paul Gates, *Air Time: The Inside Story of CBS News* (New York: Harper and Row, 1978), p. 211.

59. Johnson, *The Vantage Point*, p. 383.

60. The luncheon took place just three days after the New Hampshire primary, where Senator Eugene McCarthy received 42.4 percent of the votes against President Johnson's 49.5 percent write-in votes.

11

DÉTENTE

Thus Vietnam should teach us fundamental lessons about the intertwining of international relations and domestic politics. First, it should teach us that the traditional constitutional preeminence of the chief executive in foreign policy notwithstanding, any projection of U.S. forces into deadly quarrels abroad requires massive public support at home. Second, that the emergence of the United States as a global superpower notwithstanding, such support will be difficult to mobilize on issues involving our special interests and extremely difficult to mobilize when only our general interest in international order is at stake. Third, even when mass support is mobilized, it may prove to be a fickle consort. Its ardor may cool suddenly; unexpectedly it may feel betrayed, reverse itself, and vent its fury. It requires constant care to assure broad congressional cooperation and the persistence of a concurrent majority among the opinion-leading elements of our society. In this the exposition of a general strategy and an explanation of how specific initiatives fit into this strategy are likely to prove helpful, and so will a straightforward, honest accounting. On the other hand, any shading or covering up of evidence is a very hazardous venture. It will inevitably be found out, quite often much sooner than expected. In foreign affairs, where the patriotism of the American people is engaged, they want very much to trust and be proud of their government. They do not like at all to find that they have been misled. And lies, in our democracy, are explosives with very short fuses.

These, however, were really lessons for the future. In 1968 the issue was not whether we should intervene militarily in a distant land. We had already done so. It was not how to mobilize and sustain mass support behind a particular force projection. Public support had already been lost. The issue was not how to avoid future mistakes but how to mitigate the consequences of past mistakes and how to recover from them. Our international position had visibly deteriorated.

American prestige, at impressive heights just a decade earlier, had suffered several shocks. International order, never very sturdy, was in shambles. All in all, a rather unsatisfactory condition.

Talking of options, it was of course possible to chuck it all in disgust. We could be content to concentrate on our borders, and perhaps concern ourselves with people we like and governments worthy of our approval. It also was possible to continue to pretend that we would pay any price and bear any burden for international order. But the new realities of our external and internal environments of foreign policy decision making reduced these options to just talk. The question was: What could we do?

THE FIFTH TRY: A RETURN TO POWER POLITICS

National elections brought a new President. Richard Nixon had extraordinary talent, experience, and interest in international affairs. He served as Vice President under President Eisenhower and could observe him more or less closely in action. But his mentor was John Foster Dulles. There was no question now of decentralized world order. Ideals are useful; but the real world with real peace and real war, Nixon was—and apparently still is—convinced, rested on power. First, he selected Henry Kissinger, a brilliant academic with a keen appreciation of the practical and a marvelous sense of humor, as his chief foreign policy adviser. Kissinger, whose Ph.D dissertation was a masterly analysis of the Congress of Vienna, was (and apparently still is) convinced that there are only two alternatives for international order: hegemony or the balance of power. Then President Nixon set out to restore American position in the world and to construct "a framework of peace."[1]

By 1969 it had become perfectly clear that the United States could not impose its preferred pattern of global political arrangement. At the same time, evidence of widespread political instability throughout the world made some initiative mandatory. Almost every month a "government" was overthrown in Africa, Asia, or Latin America (not to mention Southern Europe). What made the situation especially perilous was the role of the Soviet Union. While the United States invested massive effort and wealth in building *order,*—political order within the frail newly independent (postcolonial) states and some semblance of order on the international scale—the prime purpose of Soviet policy was to accelerate *change*. Its doctrines of "world revolution" and "wars of liberation" provided ideological justification; its military assistance programs to Communist cadres and its diplomatic opposition to any and all U.S. initiatives lent support to revolutionary movements on the national and international scale.

President Roosevelt had hoped desperately to avoid such radical polarization. President Truman could find no way out of it. The question was: Had conditions changed? Stalin's police state was denounced by Khrushchev and noticeably ameliorated by Brezhnev. The differences between the values of Soviet Communism and American democracy were still very deep and the tensions were

Figure 5
Instability of Bipolarity

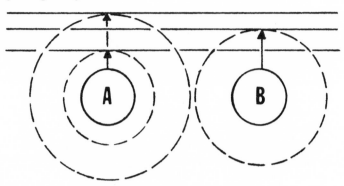

severe, but not necessarily more so than were the differences and tensions between czarist Russia and parliamentary Britain at Vienna some 150 years earlier.
By 1969 the rise of their military power may have ameliorated Soviet anxieties
that others could push them around. The Soviet system may have matured
sufficiently to recognize its vested interest in peace. If so, a stable international
order could emerge from a return to old-fashioned balance-of-power politics
by the superpowers. In any case, given the existing distressing disarray, it was
worth a try.

In order for balance-of-power politics to be built into a system, however, two
major conditions had to be met. First, the balance, while dynamic, must be
stable. A brief diversion into theory may be helpful on this point. A bipolar
system, a pattern with two groups of major powers (as in the nineteenth century)
or two superpowers (as in the second half of the twentieth) facing each other,
is inherently unstable. Predictably, each side (A,B) will be vigorously (and
perhaps covertly) striving to gain a decisive edge. There is no systemic restraint.
(See Figure 5.) The system, however, can be stabilized by a independent major
power (C), one that is significant but not quite in the same category with the
two superpowers, and one whose vital interest requires that neither of the superpowers should gain hegemony. (See Figure 6.) If either side appears to be
gaining an advantage, this "holder of the balance" will shift and join the other
pole, and together they will overwhelm the excessively ambitious power. Since
this prospect is both predictable and undesirable, it will serve as a restraint and
keep the system in rough equilibrium.

Thus the question became acute: Was there a suitable "holder of the balance"
and, as a corollary, could we integrate it into the system? India was independent
but hardly a major power. Britain, which played this role so admirably in the
nineteenth century, was now a U.S. ally, and its power was visibly declining.
The Russians feared the Germans, but with Germany divided and each part
closely attached to one of the superpowers, that would not work either. There

Figure 6
Stabilization by the Holder of Balance

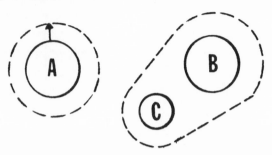

was one power that would be well suited: China had become independent of the Soviet Union, and the Russians were very much worried about it. The problem was that relations between China and the United States were almost nonexistent, and what little there was, was bad.

President Nixon set out to solve the problem. He had some assets: the unmeasurable talent in his National Security Council; his own skills, reinforced by the tendency of others (especially his enemies) to underestimate him; and his reputation as an implacable anti-Communist. Meanwhile, the Chinese had become concerned about their military vulnerability. They needed modern weapons; they needed a diplomatic counterweight to their northern, now not altogether "fraternal," neighbor. Their prime minister, Chou En-lai, was by all reports a very astute global strategist. It took some doing, false starts through Warsaw and Bucharest, but by 1971, with the help of Pakistan, the great diplomatic coup of our time was in motion. China would fill the key role of the holder of the balance.

There remained, however, a second condition for international order based on a balance between the superpowers: the credibility of their power. No one doubted the enormous power of the Soviet Union and that it was prepared to use it. No one doubted the enormous power of the United States, but would we use it? The doubts were persistent. How could a superpower become bogged down in a distant, highly complex but essentially third-rate local conflict in Vietnam? We had a serious credibility problem. How could the Soviet Union respect us and the Chinese rely on us for counterbalance when we were visibly pushed around by a third-class state like North Vietnam? For the United States to play its proper role in balance-of-power politics, it would have to regain its credibility and emerge from Vietnam with honor—a challenge which surpassed that of the "opening to China," and one which President Nixon also set out to meet.

It was an awesome task. The domestic environment was in an uproar. After a momentary lull, from every part of the country, from every element of society, people were screaming imprecations and expletives, demanding every kind of action from him regarding Vietnam. Through all the noise he had to keep a steady course. It is a wonder that he could do so. Fortunately, here, too, President Nixon had significant assets: foreign assets. Our allies in Western Europe had respect for him. More important, though, was the change in the Soviet Union and China. While in the past they saw the American model of decentralized world order as inimical to their national interest, the idea now advanced by the Americans (Nixon and Kissinger) of managing global affairs through a partnership (albeit a competitive partnership) of superpowers was decidedly to their liking. So much so that it was worth it to them that the United States should restore its credibility in Vietnam.

Soon fundamental international changes were in progress with profound repercussions throughout the globe, but especially so in Vietnam. For within a framework of a decentralized world order, North Vietnam and South Vietnam mattered. They had value of their own—indeed, in the rhetoric they were equal in their sovereignty with the major powers. Not any more. They were reduced to means, no more than pawns in power politics. Military policy options consistently rejected by President Johnson as inappropriate now became available. The President was free to press the war aggressively: to bomb North Vietnam, to search and destroy in the South, and even to invade Cambodia and Laos.

Neither Congress nor the people had any idea what was actually taking place. President Nixon chose not to enlighten them. North Vietnam was the first to recognize its brutally altered circumstances. In the face of President Nixon's evident determination, Hanoi decided to force the hand of her increasingly uncertain allies. Late in March 1972 it launched a massive invasion across the Demilitarized Zone; within a month it expanded its offensive to the Central Highlands.[2] Then, in a "brutal" secret negotiating session with Henry Kissinger, after a harangue of quotes from American domestic sources and after reciting repeatedly his "epic poem of American treachery and Vietnamese heroism," the chief North Vietnamese negotiator "laid down terms." President Thieu of South Vietnam would have to resign, and the remaining "Saigon Administration" would have to dismantle its military and police forces.[3] If the Nixon administration would give in, that was fine. Possibly American domestic opposition would compel it to do so. But if the United States chose to resist and fight back, surely the Chinese and the Soviets would have no alternative but to dramatically demonstrate their fraternal (Communist) solidarity.

Nixon, however, was made of sterner stuff. On May 8 he announced his decision. He ordered the total military isolation of North Vietnam by U.S. forces. All entrances of its ports would be mined; all internal waterways would be interdicted; all rail and other communications would be cut off. The President then made it perfectly clear to "other nations especially those which are allied with North Vietnam. The actions I have announced tonight are not directed against you." He closed his television address to the American people by asking for their support. "The world," he said, "will be watching."[4]

The congressional (Democratic) leadership, television commentators, newspaper editors and columnists, and academic experts joined in a chorus of disapproval. The North Vietnamese could not have expected better. But they were to be sadly disappointed by their allies. Surely China would feel betrayed by so massive a U.S. military action so soon after Nixon's historic visit. Surely the Soviet Union would angrily cancel the summit meeting scheduled for later that month. But the Chinese now saw the geopolitical advantages of balance-of-power politics in which the United States played a vigorous role. They saw no benefit in an American paper tiger. They protested, but only in the mildest terms, and did not challenge the U.S. blockade. The Soviet Union also saw the geopolitical advantages in a détente with the United States.[5] Official Soviet news reports were restrained. TASS even called special attention to the President's assurance that U.S. military operations were not directed at any other country. On May 10, just two days after the announcement, the Soviet Ambassador called on the President's National Security Adviser. The conversation was low key, but the position was most revealing.

Dobrynin was a good chess player. At the end of the meeting, out of the blue, he asked whether the President had as yet decided on receiving Trade Minister Patolichev (who at the time was visiting Washington). I was a little startled by the request; it could only mean that the Soviet leaders had decided to fall in with our approach of business as usual. Trying to match the Ambassador's studied casualness, I allowed that I probably would be able to arrange a meeting in the Oval Office. Playing a little chess myself, I mentioned that it was customary on these occasions to invite press photographers. Dobrynin thought this highly appropriate.[6]

Of course the meeting was arranged, and pictures of a senior Soviet delegation chatting amiably with the president, who had just closed off North Vietnam from its military supplies, were there for all to see. Evidently "all the major powers—the United States, China and the Soviet Union—were painting on a canvas larger than Indochina."[7]

The summit took place as scheduled. Treaties between the United States and the Soviet Union were signed. President Nixon was proud and pleased; Chairman Brezhnev was beaming, even playful. The Cold War was receding into the past; the era of détente was about to begin. And with it returned the international order of balance-of-power politics.

There still remained the matter of Vietnam, now a manageable nuisance. The North Vietnamese had read the signs, and just to make sure, after the conclusion of the summit Nikolai Podgorny, the President of the Soviet Union, flew to Hanoi to explain the developments. His exposition was received with "an attentive attitude, Brezhnev reported to Nixon."[8] When Henry Kissinger met the North Vietnamese negotiators on July 19, the whole atmosphere had changed. Gone were the ideological harangues, the studied discourtesies, the arrogant setting of terms. Le Duc Tho was polite, subtly deferential, eager to conciliate.

Serious negotiations were finally under way. At the next meeting (August 1) signs of a sense of urgency on Hanoi's side became discernible. Significant movement entirely by the Communists toward a settlement was taking place. September 15 brought further advance and their request for longer sessions. Next time the meetings lasted two days (September 26–27) and brought further concessions, followed by three days (October 8–10) and a basic agreement.

It was an extraordinary achievement. The terms were far better than congressional leaders, media commentators, and academic experts expected, and far, far better than the terms for which they would have settled. The South Vietnamese government was not dismantled; indeed, its military and police forces remained intact. "We thought with reason," observed Henry Kissinger, "that Saigon, generously armed and supported by the United States would be able to deal with moderate violations of the agreements; that the United States would stand by to enforce the agreement and punish major violations. . . . "[9] There were, however, concessions. Some, involving the designation of a few joint commissions, were symbolic; one was substantial. Communist forces, including North Vietnamese units, were conceded areas of control within South Vietnam. In fact, they had been holding these areas for some time. We could not dislodge them. All the same, their recognition was a visible violation of South Vietnamese sovereignty.

Looking at it from the perspective of a United States engaged in great power politics, it was no big deal. From the perspective of the President and his National Security Adviser, who were convinced that come next spring Congress would cut off appropriations for the war,[10] it was a pretty good deal. But the President of South Vietnam, General Nguyen Van Thieu, did not notice, or would not recognize, the changed American and international realities. His perspective was that of decentralized world order and of the sovereign equality of states. In those terms the U.S. concessions were intolerable.

When Kissinger arrived in Saigon to brief the Vietnamese on the negotiations, he carried with him a letter from the President that had the frank conclusion: "I believe we have no reasonable alternative but to accept this agreement." Nixon cabled instructions "that if there appeared to be no chance of obtaining Thieu's agreement, Kissinger should inform him that we would have to consider making a separate agreement with the enemy." Then quickly followed another letter to be delivered to the Vietnamese president, which included the dire warning:

Were you to find the agreement to be unacceptable at this point and the other side were to reveal the extraordinary limits to which it has gone in meeting demands put upon them, it is my judgment that your decision would have the most serious effects upon my ability to continue to provide support for you and for the government of South Vietnam.[11]

American pressure was enormous and obvious. All the same, the president of the small country and a government that since Ngo Dinh Diem had become totally dependent on us refused to act the pawn in a great power game. General Thieu rejected an agreement made by the United States, a superpower and ally, and supported (at least tacitly) by the Soviet Union, another superpower, and

China, the preeminent regional power.[12] He insisted that any settlement must contain absolute guarantees of the Demilitarized Zone, complete withdrawal of North Vietnamese forces, and the self-determination of South Vietnam.[13] After all, was not building and protecting an independent South Vietnam the purpose of U.S. military intervention in the first place? Kissinger, utterly frustrated and distressed, returned to Washington.

Perhaps it should be added to the lessons of Vietnam that when we make our grand pronouncements about freedom and equality (often for domestic consumption), many millions of people throughout the world and some of their leaders may honestly believe us.

A few days before our national elections it was a fair-sized crisis.[14] What made it worse was that most Americans had no idea what was holding up the settlement, and those who did would not worry about South Vietnam being sacrificed as a pawn in a gambit for strategic advantage. They did not care about South Vietnam at all. The Communists could have it with our compliments.

Worst of all, the Soviets and the Chinese were watching closely.[15] Each, for its own special reasons, remained curious: Just how far would the United States go in using military power to support its foreign policy? What they witnessed was a calculated, at times raw, exercise of U.S. power against friend and foe alike. North Vietnam would be forced, forced dramatically, to make further concessions. Our demands were mostly cosmetic, but the point was that they were *our* demands. Hanoi balked and had to face our military might. The President ordered the reseeding of the mines in Haiphong Harbor, the resumption of aerial reconnaissance, and, most dramatic of all: massive B–52 raids on the Hanoi-Haiphong area.[16] Within days the North Vietnamese had had enough, and were ready to settle.

South Vietnam, too, would be forced, and forced dramatically. Kissinger's deputy, General Alexander Haig, flew to Saigon with the new, somewhat improved draft of the agreement, but one that still permitted organized Communist forces to control some areas of the country. On January 16 he saw President Thieu and presented him with a letter from the President of the United States. In it Nixon made it perfectly clear that he had decided to initial the agreement on January 23 and sign it on January 27. "I will do so," he wrote, "if necessary, alone." He continued: "In that case I shall have to explain publicly that your government obstructs peace. The result will be an inevitable and immediate termination of U.S. economic and military assistance which cannot be forestalled by a change of personnel in your government."[17] It was an ultimatum, simple and brutal, with a fixed, very short time limit. You must do what we tell you, OR ELSE. President Thieu, reluctant, resisting to the very last minute, looked across his desk at the American Ambassador. "I have done my best," he said woefully. "I have done all that I can do for my country." Then he accepted the agreement. In a world where the superpowers (at least tacitly) cooperated in the settling of disputes, he had no more of a choice than his North Vietnamese counterpart.

The agreement was duly signed. U.S. forces were withdrawn from Indochina "with honor," and our foreign policy could turn to other, global matters. The United Nations was meeting regularly in New York, which was all right. What really mattered though were regular high-level exchanges among the United States, the Soviet Union, and China, and annual summit meetings between the United States and the Soviet Union.

THE UNRAVELING OF DÉTENTE

An understanding between the superpowers of a shared vested interest in world peace is surely a plus, but balance-of-power politics, though perhaps better than international anarchy, do present serious problems to American foreign policy. To begin with, it was hard on our alliances. Our friends, some until recently very powerful countries themselves, were accustomed to participate in shaping international events. With détente, when all the great issues would be discussed and possibly settled by Nixon and Brezhnev (with some assistance from China), their position in decision making would be reduced to a subsidiary role. America's allies, moreover, had their own interests, which to them were of special, a few of vital, significance. Now, in superpower politics their interests would be reduced to secondary importance. That is how it was, and under this scheme that was how it must be. All the same, our allies did not like it. Across the Pacific the Japanese were grumbling about "Nixon shocks." Across the Atlantic people were not amused when the president announced his intention to make 1973 "The Year of Europe," nor when he ordered a global military alert in October 1973 but did not consult them and (with the exception of Britain) did not even inform them until two hours after the fact. To the south, Latin Americans saw new evidence of *Yanqui* arrogance and neglect. Governments and people everywhere wondered what America was doing, what the United States and the Soviet Union (with the help of China) would decide about their fate.

Détente and balance-of-power politics also were hard on the nonaligned states of Asia and Africa. They had enjoyed much profit from the conflict of major powers—indeed, their security rested largely on it. But they had even more at stake. Until recently most had been colonies, part of an imperial system. As such they did enjoy some benefits, but they paid a very high tribute in human dignity. They had struggled for and attained independence. Now, at last, there would be no more stuff about the inferiority of the "colored races" or the "dependency" of certain peoples. In the U.N. General Assembly—the Security Council was deadlocked by the Cold War—they were equal, dramatically equal, with their former colonial rulers. Regardless of race or color: one state, one vote. As human beings, in world affairs they had a right to be treated as equals. It felt good. It felt good to be able to address the General Assembly and other international forums on imperialist exploitation while delegates from Western Europe sat in respectful silence. It felt good to assume the superior moral position against the United States.

During Jawaharlal Nehru's visit to the White House in 1961, President Kennedy tried to develop a dialogue, but "question after question [the Indian Prime Minister] answered with monosyllables or a sentence or two at most." The President found it very discouraging but he kept his good humor and kept on trying.[18] Afterward, somewhat anxiously, he asked his ambassador to India how he thought things had gone. India was important. Nehru was satisfied. His daughter, Prime Minister Indira Gandhi, used her toast at a state dinner in Washington in 1965 to instruct Lyndon B. Johnson on morality and the Vietnam War. He was furious; she was pleased. But all this was changing now. Henry Kissinger, visiting New Delhi (on his secret trip to China), was subjected to similar treatment. He did not bother to debate. She did not matter, her country was not important. She was not pleased; she was not satisfied.

Then, in 1973, while war raged in the Middle East, the United Nations Security Council was standing by helplessly until Henry Kissinger flew to Moscow and negotiated an agreement. Suddenly the two superpowers introduced a joint resolution for a cease-fire and China let it be known that while it disapproved, it would not vote against it. In less than four hours the Security Council, by unanimous vote (with one abstention), approved the resolution. This was remarkable in itself, but otherwise the debate was made noteworthy by a lament of the Indian ambassador that the smaller powers had become irrelevant. In a world order where power dominates and a concert of superpowers decides, the rhetoric on sovereign equality sounds hollow. Much of mankind could hardly help wondering whether their change from a dependent colony to a third-class independent state was really an advance. Certainly, in terms of human dignity, after the experiment in decentralized world order it represented a keenly felt retrogression.[19]

Another not insignificant problem with balance-of-power politics was that it required the periodic flexing of muscles by the United States. Conventional wisdom holds that political leaders who have risen to the top in authoritarian systems have the inclination to act forcefully and are subject to few, if any, institutional constraints. Doubts persist, however, about democracies, especially about American democracy. Our friends and foes wonder about the presidents we elect: their competence, their fortitude to make hard decisions, and their stamina to hold a steady course. They wonder also about American public opinion, whether it is really qualified to have so much influence on complex foreign policy issues. And they wonder about Congress, its legislative veto, its special ethnic biases, and its periodic distemper. When questions and doubts arise, they invite periodic testing and require firm answers; and from time to time they require the use of force.

The most unsatisfactory consequence of balance-of-power politics, however, is the strain it imposes upon the domestic environment. The heart of the difficulty is the popular attitude toward power. Most Americans are ambivalent toward it. On the one hand, they seem to enjoy it. They like to feel strong, to compete vigorously, and to win in whatever they undertake. They are proud of their country's military might and, at least until Vietnam, held a somewhat romantic view of war. Whenever presidents acted firmly and forcefully, their standing in public opinion polls invariably rose.[20] At the same time, by inclination or habit, Americans want power to be exercised, whether by their football teams or by their government, within a framework of laws and rules. They are offended by unbridled power and are troubled by force checked only by counterforce.

Americans, moreover, take a dim view of secret (personal) diplomacy, the main staple of power politics. They suspected it in the time of President Woodrow Wilson and they suspect it now. "What you don't know may kill you" has become a popular tenet. They may see the need for official secrecy on certain very special matters (troop movements or nuclear technology), but systematic and routine secrecy in the conduct of foreign relations is apt to provoke popular opinion. Worse still, the media and academics will actively resist it.

Whether a successful system of balance-of-power politics—something along the lines of the nineteenth century—could have emerged in the late twentieth century may be moot. With the Watergate scandal engulfing the Nixon administration, it became a hopeless quest. By the Second Supplemental Appropriations Act for Fiscal Year 1973, Congress tied the President's hands in Indochina. It prohibited any U.S. military action in the area. Then, at the height of the Middle East war, Congress restricted the President's authority to use military force anywhere on the globe (the War Powers Act).[21] It required no sophisticated intelligence analysis to discover that a basic component of balance-of-power politics (and détente), the credibility of U.S. power, was eroding.

President Nixon resigned in August 1974. Kissinger stayed on. His reputation helped, but American credibility continued to slide down the slippery slope under President Gerald Ford. Early in March 1975, Communist forces felt secure enough to assume the offensive in Cambodia and from their enclaves in South Vietnam. Neither the Cambodian nor the South Vietnamese army performed with distinction. What about the United States of America? How did we do? At a news conference on March 17, President Ford allowed that events in Southeast Asia tended to validate the "domino theory," and insisted that the existence of a non-Communist government in Cambodia was vital to our interests. This, five days after the House of Representatives, by a resounding margin, refused to vote any more money for the region.

By the end of the month defenses were crumbling all over Indochina. "Neither friend nor adversaries," proclaimed the President of the United States (April 3, 1975), "should interpret South Vietnamese losses as a sign that U.S. commitments will not be honored world wide." And the losses were about to become total. Panic gripped the land. Riots by South Vietnamese seeking to escape were becoming commonplace. Before the end of the month the State Department was considering the evacuation of civilian refugees. Congress had no intention to help, and was busy making sure that the president would have no chance to do so. Corralled, all President Ford could think of was the evacuation by air of Vietnamese orphans. At most, this was a faint symbolic gesture, one that even went wrong when, early in April, a U.S. transport plane crashed and burned, killing at least 100 children.

It was, of course, far too late, but on April 10 the President requested $722 million in emergency aid. Congress refused to consider any support for the South Vietnamese armed forces. To be sure, the Senate was willing to consider granting some funds, provided they were used only for humanitarian aid, and the House was willing to permit the use of U.S. forces to protect evacuation from Saigon. But it was all a charade. By April 23—in six weeks—the President had tossed in the towel. "The war in Indochina is finished as far as America is concerned," he announced. A week later Cambodia had fallen; South Vietnam surrendered.[22]

All in all, not a very impressive performance by the United States—not at all worthy of a superpower. There followed a ludicrous sequel. Two weeks later (May 12) a U.S. merchant vessel, the *Mayaguez*, was seized off the shores of Cambodia by a Communist band. Cambodia had no navy, and whatever government it had was busy murdering and forcing its own people out of the cities. At last, here was a challenge we could handle. The U.S. Navy was ordered into action. The U.S. Marines stormed an island. The *Mayaguez* was released. The "rescue" should demonstrate to the world, proclaimed Secretary of State Kissinger, that "there are limits beyond which the U.S. cannot be pushed."[23] Two days later the President complimented our military men for "the skill and courage" of those engaged in the rescue. It made only page 21 of the *New York Times*; an interview with the captain of the *Mayaguez* was on page 4. Apparently the Marines stormed the wrong island, after the ship already had been released!

And so it went. Before the year was out, there was trouble in Africa. Portugal withdrew from its colony of Angola. The Popular Movement for the Liberation of Angola was supported by the Soviet Union. Indeed, its surrogate, Cuba, had sent regular forces to the country. They were opposed by another group that the U.S. government preferred. Well, perhaps not the U.S. government, just the executive branch. On December 16 Congress voted to prohibit American military intervention in the area. Three days later the Senate felt it necessary to vote (54–22) to cut off funds even for covert operations. Undaunted by such firmness, President Fidel Castro announced that Cuban military forces would stay in Angola to keep peace.[24] When global initiatives from the Western Hemisphere came from Cuba and not the United States, international order was clearly in shambles once again.

It did not help that the public had not yet recovered from the Watergate scandal and still lacked confidence in presidential leadership. It did not help that Congressmen and Senators, senior and junior, each and all thought they knew just what to do in foreign affairs. And it did not help that the man who moved into the White House on January 20, 1977, had practically no experience in world politics.

President Jimmy Carter had ideals and definite views on American foreign policy, but if he had a broad concept, a global framework of his own, it escaped discovery. During the campaign he showed disdain for détente, but once in office he and his Secretary of State took pride in "steering a balanced course." Specifically, in the case of the Soviet Union he thought that "balancing competition with cooperation" described the proper course, a description that simply put into English what détente really means.[25] During the campaign Jimmy Carter also rejected what he called the "Lone Ranger" approach to foreign policy, but all along his National Security Adviser saw international relations as a grand power play starring the Soviet Union and the United States, with China and possibly Western Europe in supporting roles. Lesser assignments would be granted to "the newly emerging regional 'influentials,' " specified at one point as "Venezuela, Nigeria, Saudi Arabia, Iran, India and Indonesia."[26] The rest were extras—just filling the stage. It is worth noting that when Zbigniew Brzezinski published his memoirs, he chose the title *Power and Principle*. No less revealing is that the large section under the heading "On the Same Earth" (124 pages) in the President's own memoirs was devoted mostly (two-thirds) to relations with the Nixon partners, the Soviet Union and China.

Early in the Carter Administration some thought to find a clue to the President's global (macro) vision in his determination to negotiate, sign, and manage ratification of the Panama Canal treaty, which gave up our control of the Canal Zone and promised to turn over management of the canal to Panama by the end of the century. Strategically it was hazardous; in terms of domestic politics it was a controversial move. The question arose: Did the President take the security risks, was he willing to pay the enormous political price at home as an investment in hemisphere solidarity, the rock upon which he hoped to build a U.S. global design? It was certainly an interesting idea, but a closer examination revealed all kinds of contradictions.

Just a few months into his administration (March 11, 1977), Brazil, the largest South American power, felt compelled to cancel the military assistance treaty it had had with us for 25 years. By November 1978 tensions with Mexico, our closest Latin neighbor, had risen to such alarming levels that a set of new policies (Presidential Review Memo no. 41) was proposed. Then there were faux pas. Venezuela held democratic elections, the opposition won, power was transferred in a peaceful, orderly manner—quite a significant achievement. To the inauguration of the new president the democratic countries of the hemisphere sent their heads of state. The United States was represented by the wife of the Vice President. Another case was President Carter's visit to Mexico. During his toast at the state dinner, he unaccountably dragged in a reference to "Montezuma's revenge." If indeed there was an intention to build hemisphere solidarity, it was lost in the implementation.

The Carter Administration, of course, had other initiatives as well. American diplomacy mounted an offensive against white minority governments in Africa; we would set an example by being more "humane and moral" in our foreign relations. The President himself guided "the peace process" in the Middle East, leading to the Camp David accords and their partial implementation. These, however, were moves of primarily regional significance and reflected (if they were not motivated by) domestic political pressures. We were not engaged in building international order. Meanwhile, our credibility as a superpower continued to recede. In Nicaragua we helped to overthrow the pro-U.S. Somoza dictatorship but did little when its successors established a hostile Communist regime. In Ethiopia, with Soviet and *Cuban* help, a brutal Communist dictatorship was murdering its own people. The Soviet Union invaded and occupied its neighbor Afghanistan. Iran callously violated the most rudimentary international law by invading the American Embassy and holding hostage our diplomatic representatives.

During much of his first administration, President Reagan was absorbed in domestic issues. Even so, he quickly moved to restore American power and improve American credibility. He significantly accelerated the military modernization and buildup that had begun under his predecessor. Then he demonstrated that the United States was once again able and willing to project force overseas without getting trapped into escalation by it. When, during the summer of 1982, Israel, on a flimsy excuse, invaded Lebanon and then pressed on to and into Beirut, he sent in the U.S. Marines (as part of an international peacekeeping force) to help stabilize the situation. Clearly the post-Vietnam paralysis was over. When it seemed that the situation in Beirut was under control, he withdrew the Marines. When massacres suggested that his action was premature, he ordered them back. When, shortly thereafter, it appeared that the mission of the Marines helped little—indeed, their barracks were attacked and blown up by some of the Lebanese combatants—the President withdrew them once and for all. Clearly the United States had learned its lesson from Vietnam: it would not become mired in a local conflict. The United States intervened in Grenada, intercepted a plane flying terrorists to safety, and attacked Libya from the air—actions that were dramatic, quick, and successful.

Noticeably the Administration's foreign policy initiatives were military. The peace process in the Middle East was not pressed; the Caribbean Basin development never really got off the ground; the quiet diplomacy in Southern Africa was practically inaudible. And, noticeably, its foreign policy was ad hoc and reactive. Others set our agenda for action. In contrast with the days of Truman, Eisenhower, Kennedy, and Nixon, we did not project a vision of the future; our policy was an aggregate of fragments. Insofar as the Administration had a concept of the international environment, it lacked subtlety. It was a world of stark contrasts (of Communist red and true blue) where all issues were reduced to a common denominator: the mortal struggle between the forces of peace and disorder. It was a stage with only two stars and many more or less inconsequential extras.

In the fall of 1985 the President had a particularly suitable opportunity to air his view of the world. He was addressing the fortieth anniversary session of the U.N. General Assembly and was offering "a new commitment, a fresh start." It would be based on the plain and simple fact that "the differences between America and the Soviet Union are deep and abiding." The management of these differences, he explained to an audience composed mostly of representatives of the "Third World" countries, was the principal task. Conflicts in Afghanistan, Cambodia, Ethiopia, Angola, and Nicaragua all "share the common characteristic: they are the consequence of an ideology imposed from without, dividing nations and creating regimes that are, almost from the day they take power, at war with their own people."[27] The approach the President suggested was a three-tier process. First, bring together the Communist and democratic elements of the country (or region) for purposes of negotiation. Second, provide Soviet and U.S. help toward achieving agreement. Third, welcome each country back into the world economy (presumably with some economic assistance). It was not much of a design for international order. It was not an approach that was new or particularly relevant to most in the audience. They applauded politely.

NOTES

1. Whether "international" order was a main motivating force or just a by-product is somewhat of a puzzle for me. Nixon's public statements from the Guam Doctrine on indicate concern, but when I once complimented him on his achievements in this field, he gave me a most quizzical look.

2. By May 2 they had made visible progress, taking Quang Tri, surrounding An Loc, and imperiling Pleiku.

3. "When I asked him to explain why a Vietnamese government could abandon a policy of Vietnamization, he reverted again to Hanoi's unchanging demand for a tripartite coalition government in which the anticommunist government, decapitated and deprived of its police and army, was supposed to join a coalition with 'neutralists' (approved by Hanoi) and the fully armed Communists backed by the North Vietnamese army, which coalition would then negotiate with the fully armed Viet Cong, backed by Hanoi's entire field army. That is what Xuan Thuy called the 'real situation in South Vietnam.' " Henry Kissinger, *White House Years* (Boston: Little, Brown, 1979), pp. 1160–73.

4. *New York Times,* May 9, 1972, p. 19.

5. During his secret visit to Moscow on April 22, Kissinger became convinced that "Brezhnev wants a summit at almost any cost, but after the mining expected its cancellation." Kissinger, *White House Years,* pp. 1159–1200. Nixon, in turn, believed that without a strong military response in Vietnam, he would have too weak a position and could not afford to go to Moscow. At one time *he* seriously considered canceling the summit. Indeed, he ordered the May 8 measures so he *could* go to Moscow!

6. Ibid., p. 1193.

7. Ibid., p. 1105.

8. Ibid., p. 1303.

9. Ibid., p. 1359.

10. Early in January 1973 the Democratic Caucus in the House voted 154–75 to cut off all funds for Indochina military operations. The Senate Democratic Caucus more than matched it with a 36–12 vote. Richard Nixon, *RN* (New York: Grosset and Dunlap, 1978), p. 742.

11. Ibid., p. 700.

12. Some similarities with the pre-Munich negotiations are rather striking.

13. Nixon, *RN,* p. 702.

14. President Nixon instructed Kissinger "that nothing that is done should be influenced by the U.S. election deadline," and both of them make a point of this in their memoirs; but, of course, by this time all polls indicated the Nixon lead to be of landslide proportions.

15. In addition, by this time the Watergate cover-up was beginning to intrude into the President's schedule.

16. The North Vietnamese, the Soviets, and the Chinese knew what this was all about, but just in case some Americans, particularly some of our military leaders, were slow to understand, the president made it clear: "The day after the bombing began I think I shook Admiral Moore [Chairman of the Joint Chiefs of Staff] when I called him and said, 'I don't want any more of this crap about the fact that we couldn't hit this target or that one. This is your chance to use military power effectively to win this war, and if you don't, I'll consider you responsible!' I stressed that we must hit and hit hard or there was no point in doing it at all. If the enemy detected any reticence in our actions, they would discount the whole exercise." Nixon, *RN,* p. 734.

17. Ibid., p. 746.

18. John Kenneth Galbraith, *Ambassador's Journal* (Boston: Houghton Mifflin, 1969), p. 248.

19. According to Nixon, during his visit to the Nixon home at San Clemente, Brezhnev (late one night) pressed for a Middle East settlement imposed upon the weaker countries of the region by the superpowers, which he resisted. Kissinger reported similar attempts at the Moscow meeting, which he, too, rebuffed. Nixon, *RN,* p. 885; Henry Kissinger, *Years of Upheaval* (Boston: Little, Brown, 1982), pp. 553–55. Possibly they hoped to create the impression that Brezhnev sought a U.S.–Soviet joint condominium, which is probably true, and that Nixon and Kissinger did not, which perhaps is another matter.

20. Louis Harris, *The Anguish of Change* (New York: W. W. Norton, 1973), pp. 55–59, 71.

21. Kissinger, *Years of Upheaval,* pp. 338, 582.

22. *New York Times,* March 13, 18, and 29; April 4, 5, 11, 23, 24, and 30, 1975. All stories were on p. 1.

23. Ibid., May 17, 1975, p. 1.

24. Ibid., December 17, 1975, p. 1; December 20, 1975, p. 8; December 23, 1975, p. 5.

25. Cyrus Vance, *Hard Choices* (New York: Simon and Schuster, 1983), pp. 84, 120ff.

26. Zbigniew Brzezinski, *Power and Principle* (New York: Straus and Giroux, 1983), pp. 53–54.

27. *New York Times,* October 25, 1985, p. A–11.

12

NEW HORIZONS

In the twilight of the Reagan Administration the remarkable transformation in the Kremlin was matched in Washington. The President learned to trust the General Secretary, though he was still cautious. "Trust but verify" was his frequently repeated motto. After some hesitation his successor, George Bush, apparently is following the same path. In the face of continued Soviet congeniality, President Bush has let it be known that he, too, has become convinced that the new Soviet direction is irreversible. Possibly we may be gravitating toward a new détente, a less sophisticated version approaching a U.S.–Soviet condominium. More likely, though, we are still just marking time with an ad hoc, reactive foreign policy. Others continue to set our agenda for action. We do not project a vision of the future. We lack a design on the global scale. Our foreign policy remains an aggregate of fragments.

It may be that we are advancing toward a satisfactory international order anyway. The Cold War is over and democracy is on the march. Democratic countries, President Woodrow Wilson told us 70 years ago, are inherently peaceloving and are likely to be friendly to the United States. All we really have to do is to continue to encourage pro-democracy forces in the authoritarian states and try to assure that they are not thwarted by government coercion.

It could be that in the future we shall see popularly elected governments in now Communist countries and that in international relations they will subordinate their power to law. It would be a monumental departure from the past, but it is at least conceivable. When Mr. Khrushchev says that our grandchildren will live under Communism, promised Richard Nixon to the Republican Convention in 1960, I say his grandchildren will live in freedom. He may have been right. Even so, the question of just how do we get there remains. We must guard against the notion that the human journey will follow a straight line and be prepared for distractions, diversions, breakdowns, and reverses. The danger of turbulence ahead remains very real.

We cannot take progress for granted in Eastern Europe. Like snowballs rolling down a mountain, mass movements are gaining in dimension and speed. They have already swept away many a Communist leader and some repressive practices. Gathering momentum further, they may sweep away many other things as well. The question is: What else? Law and order? Much will depend on the role of the Catholic (and Lutheran) Church. Can it provide ideas and leadership in the development of democratic institutions? Much also will depend on the state of the economies, where the problems are staggering.

To be sure, some barriers to growth are structural, and reform-minded governments can do something about that. But will they? Some barriers are normative, and freedom may unleash a motivation for achievement. But will it? And one major barrier is a lack of money. Eastern European countries desperately need massive foreign investment; some suggest a new Marshall Plan. Western Europe and especially West Germany are inclined to help. At the end of 1989 all this country would offer is less than $800 million in U.S. aid to Poland and Hungary and President Bush's urging of the Japanese Prime Minister to visit Eastern Europe, steps that are hardly sufficient and not exactly in the right direction. The democracy movements will have to produce some dramatic economic achievements in the not too distant future, or the masses will turn on them and fascism will raise its ugly head.

We cannot take progress for granted in China. Until recently the Communist Party on the highest level seemed to muster a majority in support of policies that stimulated openness and rapid economic growth, but then it turned against the demands for political reforms that the openness and economic growth precipitated. American opinion leaders, with few exceptions (most notably Richard Nixon and Henry Kissinger), want to punish the Chinese rulers for the Tiananmen Square "massacre"; some wish for an apology. Congressmen have demanded, at times quite vociferously, harsh political and economic sanctions from the President. From the Chinese they demand radical changes in the top leadership and the removal of restraints on freedom.

There are at least two things wrong with this kind of approach. First, the Chinese do not take kindly to foreigners trying to impose on China the virtues of freedom. They recall only too well that during the last century Britain punished them for restraining freedom, more specifically for restraining free trade in drugs (the Opium War, 1839–42), and for over 100 years Britain, other Europeans, once the Americans, and then the Japanese kept punishing them in the name of liberty and civilization. It is doubtful that they enjoyed it. Most will quote with pride the word of Chairman Mao in Tiananmen Square 50 years ago (October 1, 1949), when he proclaimed the People's Republic of China: From today the

Chinese people have stood up (Zhongguo Renmin cong ci zhanqilaile). And all of them will remember that just recently China took on both superpowers and that both (Nixon in 1972 and Gorbachev in 1989) came to Beijing bearing olive branches.

The second thing wrong with trying to punish China is that we are not good at intimidation. We were quite unsuccessful in intimidating General Noriega. In the end we had to invade Panama to remove him from office. In the case of China our punitive actions are likely to harm the people we do not want to hurt: hundreds of millions of non-Communist poor and the many small entrepreneurs who contributed so much to economic growth. On the highest party level American knee-jerk response is not likely to strengthen the position of the modernizers; indeed it may shift the balance in favor of the hardliners. If we are not careful, China will choose a rapprochement with the Soviet Union or may go it alone. An unfriendly China will not help balance Soviet power in the Pacific; it will not help restrain Vietnamese aggressiveness in southeast Asia and it will not help restrain a pugnacious Japan. And it is difficult to see how we could have international order if a major power with more than 20 percent of the world population remains outside of it. In any case, with or without arms control agreements, we shall continue to need the secret listening posts in China for our surveillance of Soviet strategic forces. And we certainly do not want the Chinese selling missiles to the Middle East (or to anybody, for that matter).

Neither can we take progress for granted in the Soviet Union. The Russian people derived much pride from the dimensions and proclaimed glories of the Soviet Empire—an empire that far exceeded the power of its Czarist predecessors. Now almost daily they see evidence of declining national prestige. Their leaders regularly defer to the Americans: their values and their leaders. Almost daily they see signs of what might become the breakup of the empire. There are problems in Asia; minorities there are steadily growing in proportion and have become restless. There are problems in the Baltic, in the Caucasus, in Moldavia, and, most dangerous of all, in the Ukraine. If the fissiparous trends continue and accelerate, a political reaction may set in. The Communist Party leadership may react and blame democratization. The democratized institutions may react and demand firmer central control. Some speculate whether President Gorbachev will last. More to the point is the question whether the current political direction of Soviet domestic and foreign policy will persist. We just cannot be sure that his successor, or Gorbachev himself, will not revert to totalitarian methods and resume an imperialist foreign policy.

We can be sure though of this: We may continue to try our hand at a system of major power dominance; we may decide to muddle through; and, of course, we may once again devote our energies (and resources) to a decentralized world order; but whatever course we choose to follow, we shall come face to face with two pressing international realities. First, we shall have to realize that the large number of states in Asia and Africa that have gained their independence from colonial rule in recent decades are important to world peace and in all probability will become more important still. Second, we shall have to admit that these states, which we habitually call "developing," are politically highly unstable. They may move forward, but the danger is always present that they will regress into primitive conflicts and fratricidal chaos.

A story may help to illustrate their difficulty. During the nineteenth century an Irish town council passed three concurrent resolutions. First, it resolved to build a new courthouse. Second, it resolved that the new courthouse should be built with the bricks and beams of the old courthouse. Third, it resolved that while the new courthouse was being built, business would be conducted in the old courthouse. The story is, of course, only a story; but it highlights the task of newly independent states. Most want to develop a viable modern political system. They want it to be theirs, rooted in their own traditions. But while the new system with its modern institutions and structures is being established, they have to manage as best they can.

The transitional stage is loaded with problems. Many of them are unique to specific indigenous environments. But some, very important ones, are shared by most. We can identify them. And if we are to understand the colossal dimension of the obstacles to political stability and human development, we need to focus attention on them.

SOCIAL REALITIES

To begin with, there is the problem of *social cleavages*. As a matter of fact, few, if any, countries are socially homogeneous. Most are divided into groups. The number of these groups is a relevant question, but far more important is their principle of cohesion. Are the component groups held together by a common interest developed through the experience of life, or by a common characteristic ascribed at the instant of birth? There is a measure of flexibility in the former, the possibility of mobility and interchangeability. The difference between faculty and students in a university is a case in point. Each group has its own interests, but there are no radical discontinuities. A student may well become a professor, and a professor usually studies and learns for the rest of his life. It is very different with ascriptive groups. Mobility among them is minimal, and interchangeability is practically nonexistent. There is not much a person can do to change his or her race or gender. If the overriding fact for a professor is that he is a man and for his colleague that she is a woman, or that she is white and he is black, and their interests are determined by such essentially fixed characteristics, collegial relationships are apt to become nonnegotiable confrontations. In the United States ascriptive differences have always been present and potent, but with the Constitution a beginning was made to keep them out of the political process. Admittedly we are still struggling with the problem, yet it is possible for Americans, with all their diverse backgrounds, to relate to the social, economic, and political system in nonascriptive terms.

This is rather less so in much of contemporary Asia and Africa. Attributes which stamp them at birth usually define a person's identity, marriage partner, career prospects, even meal companions. In Lagos it makes all the difference whether a Nigerian is Ibo or Hausa-Fulani. In New Delhi, decades after India outlawed castes, they still form the basis of identification, and in provincial towns and 600,000 villages they still define it. In Kuala Lumpur there are lawyers, teachers, businessmen, politicians, and bureaucrats; but when the chips are down, Malaysians are primarily Malays, Chinese, or Indians. And that is putting it mildly. Ascriptive cleavages not only separate; they tend to direct hostility. The "others" are ready targets of suspicion and hatred that can turn into violence— and regularly does. Most people in Asia and Africa have to live in the shadow of communal riots and massacres.

Added to this is another social problem, that of *accelerated anomie,* a condition of rapid loss of confidence in norms. We all like to proclaim our right to make up our own minds. In fact, however, making decisions is a difficult task, and in general we would much rather avoid it. When we cannot, we look for help. Consider for a moment this scenario. You are invited to a state dinner. It is an impressive, new experience. The first course is served: a whitish mass with some mushrooms and grapes in the middle of a delicate plate. There are all kinds of knives, forks, and spoons lined up on each side. What do you do? You take a surreptitious peek at your neighbor. She, too, is puzzled and is glancing at her neighbor, who in turn is no less in need of guidance. If somewhere down the line a Texan grabs the catsup bottle, the filet de sole veronique will soon be doused with the red stuff all around the table.

In general we would much prefer to avoid such uncertainties. Consider another illustration. Approaching an intersection as the traffic signal turns red, do we ordinarily engage in a cost:benefit analysis? Do we calculate that, on the one hand, if we go through, someone may hit our car, or we may hit someone, or we may get a ticket? On the other hand, if we stop, we may be late for an important appointment. Usually we do not. "Instinctively" our foot moves from the accelerator to the brake pedal. It is, of course, not an instinct but an expression of successful socialization. All in all, we prefer it that way.

Although we do not always act accordingly, we want to know what is right and proper. For fashions we look to our neighbors, the Joneses; for political opinions, to politicians and media personalities; for knowledge, to teachers or our own experience; and for basic values, we look to our belief system, our religion or ideology. We need guidance and are disturbed when we can no longer rely confidently on our norms, when it is up to us to figure out our standards and the justification for their validity.

For many, many generations "traditional" values were preeminent and provided comfort in Asia and Africa. People lived in small communities, mostly in villages. Everyone knew everyone else personally and quite well, and could be guided by long experience. People were profoundly impressed by their vulnerability amid overwhelming and mysterious forces. They did not understand lightning and thunder, floods, drought and typhoons; they did not understand disease but knew its perils. And they knew they would have to die. They believed in the existence of supernatural powers and the wisdom of guiding their lives by the expressions of supernatural will(s).

Roles were determined accordingly. The birth of a child—a mysterious, hazardous event, in a way a bridge to the immortality of the parents—was seen as a divine message. It affected the reputation of the father and mother; it defined the proper role of the child in the future. Rulers had a mandate from heaven. Men and women knew their proper place because they believed it was ordained. Similarly, the rules of the community reflected expressions of supernatural will(s). Man did not have the temerity to make laws. They were made in heaven and revealed on earth by prophets, holy texts, and specific signs interpreted by specialists in the occult, priests, theologians, swamis, and medicine men.

All in all, it was a stable arrangement. Not that there was no dissent. There were ambitious persons who were not content with their assigned roles; there were persons who broke the rules. But they had no alternatives, no escape. The cost of mobility was enormous. Transportation was rudimentary; roads were few. In order to move to another community, a person would have to cross formidable physical barriers: rivers, forests, mountains, deserts. If he made it, he would find a community governed by very similar rules that would feel no tolerance, offer him no welcome. It would see him as a stranger, a menace, and treat him with suspicion and hostility. Quite possibly it would kill him.

The decline of traditional societies began under colonial rule. One reason was that imperial rule facilitated urbanization. As a matter of fact, not everyone had lived in villages. There were towns serving as administrative centers or marketplaces. All the same, they were fairly small in scale, very much part of the rural order, dominated by traditional hierarchies and traditional values. Under colonial rule, however, these towns were transformed and new, very different kinds of urban centers were emerging. Linked to distant lands across the sea, they were much larger in scale. As extensions of imperial power, their processes were dominated by foreign values. A growing rural-urban discontinuity soon became apparent. In need of supporting labor, European trading companies and colonial administrators attracted villagers, employed them without much inquiry into their village reputations, and paid them (by rural standards) munificent wages. People who for generations had had their fates fixed by tradition found that they had a choice. That prodigal sons could escape village discipline and sanctions was hard enough. When some of them returned after they made good in the city, flaunted more resources than they could have gathered had they stayed at home, and when young women would not resist their curiosity, the authority of the traditional hierarchy was in big trouble.

Worse still, colonial rule brought new technology. Not that the Europeans were interested in building factories in Asia and Africa. On the contrary, they looked to their colonies to supply the raw materials for their own industry and markets where their finished products could be profitably sold. There were two exceptions however: transportation and communication. To facilitate the exploitation and shipment of mineral deposits and the distribution of finished goods (not to mention military and administrative control), railroads and highways were built. Shipping was developed and the telegraph was introduced. They improved mobility, and they did more: they invited comparison, not only with their more distant neighbors but also with the imperial "mother country." People who for generations had believed that theirs was the proper—indeed, the only—way of life now saw and were sorely tempted by an alternative. That it was the way of the conqueror was bad enough. That the alternative was more effective in coping (through medicine and education) with the mysterious forces of nature, and offered more personal comfort, made it much worse. And when the traditional elites became attracted to the different way, traditional values were in deep trouble indeed.

Traditional societies did, and still do, fight back. Some sought to defend themselves by absorbing their alien rulers. After all, in India (and China), for example, they had managed armed intruders with this technique in the past. Thus British officers were assigned the status of high-caste Brahmins. But it did not work; the British were quite different from the Moghuls (or the Tartars in China). They did not "go native." Far from home, they remained committed to the values and interests of their distant homeland. It is often overlooked, but a very important motive behind the *mass* support of independence was the hope (frequently expressed by Mahatma Gandhi) that with the British gone, Indians could resume their traditional way of life.

The British did go. Soon after World War II they and other colonial powers withdrew from their Asian and African possessions. But the disintegration of traditional societies was not reversed. Mobility actually increased. People started streaming into the cities. Travel became cheaper and faster. Meanwhile, progress in communications proceeded—in fact, it accelerated at a psychedelic rate. Comparisons became very cheap and very simple.

And then came the catastrophe; then came the Americans. They did not come as soldiers and conquerors. Some came as technical advisers, many as students and tourists. Most did not set foot in Africa and Asia at all. They came through the radio, through the movies, and through television. They brought the example of their enormously high standard of living; they brought the example of their freewheeling lifestyle. And they brought the most radical, revolutionary departure from tradition: a mass culture based upon the value of the common man. Not just the elites but soon all people were losing their interest in traditional hierarchies and their respect for traditional values. People all over the world were grabbing for the catsup bottle. They wanted to emulate the Americans;[1] they wanted to share in their affluence.

Some, in desperation, have sought solace in neo-orthodox reaction. Dramatically they have turned their backs on the temptations of the foreign Satan and rededicated themselves to traditional virtues, to the traditional order. They no doubt will be followed by others. For many, though, the problem is much more complex and much more difficult. They recognize the passing of traditional society and are acutely concerned about being overwhelmed by a foreign culture.

They doubt that they can go back—indeed, they do not want to go back. They want to go forward, but where can they go? Where can they find reliable instruction about what is right and proper in a *modern society of their own*? So people just go on, in an altogether unsatisfactory anomic state, neither fish nor fowl. They feel deprived, frustrated, and insecure.

ECONOMIC REALITIES

Social causes of political instability are related to and exacerbated by economic conditions. Most African and Asian states (as well as some Latin American ones) are marked by a special kind of poverty: *mass poverty,* a poverty that is very different from what we may encounter in the United States.

To begin with, there is a quantitative difference. The poor in the United States by official definition add up to about 15 percent of the total population, too large for comfort but a manageable challenge for the other 80–plus percent who are enjoying affluence. In newly independent states the number of the poor is very much higher—40, 50, even 60 percent—posing a staggering burden to the remainder, few of whom are very much better off.

More important is the qualitative difference. The poverty line in the United States, as defined by the government, is above $12,000 annual income for a family of four. Those living on less than that exist under conditions very much below our accepted standard of living. It is an unsatisfactory, frustrating experience, made all the more so by the proximity and demonstration effect of the vast majority enjoying a plainly much better quality of life. Thus the poor in America often feel aggrieved; they complain that they do not have a "fair chance."

In Asia and Africa few families live at the $12,000 level. Indeed, per capita incomes in many countries are below $350. Theirs is not a poverty of living without some modern conveniences but of existing with the barest necessities, totally at the mercy of nature. Poverty does not mean living without heat or air conditioning, without automobiles, VCRs, or television. It means living without electric light. It means no clean drinking water. It means no medical or dental care. Teeth rot and fall out. Illness is treated by witchcraft and old-fashioned nostrums; childbirth is assisted by a midwife or an older relative. All too often the mother dies and the baby survives not much longer. Poverty means the shelter of primitive (bamboo or grass) huts with leaky roofs, no windows, and earth for the floor. Sanitation depends on vultures and scavengers. The bathroom is convenient: it is the great outdoors. Poverty means clothing amounting to a piece of course cloth wrapped around the body, scant protection in rain or cold. No shoes, of course. And poverty means a continuous state of hunger, with available food deficient in calories and the most essential nutrients. (The average protein intake in much of South Asia is below that of inmates of German concentration camps.)[2] Such deficiencies are bad enough for adults, but in infants and children they retard development of mental processes. Thus poverty in much of Africa and Asia means human beings existing at a level of animal subsistence. Men and women live, work, propagate, fight, even play. But—and this is the crucial point—due to (absolute) physical deprivation they *cannot function as human beings*: solve problems, create, or develop.

Mass poverty is a miserable condition. What makes it especially depressing is the thought that mass poverty is not just the bane of the current generation of Africans and Asians, but may be the fate of their children and grandchildren as well. So far most of these countries have been unable to manage a takeoff into self-sustained economic growth, and the odds that they can do so in the foreseeable future are not good. All too many mutually reinforcing links make up their chain of poverty.

In the countries of the West and the Pacific Rim that did succeed, economic development was usually underwritten by heavy private investment and sustained by highly rewarded individual achievement. But conditions in most of Africa and Asia do not favor the propensity to invest. Where the masses of human beings have to exist at the level of animal subsistence, few can have personal savings. Those who do may be tempted to invest abroad, for at home conditions are simply too uncertain to offer any risks worth taking. Besides, the few with disposable incomes are especially aware of the modern consumer goods enjoyed in advanced industrialized societies and are especially attracted to them. They much prefer buying cars, TVs, VCRs, refrigerators, and such to putting their money into domestic ventures building them. Government makes it worse. Whether Communist or (more or less) democratic, it has become entangled with egalitarian maxims, and is usually vulnerable to charges of corruption. It cannot offer extraordinary material incentives (profits) to those willing to take extraordinary risks in investment, nor to those demonstrating extraordinary merit with innovation. More than that, through progressive taxation and other sanctions, it will try to prevent the private sector from doing so. How could anyone of sound mind find it reasonable to forgo the pleasures of the moment for some tenuous and modest benefit in some distant years?

Moreover, in countries that have succeeded, economic development was generated by a productive combination of physical (technology) and human (skills) capital formation. Difficulties abound on both counts in most of Africa and Asia. Looking first at *physical capital* formation, it takes no profound analysis to recognize that countries chained down by mass poverty are not apt to generate on their own either technological advance or industrial growth. At least until their economies have a chance to gain acceleration, they need significant capital transfers from the industrialized countries. The trouble is that modern technology is scarce and very expensive. Not much is available for transfer to the countries of Africa and Asia, and less can be paid for it by them. Perhaps a bigger trouble is that even when the modern machines are made available, they are often unsuitable. Their efficiency, resting on their native environment, cannot be readily transferred to the very different conditions of Africa and Asia. There are many reasons for this, but three are especially worth noting.

First, we should recognize the enormous *disparity in the scale of markets*. Our market is large, the whole United States plus the foreign demand for our goods. If we try very hard, we can still think of items that we buy that are locally produced, but most come from different parts of the country or from foreign states. It is a very integrated market. Our transportation (and communication) system is phenomenal. Inland waterways are well developed, railroad tracks and multi-lane, all-weather interstate highways crisscross the land. Add to that the heavy use of air cargo. Goods can be hauled quickly and efficiently over long distances. More than that, it is a very broadly based market. Practically everyone owns and can buy cars, radios, stereo sets, whatever. All segments of society, even the poor, have sufficient disposable income to be part of the demand for manufactured goods. Advanced technology and mass production serves it well.

In contrast, the market in Africa and Asia is still small in scale. Most people live in more or less isolated villages. What they produce is usually consumed locally, and what they consume was generally produced locally. Even in large countries like India and Nigeria the market is highly fragmented. Bicycles are now spreading to the countryside, but most traffic is pedestrian, over narrow dirt roads, imperiled by hostile elements (floods) and quite often by snakes. Most goods are transported on the back of a person or in a cart pulled by man or beast. During the colonial period some long-distance railroads and hard-surface highways were built, but they were few and remain relatively few. They do not link the country together into a large-scale market. There are not nearly enough tracks for freight trains, not nearly enough wide, all-weather highways for tractor trailers, and not nearly enough bridges to cross the often unpredictable rivers. Distribution remains inadequate. It is not unusual in many countries of Africa and Asia for some villages to suffer famine while others not too far away enjoy a surplus of wheat or rice. The need for manufactured goods is general and great, but in an environment where few have disposable incomes, that market is limited to too narrow a segment to support mass production.

Second, we should recognize the enormous *disparity in the scale of production*. American family farms are generally well over 2,000 acres. To service them we have developed special machines. These agricultural combines, marvels of technology, account for the phenomenal efficiency (and surpluses) of our food production. In sharp contrast, in much of Asia family farms average just half an acre, and that is often divided into two or three parcels.[3] By the time the driver of one of these magnificent U.S. machines shifts it into gear, he has almost crossed into his neighbor's land. Much more relevant than the giant combines are simple steel plows that dig deep and turn over the soil; but such single steel plows, so useful on small plots, have not been in demand in the United States for almost a century and are rarely produced.

Third, we should recognize the far-reaching *differences in cultural norms*. For example, much of our life and practically all the production processes in the United States are organized by chronometric time. Our favorite TV shows start punctually on the hour (or half hour). Our trains and planes (supposedly) leave according to a fixed schedule. Most offices are open from nine to five, our factories work in three eight-hour shifts. Assembly lines depend on a full crew being present and being rotated at regular, predictable intervals. But people in Africa and Asia are much less devoted to the clock. They may come early, quite often arrive late, and occasionally, because of some family matter or personal mood may not show up at all. It does not make much difference for a small producer with a spinning wheel or a hand loom, but it works havoc with the assembly line of a modern textile mill.

Turning to the formation of *human capital,* we find the barriers no less formidable. Part of the problem is traditional ideologies, which still have a hold on the masses. Invariably those ideologies were based on a profound belief that human life was a vale of tears dominated by overwhelming forces of nature. Only a fool misguided by vainglory seeks to change his environment. Man's only hope is God, possibly a merciful God, Who might try us severely in this world but Who could richly reward us in Heaven. Ambition, efforts to gain special skills, and special recognition, to advance in social or economic terms— simply put, to achieve in this world—was considered antisocial behavior. Those who moved up fast were not admired; when they fell, their friends and neighbors were elated. In Chinese and Indian civilization men in pursuit of material gains were held in low esteem. Islam's Holy Prophet proclaimed poverty as a source of his pride. Clearly the past serves better as an inspiration for endurance.

Much of the problem is physical. For the masses existing at levels of animal subsistence, dietary deficiencies are a colossal handicap, and so are the low level of energy and the absence of recreational opportunities. In the tropics, within unventilated bamboo (or straw) shacks with the temperature at night in the 90s and humidity close to 100 percent, the human body perspires constantly. It uses up most of its energy keeping cool, at times leaving little even for the digestion of food. Hungry children cry throughout the night in a Bengali village, but that is not the only reason their parents sleep fitfully. They are too tired to rest, let alone think.

A significant segment of the population lives better, but for most of them as well conditions are not conducive to the generation of new ideas or the acquisition of new skills. Much of the learning in any society is through more or less informal processes. An especially favorable period for this is early childhood, and one important vehicle is toys. It may be significant that the children in Asia and Africa play with "life replicating" toys, with dolls or crude models of animals and carts that they themselves make and with which they imitate familiar situations and established patterns. In contrast, American children are soon introduced to general "problem solving" puzzles and games, which are very different. The bits and pieces of jigsaw puzzles, for example, have no meaningful shape in themselves. They pose a challenge to the mind to discover a proper relationship; and once it is accomplished, a new puzzle will present an entirely new situation and an entirely new challenge to the mind. American children barely out of infancy, moreover, now have access to computer games with the same mind- and skill-expanding qualities. And that is just the beginning. In an environment of advanced technology American children soon become accustomed to operate a car and work with computers. Meanwhile they become acquainted with the rules of a mass society, the way (and the need) to get along with strangers, to fit into and advance in a large, complex organization. Such opportunities are simply not available for most youngsters in Africa and Asia.

There is, of course, the process of more formal learning, institutional education. But the prospects are not much better. To be sure, laws requiring universal education have been passed, and governments have built many schools (mostly in the urban areas), but none of this helps much if students are not motivated. They attend classes, more or less, but given a choice, they prefer general subjects with vague content.[4] Add to this the problem of qualified teachers: they are extremely scarce. Printing diplomas and passing them out in solemn ceremonies does not address the problem. It is true the world over: those who do not know, cannot teach.

On the university level, which only a few reach, we encounter a further handicap: the political volatility of the students. That this should be so is no great surprise, but why governments thoughtlessly exacerbate it is difficult to understand. College students are still in their adolescence. They have been moving out of childhood; they have discovered new feelings; they have become aware of the realities of the adult world and are struggling to cope with them. Under the best of circumstances it is a difficult period for them and for their families. At home family solidarity helps ameliorate some of the stresses, but when young people go to universities, they have to move away. There is some distance between suburbia and the Ivy League, but an enormous distance between an Asian or African village and the university in the capital. Teenagers are physically and psychologically uprooted from their homes and moved to a strange and highly competitive environment. Their insecurity is raised to an almost unbearable level. Their anxieties and their intensified need to belong make them extremely vulnerable to peer pressure and an easy prey to political agitators. Students find little time, and have less inclination, for studies, especially for the rigorous disciplines of mathematics and the sciences. Governments that for the sake of efficiency and economy crowd thousands of young men and women into giant dormitories help build compression and should not be surprised when the lid blows off.

To be sure, the children of elites, largely unconstrained by surrounding poverty and government misjudgments, may get some education in special private schools. Often they continue their studies at American universities. Some, after demonstrated accomplishments, return home, where they are forced to contend with the hostility and jealousy of indigenously trained colleagues and pathetically skimpy financial support for research and development. Many others prefer to stay in the United States. They do contribute to human capital—the human capital of the United States.

Candor compels mentioning one other serious barrier to the acquisition of new knowledge. A very delicate matter, to be sure, but somehow, directly or indirectly, it must be faced. Language is the instrument of learning; its dynamic propensities are essential to the advancement of knowledge and skills. As it happens, the English language, with its simple grammar and vast vocabulary, is remarkably well suited. Most languages in Africa and Asia, not to mention dialects, are far more cumbersome; their vocabulary is much more limited. Indeed, some until recently lacked the written form and were entirely oral. Worse still, recent developments have exacerbated the disparity. It is English that during the twentieth century has provided the new words and phrases needed for advancing science and technology; with a few exceptions it has been English that has supplied the names for modern business practices and organizational patterns, not to mention the jargon for social sciences. With the driving edge of communications and computer technology still in English, and with a share in the North American market still an eagerly sought prize, the disparity is likely to grow.

Political pressures of national identity and pride, however, drive in a different direction: toward national languages. Some try to construct a new grammar, make up new vocabulary, and transplant English words en masse, which is not that easy. School, for example, may be changed to *sekolah* and bus to *bas* in Malaysian, but what can be done about carburetors, transistors, microchips, and superconductors—to say nothing of the marginal propensity to consume? Such artificial words can be memorized, of course, even pronounced trippingly on the tongue, but without roots in indigenous culture and tradition they often lack the precision needed in the development of new skills or the successful use of foreign technology. The alternative of learning English would prove to be a heavy burden on the young people of Africa and Asia. It would overload their already crowded curriculum. Worse still, it would separate them from their fellow citizens into a special, alien-oriented class. Like merchants in the Middle Ages, they would be suspected by their own people. All these factors combine differently in the various countries of the Third World, but, concludes a Pakistani Nobel laureate, *"the African, the Arab and the Islamic countries* by and large have a long leeway to make up. There appears to be scant future for science and technology in these societies."[5]

There *has* been economic growth in Africa and Asia. The changes, especially in the cities, leap to the eye. Progress in general, however, has largely been externally induced. In the countryside it has been painfully slow. Concluded one World Bank report (in its peculiar jargon): "The long-run trend of 'fluctuations around stagnancy,' for the rural laborer in the *average* season and place in India, seems clear."[6] Meanwhile America too, has advanced—much faster. It seems to advance perpetually, which makes slow (no) economic growth all the more politically disruptive. For as comparisons become available, people understandably become more and more impressed by the gap between our standard of living and their own, especially if the gap continues to widen.[7] As part of an international demonstration effect the people of Asia and Africa learn to want just exactly what Americans have. (All the more so since Americans never miss a chance to proclaim their basic conviction that all men are created equal.) They learn to want it not as the result of an arduous process of hard work and careful economizing, but as they see Americans have it: everything with and for pleasure. And they learn to want it not in the future, in the days of their grandchildren, but as they see Americans have it: right now. As they realize that they cannot have it, as part of the international demonstration effect they become frustrated and hostile.

POLITICAL REALITIES

What makes it all so much worse is that most governments in Africa and Asia are inefficient and ineffective. Internationally they may be recognized as sovereign. At home they may establish ministries and planning commissions. They may appoint officials who will attend joint meetings, write reports, and carry on a brisk correspondence and vigorous battles for the protection of their own turf. Governments may proclaim policies, but what most of them cannot do is implement them. As a matter of fact, few can maintain law and order, and fewer still can collect taxes.

One reason is that they have very little capacity to coerce. To be sure, they can persecute some dissidents; they can jail, torture, and murder them. But not even the most authoritarian system, the most brutal tyrant, can extort general compliance. Fascist and Communist methods do not produce the results they did in Europe.

For one thing, the long tradition in Asia and Africa is against it. Not against physical force. People regularly fought over property; they fought over women (their favors or their honor). They fought to dominate. They fought from pride, in frustration and desperation. Quite often people were very cruel; they relished the agony of others. People were accustomed to such acts of private violence. But people were not accustomed to the use of force as a instrument of public policy.

Government meant personal rule, a rule to be marked by kindness and generosity. In fact, when the ruler/subject context was translated into referents that were more familiar to the rural masses, it became analogous to a master/servant relationship. And in the latter the constraints of noblesse oblige were operative. A husband might beat his wife; but it was the height of bad form for a master to beat his servant. It is a curious consequence of this analogy that a policeman raised in a village, who has married a girl from the village, and whose income is no higher than that of a villager, nevertheless has crossed the magic line of separation. For him to use force to compel compliance with government policy does not seem right. The people resent it; he does not want to do it. Governments may bring in troops recruited in other regions, from different tribes, perhaps import troops from abroad. These "foreigners" may be more willing to fire into crowds. They may for a time improve the appearance of compliance, but more likely they will incite hostility and resistance. The Cubans did in Angola and Ethiopia, the Soviets did in Afghanistan, and too often the Americans did in Vietnam.

Not just tradition is against it. The practical realities of the present also militate against government coercion. The countries of Asia and Africa are essentially rural. Most people still live dispersed in small villages. They mind their own business and regulate their own affairs. Officials know little about them; occasionally they come to visit, but they do not stay. After a few hours they hasten back to their more comfortable, urban quarters. In fact, the government has little effective access to the masses. Communications are rudimentary. Telephones and radios are rare. There are few roads. Paths are narrow, travel is hazardous, the possibility of snakebites is always present. In case of a crime or an incident it takes hours, possibly days, for government to hear about it. By the time it can respond and get to the place of trouble, even the shouting is over.

The most fundamental reason for the ineffectiveness of governments in Africa and Asia, however, is their almost total lack of *capacity to persuade*. For that they need legitimacy, a quality that so far has proven all too elusive.

The disruption of traditional societies undermined the legitimacy of political authority based on divine selection. Meanwhile, an alternative had been suggested by the West: the right to govern rests on the consent of the governed. It was an appealing alternative, a modern idea. More important, it was the formula that overcame the power of colonialism and brought independence. Many, though not all, of the nationalist leaders were attracted to popular sovereignty and, when given the opportunity, tried very hard to build their new government on that principle. Even so, it did not seem to work. Soon elections were postponed, constitutions were abolished, and democratic governments collapsed. In the 1960s and 1970s coups took place all over Asia and Africa with disheartening regularity.

Perhaps democracy did not have a chance. The political boundaries were not suitable. During the previous centuries, when the colonial dependencies were carved out of Asia and Africa, their borders were drawn by purely external criteria: the economic advantages and the administrative conveniences of the distant (European) power. In terms of local considerations—especially for Africa—the delineations made no social sense. They artificially combined different ascriptive groups (such as tribes) that for centuries had been divided by hostility and bloody conflict. At the same time they arbitrarily divided groups that had been tied together by kinship and common tradition. Neither did the borders make economic sense. Often colonies were so small, and their configuration so peculiar, that they could not possibly contain the resources to be self-sufficient, or to generate development. Yet, remarkably, after the various European dependencies in a balkanized Africa finally gained their independence, they not only preserved these arcane borders but, through the Organization of African Unity, have repeatedly proclaimed them to be sacrosanct.

Possibly the people were not ready for democracy. After several centuries of evolution, universal suffrage has become a reality in the United States. Is it reasonable to expect that in Africa and Asia the process can be telescoped into a few decades, let alone that constructive universal suffrage could be achieved overnight? Democracy without education is hypocrisy without limitation, warned a former president of Pakistan. Perhaps more to the point: Is it reasonable to expect that democracy can function well when most people exist in abject poverty, but can see others (at home or abroad) enjoying the life of affluence? Is it reasonable to expect the masses of poor people, when they exercise their right of suffrage, to be motivated by the common good, or even by "enlightened self-interest"?

There is also the possibility that the political leaders were not ready for democracy. Democratic politics requires above all three things. First is an attitude of *moderation*. It shuns absolutes, dichotomies between right and wrong, the righteous and the ungodly, or winners and losers. At the heart of democratic conflict resolution is political bargaining, brokering of interest, and ultimately the means of settlement: compromise. It needs tolerance, a willingness to share (profits and costs), and satisfaction with incremental gains. But Asian and African leaders live with the tradition that presents issues in harsh black-and-white moral terms, and live in the present, where conflict is zero sum and its results are clear-cut: you win or you lose; you win much or you lose badly. They live in a world that is not at all conducive to moderation.

Second, democratic politics requires *respect for transcendental rules*. You cannot play a game that ends with winner take all. You cannot play football if a team, by winning this year's Super Bowl, acquires the right to change the rules of recruitment for next year (and decides to pick all the top draft choices). Some two hundred years ago the Constitution determined the basic rules of American politics. They could be changed through the careful process of amendment, but in general the Constitution remained a respected basic framework that no election winner could expropriate. Politics in Africa and Asia, however, is not a game. It is more like total war. Rules are not mental guides for proper conduct; they are weapons of combat to be used against the enemy, the opposition. Constitutions are promulgated not so much to institutionalize a stable political framework as to give advantage to the party (person) in power. When (which is not often) elections are held, the main issue is usually how the constitution must be changed. The chances that it will survive a decade are not very good.[8]

Closely related to this point is the third requirement of democratic politics: *respect for the opposition* (minority). Legitimacy is most vulnerable when it has to be transferred. In traditional systems much is made of proclamation: "The king is dead, long live the king" then followed by the coronation. A democratic system relies on elections as a means of transference of power (office). A majority vote of the electorate designates the successor. But, and this is not a widely recognized point, it is not the winning majority that actually legitimizes the succession. It is the defeated minority. In a remarkable subtlety of American (and other) democracy, legitimacy is in fact transferred when the losers admit it loud and clear; you have won fair and square. Indeed, for the steady continuation of the government's legitimacy (as well as other reasons), the minority is far more important than the majority.

Political leaders in Asia and Africa are not known for such subtlety; or perhaps conditions are not suitable for it.[9] In any case, when occasionally elections are actually held, invariably we hear charges of fraud by the losers and a chorus of "We were robbed." And we find the winners, far from cherishing the opposition, persecuting and jailing its leaders.

The point is that while few African and Asian governments now qualify for a mandate from heaven, fewer still can benefit from the consent of the governed. Governments may be tolerated by their people as long as they keep out of the way, do not get any ideas or launch any new initiatives. Frustrated, some leaders may experiment with Communism or fascism, but they do not have the resources of coercion to carry on for long. Frustrated, some people may seek escape in neo-orthodox (fundamentalist traditional) reaction. Most governments, however, do not want to turn back. Since they do not quite know how to move ahead, they have not much choice but to try to muddle through—and look for help from abroad, possibly from America.

U.S. AID AND BENIGN NEGLECT

The problem is, it is not quite clear just what we could do and how we should do it. We thought we knew two or three decades ago. In support of a decentralized world order we launched a massive effort (1) to increase the inadequate governmental capacities of newly independent states and (2) to contain the accelerating pressures of destabilization that they faced. In order to help train public officials, U.S. government agencies, private foundations, and universities established and subsidized institutes of public administration. In order to help build effective administrative structures, they provided advisory groups. At the heart of the approach, however, was economic assistance. It would help, we hoped (and believed), to generate sufficient momentum for a takeoff into self-sustained growth, alleviate mass poverty in the foreseeable future, and consequently contain demands on government and help fend off revolutionary mobilization.

The United States was prepared to invest very substantial sums. In 1965 some 90 countries received economic assistance—nearly all of Asia, Africa, and Latin America. The total cost of $4.9 billion represented a healthy chunk of the federal budget ($118.2 billion) and compared favorably with appropriations for our national defense (about $50.6 billion). The largest sums went to India and Pakistan,[10] two newly independent states important for international order and countries where hundreds of millions of human beings were barely subsisting in absolute poverty.

It is customary to separate foreign aid allocations into two categories: grants and loans. For a banker this may make considerable sense. In terms of the overall political and economic purposes of the program, however, such classifications are of little significance. More helpful are the subdivisions indicating the character of the input: project assistance, program assistance, and commodity assistance.

At first the most prominent form of American economic aid was *project assistance*. Grants or loans were made available after a careful scrutiny of specific requests. Generally directed toward the establishment of industrial plants (although at times they included major social overhead projects), they were evaluated by strict (even orthodox) economic criteria. Another substantial category of American foreign aid was *program assistance*. Officially it was defined as "the transfer of non-project resources . . . under circumstances where the totality of the resources made available, rather than their particular use, constitutes the primary United States concern." In simpler, nonbureaucratic language this meant that countries would draft their comprehensive and integrated development plans. Then, after adding up the cost and determining the shortfall of domestically available resources, they would turn to the United States to make up the difference. We would examine the soundness of the plan and then grant a credit line. Up to a certain amount, a foreign country could buy from us any commodity of its choice, provided it could be explained in terms of the general framework of the plan. It is impossible to identify exactly the specific commodities that were financed through program assistance. We may find a clue to the mix, however, in the overall import pattern. If so, it becomes apparent that while large quantities of industrial raw materials were so acquired, the lion's share of program aid financed manufactured goods, mostly consumer goods. The rewards generated were personal and material; the groups most affected were urban (middle-class) elements with high political saliency.

The third category of our aid was also called the Food for Peace program. Massive shipments of surplus agricultural products were authorized under Public Law 480. Technically they were sold to the recipients. "Payments," however, was made in nonconvertible local currency. Since we could spend only a limited amount of rupees in India or Pakistan, and none of them in the United States, the food shipments were in fact a gift. It provided a somewhat circuitous route to escape detailed congressional scrutiny.

Food for Peace did reach the poor. Project and program assistance, by focusing on industrialization as the vehicle of economic development, was designed to bring them benefits in the longer run. All the same, our foreign aid program was not an unambiguous asset. All those many, many tons of food we made freely available, we discovered, caused some problems as well. Dietary patterns are deeply rooted in tradition; there are firm taboos and well established preferences. A large portion of the poor are Muslims, who will not touch protein-rich pork. They would be horrified even to think of it.[11] Hundreds of millions in Africa and Asia are accustomed to rice as the staple of diet. They are apt to resist vigorously the merits of wheat (not to mention corn). Even the (California) rice we delivered looked different. It did not seem to taste just right. Milk and eggs were welcome, but given the distance and time they had to be shipped, were dehydrated and/or canned. They had a strange taste to GIs in World War II, and they still have a strange taste to the villagers in South Asia and Africa. When they were taken in school lunch programs, some children became violently ill.

Meanwhile, the transfer of our technology proved to have its own problems. It soon became apparent that in addition to the difficulties inherent in adjusting it to local conditions, project and program assistance was accompanied by an unfortunate side effect: it exacerbated the international demonstration effect. American machinery had to be accompanied by American technicians who had to operate it or train others to do so, but who would not have accepted foreign assignments without the incentives of high incomes and assured living conditions well above those they enjoyed at home. Meanwhile, some indigenous technicians came to the United States for special instruction. In the process the people of Africa and Asia became more familiar with the United States, its resources, and *its quality of life*. It inflated their aspirations enormously. In the process their attention was soon distracted from the achievement of their own economic gains made possible by U.S. aid. More than ever before they became impressed by the gap between what we have and what they could expect in the foreseeable future.

On balance, then, it may be said that U.S. economic assistance of the 1950s and 1960s had mixed results. It did contribute somewhat to the amelioration of mass poverty.[12] It should also be recognized, however, that it did not yield satisfaction with visible progress and an attitude of self-confidence. All too often it produced frustration, a feeling of grievance, even hostility. It did not enhance the political stability of its recipients, and it did not noticeably generate gratitude toward the United States. All the same, we had tried. When President Kennedy established the Peace Corps, when thousands of young and not so young Americans volunteered to live in and work for the development of the various countries of Africa and Asia (and Latin America) without any material gain, and when the President kept a visible, personal interest in the program, everyone could see that our fellow humans mattered to Americans. That we cared did not go unnoticed.

Our circumstances are very different now. By 1985 the federal budget had climbed precipitously to nearly $1 trillion ($946.3 billion). The annual federal deficit reached $212.3 billion that year, about 150 times the 1965 level ($1.4 billion). Our international (merchandise) trade deficit hit $132.1 billion and kept climbing.[13] We were becoming a debtor nation. Meanwhile, our foreign policy posture had changed as well. Vietnam had buried (at least for a while) thoughts about decentralized world order. Once again we thought in terms of great power politics. It is easier and cheaper that way. And with the Soviet President exuding good will, we feel quite secure and comfortable.

We still have a program of foreign aid. A perfunctory glimpse may lead one to be impressed by the more than doubling of the funds allocated over 20 years

(1965–85). The increase becomes rather less impressive, however, if we recall that this was a period of steady and at times substantial inflation and that the federal budget rose by 700 percent. Indeed, the share of economic assistance shrank from 4 percent to 1 percent of the federal budget pie.[14]

As a matter of fact, foreign aid is very different now. Since 1982 military assistance has become its largest component.[15] We now sell arms on credit and then, before payment becomes due, we cancel the debts. We did, of course, resort to a similar process in the past—under Public Law 480, for food. Now we are doing it for weapons.[16]

Meanwhile, strange things were happening to the nonmilitary components. U.S. Agency for International Development (AID) totals now include such items as American Schools and Hospitals Abroad, International Disaster Assistance, Operating Expenses, and the Foreign Service Retirement and Disability Fund! Then, there is a new giant category: the Economic Support Fund. In fiscal year 1985 it accounted for $5.2 billion of the $7.8 billion economic assistance. Any way one looks at it, no more than a third of it can be considered development aid.[17] Indeed, if we strip the economic assistance budget of the contribution of creative accounting, we find our investment in the economic development of Asian and African countries shrinking fast.

It is a fact further dramatized by a definite change in the beneficiaries. A Senate report (1985) listed 36 countries "most in need of assistance" with annual per capita in incomes below $400. Their population (including the People's Republic of China) exceeded 2.2 billion human beings. Our total dollar assistance (through U.S. AID) was $845 million, or 38 cents a person. At the same time Israel, with a per capita income of $5,360, received *economic assistance* (not including military aid and credits) of $910 billion, which works out to over $250 per person (*650* times more). The Senate report makes no bones about it: "While it is little understood by many, our foreign assistance program is largely tied to direct U.S. security interests."[18] Political stability in newly independent states has receded to secondary importance; concern for the alleviation of mass poverty can be found only by inference.

TOWARD THE NEXT AMERICAN CENTURY

The question remains open: Could we have done otherwise? Given the trauma of our massive, largely altruistic involvement in Vietnam and the constitutional crisis of Watergate, given our rapidly growing deficits and the newfound foreign policy preoccupation of congressmen who found "no constituency" for foreign aid, did we, as a practical matter, have any alternatives? Could we have continued the relatively high level of appropriations for economic assistance to underdeveloped countries year after year, decade after decade? Possibly not.

There is no doubt, however, that while superpower relations may move from harsh conflict and mutual recriminations to mutual understanding and perhaps even mutual cooperation, we can expect trouble, all kinds of trouble, in Africa and Asia in the not too distant future. We shall see more violence along ascriptive lines, among different races, ethnic groups, or tribes; we shall see border wars over disputed territories; and we shall regularly see coups and revolutions. They may be of local significance only, but they may affect regional security. Some will involve only our general interest in international order; some will jeopardize the interests of our friends and allies, and challenge our commitments. Possibly a few may threaten us directly by abetting the spread of international terrorism.

We shall need a capability to project force into distant parts of the globe. Specifically, first, we need to maintain a capability for covert operations. They may sound sinister, but they are very useful. There are circumstances when foreign governments would welcome U.S. intervention but could not say so publicly. More important, as long as they are secret, we could contain conflict at the lowest level of intensity. We could avoid overt intervention, which might trigger a process of escalation into open insurgency, warfare, and who knows what. Second, we need to build a capability to insert small, highly trained, and highly mobile units to swing the outcome of local and regional deadly quarrels in our favor, or at least to assure the evacuation of American citizens from their immediate vicinity. In fact we have some of this capability, but we need much more of it.

Actually, the rationale for a highly mobile force capable of quick deployment in Africa and Asia is not new.[19] In 1963 Secretary of Defense McNamara established a Strike Command very much for this purpose. It was vigorously opposed by the military leadership, remained not much more than a paper command, and was dissolved by the Nixon Administration in 1972. The idea, however, did not disappear. In August 1977 President Carter issued a presidential directive (PD no. 18) that called for the establishment of such a force that could be moved quickly to crisis areas outside of NATO. The Joint Chiefs did not like the idea at all, and Secretary of Defense Harold Brown was preoccupied with other matters, so the presidential directive languished in a bureaucratic limbo. The unstable, then hostile, conditions in Iran, however, produced some action, such as it was. In December 1978, without mentioning Iran, a review was ordered (PRIM no. 10) of contingency plans for the use of military force in the Persian Gulf. The review was completed at leisure (Secretary Brown was still otherwise preoccupied) and then carefully, very carefully, filed away.

The President and especially his National Security Adviser, however, kept pressing. A directive in October 1979 ordered the establishment of a U.S.-based Joint Task Force to respond to contingencies anywhere in the world, with initial concentration on southwest Asia, and asked for names of Army three star generals to be considered for its command. The Joint Chiefs most reluctantly agreed to proceed (and recommended a Marine Corps two star general for the position). When Major General P. Kelley was approved and given a third star, their resistance shifted to arguments on the location of the new force's headquarters. Somewhere close to Washington, D.C., would have made good sense, but the Army insisted on Fort Bragg, North Carolina. In a "compromise" McDill Air

Force Base in Florida was designated, and there, on March 1, 1980, the Rapid Deployment Joint Tactical Force (RDJTF) became operational.

At first glance it was an impressive concentration of power: three and a quarter Army divisions, two and a quarter of which were airborne; one and a third amphibious Marine Corps divisions (all the Navy was capable of lifting); three Navy carrier battle groups; four tactical Air Force wings; and thirty-five B–52G strategic bombers. Such a force could surely make an enormous difference in any Third World unpleasantness. While the RDJTF commander did not have operational (command) control, he did have a say in planning, training, exercise, deployment, and employment—which was all General Kelley wanted.

In fact, he was quite enthusiastic about the opportunity. Quickly he established a special liaison office at the Pentagon through which the command in Florida could be kept up to date about all the activities at the highest military levels. More than that, he insisted that the regional commanders in chief send high-level liaison officers to Florida to build the closest cooperation. Soon joint exercises were held; one of them, "Bright Star," was a cooperative effort with the Egyptian army.

Indeed, as an effective instrument of global force projection, the RDJTF never got off the ground. The resistance of the Joint Chiefs of Staff remained fierce. Possibly they were concerned that a commander with such broad geographic responsibilities might trespass on their own prerogatives. (They were seriously annoyed when the aborted Teheran rescue mission, an operation by such a joint task force, was managed directly from the Office of the Secretary of Defense.) What they said publicly was that regional commanders were much more knowledgeable about (cultural, political, economic) conditions of their region, and hence far more qualified to "employ" U.S. forces in their own area than any command located in the United States. Meanwhile, the commander of the RDJTF and his staff were developing their own doubts. There were just too many and too different kinds of trouble spots throughout the world. They could focus on one, perhaps two, at a time, but no sooner had they worked out their plans than a problem somewhere else threatened to become acute. Too much back and forth, back and forth, they complained. Then came press reports on Operation Bright Star. They had some favorable things to say, but they highlighted the high cost, the logistical difficulties, and the political sensitivity of the operation. It took 50 sorties of heavy cargo planes to get just 1,400 troops plus headquarters and Air Force personnel there. The cost amounted to $40,000 per soldier.[20]

Worst of all, even before it became organized, the RDJTF had to concentrate on the special problem of Iran. When President Carter and Zbigniew Brzezinski left office, it was an easy step to convert RDJTF into a more or less conventional regional arrangement. It was renamed Central Command, its commander was given another star, and the global mission was abandoned. By the time of the Lebanon crises, the Grenada intervention, and the raids on Libya, regional commands were in charge of "rapid deployment." The Central Command was hobbling along, one of its airborne divisions replaced by a heavy division, its war-fighting ability limited by only 83 percent readiness of the major combat support units and just 62 percent readiness of the nonmajor units.[21] It could have handled an airplane hijacking in Karachi (except that the Pakistanis took care of the problem before we could get there), and it managed the search for the downed plane of Congressman Mickey Leland.[22] It did run one major operation: the escorting of Kuwaiti tankers in the Persian Gulf (1987–88). Probably the best recent example of measured U.S. force used to accomplish political aims. It was truly a joint operation, forces were deployed quickly (the number of naval vessels rose rapidly from 5 to more than 30), and in the end success was there for all to see (American prestige in the Gulf rose markedly).

President Bush apparently is aware of the new challenges. In his first (Presidential) address to the United Nations General Assembly he made it clear:

We have not entered into an era of perpetual peace. The threats to peace that nations face may today be changing, but they have not vanished.

In fact, in a number of regions around the world, a dangerous combination is now emerging: Regimes . . . with old and unappeasable animosities . . . [armed with] modern weapons of mass destruction.

This development will raise the stakes whenever war breaks out. Regional conflicts may well threaten world peace as never before. . . .

And let me assure you the United States is determined to take an active role in settling regional conflicts.[23]

If his words are to gain meaning and credibility, however, they must be followed by action. The problem is that this is not the time to add to the defense budget. To be sure, some existing assets could be used for a rapid deployment force: aircraft carriers, transport planes, airborne troops, for example. But more of them and other things as well are needed to build it into an effective global instrument: possibly the new V–22 (Osprey), a vertical-takeoff-and-landing plane that is faster and has a greater range for delivering Marines from a carrier than the available helicopters. As a practical matter, such costs would have to be taken out of other parts of the budget. That would mean the restructuring of our armed forces, which in turn would require a major revision in the definition of their mission.

For decades we have concentrated on two major goals. First, we have sought to *deter* a nuclear attack upon us, an attack that would cause unimaginable devastation of our country and a horrendous cost in lives. Second, we hoped, if necessary, to *win* ("to terminate on favorable terms") large-scale conventional wars, similar to the last great war we had won so gloriously.

Clearly we cannot abandon the first; we must not neglect our strategic deterrence. Looking at the future, however, we may revise, quite fundamentally, our preoccupation with large-scale conventional wars. We have some 326,000 troops in Europe and another 141,000 stationed in East Asia (mostly in Japan/Okinawa and South Korea). They are part of our "forward defense." Its logic, although rarely put this crassly, is that if we have to fight a war, we would prefer to fight it on someone else's territory, far from the United States. Our usual public explanation is that we are there to help protect those countries from Communist aggression. Indeed, there may have been validity in this contention in the 1950s and 1960s.

South Korea was militarily and economically weak. It was facing North Korea, an agent of the Sino-Soviet behemoth. Lately, however, South Korea has become a significant economic power in the region, much more productive and far more wealthy than her neighbor to the north. General Louis Menetrey, Commander, Combined Forces, Korea has conceded that most U.S. forces could probably leave the peninsula by the mid 1990s. Admittedly, we can hear some dire warnings that if we reduce our troops there, South Korea will turn to the Communist power. There are at least two things wrong with this. One is that South Korea, its leaders, and its people enjoy their high standard of living. They would not want to give it up. But their newfound wealth is really the consequence of their access to the North American market. How many Hyundais could they sell in North Korea? How much profit could they make from trade with the Soviet Union? We may consider the possibility that the South Koreans want our forces there not so much because they need them for their military defense but because they serve as such convenient hostages. They really help reduce the danger that the United States will run out of patience with South Korean exclusionary trade practices and restrict South Korean access to our markets.

The second thing wrong with the argument is that the Communist powers might not welcome South Korea in their midst. The Red conglomerate has broken up. The Chinese would not like it at all if the whole Korean peninsula fell under Soviet dominion. They might well resist it—even with armed force. In turn, the Soviet Union does not look with favor on Chinese forces in North Korea, let alone Chinese domination of both Koreas. For them as well, things are right just as they are.

This is not the time unilaterally to withdraw forces from Western Europe. The Soviet Union has made public statements about going on the defensive and has actually implemented some measures that would indicate its leaders are quite serious about it. But military planning is better based on the other's actual capabilities than on its estimated intentions, and Soviet military capabilities in Europe are still awesome. All the same, there are good reasons to assume that they have leveled off. Moreover, even if Soviet forces were not steadily reduced in the future, with Eastern Europe in turmoil the Soviets' capabilities are actually declining. A surprise attack is becoming impossible for them. A more massive attack (30–22 scenario), which requires moving and supplying heavy forces across an increasingly independent Poland and an increasingly volatile East Germany, is becoming more and more difficult. The presence of U.S. troops may continue to make sense, but the need to deploy 37 percent of the Army combat forces and 42 percent of our tactical air forces in Europe is noticeably losing its rationale. It is time to begin planning for the contingency of withdrawing some of them.

The question arises: Where else, and more specifically where in Asia and Africa, could a conflict arise in which we could usefully deploy large conventional forces? And, to be realistic, where would Congress permit the deployment of such forces? In the Philippines? That would be a bad decision. In the Middle East? That would be a disastrous decision.

So a global rapid deployment force may be an idea whose time has come. The argument that regional commands in the immediate physical proximity are better suited to manage low-intensity conflict, at least as far as Africa and much of Asia are concerned, never made much sense. Given the existing political environment in recently independent (postcolonial) countries, it would be practically impossible to get the consent of any government there for the establishment of a major U.S. base within its territory—and even if one might be found, it would be constantly exposed to the possibility of insurgency and coups. The Central Command, with headquarters in Florida worked admirably in the Persian Gulf; it or a similar command, properly led, could do as well in other areas of Asia and Africa.

As a matter of fact, in the near future two conditions will greatly exacerbate the pressure for a restructuring of our armed forces. First, the popular and congressional threat perception of Soviet military might is likely to decline substantially. Consequently the need for the "forward deployment" of our heavy divisions will become increasingly controversial. But there is no place to put these forces back home. (Admittedly this is a double-edged argument. Many a congressman would be glad to support building new military installations in his own district with economic multiplier effects for his constituents and political benefits for himself.) The answer may well be a smaller, leaner, tougher, and globally mobile conventional force that, when projected into *the areas of most likely conflict in the future,* could "terminate war on favorable terms" for us.

Second, the deficit reduction requirements will become even more acute. Congress and the executive branch are running out of ideas for creative book-keeping, and the mandated cuts are getting closer and closer to the bone. The high cost of manpower will soon attract more attention. As a matter of fact, more than half of the defense budget is spent on personnel and personnel-related items. Indeed, by the end of 1989 plans were being negotiated in the Pentagon for a personnel cut of between 35,600 and 48,600 by October 1, 1990, and concerns were widely expressed that if the "sequester" in effect remained in place throughout the entire budget year, it might require a slash in manpower, something on the order of 160,000! Clearly, a general reduction, but especially a significant reduction of Army forces on active duty (perhaps from 771,847 to 500,000), could yield an almost immediate saving of $20 billion (much more than we could get by blowing up tanks).

So major a restructuring of our Armed Forces will require bold Presidential leadership. Congress is comfortable with the existing pattern. It prefers general across-the-board reductions, and recently, when it focused on specific targets, it cut the very weapons we may need most in the future: new weapons of strategic deterrence (SDI, MX, and Midgetman) and instruments of force projection (aircraft carriers, V–22). It will require the maximum use of the civilian control of the military; the Chiefs, too, are comfortable with the present arrangement of each service being assured a more or less equal piece of the pie. And they do not like joint command arrangements. The Air Force will resist the idea of its strategic bomber wings or missile batteries being commanded by anyone who is not in Air Force blue no less vigorously than the Navy would resist any attempt to put a general in charge of its ships. Most fundamentally, however—and we have now come full circle—we shall require a prepolicy consensus on our changing security needs emerging from a public discussion among our opinion leaders and within the general electorate. To be sure, we will have to move carefully and gradually—but the time to begin is now.

If we are determined to take an active role in settling regional disputes, however, we shall have to do more than be able to respond militarily to crises. It is far better to prevent them by investing in the countries' political stability. The problem is that we are talking of states and regions that are not, strictly speaking, strategically and economically significant for us. It is easy to succumb to the temptation to ignore them. But can we ignore the fate of their people?

Let us keep in mind that our democracy is based unequivocally on universal categories: "*All* men are created equal; *all* men are endowed with certain inalienable rights." Not just the strong, the rich, the intellectually brilliant; not just the white, the Anglo-Saxon, the Protestant; all men and women. Our ideology, the political tenets that made this country what it is, rejects radical discontinuities between human beings who are Americans and human beings who are not. No first-class human beings, no second-class human beings, no chosen people, no super race; just human beings.

Admittedly we have not always been faithful to our values. At times we have violated them, and for much of our history we did not think of our fellow men in distant lands. Psychologically we could cope with not thinking of them because we did not know, and had little chance of finding out, about them. They might just as well have been on another planet. This is no longer so. Phenomenal advances in modern communications technology have made the rest of the world aware of the United States and no longer permit us to remain comfortably ignorant of the rest of the world. Our information is still spotty, but when pictures of misery in Bangladesh or starvation in Ethiopia are flashed on our TV screens, we cannot wipe them out of our minds. Americans do not turn off their sets; we watch and then are galvanized into massive efforts of aid. Often it is an emotional reaction, and our ventures may not be well thought out, but the evidence is in: we cannot turn our backs on our fellow men and retain our self-respect. This does not mean that the United States, its government, and its people should become mesmerized by humanitarian responsibilities. But it does mean that the time has come when our national interest can no longer ignore the fate of about half of humanity who are of no military or economic use to us—but who, we know, are our brothers and sisters.

The truth is, however, that we do not know how to handle the consequences of our national interest in our fellow men. On this, too, we need a general discussion to explore in detail exactly what we can do, and then to build a prepolicy consensus on what we ought to do. There is no way we can provide all human beings with an economic ''safety net,'' but we could make a major contribution to the alleviation of widespread hunger and dietary deficiency. It is surely one of the great paradoxes of our time that the United States spends billions and billions of dollars year after year to reduce its agricultural production. We cannot provide social order and political stability for other countries, but our government and private foundations could help organize and support institutes and seminars devoted to the problems of political and social development at which new ideas and more effective (realistic) approaches could be generated.

We do not have much money to spare, but we could reexamine the proper composition of our foreign aid package, its excessive focus on the Near East and its neglect of South Asia and sub-Sahara Africa. Is it really true that the close diplomatic ties between the governments of India and the Soviet Union must preclude greater humanitarian involvement of the United States in the subcontinent? Is it really true that what Pakistan needs most is F–16s and armored personnel carriers? Is it really true that Black Africa has little absorptive capacity for U.S. aid, that the governments there are too incompetent and/or corrupt and the difficulties are altogether intractable?

We may consider whether it is time once again for the President of a ''kinder and gentler America'' to call upon the wellsprings of this great nation, and especially that of its youth, and reinvigorate the Peace Corps. Surely there are many things our government could do without being paralyzed by the Gramm-Rudman deficit-cutting mandate. And surely there are many things we could do through private organizations and initiatives.

The danger is that with the peril to our national survival receding, we may become complacent and (even more) self-oriented. We may be inclined to concentrate on pressing domestic issues, on social justice, urban crime, AIDS, and drugs, and become distracted from the problems and demands of our international environment. It is time for some consciousness-raising, the development of a sense of purpose. For our own sake as well, we need to demonstrate that we care. We need to learn about our fellow men, their traditions and conditions. We need political leadership: practical, effective, and inspired by what President Kennedy recognized as ''the supreme reality of our time . . . our indivisibility as children of God and our common vulnerability on this planet.''

So, as we approach the twenty-first century, as we seek to guide our foreign policy in a less perilous world, our vital national interest to assure our survival through deterrence of nuclear attack will continue to require our vigilance and attention. Our special national interest to guide our delicate relations with our friends and allies will continue to require much skill and tact; our general national interest to lead in the development of international order will continue to require dedication and imagination. But the greatest challenge to us and our children, a challenge more difficult than our program of landing on the moon in the 1960s and more urgent than our Manhattan Project during World War II, is to participate—indeed, lead—in the quest to give every person on Earth a human chance.

Admittedly it is easy to write prescriptions for what we need to do; it is very much harder actually to fill them. Can it be done? Can we do it? We shall see. The point is that we ought to try. We must not ignore our historic challenge if we want to live in peace, not precariously balanced on power but firmly founded on law and justice, and if we want our fellow men to look at America not in fear of our military might but with respect for our civilization.

NOTES

1. One can observe American influence on tastes almost everywhere. American students unintentionally set international standards by their behavior. Far, far away young people eat hamburgers, wear designer jeans, listen to rock music, and dance at discos to follow the American example. I was visiting a village chief in the very orthodox Muslim state of Kelantan. We had some refreshment. There were no women in sight. His son was present, listening almost reverently to every paternal pronouncement. Suddenly four children burst noisily into the room, ignored everyone around, and turned on the television set. "It is seven o'clock, they want to watch Mickey Mouse," explained their father. "What can we do?" the head of the family lamented.

2. One comprehensive study reports that the daily protein consumption was 106 grams in the United States, 63 in Nigeria, 52 in India, 47 in the Philippines, 38 in Indonesia, and 33 in Zaire. Sartaj Aziz, ed., *Hunger, Politics and Markets* (New York: New York University Press, 1975), pp. 117–21.

3. Children inherit a portion of their parents' land, to which they add the portion inherited by their spouses, which is rarely adjacent.

4. While in industrialized countries the proportions enrolled in "professional" and "liberal arts" programs is 50:50, in the Third World it is 10:90. Abdus Salam, *Notes on Science, Technology and Science Education in the Development of the South* (Trieste: Tipografia-Litografia Moderna, 1989), pp. 67, 69.

5. Ibid., p. 93. Emphasis added. See also pp. 42–44.

6. Michael Lipton, *Labor and Poverty,* World Bank Staff Working Paper no. 616 (Washington, D.C.: World Bank, 1983), p. 86.

7. Between 1960 and 1978 the average annual growth in GNP per capita was 2.4 percent in the United States, -0.4 percent in Bangladesh, 1.0 percent in Burma, 0.5 percent in Ghana, 1.4 percent in India, -1.4 percent in Niger, 2.0 percent in Sri Lanka, 0.7 percent in Uganda, 1.1 percent in Zaire, and 1.2 percent in Zambia. The World Bank, *Poverty and Human Development* (New York: Oxford University Press, 1980), p. 68.

8. A notable exception is the Indian Constitution, which, though battered, has survived since 1949.

9. During the winter of 1961 I tried to make this point to Prime Minister Nehru. It was not an original point, since Mahatma Gandhi had urged the Congress Party to disband on the day of independence. He dismissed the suggestion out of hand: "Professor, it would be foolish for me to help my enemies."

10. United States, Agency for International Development, *Operations Report. FY 1965* (December 1965), pp. 24–25, 35–41, 90–102.

11. They do not even like it when others do. In Malaysia, Malays (who are mainly Muslims) are irritated when they see their Chinese fellow citizens munching succulent morsels of the unclean animal, and are outright provoked when they encounter it during their own month of fasting (Ramadan).

12. "The *proportion* of people in absolute poverty in developing countries as a group is estimated to have fallen during the last two decades (though probably not in Sub-Saharan Africa in the 1970's[)]. But because population has grown, the *number* of people in absolute poverty has increased." World Bank, *Poverty and Human Development*, p. 3.

13. United States, Department of Commerce, Bureau of the Census, *Statistical Abstract of the United States, 1986* (Washington, D.C.: U.S. Government Printing Office, 1986), pp. 292, 789.

14. Calculations are based on United States, Agency for International Development, *Operations Report FY 1965*, pp. 24–25, 31–41, 90–102; United States, Agency for International Development, *Congressional Presentation Fiscal Year 1988*, main vol., pp. 6–7, 11–13; United States, Department of Commerce, Bureau of the Census, *Statistical Abstract of the United States, 1987*, p. 292.

15. United States, House of Representatives, Select Committee on Hunger, *Trends in Foreign Aid, 1977–86* (Washington, D.C.: U.S. Government Printing Office, 1986), p. 8.

16. The fiscal year 1985 actual figures were (a) total military assistance; $7,593,143,000; and (b) direct credit and forgiven loans; $4,939,500,000.

17. United States, Senate, *Foreign Assistance and Related Programs Appropriation Bill, 1986*, Report no. 99–167, October 31 (legislative day, October 28), 1985, pp. 30, 84–88.

18. Ibid., p. 27.

19. George B. Crist, "Twenty-five Years of Debate: A Look at Rapid Deployment Forces and Joint Command Arrangements for the Near East," unpublished study (1989).

20. *New York Times*, November 21, 1980, p. A–18.

21. Statement of General George B. Crist, U.S. Marine Corps, Commander in Chief, U.S. Central Command, before the Senate Armed Services Committee on the Status of the United States Central Command, March 15, 1988, pp. 31–35.

22. In 1987 a joint Special Operations Command was established with headquarters next door to the Central Command at McDill Air Force Base in Florida. Its assets (Navy SEALs, Army Delta Force and Rangers), however, are best suited for anti-terrorist, perhaps anti-drug moves, similar to and only slightly larger in scale than CIA covert operations. As an instrument of settling regional disputes its capabilities are inadequate.

23. *New York Times*, September 26, 1989, p. A–16.

Selected Bibliography

ARTICLES

Bethe, Hans, Richard L. Garwin, Kurt Gottfried, and Henry W. Kendall. "Space-based Ballistic-Missile Defense." *Scientific American,* 251, no. 4 (October 1984).

Broad, William J. "Nuclear Pulse (I): Awakening to the Chaos Factor." *Science,* 212 (May 29, 1981).

Coffee, J. I. "The ABM Debate." *Foreign Affairs,* 45 (April 1967).

Dulles, John Foster. "Policy for Security and Peace." *Foreign Affairs,* 32 (April 1954).

Erlich, P. R., M. A. Harnwell, Peter H. Raven, Carl Sagan, G. W. Woodwell, et al. "The Long-Term Biological Consequences of Nuclear War." *Science,* 222 (December 23, 1983).

Evans, Richard. "The New Nationalism and the Old History: Perspectives on the West German *Historikerstreit.*" *Journal of Modern History,* 59 (December 1987).

Garwin, Richard L., and Hans A. Bethe. "Anti-Ballistic-Missile Systems." *Scientific American,* 218, no. 3 (March 1968).

Martin, J. J. "Nuclear Weapons in NATO's Deterrent Strategy." *Orbis,* 22 (Winter 1979).

Rogers, General Bernard W. "The Atlantic Alliance: Prescription for a Difficult Decade." *Foreign Affairs,* 60 (Summer 1982).

Rothestein, R. L. "The ABM: Proliferation and International Stability." *Foreign Affairs,* 46 (April 1968).

Schlesinger, James. "The Eagle and the Bear: Ruminations on Forty Years of Superpower Relations." *Foreign Affairs,* 63 (Summer 1985).

BOOKS

Acheson, Dean. *Present at the Creation: My Years in the State Department.* New York: W. W. Norton, 1969.

Aziz, Sartaj, ed. *Hunger, Politics and Markets*. New York: New York University Press, 1975.

Bacon, Sir Francis. *The Great Instauration and New Atlantis*, edited by J. Weinberger. Arlington Heights, Ill.: AHM Publishing, 1980.

Bailey, Thomas A. *A Diplomatic History of the American People*, 3d ed. New York: Appleton-Century-Crofts, 1946.

Bismarck, Prince Otto von. *Reflections and Reminiscences*, edited by Theodore S. Hamerow. New York: Harper and Row, 1968.

Bodde, Derk. *China's First Unifier: A Study of the Ch'in Dynasty as Seen in the Life of Li Ssŭ*. Leiden: E. J. Brill, 1938.

Braley, Russ. *Bad News, the Foreign Policy of the New York Times*. Chicago: Regnery Gateway, 1984.

Brodie, Bernard. *Strategy in the Missile Age*. Princeton: Princeton University Press, 1959.

Brzezinski, Zbigniew. *Power and Principle: Memoirs of the National Security Adviser, 1977–1981*. New York: Straus and Giroux, 1983.

Carnegie Endowment for International Peace. *Challenges for U.S. National Security, Assessing the Balance: Defense Spending and Conventional Forces*. Washington, D.C.: Carnegie Endowment for International Peace, 1981.

———. *Challenges for U.S. National Security*. Washington, D.C.: Carnegie Endowment for International Peace, 1982.

Carter, Ashton B. *Directed Energy Missile Defense in Space*. Background paper. Washington, D.C.: Office of Technology Assessment, April 1984.

Chayes, Abram, and Jerome B. Wiesner, eds. *ABM: An Evaluation of the Decision to Deploy an Anti-Ballistic Missile System*. New York: Harper and Row, 1969.

Churchill, Winston S. *The Second World War: The Gathering Storm*. Boston: Houghton, Mifflin, 1948.

———. *A History of the English-Speaking Peoples*, vol. 2. New York: Dodd, Mead, 1956.

Ciano, Count Galeazzo. *The Ciano Diaries 1939–1943*, edited by Hugh Gibson. Garden City, N.Y.: Doubleday, 1946.

Cicero, Marcus Tullius. *On the Commonwealth*, translated by George Holland Sabine and Stanley Barney Smith. New York: Bobbs-Merrill, 1929.

Collins, John M. *U.S.–Soviet Military Balance: Concepts and Capabilities, 1960–1980*. New York: McGraw-Hill, 1980.

Deane, General John R. *The Strange Alliance: The Story of Our Efforts at Wartime Cooperation with Russia*. New York: Viking Press, 1948.

Eisenhower, David. *Eisenhower: At War, 1943–1945*. New York: Random House, 1986.

Fay, Sidney Bradshaw. *The Origins of the World War*, 2d ed., New York: Macmillan, 1930.

Freud, Sigmund. *Civilization and Its Discontents*. London: Hogarth, 1949.

Fung Yu-lan. *A History of Chinese Philosophy*, translated by Derk Bodde. Princeton: Princeton University Press, 1952.

———. *A Short History of Chinese Philosophy*, edited by Derk Bodde. New York: The Free Press, 1966.

Gaddis, John Lewis. *Strategies of Containment, a Critical Appraisal of Postwar American National Security Policy*. New York: Oxford University Press, 1982.

Galbraith, John Kenneth. *Ambassador's Journal*. Boston: Houghton, Mifflin, 1969.

Gallup, George H. *The Gallup Poll: Public Opinion, 1983*. Wilmington, Del.: Scholarly Resources, 1984.

Gandhi, M. K. *The Story of My Experiments with Truth*, translated by Mahadev Desai. Washington, D.C.: Public Affairs Press, 1960.

Gates, Gary Paul. *Air Time: The Inside Story of CBS News*. New York: Harper and Row, 1978.

Hadley, Arthur T. *The Straw Giant, Triumph and Failure: America's Armed Forces*. New York: Random House, 1986.

Halberstam, David. *The Best and the Brightest*. New York: Random House, 1969.

Harris, Louis. *The Anguish of Change*. New York: W. W. Norton, 1973.

Higgins, Marguerite. *Our Vietnam Nightmare*. New York: Harper and Row, 1965.

Hoffmann, Stanley. *Primacy or World Order: American Foreign Policy Since the Cold War*. New York: McGraw-Hill, 1978.

Holmes, Geoffrey, ed. *Britain After the Glorious Revolution, 1689–1714*. London: Macmillan, 1969.

The Holy Qur'an, text, translation, and commentary by A. Yusef Ali. Brentwood, Md.: Amana Corporation, 1983.

Hoopes, Townsend. *The Limits of Intervention*. New York: David McKay, 1969.

Inter-American Development Bank. *Economic and Social Progress in Latin America*. 1987 Report. Washington, D.C.: Inter-American Development Bank, n.d.

Johnson, Lyndon Baines. *The Vantage Point, Perspectives of the Presidency, 1963–1969*. New York: Holt, Rinehart and Winston, 1971.

Keddie, Nikki R. *Roots of Revolution, an Interpretive History of Modern Iran*. New Haven: Yale University Press, 1981.

Kennan, George F. *Memoirs, 1925–1950*. Boston: Little, Brown, 1967.

Kissinger, Henry A. *A World Restored*. New York: Grosset and Dunlap, 1964.

———. *The Troubled Partnership, a Re-appraisal of the Atlantic Alliance*. New York: McGraw-Hill, 1965.

———. *White House Years*. Boston: Little, Brown, 1979.

———. *Years of Upheaval*. Boston: Little, Brown, 1982.

Lipton, Michael. *Labor and Poverty*. World Bank Staff Working Paper no. 616. Washington, D.C.: World Bank, 1983.

Lowenthal, Abraham F. *Partners in Conflict, the United States and Latin America*. Baltimore: Johns Hopkins University Press, 1987.

Malraux, André. *Felled Oaks: Conversation with de Gaulle*. New York: Holt, Rinehart and Winston, 1971.

Martone, Celso L. *Macroeconomic Policies, Debt Accumulation, and Adjustment in Brazil, 1965–84*. World Bank Discussion Paper. Washington, D.C.: World Bank, 1986.

Mehrens, Bernhard. *Entstehung und Entwicklung der grossen französischen Kreditinstitute*. Stuttgart: J. G. Cotta'sche Buchhandlung, 1911.

Menaul, Stewart. *The Illustrated Encyclopedia of the Strategy, Tactics and Weapons of Russian Military Power*. New York: St. Martin's Press, 1980.

Mommsen, Theodor. *Römische Geschichte*. Berlin: Weidmannsche Buchhandlung, 1868.

Moulton, Harland B. *From Superiority to Parity: The United States and the Strategic Arms Race, 1961–1971*. Westport, Conn.: Greenwood Press, 1973.

Nixon, Richard. *RN, the Memoirs of Richard Nixon*. New York: Grosset and Dunlap, 1978.

Pahlavi, Shah Mohammed Reza. *Mission for My Country*. New York: McGraw-Hill, 1962.

———. *Answer to History*. New York: Stein and Day, 1980.

Plutarch of Chaeronea. *The Lives of Noble Grecians and Romans*, translated from Greek into French by James Amyot and from French into English by Thomas North. New York: Heritage Press, 1941.

Price, Raymond. *With Nixon*. New York: Viking Press, 1977.

Rangel, Carlos. *The Latin Americans, Their Love-Hate Relationship with the United States*. New York: Harcourt Brace Jovanovich, 1976.

Rappard, William E. *The Quest for Peace Since the World War*. Cambridge, Mass.: Harvard University Press, 1940.

Remarque, Erich Maria. *Three Comrades*. Boston: Little, Brown, 1936.

Roosevelt, Kermit. *Countercoup, the Struggle for the Control of Iran*. New York: McGraw-Hill, 1979.

Rubin, Barry. *Paved with Good Intentions, the American Experience and Iran*. Dallas, Pa.: Penguin Books, 1981.

Rubinstein, Alvin Z. *The Foreign Policy of the Soviet Union*, 3d ed. New York: Random House, 1972.

Say, Leon. *Les finances de la France sous la Troisième République*. Paris: Levy, 1898.

Schell, Jonathan. *The Fate of the Earth*. New York: Alfred A. Knopf, 1982.

Schlesinger, Arthur M., Jr. *A Thousand Days: John F. Kennedy in the White House*. Boston: Houghton, Mifflin, 1965.

Sherwood, Robert E. *Roosevelt and Hopkins: An Intimate History*. New York: Harper and Brothers, 1948.

Sick, Gary. *All Fall Down: America's Tragic Encounter with Iran*. New York: Viking Penguin, 1986.

Slessor, Sir John. *Strategy for the West*. New York: William Morrow, 1954.

Smith, Vincent A. *The Oxford History of India*. Oxford: Clarendon Press, 1923.

Spanier, John. *American Foreign Policy Since World War II*, 9th ed. New York: Holt, Rinehart and Winston, 1983.

Stempel, John D. *Inside the Iranian Revolution*. Bloomington: Indiana University Press, 1981.

Sullivan, William H. *Mission to Iran*. New York: W. W. Norton, 1981.

Summers, Harry G. *On Strategy, a Critical Analysis of the Vietnam War*. Novato, Calif.: Presidio Press, 1982.

Talbott, Strobe. *The End Game, the Inside Story of SALT II*. New York: Harper and Row, 1979.

———. *Deadly Gambits, the Reagan Administration and the Stalemate in Nuclear Arms Control*. New York: Alfred A. Knopf, 1984.

Thucydides. *The History of the Peloponnesian War*, translated by Richard Crawley. New York: Dutton, 1974.

Tierney, Brian. *Religion, Law and the Growth of Constitutional Thought, 1150–1650*. Cambridge: Cambridge University Press, 1982.

Toynbee, Arnold J. *War and Civilization*. New York: Oxford University Press, 1950.

Trommler, Frank, and Joseph McVeigh, eds. *America and the Germans: An Assessment of a Three Hundred Year History*. Philadelphia: University of Pennsylvania Press, 1985.

Truman, Harry S. *Memoirs*, 2 vols. Garden City, N.Y.: Doubleday, 1955–1956.

United States. *Treaties and Other International Agreements of the United States of America, 1776–1949,* vols. 1 and 2. Washington, D.C.: U.S. Government Printing Office, 1970, 1973.

United States, Agency for International Development. *Operations Report, FY 1965.* Washington, D.C.: U.S. Government Printing Office, December 1965.

United States, Congress, Office of Technology Assessment. *Strategic Defense, Ballistic Missile Defense Technologies, Anti-Satellite Weapons, Countermeasures and Arms Control.* Princeton: Princeton University Press, 1986.

United States, Department of Commerce, Bureau of the Census. *Statistical Abstract of the United States, 1986.* Washington, D.C.: U.S. Government Printing Office, 1986.

United States, Department of Defense. *Soviet Military Power, 1985.* Washington, D.C.: U.S. Government Printing Office, 1985.

United States, Department of State. *Foreign Relations of the United States, 1952–1954,* vol. 10, *Iran.* Washington, D.C.: U.S. Government Printing Office, 1989.

United States, House of Representatives, Committee on Armed Services. *United States-Vietnam Relations 1945–1967.* Washington, D.C.: U.S. Government Printing Office, 1971.

United States, House of Representatives, Select Committee on Hunger. *Trends in Foreign Aid, 1977–86.* Washington, D.C.: U.S. Government Printing Office, 1986.

United States, House of Representatives, Subcommittee of the Committee on Appropriations. *Readiness of the U.S. Military.* Washington, D.C.: U.S. Government Printing Office, 1983.

United States, National Bipartisan Commission. *Report of the National Bipartisan Commission on Central America.* Washington, D.C.: National Bipartisan Commission, January 1984.

United States, President's Commission on Strategic Forces. *Report.* Washington, D.C.: April 1983.

United States, Senate. *Study of Airpower.* Hearings before the Subcommittee on the Air Force of the Committee on Armed Services, 84th Congress, 2nd Session. Washington, D.C.: U.S. Government Printing Office, 1956.

———. *Foreign Assistance and Related Programs Appropriation Bill, 1986.* Report no. 99–167, October 31 (legislative day, October 28), 1985.

Vance, Cyrus. *Hard Choices: Critical Years in America's Foreign Policy.* New York: Simon and Schuster, 1983.

Wickert, Erwin. *Dramatische Tage in Hitlers Reich.* Stuttgart: Steingruber Verlag, 1952.

The World Bank. *Poverty and Human Development.* New York: Oxford University Press, 1980.

———. *World Debt Tables 1987–1988,* 1st supp. Washington, D.C.: World Bank, 1988.

Index

ABOUT THE AUTHOR

KARL von VORYS is Professor of Political Science at the University of Pennsylvania. Dr. von Vorys has been a Fulbright Lecturer in International Relations at the University of Dacca; visiting research associate at the Center of International Studies of Princeton University; and senior advisor to the Ford Foundation, Kuala Lumpur, Malaysia. He is the author of *The Political Dimensions of Foreign Aid, Political Development in Pakistan*, and *Democracy Without Consensus: Communalism and Politics in Malaysia*. His writings have appeared in several journals, among them the *American Political Science Review, The Annals of the American Academy of Social and Political Science, Die Dritte Welt, Western Political Quarterly*, and *World Politics*. His principal research interests are political development and foreign policy.